THE MARIACHI VOICE

THE MARIACHI VOICE

Dr. Juanita Ulloa

OXFORD
UNIVERSITY PRESS

Oxford University Press is a department of the University of Oxford. It furthers
the University's objective of excellence in research, scholarship, and education
by publishing worldwide. Oxford is a registered trade mark of Oxford University
Press in the UK and certain other countries.

Published in the United States of America by Oxford University Press
198 Madison Avenue, New York, NY 10016, United States of America.

© Oxford University Press 2024

All rights reserved. No part of this publication may be reproduced, stored in
a retrieval system, or transmitted, in any form or by any means, without the
prior permission in writing of Oxford University Press, or as expressly permitted
by law, by license, or under terms agreed with the appropriate reproduction
rights organization. Inquiries concerning reproduction outside the scope of the
above should be sent to the Rights Department, Oxford University Press, at the
address above.

You must not circulate this work in any other form
and you must impose this same condition on any acquirer.

Library of Congress Cataloging-in-Publication Data
Names: Ulloa, Juanita, author.
Title: The mariachi voice / Juanita Ulloa.
Description: [1.] | New York, NY : Oxford University Press, 2024. |
Includes bibliographical references and index.
Identifiers: LCCN 2023057245 (print) | LCCN 2023057246 (ebook) |
ISBN 9780190846237 (paperback) | ISBN 9780190846244 (hardback) |
ISBN 9780190846268 (epub)
Subjects: LCSH: Singing—Instruction and study. | Mariachi—Instruction and study.
Classification: LCC MT820 .N55 2024 (print) | LCC MT820 (ebook) |
DDC 783/.043—dc23/eng/20231212
LC record available at https://lccn.loc.gov/2023057245
LC ebook record available at https://lccn.loc.gov/2023057246

DOI: 10.1093/oso/9780190846244.001.0001

CONTENTS

FOREWORD BY MARK FOGELQUIST, MARIACHI DIRECTOR   XI

FOREWORD BY DR. KAREN HALL, PROFESSOR OF VOICE, SONGWERKS
VOICE STUDIO   XIII

PREFACE   XV

DEDICATIONS AND ACKNOWLEDGMENTS   XIX

AUTHOR BIO   XXIII

CHAPTER 1   MARIACHI SONG   1
Introduction: What Is Mariachi Singing?   1

Growth of Mariachi Programs and Hispanic Song in the United States and Mexico   5

Understanding Terms: Ranchera, Mariachi, Mariache, and Música Regional
Mexicana   11

Lesson Plans   14
  Lesson 1: Mariachi Song: Introduction   14
  Lesson 2: Growth of Mariachi and Understanding Terms: *Ranchera, Mariachi, Mariache,*
  and *Música Regional Mexicana*   14

CHAPTER 2   HISTORY: MARIACHI SINGERS AND THEIR SONGS   16
Ranchera Rural Folk Origins   17
  Vocal Roots   20
  Early Twentieth-Century Ranchera Songs   27
Mexico's Golden Age of Cinema, Singers, and Songs   29
Manuel M. Ponce, "The Father of Mexican Song"   31
Solo Ranchera Singers Become Celebrities through Media Expansion   35
Crossover Singing: Jorge Negrete and *Operas Rancheras*   37
  Jorge Negrete   37
  Opera Rancheras   39
Mexico's Premiere Voice Teacher: Maestro José Pierson   43
The Bolero in Mexico: History, Singers, and Composers   45
Ranchera Singing Style   48
Singer/Songwriter José Alfredo Jiménez: A Third Period in Mariachi History   50
Female Ranchera/Bolero Singers and Composers   51
Bravío Ranchera Singing-Lucha Reyes and Vocal Conditions for Female Ranchera
Singers   52

VI   CONTENTS

Vocal Conditions for Female Ranchera Singers   54

Summary   55

Chronology: Key Dates in Ranchera Voice History   57

History: Mariachi Singers and Their Songs   58

     Lesson 1: Ranchera Rural Folk Origins   58

     Lesson 2: Vocal Roots and Early Twentieth Century Ranchera Songs   58

         Vocal Roots   58

         Songs   59

     Lesson 3: Mexico's Golden Age of Cinema, Singers, and Songs   59

     Lesson 4: The Father of Mexican Song—Manuel M. Ponce   59

     Lesson 5: Solo Ranchera Singers Become Celebrities Through Media Expansion   60

     Lesson 6: Crossover Singers: Jorge Negrete and *Operas Rancheras*   60

     Lesson 7: Mexico's Premiere Voice Teacher: Maestro José Pierson   60

     Lesson 8: The Bolero in Mexico—History, Singers, and Composers   61

     Lesson 9: Ranchera Singing Style   61

     Lesson 10: Singer/Songwriter José Alfredo Jiménez: A Third Period in Mariachi History   62

     Lesson 11: Female Ranchera/Bolero Singers and Composers   62

     Lesson 12: Bravío Ranchera Song—Lucha Reyes and Vocal Conditions for Women   62

     Lesson 13: Key Dates in Mexican Voice History—Advanced Studies (Based upon Chronology)   62

Answer Key   63

     Lesson 1: Ranchera Rural Folk Origins   63

     Lesson 2: Vocal Roots and Early Twentieth Century Ranchera Songs   63

         Songs   65

     Lesson 3: Mexico's Golden Age of Cinema, Singers, and Songs   65

     Lesson 4: The Father of Mexican Song—Manuel M. Ponce   65

     Lesson 5: Solo Ranchera Singers Become Celebrities Through Media Expansion   65

     Lesson 6: Crossover Singers: Jorge Negrete and *Operas Rancheras*   66

     Lesson 7: Mexico's Premiere Voice Teacher: Maestro José Pierson   66

     Lesson 8: The Bolero in Mexico—History, Singers, and Composers   66

     Lesson 9: Ranchera Singing Style   67

     Lesson 10: Singer/Songwriter José Alfredo Jiménez: A Third Period in Mariachi History   67

     Lesson 11: Female Ranchera/Bolero Singers and Composers   67

     Lesson 12: Bravío Ranchera Song—Lucha Reyes and Vocal Conditions for Women   68

     Lesson 13: Key Dates in Mexican Voice History—Advanced Studies (Based upon Chronology)   68

CHAPTER 3   MARIACHI VOICE PEDAGOGY   70

Vocal Production and Vocal Care: A Visual Starting Place for Vocalists   72

     Voice Production in Class Exercises and Discussion   73

"Understanding Your Vocal Instrument" by Professor John Nix   73

     Vocal Cords: What Are They, and How Do They Work?   74

     Breathing: The Energy for the Voice   75

     Breathing for Singing Exercises   75

     Vocal Cords Quiz   76

CONTENTS VII

Staying Healthy as a Singer 76
The Vocal Athlete 76
We All Like to Eat! 77
Traveling and Singing 77
Minding Your Meds 78
Pacing Rehearsals 78

Differences between Men and Women's Voices 79
General Vocal Exercises for Daily Use (Men and Women) 80
Vocal Exercises Specifically for Men 80
Vocal Exercises Specifically for Women 81
Addressing Common Vocal Problems Faced by Mariachi Singers 81
If You Are a Teacher, Be a Good Example 83
Reinforce Healthy Habits 84
Final Thoughts 84
Staying Healthy as a Singer Exercises 84

A Voice Lesson: Alignment, Breath, and Vowel 85
Alignment, Breath, and Vowel Exercises 86

Voice Teacher or Voice Coach—What Is the Difference? 87

Female Mariachi Fach 88

Mariachi *Falsete*: To Bridge or to Break 90
Can Anyone Sing Falsete? 91
Where Does Falsete Come From? 92
How Do I Learn Falsete? 92
Practicing Falsete 93
Vocal Yodeling Exercises 93
Beginning Falsete Exercises 94
Advanced Falsete Exercises 94
Falsete Quiz 95

What Is the Belt Voice? 95

Handling Vocal Fatigue and Developing Mindfulness 96
Develop Mindfulness and Protect Yourself 96
In Performance 97

Mariachi Directors Provide Vocal Leadership 98
Mariachi Mindfulness Exercise 98
Mariachi Mindfulness Check-In 99

Similarities and Differences between Mariachi and Classical Voice Production 99
Similarities 99
Differences 100

Wake-up Warm-ups, Vocalises, and Practicing 101
Wake-up Warm-ups 102
Mariachi Vocalises 105
Practicing 106

Finding the Right Key for Your Song 108
Key Choices for Women 109
Key Choices for Men 111
Finding the Right Key Exercises 111

VIII   CONTENTS

Finding the Right Key Quiz   111
Choosing a Key with Falsete   112
Answer Keys to Quizzes   113

CHAPTER 4   PREPARING TO BE A MARIACHI SINGER   115

The Voice Is the Instrument Everybody Shares   115

Group Singers, Ensemble Soloist, Mariachi Soloist: Where Do You Fit In?   116
Group Singers   116
Ensemble Soloist   116
Mariachi Solo Singer   117

Costumes, Make-up, Song Studies, and Singing with a Microphone   120
Make-up and Hair   123
Song Studies   125
Singing with a Microphone   125
Preparation Tips for Auditions and Performances (Live and Online)*   128

CHAPTER 5   MARIACHI RHYTHMS AND CHOOSING SONG REPERTOIRE   131

Overview of Mariachi Rhythmic Styles   132

Why Good Singers Listen to Rhythm   133

Rhythm Exercises and Learning Songs   134

Six Basic Rhythms   136

Choosing Mariachi Voice Repertoire   136

Graded Ranchera Song Lists: Beginner, Advanced Beginner, Intermediate, Advanced Vocal Levels   139
Level 1: Beginning Solo Mariachi Songs   140
Level 2: Advanced-Beginner Mariachi Songs   141
Level 3: Intermediate Mariachi Songs   141
Level 4: Advanced Mariachi Songs (Competition Level)   142

CHAPTER 6   SONGS, DICTION, LYRICS, IPA, AND TRANSLATIONS   144

Introduction to Mexican Spanish Lyric Diction   144
Mexican Spanish Is Unique   146

Pronunciation Tips for Mexican Spanish   148

Tips on Memorizing Lyrics   149

Diction Lessons 1–5   150
Diction Lesson 1: Draw Your own IPA Letters and Short Words   150
Diction Lesson 2: IPA Short Mariachi Words in Spanish   150
Diction Lesson 3: IPA Mariachi Words in Spanish   151
Diction Lesson 4: Important Mariachi Phrases and Song Titles   151
Diction Lesson 5: Mariachi Longer Song Titles   152

Lessons: Song Studies; History, Lyrics, and Translations, Guide; Acting; Performing Artist; Composer Studies   153
Song Studies: History   153
Song Studies: Lyrics and Translations   154
Checklist for Song, Lyrics, and Translation Studies   154

CONTENTS IX

Acting Study 155
Performing Artist Study 155
Composer Study 156
Ranchera Songs List with IPA, Poetic, and Literal Translations 156

CHAPTER 7 MARIACHI MUSIC FUNDAMENTALS 262

Sheet Music in Mariachi's Urban Period 262

Ranchera Composers and Arrangers Use Sheet Music: Manuel Esperón, Ruben Fuentes, Mariachi Vargas, Jorge Negrete 263

Music Fundamentals in Schools 263

Bilingual Theory and Solfege versus Letter Note Reading 264
Solfege-Solfegio 265
Review Questions: Sheet Music in Mariachi's Urban Period, Manuel M. Ponce, Manuel Esperón, and Solfege 265

Bilingual Music Fundamentals 265
Treble Clef (Clave de sol) 266
Treble Clef in Spanish—Clave de sol en Español 267
Clave de sol 267
Bass Clef (Clave de fa) 267
Bass Clef in Spanish—Clave de fa 269

Meter and Rhythmic Note Values 269
Notes Values in Spanish 269
Transcription of Melodies and Rhythms 271
Three Basic Chords 271
Popular Mariachi Keys 272
Finding a Singer's Best Key 274
Dynamics and Tempo Terms in Spanish, Italian, and English 276

Ten Lesson Plans 278

CHAPTER 8 FOUR INTERVIEWS WITH MARIACHI ARTISTS ON VOICE 315

Linda Ronstadt: Mexican American Multi-Grammy Winner in Mariachi, twelve Grammys in diverse vocal styles, Kennedy Center and The Recording Academy's Lifetime Achievement Awards, Emmy Award, Tony, and Emmy nominations 316

Jorge Negrete: Dispelling Myths about legendary *ranchera* singer, *El charro cantor.* An interview with his grandchildren: Rafael Jorge Negrete and Diana Irene Negrete 326

Flor de Toloache: 2017 Latin Grammy Winning group based in New York with a pioneering vocal edge 329

Raul Cuellar, Jr.: Contemporary Mexican American ranchera singer and violinist with *Camperos de Nati Cano* Mariachi 336

GLOSSARY 343
Mariachi Voice Resources 343

RESOURCES AND BIBLIOGRAPHY 379

INDEX 387

FOREWORD

Mariachi teachers at all levels have struggled over the years to find materials suitable for transmitting Mexico's "national music" outside of its original cultural matrix. During the 1960s, the first mariachi teachers in US curriculums could either teach by ear, as was the norm in Mexico, or go through the laborious process of transcribing songs off of commercial recordings and copying parts by hand. As more teachers entered the field of mariachi education to meet the demands of ever-increasing enrollment, a body of transcriptions was created, with teachers often sharing their handwritten music with one another. The advent of music-notation programs for computer increased the quality of transcriptions, their legibility, and access for interested students and teachers. However, in spite of a surge of interest in mariachi music in schools in the United States over the past four or five decades, materials for teachers and students still remain scarce and sometimes of dubious quality. Few publishers have entered the field with editions of well-written resources for mariachi educators and students. For these reasons, Oxford's new book, *The Mariachi Voice*, is a very important addition to the field of mariachi education as programs continue to grow throughout the United States and now, ironically, within Mexico and beyond.

I first met Juanita Ulloa twenty years ago. Our Mariachi Estrellas de Chula Vista performed with her during her concert tour at San Diego's Centro Cultural de la Raza in Balboa Park. She later asked to visit our mariachi program site. She shared her inspiration to link her voice teaching and crossover Operachi performing to advance academic pedagogy for mariachi singers. *The Mariachi Voice* is the culmination of this labor.

Dr. Ulloa's work also has special value because it deals with the most important instrument of the mariachi ensemble: the voice. As seen in many of the early ranchera films mentioned in *The Mariachi Voice*, a lone singer with guitar accompaniment can deliver a ranchera song or bolero with heartfelt meaning and great intensity. That same song is often a standard in the repertoire of a full mariachi ensemble with up to fifteen musicians. Singers have to be ready for either setting.

The significance of *The Mariachi Voice* is doubly important as it fulfills a crucial need in the field of mariachi education: it offers comprehensive background and learning methods for the most important instrument of the mariachi. The book documents the development of the modern mariachi's vocal style and delves into the details of the technique involved in achieving success as a singer. It provides historical and cultural context for mariachi singing along with specific exercises, routines, diction, and notated songs with translations, with training in bilingual note reading.

Dr. Ulloa's credentials are impeccable. Originally from Mexico City herself, she has impressive training and experience as a crossover singer and master voice teacher in the United States, Mexico, and Spain. It is with great anticipation that mariachi educators have awaited the publication *The Mariachi Voice* by Dr. Juanita Ulloa.

Mark Fogelquist, Master Mariachi Educator
Mariachi Estrellas de Chula Vista
San Diego, California/Ajijic, Mexico
May, 2021

FOREWORD

If you are holding this book in your hands, *The Mariachi Voice*, there is a high probability that you are prompted by the title. Possibly you are a singer, or a voice teacher, and curious to learn about the technical and stylistic requirements of mariachi singing. Whatever your motivation, this book will give you the courage to pursue proficiency in the incredible world of mariachi singing, the "national music" of Mexico.

For many reasons, Dr. Juanita Ulloa is the perfect choice to write this book. She is originally from Mexico City, and her credentials, training, and experience can lead you forward. Her international experience as a crossover singer and master teacher, combined with her impressive training, ensure her work is thorough, complete, and of the highest quality.

Several years ago I came to know Dr. Ulloa by way of a phone call. She read a book I wrote about vocal pedagogy and wanted to know more. She recognized that my book had many similarities to the one she wanted to write (I am a classically trained soprano, and my doctoral research was on the similarities and differences between music theater and classical singing production and style). Through mutual musician friends we were introduced. Her enthusiasm to learn more was infectious. I answered the questions she had, and Oxford later asked me to review some of her work as part of the initial process. From there, she began writing *The Mariachi Voice*.

Her book is extensive in scope so readers can learn every aspect of mariachi singing style and vocal production. The important issues of vocal health, practicing, and choosing songs—to name only a few topics—are included. A much-needed additional feature is the inclusion of listening examples and the use of the International Phonetic Alphabet (IPA). The book is organized to give you the maximum opportunity to comprehend mariachi vocal technique and style. Her work is grounded in voice science and includes the history of mariachi singing in Mexico and the United States.

Times are changing, and *The Mariachi Voice* is now available to take its place alongside the reams of resources on singing. It is a huge and much-needed project that is long overdue!

Karen Hall, EdD
Santa Fe, New Mexico, 2021

PREFACE

My path as a singer would have been much simpler and more direct if this book had existed to guide me. Mariachi singers, teachers, and directors all deserve a mariachi voice textbook that is comprehensive, technical, educational, and yet inspirational. In this book we include Mexican Spanish lyric diction, IPA, mariachi voice history (a new perspective within mariachi music history), interviews with artists, and important pedagogical and historical differences between training male and female singers. Mariachi music educators may now shorten their lesson preparation time with graded song suggestions and lesson plans.

There is a need for mariachi vocal history materials in English for growing United States academic programs, private voice teachers, or those learning on their own. An antrhopological foundation for mariachi has been previously established with Spanish publications by Dr. Jésus Jaúregui and Dr. Álvaro Ochoa Serrano. The late musicologist Dr. Yolanda Rivas Moreno's book on Mexican popular song was also seminal. All who endeavor to learn more beyond this book should plan to read their writings in Spanish (see Bibliography).

My motivation for writing this book has been to help singers, directors, and teachers everywhere be able to access and apply this information with improved collaboration between voice and mariachi fields. I thank Oxford University Press for assisting us in creating a pathway through the publication of this book.

Even though I personally trained at some of the best universities in the world including Yale University, at the time neither Mexican nor Latin American vocal music was on anybody's radar. I settled for training in European classical voice and piano, and sought out a Master's degree in ethnomusicology of Latin America at UC Berkeley. After encouragement specific to the voice from the late Verdi scholar professor Dr. Joseph Kerman at UC Berkeley, I began more serious vocal training and performed regional opera with many California opera companies for eight years. Meanwhile, I continued to secretly collect, perform, and study my deep interest in Mexican, Latin American, and songs; songs I grew up with that were missing from academia. I knew audiences love the a rich array and prodigious volume of folk vocal styles I grew up with. I continued performing these songs from Mexico, Spain, Chile, and Peru nationally and internationally. I felt redeemed upon experiencing the great enthusiasm, appreciation, and nationalistic pride of audiences toward this huge body of folk music.

Growing up in Mexico City, Panama, and later Madrid, Spain allowed me to directly access different vocal styles including Spanish zarzuela; ultimately, however, my vocal style always sounded most unique and natural in Mexican rancheras, boleros, and my originals. I gained the title of an *Operachi* singer due to the classical background I naturally express through my vocal training and piano background. This was a novelty at the time, although readers of this book will see that men have actually been singing in a crossover "Operachi style" since Jorge Negrete hit the movie screens in Mexico's charro films in the 1930s. Why

XVI   PREFACE

not women? It is my personal path, my niche and every woman's opportunity. May this book provide all women the same access.

My own important early childhood and adolescent encounters learning mariachi songs were unusual. They took place in the backyard of my home in Mexico City. For many years, I lived next door to one of Mexico City's most famous mariachi restaurants, *El Caballo Bayo* (The Bay Horse) in the *Colonia Lomas Hipódromo*, a neighborhood of Mexico City near the racetrack. The only separation between the backyard of our home and the restaurant was a high cement wall covered with red and purple bougainvillea. The wall was too high for me to see anyone, and I was too young to be allowed in the restaurant. Nevertheless, I was able to easily listen from across the wall from my backyard. I spent countless afternoons for years absorbing and singing along to ranchera favorites. Next door, soloists and restaurant goers would passionately raise their voices in the choruses of favorite José Alfredo Jiménez songs, as in the song *El Rey-* "Con dinero o sin dinero . . . pero sigo siendo el rey," to the vocal choruses of the public with singers, accompanied by terrific mariachi ensembles.

My process was to listen, memorize the melody to one song with or without lyrics, run upstairs inside my house from the backyard to my piano to figure out how to play and sing it; then, race outside again to hear more before the song finished and double check my work. Oftentimes they were already on another song, and I would be forced to learn songs in chunks and put them together later. In the kitchen, while our cook and I made tortillas together, we would often robustly sing rancheras and ballads along with favorites on the radio. I grew to consider these songs my musical home where all passions could be released in a strong low female chest-based range.

Although my family was not involved in music, they arranged weekly visits to my home of a piano professor beginning at age four. I learned quickly, and from age eleven onward my parents would wake me up at night during their fiestas to perform a wide variety of songs that included rancheras, boleros, and sing-along favorites. On Sundays, we would eat out at restaurants and sing along with live mariachi ensembles. I was transfixed with the power, presence, and rich tone of the singers, all of them men.

Sadly, I never once saw or heard a female performer at these restaurants when growing up. I was forced to sing along with the men in vocal keys for the male voice, at the time not understanding and secretly wondering why men's voices seemed to go higher than mine (I had no head voice yet). I had not yet studied voice and did not understand how different the female range and registration is from the male voice, even though both use the same breathing technique. My later training allowed me to solve this and begin helping others. Understanding female versus male vocal pedagogy is a core issue in mariachi voice pedagogy, especially for women. Even today, commercial sheet-music publications of boleros and rancheras continue to be published in male keys without key options. This book offers two key options for twenty songs (see Chapter 6 section: "Ranchera Songs").

Later, I met my lifetime voice teacher Jane Randolph who helped me persevere technically. We spent (and continue to spend) time building air pressure, support, and stamina. With her, I learned to trust I wouldn't lose my sound, style, or lessen my interpretation by committing myself wholeheartedly to getting the right breath support. This enabled me to crossover into different styles, thus opening doors to more varied vocal opportunities including songwriting. Today, my voice students receive crossover training and each has their own unique sound.

Throughout my performing and scholarly career, I have observed and directly or indirectly experienced the lack of opportunities, recognition, and respect for women in Latin American music. It is important to address this in ranchera music, a traditionally male dominated field. Those who say we've changed need only to observe the 2023 YouTube video of extensive mariachi performances at the funeral of Vicente Fernandez whereby not one woman was featured.

Women not only sing rancheras in a different range than men, but they have their own history, pedagogy, and style. We need more educators and voice teachers to understand how to separate and isolate technique from vocal style, in order to teach and pass it on correctly. This includes special awareness of gender differences as they affect the voice. For this reason, I highlight information on the female voice and mention contributions of female ranchera and bolero singers and songwriters in this book.

Readers of this book will learn of the many styles and options a singer has to choose from, especially in the artist interviews (see Chapter 8 section: "Linda Ronstadt"). Every singer deserves to find their stylistic niche and personal sound. I wish this for you, dear reader. This is also how and why this book was born.

In this book, our focus is on solo singers, that is, soloists within ensembles and solo ranchera singers. The ensemble as a choir deserves its own separate study, although every mariachi musician will add potency to their group choir sound if studying voice.

We freely interchange the terms *ranchera* and *mariachi*. See glossary for further definitions of these terms, of which there are many. In this book new original songs with diverse vocal levels are offered and several ranchera song standards from public domain.

Our apologies in advance for any expert artist, singer, teacher, or mariachi performer or arranger overlooked in this book. We encourage all motivated readers to pick up where this book ends and continue on the brand-new field of mariachi voice scholarship.

As the mariachi song field continues to grow worldwide as one of Mexico's most treasured symbols, my hope is that *The Mariachi Voice* will offer a foundational roadmap towards better training, an appreciation of vocal history, healthy, longer careers for all singers, and more informed vocal study overall. While it may be up to future generations to carry this on, this book offers a clear starting point with many levels of study. I am humble, grateful, and at the same time bursting with pride to be able to share the spark that ignites and unites all mariachi singers with Mexico's unique style, sound, and repertoire. ¡Ajua!

DEDICATIONS AND ACKNOWLEDGMENTS

I dedicate this book in honor of Ms. Jane Randolph, voice teacher extraordinaire from the San Francisco Conservatory. Thank you for your vocal and spiritual wisdom, vocal knowledge, mentorship, and perseverance in supporting me over many years. I have learned so much and continue to learn from your dedication to my vocal transformation.

Dear friend and colleague Dario Valdelamar, your assistance and our comraderie over the years has been amazing, not to mention your incredible knowledge about the lives of so many Mexican composers. Together, we honor the memory of your amazing mother, the late and great bolero songwriter of, among others, "Mucho corazón," Ms. Ema Elena Valdelamar. Her life story and challenges as a woman songwriter in music had a great impact on me. She was an important mentor.

We also honor the memory of Belle Ortiz, who passed away in 2023. Belle was perhaps the first United States' first mariachi educator beginning in 1961–1962 with vocal/guitar/choir classes in the San Antonio schools. Thanks to Belle and performer/arranger extraordinaire, Juan Ortiz, my CD, *Canta mi son!*, became a beautiful mariachi gift for families honored by Disney! Both were kind enough to open their home to share the release together with me in a live performance. We also share Belle's dedication with every other mariachi educator who has worked to share the power of Mexico's spirit worldwide.

I extend immeasurable thanks to every contributor in this book for donating their time and sharing the spirit, beauty, and power of the mariachi voice.

I generously thank Norm, Laura, and Ms. Ganga at Oxford University Press for their patience, vision, and commitment to this project, a first in English in the mariachi field. Thank you, Ms. Nancy Taylor, music faculty colleague at the University of Texas in El Paso, for leading me to Oxford University Press.

Professor John Nix at the University of Texas at San Antonio is a former voice teacher, prolific author, and a much-esteemed colleague. He has made an invaluable contribution to this book with a section on understanding the human voice within our chapter on vocal pedagogy. Thanks, John, as well, for your teachings and uplifting me during challenging times. I am very grateful for your support. I've also received invaluable feedback from reviewers along the way: friend and Latin American musicologist colleague Dr. Mark Brill; Nevada mariachi educator Ms. Marcia Neel, whom I believe understands the need for this book; and Dr. Karen Hall, pioneer in the voice field for the development of commercial vocal music, who first inspired me to do this project through my admiration for her work.

Many thanks to Mexico City mariachi anthropologist Dr. Jesús Jáuregui and his wife, Laura, for sharing their time and expertise over the years during my dissertation crossing into the writing of this book. His writings are essential to the field and the personal music questions he often posed to me always encourage me to look for deeper meanings.

DEDICATIONS AND ACKNOWLEDGMENTS

I owe a debt of gratitude to El Paso, Texas, pianist/arranger/composer Mr. Stephen Jones for his meticulous and professional work on the sheet music for this publication. I also commend mariachi director/trumpeter/voice student José Sánchez for his Finale transcriptions and assistance with lesson plans, all the while leading Mariachi Oroazul at San Jose State University. A huge thanks goes to the amazing, patient, perseverant, and loyal Jennifer Keplinger for her dexterous and lightning fast editing skills, all the while moving around the country while we completed the book. Without her support over these last years, this project would remain incomplete.

Thanks to our incredibly talented artists in graphic design and illustration, Juan Carlos Sánchez and Marcia Cagandahan, and thanks to our independent photographers, Patrick Johnson, Andrei Paul Averbuch, Javier Vela, and Rafael Ramirez. We especially thank New York–based Javier Vela for his superb cover shot and overall coverage. We are grateful to Ms. Cynthia Muñoz, CEO of the long-running San Antonio–based Mariachi Extravaganza (annual voice, songwriting, and mariachi ensemble competitions). It is her generous spirit that allows us to share photographic access of many singers in action singing live at the annual Mariachi Extravaganza Festival.

This book features four firsthand artist interviews of professional mariachi vocalists. They shared their time with priceless and intimate vocal information. Thank you from the bottom of my heart, superstars Linda Ronstadt whom I adore, and new friends, Raul Cuellar, and *Flor de Toloache*. The fourth interview with the Negrete grandchildren, Diana and Rafael Jorge Negrete, was equally inspiring, with personal insights about their grandfather, Jorge Negrete that go beyond the tabloids into the real truth. May this book bring justice to his memory in setting the record straight and dispelling myths about him. Many thanks, as well, to important mariachi historian Jonathan Clark for sharing his valuable biography of trumpeter Miguel Martinez and for assisting in our Chapter 8 artist interview of singer Raul Cuellar.

While this book focuses on the voice and vocal training (not mariachi group programs), it also affords me the opportunity to briefly honor several mariachi pioneers in the United States. One of them is mariachi's initial and longtime program director based in Southern California, Mark Fogelquist. He was one of the first to train mariachi ensembles in the 1960s in California. In his foreword to this book, Mark shares how difficult it has been for instrumentally based mariachi directors to teach voice without available mariachi voice scholarship. Mark first inspired me when we collaborated with one of his gifted mariachi ensembles in San Diego's La Raza Cultural Center in Balboa Park. I never forgot his excellence and professionalism.

I appreciate the generous interview time afforded to me by Dr. Dahlia Guerra, excellent mariachi director and former classical pianist at the University of Texas Rio Grande Valley (UTRGV). Her mariachi program has achieved wonderful acclaim and sets a high standard for all. Thank you, Dr. Belinda Arriaga, for your compassionate spirit and for our baby steps beginning a vocal component for your mariachi program *Ayudando latinos a soñar* (ALAS— Helping Latinos Dream), in Half Moon Bay, California.

Special gratitude goes to the National Association of Teachers of Singing nationally for newly opening their hearts to the growth of Latin American song in both classical and commercial styles. The San Francisco Bay Area (SFBAC-NATS), and more recently the California Capital Chapter (CCC) have been the first to go beyond Latin American classical music to include commercial songs in Spanish and Portuguese within competition, including mariachi and boleros. Thanks to them we have had several mariachi winners over the last two years. They have also embraced diversity by sponsoring Latin American voice master classes and webinars.

Many voice colleagues and student singers have toiled diligently behind the scenes alongside me reviewing IPA, translations, and lesson plans: Lidia Chávez; San José State voice professor Jacque Scarlach Wilson; and voice students María Arenas, Connie Gonzalez, Samantha Woodsum, José B. Sánchez, Dalia Miguel, and Viridiana Vásquez for her contribution to our glossary. My respects go as well to my music students and colleagues from Laney Community College, University of Texas at El Paso, and at Texas State University.

Most of all, thanks to all the mariachi performers and educators in the United States and Mexico with whom I so enjoy working; pictured in Figure 1, in between performances for *Fiestas Patrias* with Mariachi Cuauhtemoc, working with the Mexican Consulate in El Paso, Texas.

AUTHOR BIO

Juanita Ulloa, *Operachi* singer with Mariachi Cuauhtémoc and Mexican Consulate, El Paso, Texas

Dr. Juanita Ulloa, DA, enjoys a unique niche first initiated in her trendsetting CD *Mujeres y Mariachi*. The singer has been honored as an artist in a class of her own, along with Santana (Mark Halstern, *Hispanic Magazine*). Dr. Ulloa grew up in Mexico City hearing mariachi in her home as it came from the famed Caballo Bayo restaurant next door. She also lived in Spain and Panama. She pioneers opening awareness and high vocal standards in Mariachi, and is a pedagogue, scholar, singer/songwriter, and specialist in different styles of Hispanic vocal music. Juanita Ulloa has performed in major California arts centers, is a six-time winner of the Festival de la canción latinoamericana as a singer and composer, has won classical voice competitions with the National Association of Teachers of Singing, an Addy winner for voice-overs, and her CDs have received numerous awards. She is sought after nationally as a soloists for Latin Pops Symphonic programs and has worked as a soloist with San Francisco Symphony's Adventures in Music. Dr. Ulloa has taught classical and mariachi voice at University of Texas at El Paso, Texas State University, and community colleges in Texas and California. As a professor she trains singers in commercial and classical styles, cultivating crossover and diversity. She has trained Latin Grammy winners, national Mariachi champions and finalists at Latin American, Mariachi Extravaganza, and NATS Regional Competitions, America's Got Talent and soloists at the White House.

Dr. Ulloa holds a doctorate in vocal performance from the University of Northern Colorado (emphasis in Hispanic studies), with music degrees from Yale University (BA) and the

University of California at Berkeley (MA). She is Level I, II, and III trained in commercial contemporary music (CCM). Dr. Ulloa offers master classes in ranchera and classical Hispanic song at universities nationally and at UNAM Conservatory of Music locations in Mexico City and Ciudad Juárez. She has recorded seven CDs devoted to her favorite themes championing women and bilingualism for children (Parent's Choice, Parent's Council, NAPPA, and GrIndy Disney awards), and several songbooks in collaboration with Pearson Music, Mel Bay, and MacMillan/McGraw-Hill. Dr. Ulloa published three volumes of Mexican Song on Antonio Gomezanda with Classical Vocal Reprints in 2017 and has authored The Mariachi Voice (Oxford University Press, 2024). Dr. Ulloa has served as a governor for both NARAS, National Recording Academy of Arts and Sciences (Grammys) and NATS, National Association of Teachers of Singing (SFBAC Chapter), where she advocates on diversity and advisory committees. She maintains a private voice studio, teaches at Laney Community College, and travels internationally, offering artist residencies, master classes, and concerts. Information: www.juanitamusic.com.

CHAPTER 1

MARIACHI SONG

FIGURE 1.1 Singer Chelsea Torres, vocal soloist in perfect alignment performing at the Mariachi Academy of New York City, New York.

Introduction: What Is Mariachi Singing?

One of Mexico's most prominent oral folk traditions is *ranchera* or *mariachi* music. *Ranchera* means "music in ranch style" referring to its rural origins. It originated in the western coastal states of Mexico during the early 1800s; mariachi performing is also documented farther north, going as far as San Francisco and Marin, California, in the United States.[1] Today, mariachi performers are an international symbol for Mexico. In 2011, UNESCO named Mexican mariachi music an intangible worldwide cultural heritage.

Ranchera solo singers, instrumentalists, and dancers can all be instantly spotted with their multi-colored or red-and-green-sequined costumes or black *charro* outfits, called *trajes de charro*.

---

[1] Jesús Jáuregui, *El Mariachi: El Símbolo nacional* (México, D. F.: Santillana Ediciones Generales: Taurus, 2007), 353–373.

The Mariachi Voice. Dr. Juanita Ulloa, Oxford University Press. © Oxford University Press 2024. DOI: 10.1093/oso/9780190846244.003.0001

FIGURE 1.2 Mexican singers and dancers often perform with regional costumes; Chiapanecas costume from Chiapas, Mexico. Photo taken by Rafael Ramirez.

They are lined with silver *botonadura* (buttons) running down their sides. They also often wear large Mexican sombreros. Examples of singers dressed as *charros* along with other important regional Mexican costumes used by solo singers are depicted in Figures 1.2, 1.3, and 1.4.

In the mariachi world, music, lyrics, and voice are inextricably linked; they are the core of ranchera music. The vast percentage of ranchera songs are vocal songs with lyrics and not instrumental solos. For this reason, understanding the lyrics and relaying the message are of great importance.

Mariachi singing has its own vocal style which attracts listeners all over the globe with its natural earthiness, passion, and spirited joy. A singer's sound can be instantly identified as being in mariachi style without even seeing costumes or listening to the instruments. One stylistic feature singers are taught is robust, powerful projection, often defying the suggested use of a microphone. It is unique to find impressive vocal power like this in Western folk styles. Similar vocal projection is traditionally expected only in the opera world, where classical singers train for many years and, as a result, have power and projection and often sing beyond their sixties or seventies.

Mariachi vocal projection is especially unique considering that the voice is the smallest and most delicate of all the instruments in the mariachi ensemble. Due to this requisite sound, it is important that singers wanting long, productive careers be able to access early vocal training. It allows singers to demystify breath support discovering rich tonal production, and range expansion, while avoiding vocal fatigue. Most of all, early vocal training and technical awareness allows singers to enjoy the freedom and joy of singing with vocal protection (see Chapter 3).

Mariachi songs and singing style can also be immediately identified to newcomers by famous phrases and melodies, such as *Ay, ay, ay!* from "Cielito lindo" by Mexican composers Quirino and Mendoza. This phrase goes even beyond mariachi performances into euphoric moments at soccer matches in stadiums all over the world. Audiences might also hear customary yells throughout the song, *bravío* gutsy earthiness, or crooning, or a soloist might demonstrate virtuosic falsete flips from the famous song "Malagueña Salerosa" ("falsete"—see Glossary). These vocal sounds represent part of the mariachi singing style, and they immediately identify Mexico.

FIGURE 1.3 Female singer in *china poblana* costume from Puebla, Mexico, featuring a red and green sequined skirt with the eagle, serpent, and colors from the Mexican flag highlighting the design. Design by Marcia Caganahan.

Ranchera music history represents a rich tapestry of soloists, ensembles, and colorful dancers in festive collaboration. They highlight one another by working in tandem, not competition, and there is a long history in honoring everyone working together. Mariachi instrumentalists are expected to cover solos as singers. Great singers are also actors, sometimes songwriters and arrangers, and often instrumentalists. Some musicians are also dancers. Song accompaniments include varying rhythmic patterns, some of them highly syncopated and each with their own mood, singing style, and flavor. Singers, instrumentalists, and dancers unite in performance by simultaneously following to the rhythmic groove for each song in sync.

Each group of Mexican artists represents a prism of distinct colors. While they may exist separately, each is highly integral to Mexican folk music. Whether together or apart on stage, solo singers, ensembles, and dancers are today regularly featured in solo concerts, symphonic

FIGURE 1.4 Singer Jizelle Rodriguez at the 2017 Mariachi National Champion, Mariachi Extravaganza, in San Antonio, Texas. Note how closely she holds the microphone up to her mouth. Photograph by Javier Vela.

halls, and opera arenas, while also continuing to perform in private, religious, and traditional life-celebration settings.

Ranchera's singing style has specific identifiable features present in certain songs. The listener may hear unexpected short- or long-held accented notes, called falsete, or accented register breaks in the middle of a melody or at the end of a song. Falsete is a term related to the word falsetto. In mariachi singing, the word actually refers to the head voice for women and is not purely falsetto range, although for men the term falsetto is correct (see Chapter 3 and listen to falsete in the "Duelo 'La Malagueña'" YouTube video: https://youtu.be/0kZgb6UWuQc). Long-held notes often elicit yells of appreciation and applause from the audience both during and after the song. Ranchera songs and singing style are well defined with rhythmic and melodic variety that shows off legato virtuosity while inducing passion, depth, and drama.

Mexico's vocal traditions comprise a fascinating amalgam of musical styles that reflect the country's complex history. Mexico's population is made up of indigenous peoples, imported African slaves with complex rhythms, and Spanish colonizers who ruled Mexico for over three hundred years. Musical styles from each of these cultures have elements that contribute to mariachi vocal music with syncopated rhythms, instruments, vocal expression, language, diction, inflection, movement, and costumes.

To summarize, the mariachi song tradition is visually and aurally vibrant, rich, diverse, unique, well defined, and earthy. Mariachi singers are symbols of Mexico's spirit, homeland, and identity, along with their fellow instrumentalists and dancers. Many ranchera songs evoke the nostalgic and unforgettable taste of the homeland.[2] Ranchera soloists stand center stage, leading the song, while simultaneously collaborating with the ensemble and folkloric dancers.

---

[2] Jáuregui, *El Mariachi*, 213.

All unite to share what is perhaps Mexico's most powerful and internationally celebrated mode of musical expression.

Growth of Mariachi Programs and Hispanic Song in the United States and Mexico

Well over 56 million Hispanic people live in the United States. Spanish speakers represent the largest ethnic group in the United States.[3] Despite strong representation, Mexican mariachi and Latin American classical and folk-song traditions are just beginning to find traction in university vocal music departments. Any student singer with knowledge of this immense body of classical and folkloric music is encouraged to freely suggest repertoire and courses to their faculty. As an example, the author teaches group and solo applied voice classes with a Mariachi tract as a repertoire option. All kinds of Mexican songs including rancheras can be performed in various settings: as solos with piano/guitar, solos in commercial ensembles (including or in addition to the mariachi ensemble), and solos, duets, or trios within song literature and group voice classes. With over twenty-five countries speaking different kinds of Spanish, Mexican Spanish is an important part of any comparative Spanish lyric diction class, especially considering that many college students in the United States enter college having studied some Spanish (see Chapters 4, Chapter 6 section: "Introduction to Mexican Spanish Lyric Diction," and Resources).[4] National school administrators are often unfamiliar with the size, importance, power, and popularity of ranchera music and Hispanic song. They will often welcome those who speak up with specific recommendations.

Mariachi ensembles, clubs, or some programs are thankfully emerging within music education departments in the Southwestern United States and in non-academic communities nationwide. Thanks to the hard work of these music educators and Spanish-speaking communities, they have become hugely popular since their inception during the 1960s in Texas and California.

Although it is beyond the scope of this book to cover the history of mariachi education programs, two of the earliest initiating programs during the 1960s are worthy of special mention: in 1961, Mariachi Uclatlán was born within the ethnomusicology program at UCLA in Los Angeles, California; in 1966, Mark Fogelquist joined the mariachi while studying within the program (see foreword of book by Fogelquist). The mariachi later became professional. Mark also founded a full-time mariachi middle and high school program in San Diego, California, building a foundation with the same students for five to six years in a row for over a thirty year span (see Figures 1.5 and 1.6 for Mark Fogelquist's current mariachi). Upon listening to the vocal excellence of Mariachi Vargas de Tecatitlán in Mexico, Mark hired former lead singer from that ensemble, Heriberto Molina, for annual one-week residencies. His mariachi students were thus introduced to vocal training while training on other mariachi instruments and repertoire.[5] One week per year was a start then; today, weekly private and group voice lessons are a necessity for mariachi students.

---

[3] Part of the problem might be attributed to the lack of easy availability of published sheet music. In 2017, three volumes of Mexican art song (including several rancheras) were published and are available through Classical Vocal Reprints (www.classicalvocalrep.com). Some individual rancheras and boleros can also be found at www.musicnotes.com.

[4] 91% of US high schools offer foreign language programs and Spanish is the most widely taught second language. https://www.newsdle.com/blog/foreign-language-statistics

[5] Programs are active in many major United States cities. Trumpeter and composer Jeff Nevin currently leads an instrumentally based mariachi program just north of San Diego, California, at Southwestern Community College.

FIGURE 1.5 Mark Fogelquist and his long-running mariachi program in San Diego, California, Mariachi Estrellas de Chula Vista. Courtesy of Mark Fogelquist.

CHAPTER 1: MARIACHI SONG 7

FIGURE 1.6 Lead singer Jilanie from the Mariachi Chula Vista High School Mariachi Program, led by Mark Fogelquist. Courtesy Mark Fogelquist.

Meanwhile, during this same period in San Antonio, Texas, the late Belle Ortiz was the first to Texas education in Texas schools from the early 1960s onward. Belle, who also worked with mariachi expert Juan Ortíz, first featured bilingual music with guitar. This was expanded into mariachi ensemble programs; at the same time the two built and toured with their own Mariachi "Campanas de América."[6]

Mariachi educators deserve high accolades for pioneering programs, annual conferences, and competitions in Texas, Arizona, Nevada, California, and New Mexico.

---

[6] Juan Ortiz (arranger/performer) and John López (producer) kindly collaborated with me along with Texas State University's mariachi juvenil, to record a CD, *Canta mi son!*, helping us win a *GrIndy* award from Disney. I wrote and sang fun, short originals and mariachi covers for K-12 school levels. Many of these songs have karaoke tracks.

Today, a newer Nevada mariachi program alone has over six thousand students, second only to Texas, thanks to the work of many, including Marcia Neel. To date, however, no program includes a vocal program component.

During the 1980s, Mariachi Cobre began in Arizona under the name, Los Changuitos Feos, and their lead singer Steve Carrillo has set a great contemporary standard of vocal training. The group has represented Mexico for years at Epcot Center in Florida, while, on the West Coast, the all-female Mariachi Divas have long represented Mexico at Disneyland in Southern California.

The growth and equal access to mariachi for women in United States mariachi education programs has been impressive, especially considering the traditional male dominance of mariachi ensembles since the inception of ranchera music in Mexico. Educational exposure has given female mariachi performers an edge in the United States as compared to Mexico, where programs are few and participation of women is less active; nevertheless, women in both countries still tend to find work in this style as soloists or in all-female groups. The "all-male ensemble" is still the norm and female musical talent is not yet fully respected or decently paid.

Music-education directors have been building ensembles and repertoire from their strengths, which is usually an instrumental band perspective. Our next step is to recognize that every mariachi performer plays two instruments (including the voice) not one, because the mariachi canon is largely vocally driven, and to include voice courses to support this foundation. Both voice teachers for solo and choral fields can be of assistance to mariachi directors if offering weekly voice classes independent of ensemble rehearsals that respect the authenticity of the style (see Chapter 3 section "Female Mariachi Fach" for similarities and differences between classical and vocal mariachi singing). Voice teachers can inform themselves about vocal differences between rhythms, songs, and styles in Chapter 5 "Mariachi Rhythms and Choosing Song Repertoire". A voice teacher will never know as much as a director about repertoire and ensemble intricacies, but they do know vocal production intimately. A director knows the repertoire and programming but can also inadvertently hurt a singer's voice, for example, when choosing a belt song when a student is already over yelling the belt, unable to mix head and chest voice, or choosing keys with the wrong vocal registration. Overlal, trust and collaboration is sorely needed to equalize the balance of voice development and its history alongside more established instrumental work. The current lower patterns of three-minute voice warm-ups with a cursory review of Spanish lyrics and basic melody is not a high enough standard to build, produce, and sustain great, long-lasting voices.

Several Southwestern US universities today currently boast fuller university mariachi programs, although specialized vocal inclusion is new and intermittent.[7] The Texas performance program at University of Texas at Rio Grande Valley trains several ensembles within a degree program of Bachelor of Arts in Mariachi Studies. Student mariachi ensembles tour often and regularly win vocal and ensemble awards. The university's leading ensemble, Mariachi Aztlán, appears in Figure 1.7. Its director, Dr. Dahlia Guerra, explains: "Our 30-year mariachi program [with several ensembles] credits its national achievements and success to consistently maintaining high musical standards, discipline, consistency, and an excellent work ethic."

Another important contributor to the growth of mariachi in Texas is the organization Texas Association of Mariachi Educators (TAME). While they do not yet feature solo vocal competition, this addition is a natural next step toward higher standards for many of singers.

---

[7] Southwestern Community College in Southern California offers a mariachi certificate program but without mariachi vocal training.

FIGURE 1.7 Two male soloists from national prize-winning Mariachi Aztlán. The University of Texas at Río Grande program (UTRGV) offers a bachelor of arts in mariachi studies. Courtesy of Dr. Dahlia Guerra.

During the author's tenure on the music faculty at Texas State University, mariachi vocal studies were expanded within both the undergraduate and master's degree mariachi program. Overall courses came to include applied mariachi voice, mariachi music history, mariachi class voice, and vocal coaching ensemble visits to provide acting, movement, and deeper interpretative skills before performances and competitions. They had often been ensemble winners at the annual San Antonio's Mariachi Extravaganza, had never competed vocally until my tenure. In 2009, one singer earned the university its first top national mariachi solo voice champion award in the solo voice competition. During my tenure and ever since, many others have been honored as finalists.[8] This kind of vocal program is foundational for addressing high standards of vocal excellence, whether in mariachi academia or private voice studios.

In 2018, Northern California's Bay Area chapter of the National Association of Teachers of Singing (SFBAC-NATS) began including mariachi and bolero solo competitors in their annual vocal competition as part of Contemporary Commercial Singing (CCM). They honored their first mariachi winner in the contemporary music category in virtual online finals in 2019, with other receiving honorable mention in 2018 (see Figure 1.8 for an image of winner, Lidia Chávez performing). At national and regional levels, the National Association of Teachers of Singing (NATS) has seen enthusiastic teacher and student support for master classes and recitals on ranchera and classical Mexican song.[9] Classical voice singers connect directly to

---

[8] National Vocal Mariachi Champion, Ms. Curiel, studied private voice lessons in the classical master's program, and group Hispanic voice and private mariachi lessons with the author.

[9] The author has presented regularly on mariachi, Mexican, and Latin American song at regional Cal-Western Regional and national conventions since the NATS Convention in Salt Lake City in 2010, with additional SFBAC-NATS local chapter master classes.

FIGURE 1.8 Lidia Chávez, first mariachi winner in the annual voice competition virtual finals in the Contemporary Music category (CM) at the National Association of Teachers of Singing, San Francisco Bay Area Chapter, 2020. Courtesy of Lidia Chávez.

classical Hispanic song repertoire. Increasing awareness of broader Mexican and Hispanic styles serves as an important bridge among classical singing, mariachi, and the bolero vocal worlds, and all share Italian bel canto influences (see Chapter 2 sections: "Mexico's Premiere Voice Teacher Maestro José Pierson" and "Early and Mid-Twentieth Century: Rural to Urban Contemporary Rancheras" through "Mexico's Golden Age of Cinema, Singers, and Songs").

Mexico's mariachi academic activity is currently more limited than that of the United States. Mariachi performance groups abound throughout Mexico, but with few programs and a great variety of musical levels. Guadalajara sponsors an annual mariachi festival, *Encuentro Internacional del Mariachi y la Charrería*. Toward the end of August, the streets of Guadalajara and its famed Teatro Degollado are packed with mariachi performers from many parts of the world. (Festivals have been popular for many years in U.S. cities as well, for example, Tucson, Las Cruces, San José, San Antonio, and more.) The Mexican government also began a mariachi school in Mexico City in 2012. It was first located downtown at Garibaldi Square, where mariachi is typically booked and performed, and relocated to Centro Cultural Ollin Yolitzli Cultural Center. While at Garibaldi, the voice classes for the women were classical and were not addressing the needs of female mariachi singers. The school has since moved back to Garibaldi, run by the Centro Cultural.

Separately, at the Universidad Nacional Autónoma de México (UNAM) in Mexico City, the author has had the honor of collaborating with voice faculty colleague, Veónica Murúa, to train classical voice majors in crossover ranchera singing at the *Encuentro de la canción latinoamericana* festival and to premiere Gomezanda songs and lectures. In 2012 solo singers performed rancheras in concert on the mainstage alongside classical Latin American and Mexican songs and declared it a novelty. Likewise, she has presented master classes in North Mexican border city Ciudad Juárez (sister city of El Paso, Texas), and performed with the international touring mariachi *Canto a mi Tierra* at Universidad Autónoma de Ciudad Juárez (UACJ) led by Maestro Jaime Mata. Unfortunately, regular voice classes in ranchera singing are not yet offered.

Understanding Terms: Ranchera, Mariachi, Mariache, and Música Regional Mexicana

Contemporary performers of ranchera folk music in Mexico and the United States might not yet know the many historical meanings and applications of the words *ranchera, mariachi,* or *mariache.* They are all part of a larger genre of folk music from Mexico called *música regional mexicana* (regional Mexican music).[10]

Ranchera is a common word that describes mariachi—one of Mexico's most important indigenous folk music genres. Ranchera music, that is, "music on the ranch," is an oral tradition that is sung, played, and danced. Mariachi singers who compete for Grammy and Latin Grammy awards submit in the category labeled "Regional Mexican Music."

The word *mariachi* can refer to an ensemble, especially in the United States, but it also has many other important meanings. A *mariachi* may refer to a specific body of folk-song repertory ("I sing *mariachi* songs," or "I sing *ranchera* songs"). The term can also be used to describe the singer or performer, for example, "I am a mariachi." You might also hear a performer mention the word for a *fiesta* (party) or *palenque,* as in "I am going to a mariachi." When in doubt, just remember that the word "mariachi" has become ubiquitous!

Another way to study the term mariachi is to look up words in dictionaries from specific time periods. According to Ramos y Duarte's second edition of *Diccionario de mejicanismos,* published in 1898,

> "Mariachi [. . .] Diversión en que se baila i canta al son de una orquesta compuesta de dos o tres violines, un redoblante i un bombo."[11]

> [Mariachi [. . .] Entertainment that is danced and sung, accompanied by rhythms from an orchestra made up of two or three violins, snare drum and a bombo [drum].

In 1898, mariachi instrumentation was varied and less standardized, but the inclusion of singing was quite established. We can assume there was a specific canon of songs and varied vocal styles depending on the region in Mexico, although recordings were not available at that time, and songs were passed down as an oral tradition.

In some documents, the term *mariache* is also used (see Glossary). Although most people are more familiar with the word mariachi than mariache, these words have been interchangeable throughout history, according to Dr. Jesús Jáuregui, leading anthropological scholar on this topic.[12]

---

[10] The term *música regional mexicana* is often misused by media to also include norteño and popular music that, although they are folk based, have become commercial.

[11] Jáuregui, *El Mariachi,* 52.

[12] Jáuregui, *El Mariachi,* 14, 16.

FIGURE 1.9 The manuscript title page of Gomezanda's *Mariache: Opera ranchera*. Composer and pianist Antonio Gomezanda copyrighted the world's first mariachi opera, *Mariache: Primera opera ranchera mexicana*, in 1943. It was first written in 1928–1929 under the name "La Virgen de San Juan" (see Chapter 2). Manuscript from Special Collections, Northwestern University.

The world's earliest known ranchera opera uses the word *Mariache* in its title: *Mariache: Primera ópera ranchera mexicana en tres actos* (*Mariache*: First Ranchera Mexican Opera in Three Acts). It was first written in 1928–1929 by Antonio Gomezanda under the original title *La Virgen de San Juan* (The Virgin from San Juan).[13] When Gomezanda later changed the title, he opted for nationalistic names such as *Mariache* over religious references, but the music remained virtually the same. Gomezanda was raised in Lagos de Moreno, Jalisco, in the nuclear heart of Western Mexican mariachi territory. Ranchera music proved to be a valuable folk foundation for Gomezanda throughout his life in many of his compositions. *Mariache* was copyrighted in its final form in 1943. Gomezanda's choice of the word *Mariache* for his title is unknown. His specific use of the word *Mariache*, however, draws attention to the importance of learning ranchera history. To date, this work has never been performed live, although much of it appears in the 1947 movie *Fantasía ranchera*, and several arias from *Mariache* have been published.[14] The unpublished title page for *Mariache* appears in Figure 1.9.

---

[13] Juanita Ulloa, *Gomezanda Mexican Art Songs* (Arkansas: Classical Vocal Reprints, 2018). Two arias from *Mariache* are available in the three-volume set *Gomezanda Mexican Song Collection* at www.classicalvocalreprints.com.

[14] Excerpts from the opera ranchera *Mariache* within the movie *Fantasía ranchera* are available online in DVD format.

CHAPTER 1: MARIACHI SONG   13

FIGURE 1.10 Young ranchera singer Debbie Carrillo from Mariachi Encendido of Del Sol Academy of the Performing Arts mariachi program led by Guadalupe Gonzalez, Las Vegas, Nevada. Courtesy of Mariac Neel and Guadalupe Gonzalez.

Some professionals have unintentionally promoted the word *mariachi* only as an ensemble of strolling instrumental players who incidentally happen to sing, yet readers can see that this word means so much more. Ranchera music has always been collaborative, with live, three-dimensional performances. The term *ranchera* is also useful to describe the broader, full expression of interweaving song, dance, and instrumentalists. *Ranchera* is the term most commonly used in Mexico, but it is less common in the United States.

Lesson Plans

The questions in lessons below may be used in many ways, for example:

1. Lead classroom discussions
2. In between songs during a rehearsal or break
3. Assigned as a homework
4. Special projects for event presentations
5. Display the top presentations at a school library or share them electronically

Suggestions: Presentations can be verbal, with presentation slides or a poster. Audio samples should be included.

LESSON 1: MARIACHI SONG: INTRODUCTION

1. What does the word *ranchera* mean in English?
2. When and where did ranchera music originate?
3. How did the worldwide organization UNESCO honor mariachi as a symbol of Mexico in 2011?
4. Is mariachi repertoire primarily vocal or instrumental?
5. Describe or draw and color the typical *trajes de charro* that mariachi ensembles wear.
6. What factors make the mariachi vocal sound so unique? Describe mariachi singing style in your own words.
7. Where was ranchera music traditionally performed? Where have you seen mariachi performed?
8. Are mariachi ensembles supposed to always play alone? Who do they historically collaborate with?

LESSON 2: GROWTH OF MARIACHI PROGRAMS AND UNDERSTANDING TERMS: *RANCHERA, MARIACHI, MARIACHE,* AND *MÚSICA REGIONAL MEXICANA*

1. How many Hispanic people currently live in the United States?
2. When and where did mariachi programs originate in the United States?
3. Define each term: *ranchera, mariachi,* and *mariache.*
4. Why is the phrase regional Mexican music/*música regional mexicana* slightly different from the phrase *ranchera music*? Which term is broader?
5. What is the name of the world's first ranchera opera? Who is the composer, and where was he raised? When was it written?

Answer Key

LESSON 1: MARIACHI VOICE: INTRODUCTION

1. *Ranchera* in English means "from the ranch" or rural, folk style.
2. Ranchera music originated in the 1830s in the western states of Mexico, especially Jalisco, Nayarit, and Colima, but extended up into the United States all along California up to San Francisco.

3. In 2011, UNESCO honored Mexico by naming mariachi as a worldwide musical heritage symbol of Mexico.
4. Vocal.
5. The typical *traje de charro* is black (although different solid colors are used) with botonadura in silver or gold lining the side of the pants and the jacket, moño for a tie, and a matching sombrero.
6. Use of falsete flipping into a sustained top range with a completely different sound identifies mariachi singing anywhere.
7. Life events, marriages, funerals, quinceañeras, and so on.
8. No, Mariachi ensembles more traditionally perform collaboratively with dancers and solo singers.

LESSON 2: GROWTH OF MARIACHI PROGRAMS AND UNDERSTANDING TERMS: RANCHERA, MARIACHI, MARIACHE, AND MÚSICA REGIONAL MEXICANA

1. 56 million Hispanics currently live in the United States.
2. Mariachi programs in the United States originated in Southern California at UCLA and also in San Antonio, Texas. Both programs originated in the 1960s.
3. Ranchera, from the ranch. Mariachi, performer in the style, part of ensemble, fiesta, and so on. *Mariache*, also acceptable, is an older term that has largely fallen out of use. It is also the title of the world's first opera ranchera.
4. Regional Mexican music is a broader music category used for the Grammys. It includes ranchera music, northern banda and conjunto, and other commercial and folk styles from Mexican music.
5. *Mariache: Primera opera ranchera mexicana.* Composer, Antonio Gomezanda. He was raised in Lagos de Moreno, Jalisco, in Western Mexico. He finished his score in 1928–1929 originally under another title *La Virgen de San Juan.*

CHAPTER 2
HISTORY: MARIACHI SINGERS AND THEIR SONGS

FIGURE 2.1 Female mariachi singer with eyes closed in a dramatic moment of a live performance.

Many of Mexico's classic songs and top ranchera singers are legendary household names today even though they rose to international fame over seventy years ago. These celebrities introduced songs that took Mexico and the Spanish speaking world by storm, echoing waves of nationalism felt throughout the country and beyond beginning not long after the Mexican Revolution (1910–1921).

The remarkable musical output and quality of Mexican singers, composers, and their songs during this wave of nationalism put Mexico on the world map. This era is often called *Siglo de oro del cine mexicano* (Mexico's Golden Age of Cinema) or *Siglo de oro* (Golden Age). This period ran from the mid-1930s to 1959. To date, it is the mariachi world's most important vocal period in music history. We begin this chapter by noting it as a pinnacle moment for Mexican mariachi singers and composers after a long road of oblivion. After reading this chapter and the importance of singers and their songs, readers will understand why we rename this period *Mexico's Golden Age of Cinema, Singers, and Songs.*

Studying the vocal roots of Mexican song and performance practice provides a context for understanding the actual sound and performance practice of ranchera singers. The history of vocal roots provides glimpses and context regarding ranchera song topics, styles, and celebrity singers that came together later in the twentieth century; during this precise time Mexico was defining its domestic musical identity.

Mexico City became a musical melting pot after the end of the Mexican Revolution in 1921. This period is often called the urban mariachi period, a contrast to its rural origins prior to the Revolution. Newly arrived singers in Mexico City had easier access to Spanish and Italian operatic training than rural Mexico. Folk singers also absorbed opera and other rural vocal styles, however indirectly, by being able to listen to other singers live in shows or on radio. Readers will hear of both composers and singers during the *Siglo de oro* preparing or performing both ranchera rural and urban mariachi style with subtle influences. A syncretic vocal mix and sound, uniquely Mexican, was born (See Figure 2.2 picture of Amalia Mendoza, Siglo de oro ranchera singer).

Every person mentioned in this chapter (and those we missed) contributed greatly to the growth of the ranchera singing. As a result of work that began long before all of us, dear readers, mariachi became an international symbol of Mexico. There are many more unsung and unstudied singers, teachers, composers, producers, and directors from the 1900s waiting in the wings to be researched and brought to light by those reading this book.

Ranchera Rural Folk Origins

Mariachi, or *ranchera* music as it is traditionally called (literally, "music from the ranch"), is a live, oral singing tradition with a long, post-conquest history. It has rural Western Mexico folk origins dating from the 1830s onward.[1] Ranchera songs may have existed in rural areas long before the 1800s. Performers originally wore white peasant garb with *huaraches* (sandals). Today they wear black, elegant *trajes de charro*, and singers wear the same or other colorful regional Mexican costumes (see also Chapter 4 section: "Costumes, Make-up, Song Studies, and Singing with a Microphone").[2]

In the map in Figure 2.4, the central ranchera music stronghold is pictured in pink, but ranchera music extended much farther up and down along Mexico's western coast. It also ran as far north as present-day San Francisco and San Rafael, California, in the United States.[3]

Ranchera songs have been an integral part of Mexican everyday secular lifestyle since the early days of the ranchera lifestyle in the 1830s. Ranchera songs were traditionally performed as a part of life events such as baptisms, funerals, rodeos, fairs, holidays, and weddings. Although mariachi in modern times has moved to large concert arenas and symphony halls, the rural folk tradition of accompanying life events with ranchera songs continues in full force today.

---

[1] *Ranchera* music is the tradition that specifies mariachi folk music originally from Mexico's western countries, not to be confused with other Mexican unrelated musical styles. The term *ranchera* music has also been used by some media to also describe instrumental *banda* (band) music from Northern Mexico. The word sometimes may apply to either, thanks to the media (see Glossary).

[2] Jáuregui, *El Mariachi*, 48, 177. Jáuregui has written extensively on this topic. He includes a map marking the mariachi ranch locations from 1833 forward, with photos and commentaries covering singers, dancers, and instrumentalists.

[3] Jáuregui, *El Mariachi*, 48, 177–178.

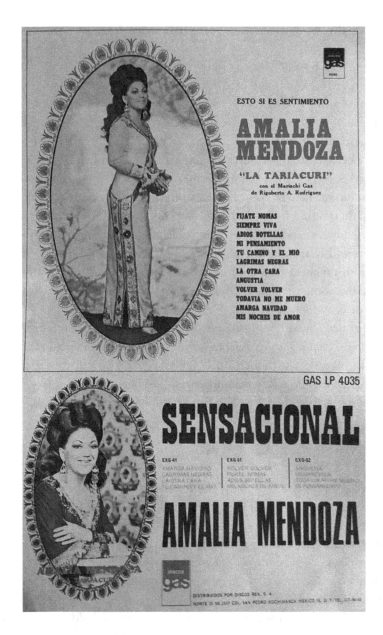

FIGURE 2.2 Ranchera soloist Amalia Mendoza was also a featured member of the Trio Tariácuri, all members of the same family. Amalia performed during Mexico's Golden Age of Cinema, Singers, and Songs.

Figure 2.5 depicts an annual Mexican *Posadas* Christmas sung celebration with rural ponchos, ranchera string instruments providing song accompaniment, young singers, and actors all in white re-enacting the story of Mary and Joseph in search of lodging before the birth of Christ.

During the mid-1800s, conservative Catholic religious leaders voiced their opposition to Spain against mariachi performers and their songs, perhaps due to their local popularity and celebrations. In 1848, Bishop Cosme Santa Ana wrote a letter to Spain, openly complaining about the mariachi "fiesta" demeanor outside the church.[4]

As of the twentieth and twenty-first centuries, however, mariachi song repertoire includes religious songs and plays an integral role in Catholic masses and services. In 1966, the bishop of Cuernavaca, Mr. Sergio Mendez Arceo, commissioned Canadian priest Juan Marco Leclerc

---

[4] https://es.w3we.com/wiki/Mariachi.

CHAPTER 2: HISTORY 19

FIGURE 2.3 Mariachi singer with traditional Mexican colored *zarape* (blanket)

FIGURE 2.4 Map of Mexico—Pictured are some of Mexico's regions with strong musical representation. Mariachi is especially prominent in Western States of Jalisco, Colima, Nayarit, and farther north, perhaps as far as San Francisco. California was originally part of Mexico. Design by Juan Carlos Diego Sánchez.

FIGURE 2.5 Typical Christmas celebration of an annual Mexican Christmas Posada produced by Mother Lode Musical Theater Company in San Rafael, California, 1992, featuring young solo singer-dancer Cristina Ulloa, accompanied by guitarrón, guitar, and requinto (smaller guitar). Photo courtesy of Juanita Ulloa.

to write the *Misa Panamericana* (Panamerican mass). Today, the mass is a standard part of Catholic masses and special events throughout the Southwest and beyond.[5]

Mariachi ensembles also sing, and soloists are featured on December 12th, an important Mexican holiday after celebrating the Virgin of Guadalupe (see Chapter 6 for a Song to the Virgin by Gomezanda). In Figure 2.6, singer and mariachi director Ramón Ponce sings while enacting a typical offering to the Virgin within the church. Ponce is the founder of today's mushrooming Mariachi Academy in New York City, New York.

VOCAL ROOTS

Ranchera music is often defined as having two broad periods in its history. This book will introduce a third period. First was rural, older, regional Mexican mariachi, or *mariachi rural* or *mariachi antiguo* up until about 1915. By the end of the Mexican Revolution (1910–1921), the situation had changed. Ranchera music had evolved into a style called contemporary, urban, or *mariachi moderno*. The second contemporary period from about 1915 onward mixed vocal techniques for ranchera singers with both classical influences and folk *bravío* singing. A third period in mariachi voice history without crossover influences is described further ahead (see "Singer/Songwriter José Alfredo Jiménez: A Third Period in Mariachi History" in this chapter).

Mariachi soloists and audiences in Mexico City during the after the Mexican Revolution (1910–1921) began to hear a wide variety of classical and regional folk music singers. The Mexican government, under Spanish rule, had long been staging Spanish nationalistic *zarzuelas* (see Glossary) since the mid-1600s. This was followed by Mexico's preference for Italian opera after its liberation from Spain in 1821. During the later twentieth-century of ranchera music from its rural roots to Mexico City's urban variety of styles, the vocal sound of composers and singers

---

[5] https://www.npr.org/2014/01/03/259389094/our-soul-is-mariachi-music-houstons-mexican-mass.

FIGURE 2.6 Ramón Ponce, director of Mariachi Academy of New York, sings to the Virgin of Guadalupe in an annual December 12th Catholic Mass. Photo courtesy of Ramón Ponce.

became more stylized, virtuosic, and sophisticated. Oftentimes the rural singing style also continued alongside the changing urban one. Where did this stylized sound specifically come from?

Many vocal roots of the mariachi world on the classical side can be traced directly and indirectly to the classical voice scene in Mexico City. Indirectly, reviews and publicity of opera performances are richly documented through newspaper reviews in Mexico City from about 1815 onward. From 1823 on, Italian operas and their singers were favored as Mexicans celebrated their newfound freedom from Spain.[6] Solo virtuosic singing became a fad in Mexico with the introduction of the bel *canto* style of singing, which literally means "beautiful singing" (see Glossary). Mexico City's socialites became obsessed with the bel canto operas of Italian composer Giacomo Rossini (1792–1868). Italian producers soon followed with imported Italian singers featured in live opera productions in Mexico City by Bellini (1802–1835), Donizetti (1797–1848), and later Giuseppi Verdi (1813–1901).

The Italian bel canto vocal style written by the above-named composers traveled worldwide, but in Mexico City, it was combined with ranchera singing in a very special way. This vocal style features rich vocal tone, virtuosic agility from note to note, and long, smoothly connected melodies without big jumps. Apart from the quick-moving *melismatic* notes (see Glossary), this vocal stylistic description greatly resembles ranchera melodic songs and the singing of top ranchera singers during Mexico's urban mariachi period, which in turn led to its Golden Age of charro musicals and celebrity singers (see further in this chapter, "Mexico's Golden Age of Cinema, Singers, and Songs").

Mexico's socialites enjoyed imported Italian productions for almost a century, thanks to the funding of Italian *empresarios* and singers by the Mexican government. Unfortunately,

---

[6] José Octavio Sosa, *La Ópera en México de la Independencia al inicio de la Revolución (1821–1910* (México D.F.: Instituto Nacional de Bellas Artes y Literatura, 2010), 22. Mexico gained its freedom from Spain in 1821.

FIGURE 2.7 Male singer/dancer dressed in *jarocho* style from Veracruz in the Gulf of Mexico. Costumes are white with *guayabera* shirts for the men due to hot weather. Design courtesy of Marcia Cangadahan.

many talented local Mexican opera singers, producers, and composers were overlooked.[7] Regardless, many Mexican singers became avid classical and operatic vocalists. Mexico City's National Conservatory of Music opened in 1866 and continues in full force today as the country's major classical music conservatory.

Before Italian opera singers became favored by Mexican socialites and the government in the 1800s, the earlier Spanish ruling government in Mexico City and Mexican socialites promoted and attended Spanish *zarzuelas* (see Glossary). The *zarzuela* genre has its own mix of Spanish folk rhythms, instruments, and songs with influence from Italian opera.[8] *Zarzuelas* were also called *sainetes* or *tonadillas*.

---

[7] Leonor Saavedra, "Staging the Nation: Race, Religion, and History in Mexican Opera of the 1940s," *Opera Quarterly* (2007): 3, 5. Mexico has its own opera history, which has been largely ignored.

[8] Spain and Italy also have a long and intertwined zarzuela-opera music history dating back to 1650, and Spain ruled parts of Italy going back as far as 1442 under Spain's Alfonso I. https://uta.alma.exlibrisgroup.com/discovery/openurl?institution=01UTAR_INST&vid=01UTAR_INST:Services&lang=en&rfr_id=info:sid%2Fsummon&rft_dat=ie%3D&rft.mms_id=996260083504911&svc_dat=CTO&u.ignore_date_coverage=true&Force_direct=false.

Spanish *zarzuela* productions of short sung comedies were called *género chico* and *comedias musicales* (one-act *zarzuela*—see Glossary.) These one-act *comedias musicales* were also sung-dramas and comedy-musicals, not unlike the mood and structure of Mexico's future charro musicals. Mexico later calls them *comedias rancheras* (see in this chapter "Mexico's Golden Age of Cinema, Singers, and Songs" and "Crossover Singing: Jorge Negrete and Operas Rancheras").

While under Spanish rule, *zarzuela* singing in Mexico was deemed a proper vocal expression, more elite, and upper class. Indirectly, this belief would falsely lead Mexicans to believe idiomatic Mexican ranchera folk song was inferior or less acceptable. Classical singing was most often performed in indoor salons, concerts, or sung dramas.

While salon performances were classical, they could include rancheras on voice and piano.[9] (See "Crossover Singing: Jorge Negrete and *Operas Rancheras*" in this chapter.) One early, important example from the mid-1800s is the sheet-music publication "Colección de Treinta Jarabes, Sones y más populares Aires Nacionales de la República Mexicana" ("Collection of Thirty Jarabes, Sones, and more National Folk Songs from the Mexican Republic"), depicted in Figures 2.8 and 2.9. The subtitle explains the folk songs were collected and arranged for voice and piano by Miguel Ríos Toledano. These folk songs, which were specifically from the ranchera tradition, consisted of *sones* and *jarabes*, both popular and highly syncopated rhythmic styles cultivated by mariachi ensembles (see Glossary).

Another crossover performance situation during indoor *zarzuela* productions was when solo ranchera singers and Mexican folk dancers were allowed to perform during interludes between acts.[10] Ranchera songs were otherwise active outside of the theater in Mexico's indoor and outdoor community celebrations and family events from the 1830s forward.

Ranchera singing has always been an oral tradition. This explains why, contrary to classical singing, there is scant audio and written information describing early rural singing sound prior to 1900. Nevertheless, readers, just for one minute, imagine days in the past without internet, radio, television, cars, or airplanes, along with less access to mobility and transportation. Different regional stylistic variations probably existed then due to Mexico's large geographic size and lack of easy transportation access. Pictorial images of social and musical gatherings from before the 1900s, resemble singers alongside instrumentalists and dancers and Mexican culture has always included singing, even in pre-conquest times.[11]

Before and after the conquest in 1521, each of Mexico's regions had its own vocal styles for speech and singing with a syncretic mix of indigenous roots. Spanish and African elements were added after the conquest. It is also important to know that prior to the 1521 conquest, poetry and song were hugely valued by the Nahua indigenous cultures, as seen in the extant pre-1521 poetry from the *Flower Songs of King Nezahualcoyotl* published in Nahuatl (see Glossary) and Spanish.[12]

While we don't know exactly how singers sounded prior to the advent of radio and recordings in the twentieth century, we know the linguistic sound was different. As an example, consider

---

[9] Later, many charro musical composers such as Tata Nacho were classically trained but also composed rancheras, showing perhaps a continuous tradition. Nationalistic classical composer Antonio Gomezanda also wrote many rancheras and the world's first ranchera opera, *Mariache* (see "Crossover Singing: Jorge Negrete and Operas Rancheras" in this chapter).

[10] Ironically, the *zarzuela* musical tradition originally got its own start in Spain as a song interlude within larger presentations of full plays during Spain's *Siglo de oro* (Spanish Golden Age). Yolanda Moreno Rivas, *Historia música popular Mexicana* (Mexico City: Editorial Oceano, 2008), 56–57.

[11] Jáuregui, *El mariachi*, pictures on pp. 34, 47, 49, 53, 90, 149.

[12] The author notes that even before the arrival of sung traditions from Spain and opera from Italy, Mexico's indigenous Aztec tradition left important Náhuatl poems that were clearly sung. See, for example, "Flower Songs of Nezahualcoyotl," http://www.famsi.org/research/curl/nezahualcoyotl_intro.html.

FIGURE 2.8 Mid-1800s Publication of Mexican rancheras for voice and piano entitled "Colección de Treinta Jarabes, Sones, y más Aires Nacionales de la República Mexicana" (Collection of Thirty Jarabes, Sones, and more National Folk Songs from the Mexican Republic) (see Figure 2.10 for sheet-music sample). Courtesy of Biblioteca Cuicamatini, Facultad de música, Universidad Nacional Autónoma de México (UNAM), Mexico.

that today's actual sound and projection of Spaniards speaking Spanish has a darker back placement with head/chest mix in sound than do Indian dialects in Mexico. Many Mexican dialects have forward placement and sit consistently high in pure head voice. The blending of the Spanish language with dialects since the conquest in 1521 has resulted in what we hear

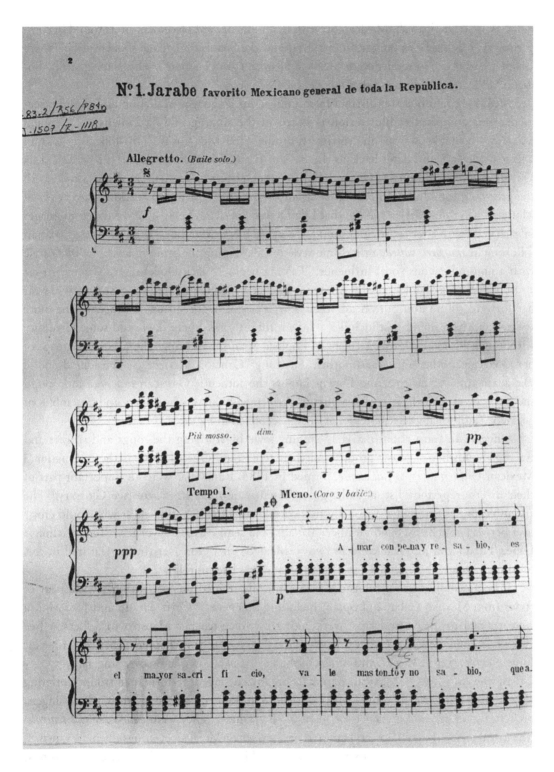

FIGURE 2.9 Sheet Music Sample from first Jarabe in Collection listed in Figure 2.9. Note the virtuosity of the instrumental melodic lines and the rhythmic and meter changes between sections of the song. There is also call and response between the singing choir and instrumental sections, as well as the integration of dancers throughout, contrasting solo dancers with a fuller dance ensemble.

today as Mexican Spanish. Mexican Spanish has more forward placement in its sound in comparison with other Latin American countries and the Spanish language spoken in Spain (see Chapter 8 section: "Introduction to Mexican Spanish Lyrics Diction"). This is the general idiomatic Mexican Spanish sound that ranchera singers use.

Mexican Spanish is also distinct from indigenous languages in diction and sound placement. One comparative illustration is heard in the singing of Lila Downs in "Canción Mixteca," available on YouTube (https://youtu.be/TIo9fMcKQwY). This folk song is from Oaxaca, Mexico, and dates back to the days of the Mexican Revolution (1910–1921). Lila Downs chooses traditional Oaxacan folk instrumental accompaniment in this example, with the groove of a traditional *ranchera valseada* rhythm (see Chapter 5 section: "Overview of Mariachi Rhythmic Styles"). Note that Lila Downs alternates Spanish and Mixtec languages in each verse with a very particular sound. Compare Lila's vocal sound in this Mixtec Oaxacan folk song in *ranchera valseada* rhythmic style to Lila singing the same *ranchera valseada* style with a non-indigenous vocal influence: "Paloma negra" (Black Dove) on YouTube: https://youtu.be/OQVJaZPdofA. In the Mixtec-influenced "Canción Mixteca," listeners will hear her forward sound and pure head voice. On "Paloma negra" listeners can hear the more stylized ranchera sound that includes a darker, robust tone, legato lines, and some virtuosity with long held notes. Downs is fluent in English, Spanish, and sings the Mixtec language of her Oaxacan mother and grandmother. The song "Canción Mixteca" is considered one of Oaxaca's primary anthems, and Downs honors the authentic Oaxacan ranchera folk sound she has grown up with. It is also regularly performed by mariachi singers and ensembles in Mexico. Traditional Oaxacan regional dress is depicted in Figure 2.10.

Singers can learn about mariachi singing style by studying the songs and singers and tracing the history of music groups and their repertoire. One example is the international Mexican *Orquesta Típica Jalisciense*, formed in 1884. Rancheras were an important part of their diverse repertoire list, and the group often wore *trajes de charro* (see Glossary.) The ensemble always featured a classically trained solo singer with acting skills who could crossover between rancheras, band numbers, ballads, and semi-classical favorites.[13] Tenors Alfonso López Tirado and José Mojica were two of Mexico's first crossover singers featured in this touring pre-mariachi ensemble, and Pedro Vargas was later to follow.

It became common for soloists to be technically trained to shift within a wide array of styles from Mexico, Cuba, and Spain, including rancheras.[14] Ortíz Tirado and José Mojica were trained for opera and crossover singing by voice teacher Maestro José Pierson (see "Mexico's Premiere Voice Teacher: Maestro José Pierson" in this chapter). They set a tone for Jorge Negrete, Pedro Vargas, and others in the next generation of crossover singers.

By the early 1900s, Mexican nationals organized staged performance troupes offering variety shows. Performers toured Mexico under outdoor *carpas* (tents) with ranchera singers, orchestras, comics, and a wide assortment of entertainers. They were called *revistas teatrales* (theatrical reviews)[15] (see Glossary) and *Noches mexicanas* (Mexican evenings). Female ranchera singer Lucha Reyes, mariachi ensembles, and a world-famous comic Cantinflas all performed in these shows. During their touring, urban ranchera singers now living in Mexico City cross-pollinated their vocal styles back into rural areas.[16]

---

[13] Jáuregui, *El mariachi*, 52–53, 58. Note that the pictures often reflect only the instrumentalists and singing style is generally not covered.

[14] Jáuregui, *El Mariachi*, 52.

[15] Yolanda Moreno Rivas, *Historia música popular Mexicana* (Mexico City: Editorial Oceano, 2008), 56–57.

[16] Jáuregui, *El Mariachi*, 69.

FIGURE 2.10 Tehuana costume from Oaxaca, Mexico. Modeled by Laryssa Ramos. Photo courtesy of Laryssa Ramos.

EARLY TWENTIETH-CENTURY RANCHERA SONGS

An important Mexican folk-song style from before and during the Mexican Revolution (1910–1921) is the corrido. The corrido is a song that narrates stories, similar to US country ballads (see Glossary). The songs can be lively polkas in 2/4 meter or slower in a 3/4 *ranchera valseada* rhythm (see Chapter 5 sections: "Overview of Mariachi Rhythmic Styles" and "Six Basic Rhythms"). Corridos have fascinating histories and often describe soldiers, leaders, and legendary figures on or near the Northern Mexican border where a good deal of the fighting took place during the Mexican Revolution. Corridos are often sung today by soloists, duos, and ensembles. Some corrido examples are "La Cucaracha," "La Adelita," "La Valentina," "La Chancla," and "Carabina 30-30."[17] Figure 2.11 features a typical norteña costume.

---

[17] Jáuregui, *El Mariachi*, 66.

FIGURE 2.11 Traditional Attire for Singers and Dancers from Chihuahua in Northern Mexico. This regional costume is perfect for those performing corridos. Design courtesy of Marcia Cangadahan.

In 1882, today's ubiquitous song "Cielito lindo" was written by Quirino Mendoza y Cortés (c. 1859–1957). This song is a *ranchera valseada* (see Glossary), and it is well known for its *Ay, ay, ay* chorus, which is sung all over the world. Despite its popularity, it is not as easy to sing as one might think, especially as a solo. There is a large jump and with an octave range which requires good breath support. One option is to assign two beginning singers with different vocal ranges to share the song, one on the verses and one on the chorus (see Chapter 5 section: "Choosing Mariachi Voice Repertoire").

The previously mentioned *ranchera valseada* "Canción Mixteca" (Mixtec song) from Oaxaca, México was written in 1916. This nationalistic song expresses longing for one's homeland. It was written by José López Alavéz (1889–1974), who won a composition competition with this song. The song has one sustained falsete note in the chorus, making it somewhat of a showpiece for beginning or intermediate students with an octave range, arpeggio jump experience, and initial exposure to falsete (see Chapter 3 section: "To Bridge or to Break").

CHAPTER 2: HISTORY   29

Another important song from this early twentieth-century era was "La borrachita," composed in 1918 by Ignacio Fernández Esperón (1894–1968; also known as "Tata Nacho"). This song can be tackled by beginning singers as its range and melodic movement are small. Listen first to Javier Solis, and then listen to Lola Beltrán later turn this song into a showpiece in film and in concert. Note each uses their own phrasing, on YouTube (https://youtu.be/9NPNpmslLlc and https://youtu.be/nSu7e9Nyb8U).

Mexico's Golden Age of Cinema, Singers, and Songs

Mexico's *Siglo de oro del cine mexicano*, or Golden Age of Cinema as it is commonly called, began during the mid-1930s and lasted until approximately 1959. There was a heightened sense of nationalism in Mexico, and this was expressed powerfully through singers, songs, and film.

Some say it all began with live music programming on XEW Radio in Mexico City. The station was inaugurated in 1930, as radio was new and microphones were first being used in radio broadcasts.[18] The first microphone was invented in 1876, followed by the first radio with limited use in the 1890s. Live music shows immediately took hold on XEW radio, presenting singers and composers, and premiering new songs.[19] Song hits were quickly incorporated into films and recordings. For many years to come, no performing artist could hope to have a successful career without performing at XEW Radio.

The film industry soon followed with new ideas, led by the same directors of XEW Radio and funding from the Mexican government to support nationalism through the arts. Mexico's secretary of public education of Mexico, Mr. José Vasconcelos, worked with the media from 1921 to 1924 to launch Mexico as an important center of future films. Mr. Vasconcelos was also a writer, politician, and philosopher. In this way the Mexican Department of Education cemented Mexico's cultural and musical identity using ranchera singers, songs, and lifestyle themes in music, all wrapped up in film.

Through the promotion of these films, singers, and songs, the mariachi vocal style also became instantly recognizable as a worldwide symbol of Mexico, alongside the instrumental ensemble, sombreros, and black *trajes de charro* (see Chapter 4 sections: "Costumes," "Make-up," "Song Studies," and "Singing with a Microphone").

The films were structured as *comedias rancheras*, literally meaning "charro comedies" (see Glossary). The term *comedia* had been used for many years whether the production was a drama or comedy. Mexicans built upon the concept of *comedias musicales* from Spain to create *comedias rancheras*, supplanting local culture and music. References to Spain were dropped, evoking instead the nostalgia and exoticism of Mexican rural life on the ranch. Plot themes also juxtaposed differences between Mexico's urban and rural lifestyles. *Comedia ranchera* plots mixed dialogue, original songs, seasoned singer-actors, and nationalistic Mexican themes to create charro films with accompanying recordings. Some films also featured contrasts between urban and rural lifestyles.

The unused availability of Mexican opera singers suddenly became a gift to the ranchera song and film world. They needed skilled singer-actors who sounded Mexican, knew Mexican culture, and could learn and perform songs quickly. The training of the opera singers included

---

[18] 1930 marks the date of Mexico's first adoption of the microphone for radio broadcasts, but the microphone was first patented as early as 1875 in earlier forms. Broadcasters began implementing them on radio beginning around 1917. For more information: https://digilab.libs.uga.edu/scl/exhibits/show/steel_vintage_mics/advent_of_broadcasting.

[19] Yolanda Moreno Rivas, *Historia de la música popular mexicana*, Editorial Océano de México, 2008, 94–95.

already developed interpretation techniques. Good interpretation included allowing intent to directly dictate the mood, movements, and stage choreography for any song or scene. Singers did not simply walk or move around to "use the stage." Many of these singers were trained at vocal technical levels that have yet to be surpassed today, and their acting skills were already high.

During the *Siglo de oro*, film production and recordings had very quick turnarounds. With this came a sudden demand for skilled technical solo singers with acting skills. Soloists were often judged on their looks for film. They were also responsible for beautiful tone, transmitting song interpretation, and fully developed acting roles aurally and visually on the big screen.

Jorge Negrete was a highly proficient opera singer and actor with equestrian skills from military school. This was useful for ranchera roles (see "Crossover singing: Jorge Negrete and *Operas rancheras*" in this chapter, and Chapter 8 section: "Jorge Negrete"). Some of the many talented cinema solo singers apart from Jorge Negrete include Pedro Vargas, Pedro Infante, Lucha Villa, Manolita Arriola, and Javier Solis, as well as Amalia Mendoza, Lucha Reyes, Irma Vila, Elena Sandoval, and Lola Beltrán (see the "Female Ranchera Singers" and "Crossover Ranchera Singers" sections in this chapter). Another ranchera soloist famous for his huapangos (see Glossary) was Miguel Aceves Mejía (1915–2006).

The superior quality of film production, acting, original songs, and singers during Mexico's *Siglo de oro* revealed Mexico's identity and greatness to the world in a novel and far-reaching way. This was especially important to Mexico after centuries of being conquered and governed by other countries. The singers, songs, producers, ensembles, and composers all played an important role in creating timeless classics that continue to be a part of the mariachi song canon today. Many also believe that the technical level reached by many of the singers during the Golden Age of Cinema, Singers, and Songs has not yet been surpassed.

Fortunately, many charro films from this epoch are easily accessible online today for singers to watch and study. By studying the acting and singing skills of these singers and their songs in film, teachers and singers will directly experience Mexican singers, singing style, acting, and the songs themselves.

Mexico's first international *Siglo de oro* charro hit was the 1936 musical film *Allá en el rancho grande* (Over There on the Big Ranch). The film's hit song with the same title quickly made its way to Hollywood in the United States and later became immortalized. "*Allá en el rancho grande*" is an up-tempo 2/4 polka, a popular rhythmic style from Northern Mexico (see Chapter 5 section: "Six Basic Rhythms"). This song was originally composed much earlier during the 1920s by Emilio Uranga, with lyrics by Jorge del Moral. Both were highly recognized classical composers of their time. "*Allá en el rancho grande*" was first recorded by Tito Guizar (1908–1999) of Guadalajara, Jalisco. The popularity of the song and film was so great, it was later re-recorded with the voice of legendary baritone Jorge Negrete (See Negrete on YouTube: https://youtu.be/SiHgY7LWa6s).

When "*Allá en el rancho grande*" crossed into the United States market, English lyrics were added. It became an international hit, sung by Elvis Presly, Dean Martin, Bing Crosby, and Gene Autry. In 1944, the same song was featured in the Disney cartoon movie *Los Tres Caballeros* (watch it on YouTube: https://youtu.be/dbCh3qTFZK8). The song has crossed through many generations and different markets throughout the world. "*Allá en el rancho grande*" automatically brings smiles to the lips and clapping to the hearts of singers and audiences everywhere; this is a true expression of the spirit of Mexican song.

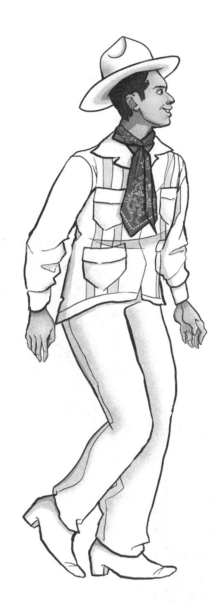

FIGURE 2.12 Male performer dressed in *jarocho* style from Veracruz in the Gulf of Mexico. *Jarocho* dancers are known for their solo footwork, not unlike *zapateado* from the flamenco world in Southern Spain. Design by Marcia Caganadan.

Manuel M. Ponce, "The Father of Mexican Song"

At the time of the Mexican Revolution, composer, pianist, music educator, and scholar Manuel M. Ponce (1882–1948) was thirty years old. Besides playing and teaching piano, he also published articles, composed, gathered songs, and wrote arrangements for folk songs. As the Revolution started in 1910, he began writing about Mexican nationalistic music topics. He stressed the importance of collecting and defining elements of Mexican folk song. Manuel M. Ponce is known for his compositions for piano, voice, and guitar. While he did not specifically compose for mariachi, his song "Estrellita" is one of the top songs performed by top mariachi soloists. Ponce was an important pedagogue, collector of songs, and a prolific composer for Mexico. For this reason, he is known as the "Father of Mexican Song." He is pictured in Figure 2.13.

Ponce and others published ranchera song collections from this period. The song cover pictured in Figure 2.15 is insightful. It lists titles with a mixture of folk songs with rancheras, ballads, and classical songs published for voice and piano. Ranchera folk songs were obviously very

FIGURE 2.13 Composer, pianist, pedagogue, and scholar Manuel María Ponce, also known as the "Father of Mexican Song." Courtesy of Biblioteca Cuicamatini, Facultad de música, Universidad Nacional Autónoma de México (UNAM), Mexico.

important to classical vocal composers. These songs were promoted worldwide, as noted in the cities listed on the cover of the publication collected by Manuel M. Ponce in Figure 2.14.

In Ponce's writings, he advocated for a new starting place for Mexican song. He did not include pre-Columbian music from before the Spanish conquest. Ponce asked musicians to collect, establish, and follow a song structure with an amalgam of folk and classical elements. The song style consisted of a combination of *Italiante* long, legato melodic lines, Western European song structure of AABA, and the direct simplicity of Mexican local folk poetry as lyrics. It is unclear why Ponce did not consider any pre-conquest vocal elements, indigenous languages, or pre-Columbian poetry. What is obvious is that he avoided Spanish melodic ornaments, showing deference to Italian musical influences. Some suggest that Mexicans at the time showed preference for Italian opera styles over Spanish singing styles because of the three-hundred-year conquest by Spaniards. While the Italian influence may seem curious with respect to Mexican song, Ponce received musical training in Italy and noted that Mexico had lost its indigenous Aztec musical roots during the Spanish

FIGURE 2.14 Manuel M. Ponce is considered the "Father of Mexican Song," as he collected and published many Mexican folk songs. This song was published in Germany and in New York as early as 1912. Courtesy of Biblioteca Cuicamatini, Facultad de música, Universidad Nacional Autónoma de México (UNAM), Mexico.

Conquest in Mexico in 1521. Perhaps Ponce felt Mexican society was not ready to accept its indigenous roots, or he may have been unwilling to research and take on reconstructing Aztec poetry into song. Another factor is that, at this same time, Mexican society and the government continued to follow Rossini, Bellini, and Italian opera with no interest in or support of Mexican song heritage.

Almost three hundred years after the conquest in 1521, Ponce wrote his best-known song, "Estrellita." In the song, he adopted the legato lines and song structure previously recommended. This song is still interpreted today as a timeless classic in both folkloric and classical styles with either mariachi or classical accompaniment. "Estrellita" perfectly symbolizes Mexico's naturally syncretic crossover song style. The melodic development and harmonic movement also reflect a similar foundation used in ranchera songs.

Ponce collected and arranged many Mexican folk songs, including "La Valentina," "A la orilla de un palmar," and "Lejos de ti." Mexico's published collection, *Doce Canciones Mexicanas*,

FIGURE 2.15 Manuel M. Ponce collected, arranged, and published many Mexican song collections such as this one: *Canciones mexicanas*, including "Cielito Lindo" and "Estrellita." Ponce was instrumental in helping Mexican musicians collect, organize, and arrange Mexican songs before composers Manuel Esperón, Ignacio "Tata" Nacho Esperón, wrote song classics for charro films. Courtesy of Biblioteca Cuicamatini, Facultad de música, Universidad Nacional Autónoma de México (UNAM), Mexico.

offers some of these short folk-song choices for singers with less range than "Estrellita."[20] Figure 2.15 depicts the publication of a song collection with "Cielito Lindo" and his composition "Estrellita," along with other well-known folk songs that continue to be performed today.

---

[20] *Doce Canciones Mexicanas. Obras para canto y piano*, UNAM, Escuela de música, 2008.

Solo Ranchera Singers Become Celebrities through Media Expansion

Beginning in the 1920s and 1930s in Mexico City, programs featuring live song performances on XEW Radio attracted singers and performers from all over Mexico, Cuba, and even South America.[21] The radio emerged in Mexico between 1920 and 1923, along with the microphone, a new invention.[22] By 1932, Mexico had over forty radio stations, ten of them in Mexico City.[23] Entrepreneur Emilio Azcárraga Vidaurreta first purchased XEW Radio in the early 1920s and began promoting solo artists and groups on live shows as he purchased additional stations.[24]

Thanks to the advent of radio and its popularity, audiences could now enjoy live audio concerts and song competitions of *ranchera* singers. Azcárraga then expanded into film and slowly built a monopoly that also included recording studios. Artists recorded and filmed at his *Estudios Churubusco* (Churubusco Recording Studios) on the south side of Mexico City. Azcárraga monopolized the careers of *ranchera* singers, groups, and composers through his Mexican media *tour de force*.[25]

Azcárraga's media expansion was able to mushroom quickly during the 1930s because it coincided with Mexico's surge in nationalistic music. The Mexican musical film industry was hugely successful, producing folk-driven *charro* films around the globe. Rural Mexican life on the ranch was depicted with nostalgic exoticism.

Solo artist celebrities such as Jorge Negrete, Pedro Vargas, Pedro Infante, and Lucha Reyes; composer/producers Manuel Esperón, Ignacio "Tata" Nacho, "Bésame mucho'" composer and pianist Consuelo Velásquez; and many others launched or promoted their careers through Azcárraga's conglomerate. *Ranchera* singer Lola Beltrán (1929–1996) worked at XEW Radio as a secretary before being discovered by Tata Nacho as a singer. This led to her meteoric rise as one of Mexico's leading *ranchera* ladies and film stars. Female singer and musician Amalia Mendoza, nicknamed "La Tariacuri," was also represented. She is depicted in Figure 2.16, and Jorge Negrete is depicted in Figure 2.17.

Another important soloist was ranchera tenor Miguel Aceves Mejía (1916–2006). While learning to be an auto mechanic in Mexico City, he sang at radio song competitions and was hired by XEW to sing salsa. Despite not having vocal training, his upper tenor range was fluid, easy, and innate. Producers at XEW were already promoting the career of the elegant and charismatic urban singer, Jorge Negrete. As a contrast to Negrete, they produced a campaign shifting Miguel Aceves Mejía away from salsa to a ranchera singer dressed in a zarape and sombrero, with a rural folk feel. His impressive lyric voice allowed him to sustain continuous long lines with falsetto flips in and out of a high tenor range, primarily singing huapangos. Aceves Mejía was a national hit. The rural vocal style he evoked seemed exotic to audiences. The successful singing of Aceves Mejía earned him

---

[21] Rivas, *Historia Música Popular Mexicana*, 71.

[22] https://www.britannica.com > topic > radio, 40.

[23] https://en.wikipedia.org > wiki > Radio_in_Mexico.

[24] "Historia," Televisa, accessed September 1, 2018. http://www.televisa.com/corporativo/quienes-somos/historia/.

[25] Donald Henriques, "Performing Nationalism: Mariachi, Media and Transformation of a Tradition (1920–1942)" (PhD diss., University of Texas at Austin, 2006), 20–21 and 113.

FIGURE 2.16 Solo singer, film actress, and musician Amalia Mendoza (1923–2001), nicknamed "La Tariacuri," came from a family of musicians. Courtesy of Amalia's nephew, Mexican singer Juan Mendoza, Los Angeles, California, and Dario Valdelamar Collection, Mexico.

the titles "El falsete de oro" (The Golden Falsete Voice) and later "El rey del falsete" (The King of Falsete).[26]

In film, singer celebrities were featured, especially if they were good actors with good looks; men were given preferential treatment. Mariachi ensembles were also featured but less so, despite being absolutely integral to the project. Many garnered steady work as top-of-the-line accompanists, notably the all-male group Mariachi Vargas. They recorded for at least forty ranchera singers. Miguel Martinez, trumpeter for the ensemble, remembers recording at least fifty songs directly with Jorge Negrete.[27]

Jorge Negrete's sophisticated acting delivery was so convincing that some believed he was an arrogant person. The real Jorge Negrete was a superior actor who knew how to develop and sustain a character as his media persona. This is confirmed in this book's interview with two of his grandchildren, Diana and Rafael Jorge Negrete (see Chapter 8 Interview: "Jorge Negrete").

During the second half of the twentieth century, ranchera music films gradually declined in popularity, especially after the 1960s. Mariachi concert performances today, however, have increased around the United States in communities, concert venues, symphonies, television, and radio. Mariachi performing continues to grow as an international symbol of Mexican identity.

---

[26] Miguel Martinez, *Mi vida, mis viajes, mis vivencias. Siete décadas en la música del mariachi* (México, D.F.: Consejo Nacional para la Cultural y las Artes, 2012, 2nd ed. 2013), 94–97.

[27] Martinez, *Mi vida, mis viajes, mis vivencias. Siete décadas en la música del mariachi*, 91–92.

FIGURE 2.17 Legendary singer/actor Jorge Alberto Negrete (1911–1953) was also a military horseman. His nickname was *El Charro Cantor* (The Singing Horseman). Collection of Darío Valdelamar and Negrete grandchildren, Diana and Rafael Negrete.

Crossover Singing: Jorge Negrete and *Operas Rancheras*

The natural mix of folkloric and classical vocal styles in Mexican twentieth-century ranchera songs makes it attractive to many kinds of singers and actors. This includes the long, rubato lines, wide range, rich tone, overall virtuosity, and creative acting possibilities within the songs themselves. The superior talent of early twentieth-century Mexican male singers knew how to show this off. Important stars included: Alfonso Luis Tirado, José Mojica, Juan Arvizu, Pedro Vargas and Jorge Negrete.

JORGE NEGRETE

The singing of Jorge Negrete (1911–1953) highlights the healthy crossover singing using elements of opera mixed into ranchera singing. Negrete had a rich, baritone voice. He was also known as *El Charro Cantor* (The Singing Mexican Horseman) for his many heroic roles in popular ranchera movie musicals. After finishing a military career, Negrete studied opera and Mexican song with voice teacher José Pierson in Mexico City. Although Negrete received standard Italian operatic vocal training, he also studied Italian Neapolitan songs, Mexican ballads by María Grever, and ranchera songs. Negrete's beautiful legato singing, novel crooning or bravío vocal production, acting skills, good looks, and ability to deftly

FIGURE 2.18 Legendary singer/actor Jorge Alberto Negrete (1911–1953) was also a philanthropist. He co-founded ANDA, Mexico's union to protect the rights of singers and actors. Collection of Darío Valdelamar and Negrete's grandchildren, Rafael and Diana Negrete.

ride a horse (which he learned through his military training) made him an instant international celebrity in ranchera movies. Jorge Negrete is depicted in Figure 2.18. He leaves a rich vocal legacy for singers, mariachi educators, and voice teachers (see Chapter 8 section: "Jorge Negrete").

Negrete interpreted rancheras in his own Operachi style (see Glossary), often using less vibrato and backspace than an opera singer. He could contrast bravío robust singing with an occasional opera sound, or employ a lighter crooning production. His vocal predecessors were singers Alfonso Ortíz Tirado, Jose Mojica, and Miguel Fleta.[28] The crooner influence is also reminiscent of popular male singers at the time from the United States, such as Bing Crosby, but ranchera singing lines are generally longer than song styles in American song. Jorge Negrete, Pedro Infante, and later Javier Solis added their own crooning touches to romantic bolero rancheros. Each made them inviting, intimate, and unforgettable. (Listen to Negrete's crooning style on YouTube with "Yo soy Mexicano": https://youtu.be/sVinVgCrhQY.)

Negrete adapted his trained operatic sound by lessening the operatic vibrato and sometimes softening his vocal production, always taking advantage of his developed wide range of tonal

---

[28] The author has often been reviewed in the press as an *Operachi* singer. She uses this term to define crossover between ranchera singing and the use of classical technique to develop vocal range and promote vocal health. Male ranchera singers have always done this, but females have not.

colors and expression. Jorge Negrete chose select moments to employ the fuller depth in his sound, revealing his large, operatically developed instrument as one of the many expressive elements in his vocal toolbox. His array of vocal techniques can be heard in the robust "Ay Jalisco no te rajes" or different acting moods in sections of "Mexico lindo y querido." Negrete's version of "Mexico lindo y querido" is still revered today by Mexicans. This song is one of Mexico's important anthems. It is multi-sectioned with various rhythms and was written by Chucho Monge. Negrete's distinguished performances and varied vocal interpretation gave Mexico one of its first nationalistic representations of identity. He toured globally, representing a Mexico that now fostered equality and a symbolic national reconciliation between the previously separated classes.[29]

OPERA RANCHERAS

While Manuel M. Ponce was writing about Mexican Song during the Mexican Revolution, many lesser-known composers of equal talent were also publishing folk songs and writing operas. A classical salon performance tradition also existed in Mexico City that in Spanish is often called *tertulias*. Composers presented songs of many types in small, intimate settings with primarily singers, pianists, and guitarists. Ranchera songs were also included in classical salon programs. One such location was the *Instituto Musical* "Gomezanda," which featured a piano, stage, and auditorium seating for approximately seventy-five people at Avenida Chapultepec 327 in central Mexico City (1915 to 1960). Composer and pianist Antonio Gomezanda (1894–1961) often held soft and full composition premieres as well as student performances of classical and ranchera works.

These Mexico City performances describe an evolution of nationalistic ranchera song expression beyond rural ranchera typical lifetime celebrations and *charreadas* (rodeos—see Glossary). Many salon and charro film composers also composed at the piano for films. Singers and pianists in today's music world need not always be limited to guitar or ensembles when performing ranchera songs, upon learning of this historical precedent (see Chapter 5 section: "Common Mariachi Rhythms").

Gomezanda composed ranchera and classical nationalistic music at the piano. Mariachi folk rhythms and cultural topics are at the core of all his music. One of his pieces de resistance is Mexico's first-known mariachi opera, *Mariache: Primera opera ranchera Mexicana*. The *opera ranchera* began as a three-act work under the name *La Virgen de San Juan* in 1928. It was later published in 1943 under the *Mariache* title. The opera ranchera is scored for full orchestra, solo singers, and mariachi ensemble with ranchera rhythms throughout the opera. The leading baritone (originally sung by Metropolitan Opera tenor from Chile, Ramón Viñay) switches styles between ranchera and classical song, the soprano sings in bel canto Italian style, and Pedro Vargas croons the *sotto voce* tenor aria almost like a bolero. The mezzo-soprano role is sung by Josefina "Cha Cha" Aguilar with a gutsy ranchera feel, but she leans on classical technique, without *bravío* singing (see Glossary).

The main theme of *Mariache* is expressing Mexican identity after the Mexican Revolution and finding love. To date, it has never been performed live, although a limited movie version (with cuts) was released in 1947 entitled *Fantasía ranchera*.[30]

Composer and pianist Gomezanda also composed over ninety short songs in both classical and ranchera styles. He wrote short ranchera gems, such as "Soy Mexicana," "Plegaria de una Indita a la virgencita morena" (see Chapter 6), and "Amor ranchero." Each song speaks to

---

[29] Jáuregui, *El Mariachi*, 153.

[30] The soprano aria "Lupe's Aria" has been premiered by the author in concert.

FIGURE 2.19 Nationalistic composer and pianist from Lagos de Moreno, Jalisco, Antonio Gomezanda (1894–1961) honors his own Mexican Indian heritage in a somewhat satirical autobiographical drawing on the cover of one of his many self-published songs. Courtesy of the Gomezanda family.

Mexican identity and pride.[31] Figures 2.19 and 2.20 depict two of his early self-published songs, each with a striking visual message of indigenous pride in the picture and titles on the song covers.

Figure 2.21 depicts famed singer Pedro Vargas, featured in one of his early crooning tenor movie roles in the ranchera movie *Fantasía ranchera*.[32] The film includes large sections of Antonio Gomezanda's *Mariache: Primera opera ranchera Mexicana.*"[33] In the original *Mariache* script, the tenor has just returned from fighting at the end of the Mexican Revolution in 1921. The tenor's very tender aria, "Como una amapolita" (Like a Little Poppy Flower), describes him still being hopelessly in love with Lupe, the soprano, despite their many years of separation. His crooning, legato singing style is on full display and, with the song itself, marks an important moment in mariachi voice history.[34] The singers in *Mariache* sing with slightly different styles, all highlighting Mexican flavor and different stylistic uses based upon classical foundation. Pedro Vargas applied his personal mix of operatic training and crooning vocal style to

---

[31] The author has published three volumes of Gomezanda songs, all available at www.classicalvocalrep.com and upcoming on her website in mid-2023.

[32] The score for the film was first copyrighted in 1943 and the film was released in 1947.

[33] Juanita Ulloa, *The Songs of Mexican Nationalist, Antonio Gomezanda* (DA diss., University of Northern Colorado, 2015). See Appendix Chronology.

[34] The tenor and soprano arias from *Mariache: Primera opera ranchera mexicana* can be found in the three volumes of *Gomezanda Mexican Art Songs and Rancheras* (www.classicalvocalrep.com and upcoming in 2024 on author's websites).

FIGURE 2.20 Antonio Gomezanda (1894–1961) composed the ranchera "Plegaria de una indita a la Virgencita morena" as a prayer to the Virgin of Guadalupe (see Chapter 6 section on songs for sheet music). Courtesy of Gomezanda Family.

Mariache, when singing romantic *bolero rancheros*, and as the lead soloist with the *Orquesta Típica Jalisciense* (see Glossary and the "The Bolero in Mexico" section in this chapter).

Since 2000, several one-act mariachi operas have been written by the late director of Mariachi Vargas, José "Pepe" Martinez. They were commissioned and produced by Houston Grand Opera. The first one, *Al cruzar la cara de la luna*, has a contemporary and intriguing theme addressing border and immigration issues. This is of great importance to Mexicans in the United States. Both productions feature classical and ranchera soloists. The contemporary mariachi opera consists of one act accompanied by mariachi without orchestra, instead of Antonio Gomezanda's three acts using orchestra with guitar and select folkloric instruments and rhythms with additional use of the mariachi ensemble in Act III. In the contemporary Pepe Martinez mariachi opera, singers are always accompanied by a mariachi ensemble. In *Mariache*, Maestro Gomezanda uses both at different times varying the musical texture.

FIGURE 2.21 Pedro Vargas (1906–1989) in one of his earliest movie roles as a ranchera tenor. *Fantasía ranchera* (1947) is an adapted movie version of Antonio Gomezanda's full ranchera opera: *Mariache: Primera opera ranchera Mexicana*. Courtesy of Gomezanda Family.

Ranchera opera crossover productions are of great significance to the mariachi field. The time span between the two productions named above is almost a hundred years.[35] While there are differences, there are also many similarities, along with opportunities to suggest and encourage future research, exploration, and future compositions. They are also a testament to the vocal flexibility of the ranchera vocal tradition. Mexican song continues to resound and grow with nationalistic pride and extraordinary vibrancy.

Classical soloists continue to crossover into ranchera singing today. A contemporary Mexican opera tenor from Veracruz, Enrique Camarena (b. 1976–), sings operas and art-song recitals; he also wears a *traje de charro* outfit for Madrid audiences singing the huapango *Deja que salga la luna* by José Alfredo Jiménez. (Watch him perform on YouTube: https://youtu.be/LkXGtAls4ek.)

The crossover flexibility inherent in the ranchera vocal style can also be heard in 2019 YouTube version of "Cu-cu-rru-cu-cu Paloma" by Tomás Méndez, sung by Peruvian opera singer Juan Diego Flores (https://youtu.be/Q7yfsNFoUvk). Rather than singing in full-voiced operatic style as Placido Domingo did in his opera recording of rancheras, Juan Diego delivers virtuosic long lines with a very gentle, crooning vocal style more reminiscent of a bolero through the first half of the song. He opts for a 3/4 accompaniment in the first half of the

---

[35] When the author first contacted Houston Grand Opera prior to the release of *Al cruzar la cara de la luna,* they were unaware of the existence of *Mariache*.

CHAPTER 2: HISTORY   43

song and not strict huapango accompaniment. (Watch his performance on YouTube: https://youtu.be/Q7yfsNFoUvk.)

Although men have traditionally had more access than women to classical training and have dominated the mariachi scene, this has now changed. Women also tend to crossover less with classical music because they sing rancheras primarily in the bottom half of their overall range. This honors the authenticity of the contralto-based female mariachi fach (see Chapter 3 section: "Mariachi Fach"). As a result of the lower range, women can more easily crossover with other commercial vocal styles, rather than classical. Women with accelerated voice training will be able to contemplate all styles, however, with new vocal possibilities around increased range and style while honoring the fach. This can be seen in the commercial and mariachi explorations of the female Latin Grammy-winning group Flor de Toloache (see Chapter 8 Interview: "Flor de Toloache").[36]

Crossover ranchera singing continues alive and well today because the stylistic mix already existed. These songs are sure to continue to resonate globally with new creative perspectives that juxtapose the robust beauty, constant growth, proud tradition, and empowerment of the mariachi style.

Mexico's Premiere Voice Teacher: Maestro José Pierson

José Eduardo Pierson (1861–1957) was Mexico City's leading voice teacher during the first half of the twentieth century.[37] Maestro José Pierson was born in Hacienda El Molino in Sonora, Northern Mexico. He studied abroad in England and completed university studies in the United States at the University of Santa Clara, California. After returning to Mexico, he staged shows and founded his own vocal academy in Mexico City. During this time, he continued his own vocal studies with Enrico Testa, while also traveling to Italy to train with voice teacher Vittorio de Vidal in Milan. In Mexico, Pierson was involved in and produced many opera, operetta, and zarzuela productions. He later became the artistic director at the following Mexico City theaters: Arbeu, Iris, Olimpia, and Colón. Maestro Pierson appears with his studio of students in Figure 2.22.

The key to Pierson's success was his training of students in various repertoires and styles, alongside technical expertise in breath support and customized voice building. The maestro's modifications for more popular styles included slightly less intense breath compression, less vibrato, less backspace, and staying close to the character and interpretation for each song regardless of style. All those studying with him received operatic training with varying combinations of Neapolitan and Mexican song, alongside operas and *zarzuelas* and including *rancheras*.[38] This flexibility would be useful for all voice teachers training mariachi singers.

José Pierson was responsible for training and early promotion of the voices of international *ranchera* singers Jorge Negrete (1911–1953) and Pedro Vargas (1904–1989), Ramon Vinay, José Mojica, Francisco Avitia, Alfonso Ortíz Tirado, among other top singers of the day. Singers received crossover technical and repertoire training from Maestro Pierson. Negrete's vocal training was more extensive, as he independently accessed and cultivated both operatic and *ranchera* styles, separately and together.

Pierson customized his vocal training, as seen in the authentically different-sounding vocal instruments of Pedro Vargas and Jorge Negrete. Vargas' voice is slightly smaller and

---

[36] The author also pioneers the *Operachi* sound for women using the Female mariachi fach with classical crossover.

[37] Pamela Corella Romero. "Paréntesis | José Eduardo Pierson en la memoria: la vida y obra del forjador de talentos." *El Sol de Hermosillo, Cultura.* April 8, 2024. https://www.elsoldehermosillo.com.mx/cultura/parentesis-jose-eduardo-pierson-en-la-memoria-la-vida-y-obra-del-forjador-de-talentos-11724678.html.

[38] Diana Negrete, *Jorge Negrete* (México: Editorial Diana, 1987), 45.

FIGURE 2.22 Sitting at the piano is master teacher José Pierson (1861–1957), Mexico's most famous and revered voice teacher. Directly behind him is Ema Elena Valdelamar, who briefly studied with him and was to become one of Mexico's premiere female bolero composers. Collection of Darío Valdelamar.

higher, and reflects gentler vocal production as if trained for an intimate, popular sound. Both Negrete and Vargas employ supported slides connecting the phrases, using less intense breath pressure than opera. On YouTube, Pedro Vargas may be heard singing "La Noche de mi mal" (https://youtu.be/CdwBgx23Xvc) and "Por que volviste a mi" (https://youtu.be/WKKQXtVeMvg). It is noteworthy, however, that at some point Vargas left the Pierson studio in 1928 to study with Alejandro Cuevas.[39]

Maestro Pierson built the careers of other Mexican professional singers beyond the aforementioned ones.[40] The last two names Juan Arvizu (1900–1985), and Mario Talavera (1885–1960).[41] In fact, Pedro Vargas lived in the Pierson household along with Mario Talavera, probably to intensify vocal training and defray expenses.[42]

The Mexican songstress Ema Elena Valdelamar (1925–2012) initiated training as a budding lyric soprano with the maestro for three to six months, but her mother refused to pay for lessons after her father's death.[43] Valdelamar was led to write popular romantic popular

---

[39] José Ramón Garmabella, *Pedro Vargas* (México: Ediciones de Comunicación S.A. de C.V.,1984), 48–49.

[40] Gabriel Pareyón, *Enciclopedia de la música Mexicana* (Guadalajara: Universidad Panamericana, 2007), 833.

[41] Ibid., 42. Mario Talavera was both a tenor and a songwriter. Dr. Ortíz Tirado premiered many of María Grever's songs.

[42] Garmabella, *Pedro Vargas*.

[43] The author heard Ms. Valdelamar sing many times. She retained a light lyric soprano sound throughout her life but always sang boleros and did not dedicate her career to pure ranchera singing or performance.

boleros instead. The lack of support she received for vocal training is a worthy reminder of the numerous obstacles women faced during this time in history.[44] It also explains why more men than women received vocal training, making it easier to achieve artistic celebrity status.

There is no record of Maestro Pierson promoting ranchera belt vocal training for women, or working with them exclusively in the lower mariachi fach. Among others, Maestro Pierson trained two operatic contraltos who sang internationally, contralto Ms. Fanny Anitúa Medrano (1887–1968) and mezzo-soprano Ms. Josefina "Cha Cha" Aguilar. After Ms. Anitúa's training with José Pierson in Mexico City, she launched her major opera career from Europe. Ms. Josefina "Cha Cha" Aguilar was trained for opera, but she also performed and recorded some rancheras. She adds robust ranchera flavor in her song interpretation but leans on intact operatic production and sound without any falsete register flips in her recordings, as evidenced in the mariachi standards "La borrachita" (https://youtu.be/B_OpeljKGeE) and "Atotonilco" (https://youtu.be/naneDeKJ2co).[45] Ms. Aguilar also sings with a robust ranchera contralto sound as the mother of lead soprano, Lupe, in the movie version of Gomezanda's *Mariache: Primera opera ranchera Mexicana*. She favors less vibrato but does not adjust to slightly less backspace or add falsete, although the latter expressive gesture might not have been favored stylistically by the producers or the composer.

Maestro José Pierson is still revered today as perhaps Mexico's most memorable voice teacher.[46] He built rich, healthy, and stylistically diverse voices, mostly with men. The results are undeniable and can be heard in the sounds of his singers' voices. Pierson built a huge legacy for Mexican singers, creating uniquely timbred voices that delivered consistency and ease, regardless of the style. Pierson's teaching led to a high standard of *ranchera* solo performance, one that can and hopefully will be used as a model for future generations.

The Bolero in Mexico: History, Singers, and Composers

Latin American boleros are popular romantic songs in 4/4 meter. They are popular throughout Latin America, and many boleros are song standards in different styles ranging from salsa, cumbia, pop, classical, and mariachi. While boleros exist independently of mariachi, the *bolero ranchero* vocal style evolved from the bolero into Mexican ranchera song repertoire.

The bolero arrived in Mexico from Cuba at least by the 1940s through Mexico's Eastern Yucatán Peninsula. Cuba and the Caribbean Islands are credited with originating the bolero genre during the second half of the 1800s. While Latin American boleros are considered the most intimate romantic of most rhythmic styles, the waltz in 3/4 meter was also considered a song of romance in the 1920s and 1930s in different Latin American countries.[47]

Cuba and Caribbean song styles are noteworthy for the predominance and importance of rhythm. Feeling the rhythmic groove in a bolero is paramount to singing it well. It helps singers vary their singing melodically and rhythmically while never losing the center of the instrumental groove (see Chapter 5 section: "Overview of Mariachi Rhythmic Styles"). While

---

[44] The author shared a mentorship relationship with Ms. Valdelamar between 1995 and 2012. During that time, Ms. Valdelamar related many such cases of obstacles in receiving training as well as when trying to get her songs even listened to by XEW Radio because she was a female.

[45] The film *Fantasía ranchera* appears periodically on Mexican television stations.

[46] Negrete, *Jorge Negrete*, 44–45.

[47] Salazar, *Cien Años de Boleros*, 109.

the Latin American classic ballad has free accompaniment, the bolero is a slow couples dance accompanied with a pattern of repeating 1/8th notes. The 1/8th notes can be usually heard in the bongos in Caribbean music. In the bolero ranchero, the mariachi ensemble designates the armonía section (guitars and vihuela) to do the same accompaniment.

The Latin American bolero from Cuba has no connection to the use of the word "bolero" in Spain and Europe.[48] Some say its precursor is the *danzón* rhythm, an intimate couple's dance felt in 2/4 meter with a dotted rhythm that is similar to the *habanera* rhythm.[49] Some danzones from prior to 1930 are still a part of ranchera repertoire today, including "La negra noche," "La barca de oro," and the ubiquitous "La Paloma."

The bolero first became popular with trios, not just soloists. A classic guitar/vocal trio that achieved worldwide fame for Mexico was *Los Panchos*. (Watch *Reloj* on YouTube: https://youtu. be/upGQr6H8DRk.) *Los Panchos* crooned in three-part harmony with occasional solo lines, while also accompanying the singing with 1/8th note bolero rhythmic pattern, all using intricate guitar arrangements. *Los Panchos* established the intimate mood of the bolero in Mexico and became internationally known, working between Mexico and New York. Their first big hit was the bolero "Sin ti" (Without You). (Watch their performance on YouTube: https:// youtu.be/a5tcLf8PXTY.)

The bolero soloist often has a rich voice and can croon or sing out over bolero ranchero accompaniment. Two popular bolero rancheros are "Si nos dejan" and "La media Vuelta." (Listen to Javier Solis perform them on YouTube: https://youtu.be/8uUhM7GT7Mk and https://youtu.be/Rjre8wwvg_o.) Bolero guitar trios cultivate a crooning style through most of the bolero in three-part harmony. They occasionally alternate three-part harmony with some solo lines. Guitar trio ensembles are often dressed in suits but sometimes wear regional dress—*trajes típicos* with either *trajes de charro* or colored *zarapes*—making sure to highlight the nationalistic flavor of the Mexican bolero.

Many Mexican ranchera soloists developed their individual vocal style around the popularity of the bolero ranchero. This genre was also heavily promoted by XEW Radio, and many artists were featured singing bolero rancheros in films. Pedro Infante and Javier Solis are celebrated for excelling at this style. Jorge Negrete also crooned more intimately when singing boleros. Singer/songwriter José Alfredo Jiménez wrote bolero ranchero songs with great expression. One of his most intimate boleros is "Amanecí otra vez en tus brazos," sung in the accompanying sample by Lucha Villa. (Watch it on YouTube: https://youtu.be/fEHC k3Qac5s).

Pedro Infante (1917–1957) was a leading interpreter of the bolero ranchero. His pseudonym was "The Romantic Charro." Infante was from a family of humble means but was highly musical, playing guitar, piano, violin, trumpet, and drums. Infante showed his superior singing and acting skills worldwide in over sixty films. (Listen to his interpretation of the Rubén Fuentes romantic bolero "Cien años" [One Hundred Years) on YouTube: https://youtu. be/diSAz7xfpvE.) He is also known for his songs "La que se fue" (The One Who Got Away) and "La suerte mia" (My Luck).

Javier Solis (1931–1966) was originally named Gabriel Siria Levario. While his charro film roles were more limited than that of Infante, he nevertheless earned the title "El rey del bolero ranchero" (The King of the Ranchera Bolero). Solo singers such as Solis often begin songs in the bolero ranchero style with intimacy, but open up the sound with a full mariachi rounded

---

[48] Many think of the rhythm in Ravel's composition entitled "Bolero," but that European rhythm is not in 4/4 meter and has nothing to do with the Latin American bolero.

[49] The *habanera* rhythm is from Habana, Cuba, and not Spain. Some wrongly assume this, thinking of Bizet's famous habanera aria in the opera *Carmen*. Bizet was French, the script is in French, and the opera takes place in Spain.

CHAPTER 2: HISTORY 47

tone expressive sound as the song progresses. (Listen to him perform it on YouTube: https://youtu.be/s2xXKiwBa78.) Some of his hit songs include "Sombras nada más" (Just Shadows) (https://youtu.be/UHAwnbE7sYk) and "Recordarás" (You Will Remember).

Women also express the intimacy of boleros completely naturally in their bolero interpretation. María Elena Sandoval (1940–2005) was a contemporary of Pedro Infante and Javier Solis. She excelled in the bolero style. In the song "Acuérdate de mi" (Remember Me), Sandoval switches to head voice with a chest mix in the rising melodic lines, but in the same range several bars later, she switches into a punched, full-belted bravío sound for the climax of the song. (Listen to her performance on YouTube: https://youtu.be/aqlHbZuMNNg.) Ms. Sandoval accesses a wide palette of color choices for expression. She simultaneously protects her voice from going flat by avoiding leaning hard on bravío and avoiding pure bravío all the time. This judicious mix of both techniques within the same register balances artistic expression with vocal health, and presents a fantastic listening model for female ranchera singers.

The bolero ranchero may be interpreted in different ways depending on the artist's style and general styles during their lifetimes. For example, Ignacio "Tata Nacho" Esperón's song "La borrachita" is a representative 1918 example of mariachi accompaniment in bolero ranchero style recorded in the very same year as María Grever's hit ballad "Júrame," also often performed as a bolero ranchero. (Listen to it on YouTube: https://youtu.be/HWLGfQiYyMc.) Notice the difficulty of the sustained, long phrases with no breaks for the singer in "La borrachita." Compare this to Lucha Villa's singing of other Tata Nacho songs twenty-five years later. Lucha Villa sings shorter lines and includes an instrumental to vocal "call and response" on each phrase of the Mexican song medley "No volveré, Flor de azalea" and "Amorcito corazón." (Listen to her performance on YouTube: https://youtu.be/eJPgf4TQNbg.)

After the Mexican Revolution, numerous male songwriters contributed to the growth of Mexican rancheras, including bolero rancheros. Some noteworthy composers are: Manuel Esperón (1911–2011), Ernesto Cortazar (1940–2004), Jesus "Chucho" Monge (1910–1964), Alfonzo Esparza Oteo (1898–1950), Jorge del Moral (1900–1941), Alberto Dominguez (1913–1975), Gabriel Ruiz (1912–1999), Gonzalo Curiel (1904–1958), and Ignacio Esperón, known as Tata Nacho (1892–1968). Perhaps the most important male Mexican commercial ballad and bolero composer was Agustín Lara (1897–1970) with approximately 408 songs, of which perhaps 162 are boleros.[50] Many of his songs, including "María Bonita," "Veracruz," "Solamente una vez," and "Granada," are interpreted as boleros rancheros with mariachi ensemble. These songs are timeless classics. They continue to be equally popular sung as boleros with guitar trios, or performed as classical solos with piano or orchestra.

While Mexico boasts a plethora of musically trained male bolero composers, three female songwriters brought Mexican boleros/ballads to international heights. They are often overlooked and deserve special mention. These three composers wrote bolero gems with a unique feminine perspective. Many are interpreted today as boleros rancheros.

The first early twentieth-century female composer is María Grever (1885–1951). Her first hit ballad, "Júrame" (Promise Me), was originally recorded in 1928. At the time, the male-dominated media could not fathom that the song was written by a woman.[51] This song is considered a showpiece, as it has extended range and a sustained climax on the top end of the range during the last portion of the song (see Chapter 5 section: "Advanced Vocal Level").

"Júrame" is the Grever ballad most often sung by mariachi ensembles as a bolero ranchero. Still a favorite today, it has transcended almost a century of diverse, beautiful solo interpretations, all of them beautiful in their own way. Listen to the hit premiere 1928

---

[50] Salazar, *Cien años de Boleros*, 109–110.

[51] https://calibbr.com/maria-grever-early-life-career-popular-songs-more.

recording of "Júrame" by the lead Mexican tenor from the Mexican Orquesta Típica Jalisciense, featuring José Mojica,[52] on YouTube: https://youtu.be/QlXR9oj0gZk. Then, compare it to an early twentieth-century urban mariachi standard female belt version by Mariachi Divas of Cindy Shea from a hundred years later: https://youtu.be/GeqZEUsN5y8.

Grever wrote approximately eight hundred songs, most of them romantic and adaptable to mariachi soloists performing in bolero ranchero style (or commercial singers in popular ballad style). Ensembles are trained to accompany boleros and may also know Grever's 1930 hit song "Muñequita linda" (Beautiful Doll) (also called "Te quiero dijiste" [You Said I Love You]), premiered by tenor Alfonso Ortíz Tirado (see Chapter 5 section: "Six Basic Rhythms with Accompaniment"). Overall, remarkably few realize María Grever was so prolific and activated her own film career writing songs for Hollywood. Likewise, they do not know that the classic ballad in English, "What a Difference a Day Made," is equally famous in Spanish with a different set of lyrics and meaning ("Cuando vuelva a tu lado"). She is definitely an unsung musical heroine of Mexico.

Virtuoso classical pianist Consuelo Velásquez (1916–2005) was also a songwriter. She composed the unforgettable 1941 ballad "Bésame mucho," often accompanied as a bolero ranchero. This song has been named by many as "the song of the century" and is a terrific beginning bolero for many singers. Her song "Que seas feliz" is slightly harder to sing, placing it at an intermediate vocal level. It is also better known in Mexico than the United States, and it is accompanied as a 3/4 ranchera valseada (see Chapter 5 section: "Overview of Mariachi Rhythmic Styles"). Velásquez had formidable skills as a pianist. Consuelito, as she was often called, married the XEW Radio executive Mariano Rivera Conde. Part of his job was focused upon promoting her songs. Listen to Consuelito Velásquez play the bolero/ballad "Bésame mucho" as a powerful and rhythmically diverse piano concert solo on Mexico's long-running variety television show "Siempre en domingo" on YouTube: https://youtu.be/0u0bX5gBCRw.

The third Mexican female bolero composer is Ema Elena Valdelamar (1925–2012). She began winning song contests on the radio for her boleros beginning in the late 1950s. Her bolero "Mucho corazón" is a classic with many decades of rebirths, from its premiere release with the Los Bribones trio, to a Grammy-winning recording by Luis Miguel, to the two-CD collection, *Romance* (https://youtu.be/-8U3kGs8ETQ). Valdelamar's prize-winning boleros "Mil besos," "Cheque en blanco," and "Devuélveme el corazón" have been popular bolero ranchero and trio bolero requests at several different points in history as bolero rancheros (https://youtu.be/VB39j-WZ2wU, https://youtu.be/qsokyskoGac, https://youtu.be/io_NHXhcdQ) and as boleros with guitar trio (https://youtu.be/SYBoxdtV-Rc). Singers Lucha Villa and Paquita la del Barrio were the best-known singers of her "feminist" song "Cheque en blanco."

Both Valdelamar and Velásquez were also longtime, dedicated board members of the *Sociedad de autores y compositores de México* (SACM). This organization is Mexico's equivalent to companies that protect composers, known in the United States as ASCAP and BMI. Together, these three important women span the twentieth century of bolero songwriting with hugely valuable, yet sometimes underappreciated songs.

Ranchera Singing Style

Ranchera singing style and its vocal evolution over the nineteenth and twentieth centuries is a little-studied but fascinating topic. Some influences were the interchange of folk and classical

---

[52] Salazar, *Cien años de Boleros*, 112. Despite his amazing voice, Mojica later gave up his performance career and finished his years in Peru as a monk.

singing with Orquestas Típicas and both urban and rural mariachi ensembles. The song structure and collection of Mexican folk songs initiated by Manuel M. Ponce and followed by other composers in charro films influenced ranchera song composition. Another factor that influenced ranchera solo singing style was the availability and subsequent employment of Mexican trained opera singers with the advent of charro films. The female singing style evolved separately but shares robust tone, legato lines, crooning, and bravío singing with male singers (see "Female Ranchera Singers and Composers" through "Vocal Conditions for Female Ranchera Singers" in this chapter).

Ranchera singing style can be immediately identified with a robust and rounded sound with falsete flips, long vocal lines, customary and celebratory yells, and a particular song repertoire. This singing style and its canon of songs are indigenous to Mexico. Mariachi vocal features are distinct from Spanish vocal expressions brought over from Europe when Spain ruled Mexico as "Nueva España" (1521–1821); as an example, songs from Spain often feature triplet melodic ornaments, and mariachi songs do not. Mariachi songs can be distinctive in that they often feature long lines that end with downward slides, especially those with influence from Northern Mexican states (Sonora, Chihuahua, Tamaulipas, Sinaloa, Nuevo León.) Listen to the long vocal lines with downward slides at the end of certain phrases along with typical yells, in a song sample from Pedro Infante's "Camino a Guanajuato": https://youtu.be/rjC6UP27-4o.

An exception today to Mexico's typical pre-1950 ranchera song style that became commercially popular in 1995 is the song "Como quien pierde una estrella." This song features some vocal virtuosity, as the melody has fast-moving Spanish melodic ornaments, although they are quadruplets instead of the more common triplets used in classical music from Spain. The accompanying rhythm is a fusion evoking both Spain and Mexico with the name *bolero moruno*. Listen to the chorus of this song sung by Alejandro Fernandez on YouTube: https://youtu.be/MXlwuZ_nEk0.

Mariachi vocal music has always been sung primarily in the Spanish language. Spanish has remained the official language of Mexico since it was first imposed by Spain when they began to rule Mexico in 1521. Contemporary Mexican Spanish has a sound and accent unique and distinct from Castilian Spanish. Mexican Spanish uses more frontal resonance and forward placement than Castilian Spanish, and this is noticeable when listening to ranchera lyrics (see Chapter 6).

What exactly is the ranchera singing style? The answer is partly based upon vocal technique and its subsequent sound production, along with the singer's phrasing, diction, and natural intonation. It can also depend on the rhythm defining the song style and the mood of the lyrics. Well-trained mariachi singers may choose to alternate in a concert between their gutsy and robust ranchera style in one song, and the crooning delivery of an intimate bolero in the next (see the "Bolero" section in this chapter). Some of the same classic Mexican songs in Spanish have also been popularized by jazz trios, or in popular style but sound completely different. When interpreted in popular singing style and less legato, singers tend to work in lower keys with short vocal lines. This evokes a call-and-response with the instrumentalists. In the case of classical singers, female singers prefer higher keys that mix in more head voice, and both women and men sustain ongoing continuous legato singing. Pepe Aguilar, singer and son of two celebrity ranchera singers, Flor Silvestre and Antonio Aguilar, evolved his own ranchera style mixing commercial music and rock to create his own sound in commercial style. In summary, ranchera singing style can be uniquely developed by each singer depending on their background and interests.

Singer/Songwriter José Alfredo Jiménez: A Third Period in Mariachi History

Beginning in the 1950s, a new phase in contemporary Mexican ranchera song began with the earthy and pioneering songwriting style of solo singer-songwriter José Alfredo Jiménez (1926–1973). Contrary to Vargas and Negrete, Jiménez did not possess vocal training, nor was he an actor; instead, he wrote unforgettable boleros and songs with simple words and an intimate yet very direct message. His lyrics often hold an ironic twist and are known to represent the emotions of everyday middle-class people, known in Spanish as "el pueblo" (see Glossary). His solo singer-songwriter style was uniquely Mexican in a novel style, leading to a new third period of mariachi vocal history.

Jiménez's voice sits in a medium to medium-high baritone range. His songs are set in a small vocal range. He sings with a talking style that communicates everyday stories with remarkable effectiveness. Rather than evoke bullfighting, palenques, and other nationalistic song topics, José Alfredo chose to reflect on relationship issues and contemporary love themes.

Jiménez's melodic writing style continues the long, legato lines and song structure from Ponce's first generation of songwriters. He skips melodic jumps and chooses only occasional long-held notes at the end of his huapangos, as in "Cielo rojo" (Red Sky) and "El jinete" (The Horseback Rider) rather than sustain falsete throughout the song as one might hear in the song "Malagueña salerosa" (Bewitching Woman from Málaga). One exception is "Deja que salga la luna," which has two extended falsetes. In this case, he expertly heightens the drama by linking falsetes to the lyrics, specifically on the word *creciendo* (growing). Jiménez also uses a less-syncopated rhythmic texture in his accompaniment, creating a transparency that allows the listener to stay closer to the message of the song. In short, José Alfredo Jiménez trades in vocal virtuosity to communicate the story of the song with laser focus. Lyric expression and intimacy in interpretation of his songs is paramount as compared to other ranchera composers.

José Alfredo's many songs are important mariachi standards today. The smaller range of many of his songs makes them attractive for beginner and intermediate-level ranchera singers. When singers are learning syncopation, they will easily shine with *ranchera valseada* and 2/4 *ranchera lenta* rhythmic styles, two of José Alfredo's favorite settings (see Chapter 5 section: "Six Basic Rhythms"). Some of Jiménez's most famous titles are "*Que bonito amor, Ella, Que suerte la mía,*" and the unforgettable classic, "El Rey." One YouTube example of his lyric song style and composition is the song "Vámonos" (Let's Go) (https://youtu.be/qSNe QOlkRYo).

While José Alfredo built his fame and unforgettable body of songs, other showpiece rancheras and their singers from earlier times continued to shine. One example is the huapango "El Pastor," composed by Cuates Castilla in 1955, a song with extended falsete virtuosity that tenor Miguel Aceves Mejía made famous, as did the youthful Spaniard whose artistic name was Joselito. (Watch him perform on YouTube: https://youtu.be/vime5i3krtU.)

Juan Gabriel (1950–2016) followed José Alfredo Jiménez and was also a singer/songwriter. He is worthy of mention even though he found more success mixing commercial vocal music in Spanish with rancheras. Born Alberto Aguilera Vásquez, he went by his artistic name along with the nicknames *Juanga* and *El Divo de Juárez*. Juan Gabriel challenged the macho stereotype as a gay singer touching the skirts of the ranchera performance circuit. He wrote over a thousand songs, many of them revered. Similar to José Alfredo, he had no vocal training, but his interpretation and the deep messages of his songs made him

CHAPTER 2: HISTORY 51

unforgettable. His bolero *Amor eterno* and his ranchera *La Diferencia* are classic staples of mariachi song repertoire.

Female Ranchera/Bolero Singers and Composers

Women have a distinct, complex, important, yet little-studied *ranchera* singing history, especially the soloists. In Mexico, women only received the right to vote in 1953–1954. Until recently, women have had less access to vocal training, composing, artist promotion, and general support for success. Female voices also sit in a distinct range from men's voices and must be trained differently for earthy mariachi singing. Their physique is smaller, and their smaller vocal cords overlap only with the mid to high end of male tenors, but almost all healthy female voices have a large head-voice range available for development of falsete (see Chapter 3 section: "Female Mariachi Fach"). These pedagogical facts explain any complications women have faced with mariachi low-register belting outdoors without microphones since the early 1900s. Women have always been valued, however, for their beauty and have many costume choices for the stage, although this has generally been given far more preference than their true vocal talents (see Chapter 3 sections: "Female Mariachi Fach" to "Handling Vocal Fatigue and Developing Mindfulness" and see Chapter 4 section: "Costumes, Make-up, Song Studies, and Singing with a Microphone").

Despite the challenges constantly facing women in the ranchera world, there are premiere soloists who have faced it head on and taken important steps for all women. Some of the many unsung heroines include Lucha Reyes in the early twentieth century (see the "Lucha Reyes—Bravío Ranchera Singing" section in this chapter), followed by María Elena Sandoval, María de Lourdes, Amalia Mendoza, Matilde Sánchez (La Torcacita), and Irma Vila, to name a few. Some sang with sweetness, others with depths of sorrow. Listen to the bravío singing of Lucha Reyes at a charreada (rodeo—see Glossary) in the charro film *El Herradero* from 1943, just one year before she committed suicide: https://youtu.be/WwhSu0Ietmk.

During the 1950s and beyond, two of perhaps the most highly revered and memorable female soloists have been Lola Beltrán "Lola la Grande" (1935–1996) and Lucha Villa (1936–).[53] Lola's lyric voice offers sweetness even while describing pain with unique phrasing. Lucha Villa's voice is a powerhouse, dramatic tenor/contralto instrument, probably the lowest of all female ranchera singers and simultaneously passionate and earthy with a touch of femininity.

More contemporary soloists include Guadalupe Pineda, Aída Cuevas, multi-Grammy winner Linda Ronstadt, Graciela Beltán, Eugenia León, Lila Downs, Flor de Toloache, Mon Laferte, and the author, among others (see Chapter 8 sections: "Linda Ronstadt" and "Flor de Toloache").

During the twentieth century, women were traditionally more active in the bolero and romantic trio tradition, as seen in the United States success of the Grammy-winning CD of singer Edie Gormé with the many CDs of the famous bolero Trío Los Panchos. This is also true of three top female twentieth-century Mexican composers María Grever, Consuelo Velásquez, and Ema Elena Valdelamar, all of whom leaned on the bolero and ballad genres (see earlier in this chapter: "The Bolero in Mexico: History, Singers, and Composers").

Early ranchera female singers were also pioneers of the duo sound. They began a unique duo singing tradition with ranchera style, sound, and repertoire. The Hermanas Padilla (Padilla Sisters) and Hermanas Nuñez (Nuñez Sisters) were huge talents and clearly deserve

---

[53] Obituary of Lola Beltrán: https://www.nytimes.com/1996/03/26/nyregion/lola-beltran-singer-dies-mexico-s-ado red-grande.html.

their place in history.[54] (Listen to Hermanas Padilla sing "Andale" on YouTube: https://youtu.be/aaZQEjygYpk.) The duos accompanied themselves on guitars. Singular ranchera soloists with guitar skills did the same, for example Tex-Mex sensation Lydia Mendoza (1916–2007), also known as "Lark of the Border" (https://youtu.be/eFnxvWgX73Y). These singers often sang with slightly less use of the *bravío*, or belt singing style, as compared to solo female singers working outdoors with mariachi ensembles. Their voices did not have to compete with a larger mariachi ensemble. The female duo tradition is rich in sound yet little studied and rarely emulated.

Mariachi ensembles have a long history of success focused until recently on male exclusivity; nevertheless, female ensembles have done excellent work, especially considering the resistance to women in mariachi ensembles since the 1900s.[55] The earliest singer/violinist known to have taken vocal solos while playing in an all-male mariachi group was violinist Rosa Quirino in 1903.[56] The first all-female group, *Las Adelitas*, was formed in Mexico City in 1948, followed by *Las Estrellas* in 1951 and *Las Coronelas* in 1953. Some of them performed in charro musical films as well. The first US all-female mariachi group formed in 1967 in Alamo, Texas, under the name *Las Rancheritas*. Today, women have equal footing in university and community mariachi ensembles in the United States. They have become a powerful force, although many are not yet directors.

During the past ten years, two all-female ensembles in the United States have won Grammy awards, and several have won Latin Grammys, Mariachi Divas and Flor de Toloache (see Chapter 8 sections: "Linda Ronstadt" and "Flor de Toloache"). The latter group's founding duo demonstrates diligent and unique vocal work with equal attention between the solo and duo voices with instruments, all while accompanying themselves instrumentally. The all-female ensemble *Mariachi Reyna* from Los Angeles, originally begun by trumpeter, arranger, and mariachi director José Hernández, is more traditional and was nominated for a Latin Grammy in 2009.

Bravío Ranchera Singing-Lucha Reyes and Vocal Conditions for Female Ranchera Singers

Lucha Reyes (1906–1944) is remembered as Mexico's first female solo *ranchera* singer to front an all-male mariachi beginning sometime between 1912 and 1919.[57] Her original name was María de Luz Flores Aceves, and she was born in Guadalajara, Jalisco.[58] She was a true pioneer, and can also be credited for initiating the *bravío* singing style (literally, brave, defiant, wild, ferocious).[59]

The term *bravío* refers to a robust and gutsy style of singing with both expressive and technical elements. Expressive yells and gasps are weaved into the singing and between the lines of any given song. The *bravío* belt style of Lucha Reyes transmits an earthy, passionate,

---

[54] For more information on the history of women ensembles in mariachi, read the program notes for the CD *Mujeres & Mariachi* by this author. Used with permission from Laura Sobrino and Leonor Xochitl Pérez. https://www.sandiegouniontribune.com/entertainment/music/sdut-groundbreaking-women-in-mariachi-2013oct05-htmlstory.html. Dr. Leonor Perez has done valuable research on female mariachi ensembles.

[55] As an example, Mariachi Vargas is over a hundred years old and has always committed to being male only.

[56] George Varga, "Women in Mariachi Shatter Stereotypes," *San Diego Tribune*, 2013.

[57] People disagree about the exact date, but sometime between 1912 and 1919.

[58] Jáuregui, *El Mariachi*, 111.

[59] Rivas, *Historia Músical Popular Mexicana*, 60.

CHAPTER 2: HISTORY   53

and aggressive confidence about who she is and how to defend herself in the male mariachi world, while always nationalistic in honoring Mexico.[60] *Bravío* can refer to a specific female archetype in mariachi—a woman who may have been through a lot, even abandonment, but is neither submissive nor obedient. Lucha embodied this persona in her performances.

Pedagogically speaking, the term *bravío* draws on different belt colors in the voice (often called *timbre*—see Glossary) with intense breath pressure. This produces a strong and driven sound. In bravío singing it is common to fill in expressive gestures and sounds, and the songs are centered in the lower half of the full female range, often without needing falsete. The sound is chest based, but when using a fully supported belt voice in lieu of pure chest from c4–c5, the sound produced is safer and projects better. In this case, the actual production *feels*, but doesn't *sound*, lighter (see Chapter 3 section: "The Female Mariachi Fach").

Lucha Reyes was discovered as a young girl living in poverty in Mexico City, where she sang at the Plazuela de San Sebastián. She was then invited to tour with a traveling troupe of performers in outdoor tents, commonly called *carpas*.[61] In 1920, she was promised a tour in the United States with voice training in Los Angeles.[62] After performing in Mexico and beyond, in 1930, she returned to successful concerts in Los Angeles, California. Despite Reyes' tremendous talent and extended touring with both trios and mariachi ensembles, she also had limited funds and battled alcoholism. The door opened for concerts, films, radio performances, and cabaret, although this began to take a toll on her voice and her health.[63]

In approximately 1927, Lucha Reyes lost her voice and stopped singing for one year.[64] It is unclear if she received vocal support. After that, she resorted to lower, breathy singing with a rasp. It is common to lose one's range and power when the voice is unhealthy, stressed, or misused. She was only twenty-one years old at the time but had been singing since about age fourteen outdoors in a wide variety of challenging conditions. For those who are listening to Reyes' later recordings, one must take into account that she fronted full mariachi ensembles outdoors with no microphone at loud party-type settings: *charreadas* and *palenques* (rodeos—see Glossary). She leaned constantly on her belt voice for power and natural amplification but often with pure chest instead of a mixed voice or perhaps enough breath support (see Chapter 3 section: "Belt Singing"). Her later recordings continue with *bravío* belt but lack the silvery head resonance mix and natural support from her earlier vocal production. Some later recordings show the wear and tear of her challenging lifestyle, although her intensity and song interpretation continue as magnetic and power-driven.

Lucha's style made use of yells, passionate gasps and openly sang of alcohol use as part of the bravío vocal style. Some of Reyes' most memorable belt songs are: "El Herradero," "La Tequilera," "Juan Charrasqueado," "La Feria de San Marcos" (Pelea de Gallos), and "La Charreada" (listen to "Corrido de Chihuahua" on YouTube: https://youtu.be/n-XZoIIrSF4). The lyrics to these songs spoke bravely of extraordinary bravío topics of nationalism, tough females, alcohol, and abandonment.[65]

Around this same time, there were other female ranchera singers using rounder, richer, and darker tones. Some examples are the female vocal/guitar duos such as the Hermanas Padilla, who, besides singing with mariachi ensembles, may have sung more indoors and could control the volume of their own guitars when accompanying themselves. Conditions

---

[60] Jáuregui, *El Mariachi*, 111.

[61] Rivas, *Historia Música Popular Mexicana*, 146.

[62] Jáuregui, *El Mariachi*, 111–112.

[63] Rivas, *Historia Música Popular Mexicana*, 146–147.

[64] Rivas, *Historia Música Popular Mexicana*, 146.

[65] Rivas, *Historia Música Popular Mexicana*, 112.

for Mexican ranchera soloist Irma Vila were also different from the outdoor singing of Lucha Reyes. Much of Irma Vila's ranchera career took place in Spain, where conditions may have included more indoor theaters and safely amplified performance spaces. (Listen on YouTube to Irma Vila https://youtu.be/mTi7imCQyYU and Hermanas Padilla https://youtu.be/RNUN jTjOQwk.) Regardless, Lucha's *bravío* belt-singing style was essential for projecting in outdoor venues with full mariachi ensembles. Neither the Hermanas Padilla nor Irma Vila leaned as consistently on the bravío style and technique as Lucha. Fortunately, singers today have access to both vocal training and powerful microphones.[66] Today, singers can shine more easily with safer singing power into full bravío sound if technically supported.

Lucha Reyes also sang roles in *ranchera* charro musicals. Lucha Villa, Lola Beltrán, Amalia Mendoza, Iram Vila, Flor Silvestre, and other women were also given limited roles. Lucha can be heard in the following charro music films: *Con los dorados de Villa* (1939), *El Zorro de Jalisco* (1941), *¡Ay Jalisco . . . no te rajes!* (1941), and *Flor Silvestre* (1943).

Despite the hardships Lucha Reyes endured, her singing created a new path for female singers of her day. Women entered the mariachi world with a new style and sound that was different from the men. In fact, it was the bravío style set by a ranchera female, namely Lucha Reyes, that led to José Alfredo Jiménez's bravío singer-songwriter style with hits such as the immortal ranchera classic, "El Rey" (The King).

Reyes and her female contemporaries set a standard for highly expressive robust female mariachi singing in a specific low range and tessitura, timbre, production, and repertoire while developing any female ranchera voice. Lucha's lower raspy sound in bravío style became a symbol of female expression and sound in the mariachi world. This is not unlike Ella Fitzgerald's inadvertent creation of scat singing in jazz when, according to legend, one night in performance she forgot the lyrics and improvised them with syllables.

Despite the hard work and pioneering steps of Lucha Reyes, her health suffered and she died of a drug overdose in 1944. Her situation was the very definition of vocal stress. Her story is one everyone can learn from.[67] Her bravío style of singing earned her the title "la madre de la canción ranchera" (The Mother of Ranchera Song), and Reyes' robust female belt style of singing continues today.

VOCAL CONDITIONS FOR FEMALE RANCHERA SINGERS

During the popularity of Golden Age charro musicals, female singers were not featured as often as male singers in films, despite the fact that Lucha Reyes and others demonstrated high-level acting skills. Actresses María Felix and Dolores del Río, along with actress/singer María Victoria, were often preferred over dedicated singers due to their glamor and beauty. Some singers had to provide audio while the actresses were pictured.[68] This situation was repeated in the 1997 movie "Selena" about the Texas crossover ranchera-pop singer Selena Quintanilla. Warner Brothers cast Graciela Beltrán to sing, yet Jennifer López was chosen as the on-screen actress (see the section "Female Ranchera Singers and Composers" for further information).

---

[66] The singer's microphone was not yet available when Lucha began her singing in the early 1900s. See "The History of Microphones," https://www.thoughtco.com/history-of-microphones-1992144.

[67] Jáuregui, *El Mariachi*, 111–112.

[68] Unfortunately, this is still sometimes the case today, as in the movie" Selena" a biography of the rising Tex-Mex pop singer Selena Quintanilla from Corpus Christi, Texas, acted by Jennifer López and sung by Graciela Beltrán.

In 2010, the author presented on female and male mariachi singers at the National Convention for the National Association of Teachers of Singing Convention (NATS) in Salt Lake City, Utah. Audio samples of Lucha Reyes were presented among other female and male ranchera singers.[69] Singers, voice teachers, and voice scientists attended and responded with great enthusiasm to most of the singers. Everything changed when several voice scientists responded with concern within three to five seconds of listening to the voices of Lucha Reyes and Amalia Mendoza. Several immediately identified vocal nodes in the raspy singing of the two. The same scientists loved the eight other audio samples of both female and male ranchera singers. In short, the field of female mariachi pedagogy is young, and there is much to learn from studying more about the singing of Lucha Reyes and her female singing colleagues.

Summary

Solo singers and ranchera songs were one of the most popular symbols of Mexican nationalism in the twentieth century. Nationalism became popular after the Mexican Revolution, thanks to support from the media and Mexican government. Singing in Italian opera and Spanish zarzuelas in Mexico during the 1800s influenced Mexican song composition, comedias rancheras, and the rich toned legato singing style used by vocalists in rancheras. Solo Mexican nationals no longer lost singing opportunities in film, radio, and recordings to imported Italian opera singers. Male opera and ranchera singers had easier access to training than women. This enabled them to easily switch between styles, whether switching between boleros and rancheras within the mariachi tradition, or from mariachi to opera and back. Master voice teacher José Pierson played a pivotal role for men in helping singers train and cross-train between European classical singing and Mexican ballads, boleros, and *rancheras*.

The bolero became popular in Mexico in the 1940s, accompanied by ranchera trios as well as mariachi ensembles. While many women composed, recorded, and sang boleros, two men gained the most prominence as singing stars of the bolero ranchero, namely, Pedro Infante and Javier Solis. The bolero ranchero was a commercial media product of the 1950s.

Jose Alfredo Jiménez began a new style of mariachi original contemporary singing as a singer-songwriter with his guitar and was especially popular during the 1960s until his death in 1973. His bravío songs are legendary to Mexican audiences, one notable example being *El Rey*.

Female *ranchera* singers had less support than their male counterparts with more barriers to overcome as they sang in a world dominated by men. Thanks to female bolero composers, all-female mariachi ensembles, the *bravío* style of Lucha Reyes and every female solo singer colleague since, women have now cemented their place in the ranchera world. Women today can access vocal training and now often outnumber the men in many educational mariachi ensembles in the United States with many new female ranchera soloists to come.

---

[69] The author presented audio samples including Lucha Reyes, Amalia Mendoza, Linda Ronstadt, Lucha Villa, the author herself, Jorge Negrete, Pedro Vargas, and Javier Solis.

56 THE MARIACHI VOICE

FIGURE 2.23 Woman in regional *huipil* from Yucatán, Eastern Mexico, with a *rebozo* wrapped around her. Design by Marcia Cagadahan.

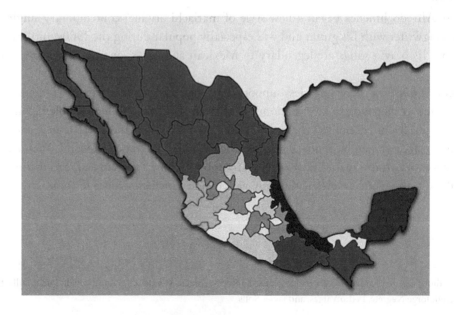

FIGURE 2.24 Unlabeled map to fill in for this lesson.

Chronology: Key Dates in Ranchera Voice History

1521: Spain conquers the Indigenous Mexican Empire and calls it "Nueva España."

1821: Three hundred years later, Mexico overthrows Spanish rule, and the Republic of Mexico is established.

1830s: Mariachi origins can be traced along the West Coast of Mexico and the United States as far north as San Francisco and San Rafael, California.

1884–ca. 1935: The Orquesta Típica Jalisciense features mariachi and classically trained solo singers who can perform many kinds of Mexican song.

1910–1921: During and after the Mexican Revolution, the quest for Mexican identity begins in earnest. The Mexican government and the media support this cause. Mexican nationalism flowers in music.

1913: Manuel M. Ponce publishes, defines, composes, and collects Mexican songs. He is known as "The Father of Mexican Song" and is the composer of "Estrellita," among many other songs.

1910–1915: Lucha Reyes is credited as the first female soloist to front an all-male mariachi ensemble. Singing was often outdoors, with the microphone not yet invented. Reyes inadvertently creates a belt or bravío style to compensate and improve her vocal projection.

1910–1921: Many move from rural areas in Mexico to its capital, Mexico City. This shift changes Mariachi style from "ranchera" rural or antiguo mariachi to modern, urban, or contemporary mariachi. Singers from all parts of Mexico come into contact with Italian opera and Spanish zarzuela live productions, creating a more stylized and mixed mariachi-classical vocal production. A cross-pollination also occurs when these styles are carried back to rural areas. Both rural and urban styles co-exist.

1920–1930s: The microphone (first invented in 1887) is used to launch radio stations and later by individual singers.

1930: Inauguration of XEW Radio in Mexico City.

1935–1960: *Siglo de oro del cine mexicano* (Golden Age of Mexican cinema) features solo mariachi and classical singers in Mexico City on XEW radio shows, movies, tours, and in recordings. The soloists are versatile, often covering classical songs, rancheras, Cuban boleros, and international Latin American hits. Charro films became a worldwide phenomenon. Solo singers and composers with vocal and acting training, stamina, and quick learning skills became celebrities, especially men. The composer Manuel Esperón and solo opera singer Jorge Negrete are especially prominent.

Urban ranchera solo huapango singing became stylized with long, virtuosic notes sustained in the upper range. Rural huapangos from the huasteca region use the register flip without sustaining the high note. Miguel Aceves Mejía (formerly a salsa singer) is especially loved in this style, considered "El Rey del falsete" (The King of falsete).

1930s–1966: Boleros from Cuba arrive in Mexico and become commercially popular. They are adapted into mariachi as the bolero ranchero style. A new intimate singing style contrasting robust ranchera singing is established; Los Panchos establishes the trio vocal style in Mexico and New York with three-part harmony, several guitars, and maracas. Soloists Javier Solis, Pedro Vargas, and Pedro Infante were celebrity bolero soloists until the death of Solis in 1966.

1954: Women receive the right to vote. Before then, women had fewer opportunities. Female singer celebrities at this time include Lucha Reyes, Amalia Mendoza, Lola Beltran, and Lucha Villa. Female singers with appreciable vocal technique were

Hermanas Padilla and other female duos, Irma Vila, Sofía Álvarez Caicedo, Matilde Sáchez "La Torcacita," and María Elena Sandoval.

1950–1973: Just after 1960, we see the rise of songwriter José Alfredo Jiménez triggered a third phase of mariachi voice history. His new singer-songwriter style includes guitar accompaniment and message over extensive vocal training, falsete, and choreographed acting skills. His original songs are classics that tell a poignant story with simple yet unforgettably personal lyrics. His songs are often less difficult to sing than songs from the previous ranchera era and therefore more accessible to beginning and intermediate singers.

1947–1996: Two important ranchera female soloists, Lola Beltrán and later Lucha Villa, achieve celebrity status in movies, recordings, and tours. Lucha Villa has the lowest female voice in ranchera singing (male tenor range).

1966–2016: The late Vicente Fernandez and later his son, Alejandro Fernandez, rise to popularity. Vicente, or "Chente" as he was affectionately called, was one of the few soloists to enjoy a very long singing and film career. His singing gift was natural without much vocal training, not unlike Pedro Infante. "Chente" shrewdly emphasized his acting talents on television and won many Grammys and recorded over fifty albums, including many songs by José Alfredo Jiménez. His son, Alejandro has a lower voice in mid-baritone range and continues his solo career today in a contemporary romantic ranchera-bolero-pop style.

History: Mariachi Singers and Their Songs

Thirteen Lessons (see Answer Key after Lessons to check answers)

LESSON 1: RANCHERA RURAL FOLK ORIGINS

1. Translate the term "ranchera music" into English.
2. When is ranchera music first documented in Mexico?
3. Describe the attire early ranchera musicians wore to perform.
4. Was mariachi singing always connected to the church? Explain.
5. What kind of secular life events always included and still includes mariachi performers?
6. Where is the center of mariachi activity in Mexico? Which Mexican states?
7. How large an area does mariachi music cover in its early history?
8. Fill out the map below in Figure 2.24. Draw and color in the two areas described in questions two and three.

LESSON 2: VOCAL ROOTS AND EARLY TWENTIETH CENTURY RANCHERA SONGS

VOCAL ROOTS

1. Name the different terms for the first two periods in mariachi music history.
2. Name the dates of these two initial periods. (Extra Credit: Is there a third period?)
3. What major event triggered everyone looking for work in Mexico City in 1910?
4. How was the singing in the urban mariachi contemporary period different from the other period? What vocal elements mixed into the ranchera singing style and can you name how?

5. What styles of vocal music had long existed in Mexico City that might have influenced ranchera singing between 1910 and the 1930s?
6. When did Italian opera come to Mexico City? What elements of Italian opera singing are similar to ranchera vocal melodies and their singers?
7. Which Italian composer did Mexico City socialites fall in love with and what is the style of singing called?
8. What do Spanish one-act zarzuelas, or *comedias musicales*, have in common with ranchera music?
9. What is the earliest date we have of published ranchera sheet music for voice and piano? (Hint: It includes jarabes and sones.)
10. What language is sung in ranchera performances? Was this Mexico's original language? If so, when did it change?
11. What is the difference in sound between many Mexican indigenous dialects and the Spanish language? Can you describe how each sounds?
12. In 1884, the famous touring Mexican orchestra, Orquesta Típica Jalisicence was formed.
13. Alfonso López Tirado and José Mojica. Their repertoire was extremely varied and the singers had to crossover between styles. They were both operatically trained.

SONGS

1. What is a corrido? What rhythms typically accompany corridos?
2. Where is the Mexican corrido from? Name three famous corrido song titles.
3. Who wrote the Mexican *ranchera valseada* "Cielito Lindo"? When was it composed?
4. What is one of the most famous *ranchera valseada* songs from Oaxaca, Mexico? Who composed it and when?
5. Who wrote "La Borrachita" in 1918? What is his full name as well as his nickname?

LESSON 3: MEXICO'S GOLDEN AGE OF CINEMA, SINGERS, AND SONGS

1. What is the name for the Golden Age of Mexican Cinema in Spanish? What is the full name that also recognizes the songs and singers? List in both languages.
2. What is the name for charro musicals in Spanish?
3. When were the microphone and the radio invented? When did radio become important for transmitting music in Mexico, and what was the name of the radio station?
4. What is the name of the first international charro film and its corresponding song?
5. Name three charro films and three ranchera songs from these films. Activate a computer search with the terms "Charro film," "Jorge Negrete," and/or "Mexico's Golden Age of Cinema."
6. Were the ranchera film singers only solo singers, or did they need to develop other talents as well? Which ones?
7. Name four ranchera singers who performed in *comedias rancheras* (charro musical dramas).

LESSON 4: THE FATHER OF MEXICAN SONG—MANUEL M. PONCE

1. Who was Manuel M. Ponce?
2. How is Manuel M. Ponce linked to Mexican folk songs? Why do they call him the Father of Mexican Song?

3. Name the Mexican indigenous group that ruled much of Mexico just prior to the Spanish Conquest in 1521. Did this group have music?
4. Name several traditional features of Mexican song as described by Manuel M. Ponce.
5. Listen to the song "Estrellita" by Manuel M. Ponce as sung by Mariachi Cobre: https://youtu.be/fXgfjMAg0Ps. What is the melodic range of the melody? Are the music phrases legato or staccato (see Glossary)? Find a student partner to transcribe the melody together. Is this a song for beginning or advanced singers? Why or why not?
6. Listen to another version of "Estrellita" by Encarnation Vasquez: https://youtu.be/JS8dannyWGg. What are the similarities between this version and the version by Mariachi Cobre? What are the differences?

LESSON 5: SOLO RANCHERA SINGERS BECOME CELEBRITIES THROUGH MEDIA EXPANSION

1. What is the name of the Mexico City Radio Station that in the early 1930s became central to Mexican singers for live concerts and promotion? Who owned the media conglomerate?
2. Prior to Mexico's nationalistic period, singers from which country dominated performances and the airwaves in Mexico?
3. What celebrity ranchera singer began at XEW working as a secretary?
4. What are *comedias rancheras*? Are they nationalistic? Why are they important to the mariachi music field? Have you seen one on YouTube?
5. What other media besides radio did Emilio Azcárraga own and control?
6. *Project:* Have students organize a monthly movie night to watch a selected comedia ranchera such as ¡*Ay Jalisco no te rajes!* featuring Jorge Negrete when he first released the title song "¡Ay Jalisco no te rajes!" Show movies that include songs from current or future song repertoire. How well does each singer act? Do they take on a character or persona? Does that character change during the course of the musical?

LESSON 6: CROSSOVER SINGERS: JORGE NEGRETE AND *OPERAS RANCHERAS*

1. What was Jorge Negrete's nickname?
2. Was he also an actor? What else did he do besides sing?
3. What song repertoire did Negrete study? All rancheras?
4. Who was Jorge Negrete's voice teacher?
5. Did Negrete's voice studies give him an advantage in pursuing a solo ranchera career? How?
6. Study Jorge Negrete. Choose either of his vocal styles by comparing and contrasting several of his songs with different vocal styles.
7. Read Chapter 8 section: "Jorge Negrete." Write less than one page describing the difficulties of being a celebrity performer and dealing with the media.
8. Compare and contrast one of Mexico's early crossover singers with a contemporary one. What is different and what is the same?

LESSON 7: MEXICO'S PREMIERE VOICE TEACHER: MAESTRO JOSÉ PIERSON

1. Who was Maestro José Pierson, and why is he so important to Mexican vocal history?
2. Did Pierson teach purely opera, or did he mix repertoires as he taught technique? If so, which styles?

3. Where and how did José Pierson vocally train?
4. Was Pierson from Mexico City?
5. How did Pierson have students achieve crossover when training them? What technical component always stayed the same?
6. Did José Pierson only teach voice? If not, what related field did he also work in?
7. How did Maestro Pierson train female singers? Did he train them the same way he as male singers?

LESSON 8: THE BOLERO IN MEXICO—HISTORY, SINGERS, AND COMPOSERS

1. What is a bolero? Describe.
2. Where did the bolero come from, and when did it arrive in Mexico?
3. What is a bolero ranchero? Is it indigenous to Mexico?
4. Describe the bolero sound using two adjectives.
5. Name five bolero composers including both women and men.
6. Name the three female bolero composers that span the twentieth century.
7. What is "crooning"? Does one need to keep their breath support active while crooning or singing gently?
8. Why do we remember Pedro Infante and Javier Solis?
9. What was Pedro Infante's musical and personal background?
10. Compare vocal sounds of Lucha Reyes and María Elena Sandoval. Does María Elena Sandoval croon like the men or use a full bravío style similar to Lucha Reyes? How are they different from each other?
11. Name your favorite ten boleros from any period in history. Compare and contrast your songs with another classmate (see Chapter 5 for a list of boleros at different vocal levels).
12. Create a quiz on the bolero with small sheets of folded-over paper naming famous boleros from Mexico (or Latin America). Keep an answer key with the name of the composer for each bolero and the year it was composed. Create two teams in class to quiz each other.

LESSON 9: RANCHERA SINGING STYLE

1. What features identify the ranchera singing style? Are you able to make some of these sounds?
2. What historical events led to the formation of a ranchera singing style?
3. What is the official language in ranchera singing?
4. What kind of fusion is the bolero moruno rhythm in the song *Como Quien Pierde una Estrella*? (What styles are mixed together?)
5. Is ranchera singing a question of personal style and training? What are your influences?
6. *Project:* Choose your favorite two ranchera singers, either two men or two women. If you are unsure, you may choose either Lucha Villa with Lola Beltrán or Jorge Negrete with Pedro Vargas. Listen, describe, and compare the sound and style of two female or male ranchera singers. You may even find them both singing the same song differently, although that is not necessary. Use adjectives to describe their sound such as rich, robust, aggressive, mellow, crooning, gutsy, velvet, intense, laid back, and rounded. For style, compare their phrasing, acting, song repertoire choices, diversity of styles, and overall presentation. Write one to two paragraphs comparing and contrasting your results.

LESSON 10: SINGER/SONGWRITER JOSÉ ALFREDO JIMÉNEZ: A THIRD PERIOD IN MARIACHI HISTORY

1. How is José Alfredo Jiménez's singing different from the ranchera singers before him?
2. Is a singer/actor different from a singer/songwriter? Explain.
3. Name three of José Alfredo's songs.
4. Describe the songwriting style of José Alfredo Jiménez. What musical techniques did he use to highlight the message of the song? What does he do differently from earlier singer celebrities?
5. Name two artists that sing songs by José Alfredo Jiménez.

LESSON 11: FEMALE RANCHERA/BOLERO SINGERS AND COMPOSERS

1. Name Mexico's three most important female bolero composers. Did they live at the same time?
2. Can you name a song by each of the three female bolero composers?
3. Which of Mexico's twentieth-century female composers grew up primarily outside of Mexico?
4. A bolero from the 1950s was written by a woman, made famous many times, and then resurfaced again when recorded by Luis Miguel on his *Romance* CD of timeless bolero classics. Name the bolero and the woman who wrote it.
5. Name two Mexican all female mariachi ensembles. When were they active?
6. Name two all-female mariachi ensembles who recently won Grammys or Latin Grammys in the United States.

LESSON 12: BRAVÍO RANCHERA SONG—LUCHA REYES AND VOCAL CONDITIONS FOR WOMEN

1. What was the real name of Lucha Reyes, and where was she originally from?
2. What is bravío singing? How did it evolve? Is it exactly the same as belt singing in musical theater in the United States?
3. Do you consider Lucha Reyes a pioneer? Why or why not?
4. Do all women sing rancheras in bravío style? Name two songs that are in bravío style and two that are not.
5. Why were vocal conditions particularly difficult for female ranchera singers until the advent of the microphone in the 1920s–1930s?

LESSON 13: KEY DATES IN MEXICAN VOICE HISTORY— ADVANCED STUDIES (BASED UPON CHRONOLOGY)

1. Who invaded Mexico in 1521 and renamed the country? What was Mexico called?
2. How long was Mexico ruled by this foreign country? In what year did Mexicans gain their freedom?
3. Was the Mexican Revolution different from the Fight for Independence from foreign rule? When was the Mexican Revolution?
4. Who was Lucha Reyes, and why is she so important to mariachi voice history?
5. Who is known in Mexico as "The Father of Mexican Song"? What did he accomplish?

6. What is the name of Mexico's first and most famous orchestra featuring trained solo singers who sang in both mariachi and classical styles? When did the orchestra begin?
7. Where is the bolero originally from? Is the bolero Mexican, Cuban, or Latin American? Explain.
8. Name two or three celebrity bolero ranchero singers who helped make the bolero famous during the 1900s.
9. When was Mexico's *Siglo de oro* (Golden Age) for movie musicals, and why was it so important for mariachi singers, composers, and the genre as a whole?
10. What is the difference between rural versus contemporary/urban mariachi? Are mariachi singing styles different?
11. Which high male singer made the huapango 6/8 rhythmic style internationally famous?
12. When did women receive the right to vote in Mexico? When did women receive the right to vote in the United States? Do you believe this basic right might have affected musical careers for women in Mexico? Why or why not?
13. Name three female singing celebrities who reached fame during the 1900s.
14. Is the singing style of José Alfredo Jiménez the same as male celebrities during the Golden Age of charro musicals? Why or why not? Why is he very important to the field of Mexican song and, in particular, ranchera singing? Name three of his songs.
15. Are the singing careers of Vicente and/or Alejandro Fernandez similar to or different from that of José Alfredo Jiménez? Describe similarities or differences in the talents of each singer.

Answer Key

LESSON 1: RANCHERA RURAL FOLK ORIGINS

1. 1830s, although it could have existed long before.
2. Nayarit, Jalisco, and Colima.
3. In the 1830s, as far as parts of present day California and Texas; today, it is worldwide.
4. Figure 2.25 [FILLED OUT MAP]
5. During the rural period ranchera performers often wore white peasant garb and huaraches (sandals).
6. Mariachi singing was not always part of the church; in fact, in 1848, Bishop Cosme wrote a letter to Spain complaining of the mariachis making too much noise outside his church, so mariachi was clearly secular only. Today, mariachi is an important part of Catholic services for life events and holidays from funerals to weddings, also including the Virgin of Guadalupe on December 12th of each year.
7. Baptisms, weddings, funerals, rodeos, fairs, birthdays, holidays, and posadas.

LESSON 2: VOCAL ROOTS AND EARLY TWENTIETH CENTURY RANCHERA SONGS

Vocal Roots

1. Names: Period 1: Mariachi rural, antiguo. Period 2: Mariachi urbano, moderno, contemporáneo.
2. Dates: Period 1: 1830s to ca. 1915. Period 2: 1915–1960. (See "Singer/songwriter: José Alfredo Jiménez: Third Period in Mariachi History" in this chapter for Period 3.)

FIGURE 2.25 Filled-in map with answers for answer key.

3. The Mexican Revolution (1910–1921) triggered the migration of people toward the urban center of Mexico City, all searching for work.
4. In mariachi urbano after 1915, singing styles became quite varied. Italian operatic singing styles influenced ranchera vocal styles, adding long legato lines, a stylization and sophisticated style to many songs. One example is the huapango.
5. Other regional folk styles from many Mexican states, Italian opera, Spanish zarzuela, and music in Spanish from other Latin American countries.
6. Italian opera with virtuosic singing lines was performed regularly in Mexico City from at least 1823 onward.
7. Mexico's audiences were entranced by the operas of Giacomo Rossini (1792–1868) and the bel canto singing style he wrote for his opera singers.
8. Spain's one-act zarzuelas were often called by other names as well, including *comedias musicales*. *Comedias rancheras* are similar in structure to comedias musicales, but with ranchera plots, themes, and singing style.
9. 1850s published *Collections of Sones and Jarabes* by Miguel Toledano for voice and piano.
10. Spanish was imposed as a language in Mexico in 1521 by the Spaniards (but Mexico has always maintained many indigenous dialects as well).
11. Mexican Indian dialects almost always lean on pure head voice and forward placement, while Spanish is placed farther back in the mouth and mixes more chest in with head voice.
12. In 1884, the famous touring Mexican orchestra, Orquesta Típica Jalisicence was formed.
13. Alfonso López Tirado and José Mojica. Their repertoire was extremely varied and the singers had to crossover between styles. They were both operatically trained.

CHAPTER 2: HISTORY 65

Songs

1. The corrido is a pre-1900 historical ballad that tells a story in Spanish. Many date back to the Mexican revolution and earlier.
2. Corridos are said to have originated in Northern Mexico as part of Mexico's música ranchera norteña tradition (Northern Mexican norteño ranch-style music). Three possible song titles are: La Adelita, La Chancla, La Valentina.
3. Quirino Mendoza y Cortes, 1882.
4. Canción Mixteca is one of Oaxaca, Mexico's important anthems.
5. Ignacio Fernández Esperón (1894–1968) had a childhood nickname of "Tata nacho."

LESSON 3: MEXICO'S GOLDEN AGE OF CINEMA, SINGERS, AND SONGS

1. *Siglo de oro del cine mexicano*
2. Comedias rancheras
3. The radio was first invented in the 1890s, and the first microphone was invented in 1876. They were first introduced in Mexico City with the inauguration of XEW Radio in 1930.
4. "Allá en el rancho grande" (Over There on the Big Ranch).
5. Answers may include but are not limited to: *Juan sin miedo*—"La Tequilera"; *Fantasía ranchera*—"Como una amapolita"; *Allá en el rancho grande*; "Allá en el rancho grande."
6. No; Alfonso Ortiz Tirado, José Mojica, Pedro Vargas, and Jorge Negrete all had to act and crossover stylistically, and Negrete was also a skilled horseback rider, which was useful in charro films.
7. Answers may include but are not limited to: Pedro Infante, Lucha Villa, Manolita Arriola, Javier Solís, Amalia Mendoza, Lucha Reyes, Irma Vila, Elena Sandoval, Lola Beltran, and Miguel Aceves Mejia.

LESSON 4: THE FATHER OF MEXICAN SONG—MANUEL M. PONCE

1. Mexican composer, pianist, music educator, and scholar.
2. He wrote about Mexican nationalistic music topics and stressed the importance of collecting and defining elements of Mexican folk song. Ponce was an important pedagogue and a prolific composer for Mexico.
3. The Aztecs; yes.
4. Traditional features include a combination of *Italiante* long and legato melodic lines, Western European song structure of AABA, and the direct simplicity of Mexican local folk poetry as lyrics.
5. C3 to G4 (octave and a half). Legato. Advanced singer.
6. Answers may include: similar legato, tempo, emotion—different singing styles, vibratos, and phrasing.

LESSON 5: SOLO RANCHERA SINGERS BECOME CELEBRITIES THROUGH MEDIA EXPANSION

1. 1895; starting in the 1930s.
2. XEW; Emilio Azcárraga Vidaurreta.

66 THE MARIACHI VOICE

3. Italy.
4. Lola Beltrán.
5. Charro film; showcases solo mariachi ranchera and bolero singing styles and popularized the style.
6. Film and recording studio.

LESSON 6: CROSSOVER SINGERS: JORGE NEGRETE AND *OPERAS RANCHERAS*

1. *El Charro Cantor* (The Singing Charro or Mexican Horseman).
2. Yes; horse riding.
3. Italian Opera, Mexican ballads and rancheras; no.
4. José Pierson.
5. Yes; building a healthy, rich-sounding tone and technique that made him unique.
6. Answers will vary.
7. Answers will vary.
8. Answers will vary.

LESSON 7: MEXICO'S PREMIERE VOICE TEACHER: MAESTRO JOSÉ PIERSON

1. He was Mexico City's leading voice teacher during the first half of the twentieth century.
2. No; he also taught Neapolitan and Mexican songs, operettas, *zarzuelas*, and *rancheras*.
3. He studied music and classical singing in England; University of Santa Clara, California; and Italy.
4. No.
5. Focus in various repertoires and styles, alongside technical expertise in breath support and customized voice building. The technical component that was always consistent was slightly less intense breath compression, less vibrato, less backspace, and staying close to the character and interpretation for each song regardless of style.
6. No; he also worked in promotion, productions and advertising singers.
7. Without emphasis on the ranchera belt or the lower mariachi fach. No, he trained the women differently than the men.

LESSON 8: THE BOLERO IN MEXICO—HISTORY, SINGERS, AND COMPOSERS

1. A romantic ballad in 4/4 meter.
2. Came from Cuba and several other Caribbean islands; 1940s but perhaps earlier.
3. Boleros in the ranchera tradition were accompanied with armonía (strumming rhythm instruments) using steady eighth notes. No.
4. Answers will vary.
5. Answers may include: Ema Elena Valdelamar, Consuelo Velásquez, María Grever, Manuel Esperón, Ernesto Cortazar, Jesus "Chucho" Monge, Alfonzo Esparza Oteo, Jorge del Moral, Alberto Dominguez, Gabriel Ruiz, Gonzalo Curiel, and Ignacio Esperón (a.k.a. Tata Nacho), and Agustín Lara.
6. Ema Elena Valdelamar, Consuelo Velásquez, and María Grever.
7. Intimate legato singing with bravío production. Yes.

CHAPTER 2: HISTORY 67

8. They created a vocal style centered around the bolero and starred in a plethora of charro films.
9. He was from a family of humble means but was highly musical, playing guitar, piano, violin, trumpet, and drums.
10. Answers can vary. Maria Elena Sandoval croons like the men but occasionally switches to a full bravío style usually for the climax of a song.
11. Answers will vary.
12. Create a quiz.

LESSON 9: RANCHERA SINGING STYLE

1. A robust and rounded sound with falsete flips, long vocal lines, customary and celebratory yells, and a particular song repertoire.
2. Mexican Revolution; Mexican Independence; entrance of Cuban boleros; invention of microphone, sound amps, and radio.
3. Spanish.
4. Romantic bolero with Spanish flamenco feel.
5. Yes, because training matters; where they are raised, teachers, finances, etc.
6. Project.

LESSON 10: SINGER/SONGWRITER JOSÉ ALFREDO JIMÉNEZ: A THIRD PERIOD IN MARIACHI HISTORY

1. Jiménez did not possess vocal training, nor was he an actor, but he wrote unforgettable boleros and songs with simple words and an intimate, yet direct message. His songs are set in a small voice range, and he sings with almost a talking style that communicates everyday stories with remarkable effectiveness.
2. Singer/songwriters are often less trained vocally.
3. Answers will vary but may include: *El Rey*, *Que bonito amor*, *Ella*, *Que suerte la mía*, *Vámonos*, and *Deja que salga la luna*.
4. Jimenez's melodic writing style continues the long, legato lines and song structure from Ponce's first generation of songwriters. He skips melodic jumps and chooses only occasional long-held notes at the end of his huapangos. Jiménez also uses a less syncopated rhythmic texture in his accompaniment, creating a transparency that allows the listener to stay closer to the message of the song.
5. Answers will vary but may include: Selena Quintanilla, Miguel Aceves Mejía, Enrique Bunbury, Antonio Aguilar, Luis Aguilar, Lola Beltrán, Vikki Carr, Gualberto Castro, Rocío Dúrcal, Alejandro Fernández, Pedro Fernández, Vicente Fernández, Los Tigres del Norte, Manolo García, Little Joe Hernández & The Latinaires, Julio Iglesias, Pedro Infante, the Mexican rock group Maná, Luis Miguel, Jorge Negrete, Sunny Ozuna & The Sunliners, María Dolores Pradera, Javier Solís, and Chavela Vargas.

LESSON 11: FEMALE RANCHERA/BOLERO SINGERS AND COMPOSERS

1. Ema Elena Valdelamar, Consuelo Velásquez, and María Grever. No.
2. Júrame, Bésame mucho, Mil besos.
3. Maria Grever.

68 THE MARIACHI VOICE

4. Mucho Corazón by Ema Elena Valdelamar.
5. Answers will vary but may include: *Las Adelitas* in 1948; *Las Estrellas* in 1951; and *Las Coronelas* in 1953.
6. Flor de Toloaoche and Mariachi Divas. Also, *Mariachi Mujer 2000* and Mariachi Reyna.

LESSON 12: BRAVÍO RANCHERA SONG—LUCHA REYES AND VOCAL CONDITIONS FOR WOMEN

1. Maria de Luz Flores Aceves; Guadalajara, Jalisco.
2. Pedagogically speaking, bravío is belt singing with gutsy expressive sounds and gestures. The technique refers to a particular timbre in the sound and intense breath pressure for either gender. For women it should be delivered in the lower half of the full female range. For men bravío can be expressed anywhere in their chest range, which is most of the male voice. Bravío interpretation includes adopting a character that is brave, robust, earthy, defiant, and aggressive. Yes.
3. Yes, she invented the belt style inadvertently. Lucha Reyes' strength, perseverance, and passion for singing add to the bravio/belting mariachi female singing style.
4. No, not all women sing ranchers in bravio style. Those who have not yet developed their falsete often lean on the expressiveness of the bravío style. Answers will vary.
5. Female ranchera singers fronted mariachi ensembles outdoors and in keys that were traditionally easy for male singers and the musicians. They honored the robust bravío sound by singing only in the bottom half of their vocal range, all prior to the standard use of the microphone in outdoor performances.

LESSON 13: KEY DATES IN MEXICAN VOICE HISTORY— ADVANCED STUDIES (BASED UPON CHRONOLOGY)

1. Spain; "Nueva España."
2. Three hundred years; 1821.
3. Yes; 1910–1921.
4. Lucha Reyes is credited as the first female soloist to front an all-male mariachi ensemble and inadvertently created a belt or bravío style to compensate and improve her vocal projection in large outdoor venues before the microphone was in full use.
5. Manuel M. Ponce; he helped promote nationalistic Mexican song writing traditions.
6. Orquesta Típica Jalisciense; 1884.
7. Cuba; there are different types of boleros depending on the rhythmic and vocal style. Mexican bolero rancheras are adopted by mariachis and soloists.
8. Javier Solis, Pedro Vargas, and Pedro Infante
9. 1935–1960; singers, composers, and producers quickly improve skills and rapidly create new repertoire to keep up with high demands and competition.
10. What is the difference between rural versus contemporary/urban mariachi? Are mariachi singing styles different? Rural mariachi is based on the oral traditions passed on from others and contemporary mariachi incorporates training singers, written music, and the addition of trumpets.
11. Miguel Aceves Mejía.
12. 1954; 1920; Yes; answers will vary.

13. Lucha Reyes, Amalia Mendoza, Lola Beltran, and Lucha Villa.
14. No; his songs are simple yet memorable. They are often less difficult to sing than songs from the previous ranchera era. Emphasis is put on the message instead of acting or vocal virtuosity.
15. They are similar in the sense that they did not have much classical vocal training but have different ranges. He sings in a lower range than his father. Answers can vary.

CHAPTER 3

MARIACHI VOICE PEDAGOGY

Vocal pedagogy is the study of general voice instruction. It can include both artistic and scientific approaches to vocal technique, range, tone, registration, song assignments based upon vocal difficulty, vocal health, and more. The study of vocal technique is designed to provide vocal freedom for singers in any style. It need not be applied only to classical singing or particular songs. Voice pedagogy comes from a many-centuries-old Italian classical tradition whereby singers practiced exercises often for years before tackling opera arias. Everyone can benefit from healthy voice production and learning habits to protect the voice. This allows the voice to blossom, rather than feel tight, tense, or limited. In this chapter we will describe vocal awareness, technique, healthy vocal habits, and pedagogy as applied to mariachi.

The uniqueness of ranchera sound and style is an important topic from both a technical and aesthetic point of view. It is helpful to become aware of the ranchera style's vocal color and head/chest balance in vocal production. Beautifully sustained floating falsete in the top end of the voice is a pedagogical topic unique to mariachi singing. Contrary to classical singing, high notes should not be top volume, and mariachi singers play with color contrasts when changing registers. Most importantly, training for the female mariachi voice differs greatly from classical vocal training and from the male voice.

It is common to see contemporary mariachi vocal professionals today training less than those of the early twentieth century. This can be heard in the sound of the voice itself and changes in the vocal sound of artists over time. Today's commercial solo singers (including mariachi) don't tend to train their voices until they encounter vocal problems. Many are also unaware that they can avoid fatigue and other issues with general vocal training (see the section: "Avoid Fatigue" in this chapter as well as Chapter 8). Voices can also be harmed by singing songs too difficult for the current level of the singer or by forcing a singer to perform out of their comfort range. Range is built with training. For these reasons and much more, it is always helpful to learn about vocal pedagogy.

Contemporary mariachi professionals often run into technical issues and have shorter solo singing careers than did some of Mexico's solo singers before and during Mexico's Golden Age of charro musicals from the first half of the twentieth century (see Chapter 2 section: "Mariachi Singers and their Songs"). The operatic and ranchera voice training of charro film solo artists Jorge Negrete (1911–1953), Pedro Vargas (1906–1989), and earlier Mexican solo singers Juan Arvizu (1900–1985), Alfonso Ortíz Tirado (1893–1960), and José Mojica (1895–1974) was clearly extensive. Vocal training gave each of them beautiful voices, which allowed them to cross over from opera to mariachi and back. Their training led to consistency in tone and performance, with technical resilience to sing longer and under difficult conditions, along with stamina under the pressures of stardom. The majority of mariachi singers during this time were men. Many of them studied with master voice teacher José Pierson before and/or during their ascent to stardom (see Chapter 2 section: "Mexico's Premiere Voice Teacher: José Pierson"). Maestro Pierson trained his singers with crossover songs. Female singers of the same time period in Mexico received

The Mariachi Voice. Dr. Juanita Ulloa, Oxford University Press. © Oxford University Press 2024. DOI: 10.1093/oso/9780190846244.003.0003

less encouragement and financial support. This must always be taken into account when researching ranchera voice history.[1] Overall, the ranchera world of singing has a great vocal standard already set in history. Those aspiring to a singing career with longevity can begin by listening to many of these singers.

There are singers who have courageously sought out vocal training but have not found voice teachers familiar with the ranchera style. This is why this book is being written. Some singers have experienced classical voice teachers assigning and insisting upon classical song repertoire in classical higher keys, too high for mariachi women. This can cause mariachi performers to mistrust or avoid classical voice training as a foundation, however unintentional. Luckily, this is changing in the United States, and voice teachers are more openly embracing crossover and commercial singing (CM), separate from classical styles. Singers can use this book for self-study and/or share it with a voice teacher who has technical expertise for breath production and support, albeit unfamiliar with mariachi.

Classical voice teachers new to the style can help students develop by focusing on voice-building exercises instead of classical songs. They can also include ranchera songs and boleros in commercial keys with less vibrato and backspace in the sound. Teaching the male voice is generally easier, as the mariachi male range corresponds to standard operatic fach classifications (see section: "Similarities and Differences in Classical and Ranchera Singing" ahead in this chapter).

The female voice requires both classical and commercial contemporary music training. Classical teachers have unknowingly assigned classical soprano fach repertoire to mariachi singers who have a natural soprano range because they are unaware that the low mariachi female tessitura is its own non-negotiable fach (see the "Female Mariachi Fach" section in this chapter). Contrary to head-voice dominance in classical singing, ranchera singing requires a strong 60–70 percent blend of female chest- to head-voice mix almost all the time. Otherwise, it sounds stylistically incorrect. Breath-support exercises and folk songs that help build the middle range are actually more useful to female mariachi singers than assigning them a separate fach for classical singing. Otherwise, mariachi singers end up with two distinct voices and repertoires with no unity to the voice with a weak middle range. Learning to negotiate the middle voice to shift between a chest/head blend and soft belt singing liberates female ranchera singers.

Mariachi instrumentalists who have yet to sing solos can embrace the contents of this book within mariachi's stylistic voice tradition and begin their journey step by step. Or perhaps you are a shy soloist not knowing how to begin. After reading this chapter, you can build confidence by singing solos in unison with another singer or in collaborative duos in harmony. Try out solos first with friends, family, and neighbors, and then in rehearsals or other low-pressure situations. Taking solos on gigs is an important way to support mariachi colleagues during long performance stints. Think about it as supporting your colleagues instead of making it

---

[1] A prime example is the case of Mexican songwriter Emma Elena Valdelamar (1925–2012), who wrote boleros that became hits beginning in the late 1950s. She shared with the author that her family never supported her vocal training beyond six months of voice study with Maestro Pierson (see Chapter 2 section: Mexico's Premiere Voice Teacher: Maestro José Pierson). When she later tried to get her original songs played by XEW Radio, she was told that they would not listen to any songs by women. Nevertheless, some of her boleros, "Mucho corazón," "Mil besos," and "Cheque en blanco," became classic hits because she entered them into live radio songwriting contests anonymously, and the public chose them as winning songs.

personal. Most of all, don't be afraid to seek vocal training sooner rather than later. Keep in mind that many professional mariachi ensembles pay instrumentalists better when they also accomplished soloists.

Mexicans have always been known for their beautiful singing. Singing is a vibrant and natural part of the culture. Even in Mexican grocery stores in the United States it is not uncommon to hear the butcher's voice booming out rancheras or boleros, projecting through the market from his back station. Ranchera singers of today also have an amazing historical precedent of solo singers in charro musicals on film available for listening online. Let us begin our study of the voice!

Vocal Production and Vocal Care: A Visual Starting Place for Vocalists

Have you thought about your body as a musical instrument? Did you know your body actually functions as a wind instrument? Take a minute to contemplate and visualize this in your awareness. Then, study the diagram depicted in Figure 3.1. The human body is a wind instrument with its own motor, phonator, and resonator.

The air for your wind instrument is stored in your lungs. This air is your *motor* for singing; it is your energy source for sound. You always have quite a bit of air in your lungs

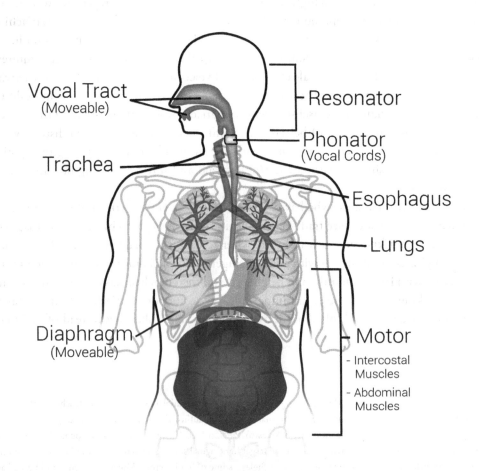

FIGURE 3.1 Diagram of a singer's body as a wind instrument. The motor, phonator, and resonator are essential parts of the singing instrument. Diagram illustrated by Juan Carlos Sánchez.

even though you cannot see, feel, or touch it. Even when you feel out of air, you are not. The sensation is only temporary as your breath turns over naturally from exhale back to inhale. If there were no air at all in your lungs, they would lose their shape. Your lungs are surrounded and protected by your ribcage. You also have muscles around your back and the sides of your ribs called intercostal muscles. They expand when you inhale and support your sound by sustaining the air in your lungs as you sing.

Your vocal folds (also called *voice box*—see Glossary) produce sound and are called a *phonator*. The phonator is the source of your sound. Feel your Adam's apple and hum for several seconds. You have located your phonator. (Watch Plural Publishing's "Finding the Larynx" video on YouTube (https://youtu.be/WbJUdF0S9ys to learn more.) While the throat area houses the source of vocal sound, it never pushes out the sound; rather, it lets the breath energize and move it. A long narrow windpipe carries the air up to your vocal tract. The vocal tract is hollow and movable. It includes the inside of your mouth. The vocal tract resonates and naturally changes shape for different vowels and consonants as your brain thinks of the vowels and words. Can you identify the motor, phonator, and resonator in the diagram depicted in Figure 3.1? (See the "Understand your Vocal Instrument" section in this chapter.)

Many mariachi singers also play an instrument and understand how sound functions on their non-vocal instrument. Sounds can function differently for each instrument, however. The voice is also an instrument. The human body does amazing things no one can see when a singer is actively making sounds. Visualize how your body works as a musical instrument inside you. As you begin to build awareness of your voice functioning as a wind instrument, you will begin to hear a richer vocal tone, your range will expand, and you will experience constant breath flow and better breath support.

VOICE PRODUCTION IN CLASS EXERCISES AND DISCUSSION

1. Trace the diagram in Figure 3.1, marking the motor, phonator, and resonator.
2. Discuss and compare the voice to other mariachi instruments. Can you identify the motor, phonator, and resonator for each mariachi instrument? What are their similarities and differences to the voice?
3. After studying the voice diagram, memorize it and draw it from memory.
4. Draw a similar diagram for your favorite mariachi instrument.

Here is one possible answer if you chose the trumpet for number 2: consider that the trumpet is also a wind instrument and uses the same motor as the voice—the air in the lungs. The trumpet phonator is the lips, while for a singer, the phonator is the vocal cords. The trumpet resonator falls in the vocal tract (which changes shape) and/or the trumpet tube or both. Trumpet vibration varies depending on the shape of the vocal tract cavity or the tube. Vibrations radiate at the mouth of the trumpet, bell of the trumpet, or the space between the two. One big difference between these two wind instruments is that trumpeters apply stronger breath pressure than singers, and they do not allow their bodies to resonate exactly the way a singer does.

Understanding Your Vocal Instrument

(Contributed by Professor John Nix)
If you play the guitar, you probably know the basics of how the guitar works: you pluck or strum the strings to make a sound, and to change the pitch, you push the string down on a

different fret.[2] If a string breaks, you get the right-size string and put it on the guitar, being careful to slowly wind the string on the tuning peg while plucking it gently. When you aren't playing, you put your guitar in a protective case. The same is true if you play the trumpet: you know that to make a sound, you have to put your puckered lips on the mouthpiece and blow. By changing your lip tension and fingering the valves, you make different pitches. You blow harder to get louder, but if you play too high and too loud for too long, your lips get beat up, and you have to stop playing. Like the guitar, you take care of your trumpet by blowing out moisture after you play, by wiping the instrument down after use, and by keeping your trumpet in a case whenever you need to travel.

But what about your voice: do you know what is involved in making a sound? How do we change pitch or loudness? What do we need to do if our voice is not working right? How do we tell when it is time to stop singing, just like the trumpet player with "no chops?" How does travel impact our voice? This next section is for you. We will start with the vocal cords—the part of your body that generates the sound. As you read along, you will see places in the text where you are asked to do something. I urge you to try each exercise, so you can feel in your body what the text is describing.

VOCAL CORDS: WHAT ARE THEY, AND HOW DO THEY WORK?

The vocal cords, or to be more precise vocal folds, are a combination of a ligament, which makes the edge strong and makes bundles of muscle. They are positioned in your larynx or voice box on top of your windpipe. The vocal folds are small (usually no longer than a penny for a woman and maybe the length of a quarter for a low-voiced man), but they generate the basic sound we need for speech and singing. The length of the vocal folds can change; other muscles that act on them can stretch them longer and stiffer for high notes (think about stretching a rubber band: the pitch goes up even though it gets longer) or allow them to shorten and thicken for lower notes.

Try it out: Let your voice glide up from low to high, and back down again. Still other muscles help turn our voice on and off by bringing the folds close together ("on") or separating them ("off").

You can try this out, too: Breathe in deep, and say "ha, ha, ha" in a good, strong laugh.

Both actions can happen at once: *Try singing* "ha, ha, ha, ha, ha" using the first five notes of a scale. We can start and stop making a sound, change pitch, and change how loudly we are singing, many, many times in a single song.

The "Normal Larynx Without and With Stroboscopy" video on YouTube (https://youtu.be/Ddal_OAzkLQ) shows what the vocal folds look like as they make sound. The video shows a woman's vocal folds (the pearly gray part that vibrates), but men's are much the same, only slightly longer. Most of the video is recorded with a normal light, but at the end, a strobe light is used to create a "slow-motion" look.

As you can see in the video, the vocal folds vibrate very fast while singing: from about 100 to 500 times per second for men, and from 200 to 1,000 times per second for women. Higher pitches mean more vibrations per second. No other part of the human body moves this rapidly. But what makes the vocal folds vibrate? Air flowing up from your lungs and through your vocal folds makes them vibrate, somewhat like a flag moves in the wind. One of the keys to singing your best, then, is learning how to feed the air through right. Just like a violin player

---

[2] Portions of this chapter have been adapted (with permission) from "Voice Health and Voice Education," by John Nix and Nelson Roy, in *The Oxford Handbook of Music Education*, ed. Graham Welch and Gary MacPherson.

CHAPTER 3: MARIACHI VOICE PEDAGOGY   75

has to control how fast the bow moves for a long note and must carefully keep the bow on the string (not pressing too hard or light) when they play, a singer has to balance a lot of things in their body alignment and breathing to sing. Next, we examine how the breathing system works, especially when we want to sing.

BREATHING: THE ENERGY FOR THE VOICE

The air for speaking and singing is in your lungs, of course! You breathe thousands of times a day without thinking about it, but when you go to sing, you need to bring something that happens unconsciously more into your attention.

Try this: Start counting aloud, beginning at 1, 2, 3, and so on, and see how long you can count on one breath. Remember that number. Now stand up (if you are sitting), and breathe in slowly through your nose, then start counting again. Did you get to a higher number? The slow, calm, expanding-lower-in-your-body breath probably helped you go further in one breath.

Now, try the same kind of breath in, but speak hushed and softly; did your number change? Use the same, calm breath, but this time, speak strongly, like you were talking to a friend in another room; did your number go back up? So how we breathe and how we coordinate that breathing with what our vocal folds are doing (breathier for soft speech and tender singing, less breathy for loud speaking and heroic singing) can really affect how long we can sing in one breath and how loud or soft we sing.

Well-trained singers learn how to balance the action of the muscles that bring air into our bodies with the muscles that help send the air back out. The key is learning how to feel expanded, as if you are still breathing in while singing out. It is a real balancing act! Watch the "Mechanics of Breathing" video on YouTube (https://youtu.be/OmoU3EexFQQ) to learn more about the components of the breathing system.

BREATHING FOR SINGING EXERCISES

1. Stand with your arms straight out, scarecrow-fashion. While maintaining a "proud" but not rigid stance, with your arms still out, blow out all of your air—every bit. Pause five seconds. Now release your belly area, and let the air in. It comes in without any apparent effort. Repeat five times to sense this quick release that lets air in.

2. Put your hands on your sides. Feel your ribs move as you breathe in. Breathe in through your nose slowly—do you feel your ribs move up and out when you breathe in? Now let your hands drop to your lower back, and bend over. Breathe in deeply. Do your hands on your back move as you breathe in? Pretend to "breathe into your hands"—does this help you feel that lower, wide expansion?

3. Return to standing. Breathe in slowly for a count of four, then hiss on an "s" sound for four counts. Repeat. Check in to see if you are still standing with a "proud" but not stiff posture. Then, try breathing in for four counts, and hissing for eight counts. Repeat. Check in on your posture again—tall and "noble," not tense. Then, try breathing in for four, hiss for twelve counts, and so forth, continuing to extend the length of time you hiss.

4. Repeat the exercise in number 3 but try humming on a comfortable pitch instead of hissing. Follow the same pattern of building up the length of time you can hum as you did on the hissing. Don't forget to check in on your noble, proud, buoyant stance periodically. Does the hum feel very buzzy and forward in your face?

5. Repeat the exercise in number 3, but this time, instead of humming, sing a sustained note in a comfortable part of your range on an "ah" vowel. Try other vowels. Does the amount of time you can sustain the note change when you do different vowels?

6. Try singing the refrain of a familiar song at normal speed, then slow it down and try again. Slow it down even more, so that the phrases are longer. Slow it down one more time. Can you still finish the phrases? Continue to check in on your posture: tall, proud, noble, buoyant? Use a mirror or have a friend watch you. You don't want to be gasping for breath at any time.

VOCAL CORDS QUIZ

Test how well you remember what you have read so far. Answers are listed at the end of this chapter.

1. True or false: Your vocal folds are about two inches long.
2. True or false: Your vocal folds get longer when you sing a high note.
3. True or false: The vocal folds come together when you breathe in and separate when you start to sing.
4. True or false: Your vocal folds become stiffer when you want to sing louder.
5. True or false: Men's vocal folds are shorter than women's vocal folds.

Staying Healthy as a Singer

Earlier in this chapter, we discussed other instruments to introduce vocal concepts. We can use the same instruments, plus your car, to discuss ways to stay healthy as a singer.

Your vocal folds are sort of like a trumpet player's lips. As we mentioned earlier, if you play too loud and too high for too long, or just play for too long in general, your lips get sore. Like your lips, your vocal folds have muscle on the inside and a moist kind of skin on the outside. Too much singing can damage the outer skin-like layer of your vocal folds. If they get continually damaged over and over, you might develop voice problems, like a polyp (which is like a blister) or a nodule (which is like a callous). Problems like these require specialized care, so you want to avoid those kinds of things by practicing smart (not too long!). While calluses on your fingers might be normal for a guitarist or a violinist, vocal fold callouses aren't normal for a singer!

How you start notes is also important. If you play the violin, you know that if you dig in too hard with your bow, you can get a scraping kind of tone, and the hairs on the bow start to come loose. With your voice, lots of loud hard onsets, like in the word "ask" or "apple," need to be avoided. These, too, can cause damage to that outer "skin" of the vocal folds.

Drinking lots of liquids (water is best) is very important as a singer. If you drove your car without oil in the engine, it would seize up, right? Keeping your voice "well oiled" by hydrating throughout the day, especially before and during rehearsals, will keep that moist, outside "skin" of your vocal folds healthy. The drier the climate you live in, the more you need to stay hydrated. And by being hydrated, you are less likely to clear your throat or cough, both of which tend to bang your vocal folds together very hard.

THE VOCAL ATHLETE

Being a singer means you are essentially a vocal athlete, and like any athlete, you have to train in order to get in shape and stay in shape. You can do this by sticking to a daily schedule of warming up your body (stretching, shoulder shrugs, trunk twists, etc.) and your voice before rehearsing, teaching, or performing, then by warming down vocally after a long rehearsal or

CHAPTER 3: MARIACHI VOICE PEDAGOGY   77

performance. Yes, just like any athlete, you warm up and warm down to avoid injuries! A list of suggested vocal exercises is provided later in this chapter. You can also keep yourself on track vocally throughout the day by doing little mini-practice breaks. For example, if you commute by car to work each day, you can do a few daily warm-up exercises in the car while stopped at a traffic signal on the way to work, on the way to lunch, or on an errand. And during long rehearsals, you can massage your neck and jaw, and do some easy humming to release tensions between songs.

WE ALL LIKE TO EAT!

We all love eating, but eating the wrong things at the wrong times can have an effect on your singing voice. Reflux of stomach acid and enzymes can affect one's vocal health. The acid can irritate your esophagus and possibly splash up to your larynx, irritating your vocal folds. Some singers may be at particular risk for problems due to the heavy demands they put on their voice and their use of abdominal-muscle activity during breathing for singing. Dietary and lifestyle behaviors should be carefully balanced. Avoiding the following can help:

- Excess body weight. Being overweight can aggravate reflux.
- Large amounts of red meats and fatty or spicy foods. They can also aggravate reflux.
- Eating within three hours of sleeping, before lots of singing or trumpet playing, and before hard aerobic exercise. It is uncomfortable and can also lead to reflux.
- Drinking large amounts of caffeinated, carbonated, or alcoholic beverages.
- Eating overly large meals.

Dietary and lifestyle behaviors to be *encouraged* include:

- Eating a balanced, low-fat diet.
- Eating smaller meals more frequently in place of a few large meals.
- Elevating the head of your bed to raise your head, neck, and upper torso above the level of your stomach.
- Consult with a doctor, and if necessary, use appropriate medications to reduce acid levels.

TRAVELING AND SINGING

Traveling is a fact of life for many performers. For the vocalist, travel has risks associated with it that warrant special attention. If you travel by car, van, or bus, just staying rested and comfortable during long hours on the highways is tricky. Often, we might like to pass the time by talking, singing, playing cards, and listening to music—but remember that travel time may be your only chance for vocal rest between performances—so it is best to probably read or sleep instead! If you travel by plane, still other factors must be considered. Here are a few "reminders for the road" for the next time you travel.

Risks

- Flying long distances can disrupt your sleep/wake cycle ("jet lag").
- Dehydration from long hours in a car, van, bus, or plane can seriously affect your voice. In planes, there is very dry air (below 10% relative humidity) in the passenger cabin.
- Long trips in a bus or plane may expose you to irritants (diesel smoke, other fuel fumes, cleansers, bacteria).

- Your ears may be exposed to loud noise (especially in airplanes if you are near the engines).
- You may strain to be heard when you speak over noise in the car, van, bus, or plane.

Coping Strategies

- Maintain a regular diet, exercise schedule, and sleep pattern as much as possible during traveling.
- Wash your hands frequently with hot, soapy water.
- Hydrate at normal if not extra levels before, during, and after long drives and flights.
- Avoid sitting near engines, which are noisy and can cause hearing damage.
- Avoid speaking over background noise, loud conversations, radios, and so on.

MINDING YOUR MEDS

Taking medications correctly is essential for your health. Some medications can have a beneficial impact on your voice, while others can cause vocal difficulties. One of the most common types of medications people take is pain medication. For singers, it is important to know which pain relievers do and do not have vocal risks for the user. Both aspirin and ibuprofen (Advil, Motrin) suppress the action of blood platelets in clotting. While this can be very helpful in preventing heart attacks and strokes, it can make your vocal folds more prone to hemorrhaging under heavy use. For that reason, when taking medication for short-term pain relief, use one that contains acetaminophen (Tylenol). The National Center for Voice and Speech website (http://ncvs.org/) provides information about the vocal side effects of hundreds of medications.

Finally, the most important health question: when should you not sing? Pain is the most important indicator you have. If it hurts to swallow, avoid singing. If it hurts to talk, *do not talk or sing* until the pain is gone (which may be several days). Do not use throat sprays to numb the pain and sing anyway. Also, if you are singing and notice that singing softly is very difficult, that your voice is cracking where it normally would not, and that there is a delay or "catch" in your voice starting when you go to sing, stop singing. That is a warning sign that your vocal folds are swollen. If any of those symptoms do not clear up after a few days of rest, see a doctor.

PACING REHEARSALS

Musicians, as a general rule, wear many hats, and I don't mean just the hats you might wear as part of a performance costume! We tend to have busy, active lives and multiple jobs. As a result, it is hard to find time to get an ensemble together to rehearse. Then, when you do find a time, the temptation is to do a marathon rehearsal that lasts for hours, which leaves everyone involved vocally exhausted. There is a better way. Here are some suggestions to rehearse smart and healthy:

- Have a plan for the rehearsal—which songs will be worked on, for how long, what aspects will be addressed, and so on—and stick to your plan! Make sure the rehearsal plan includes time for a vocal warm up, and plan an alternation of singing work and instrumental work in order to give voice rest.
- Take frequent rest breaks to drink water, stretch, and not talk or sing.
- Alternate who takes the lead in singing from one song to the next, so that no one person is carrying the load for every song.

- If there are instrumental difficulties to be worked out, work them out without having people sing over and over. You will be able to solve the instrumental issues faster because you'll be able to hear them clearly, and you'll avoid fatiguing everyone who is singing.
- If you are leading a group, limit your demonstration singing as much as possible rather than constantly modeling the pitch of musical lines. Ensemble leaders can also use a performer's tactic, "marking," by singing in a comfortable range and avoiding pitch and intensity extremes. You sing the high notes down one octave and low ones up an octave. Most importantly, leaders should not try to sing over students; doing so only limits your ability to monitor your own voice and clearly hear the students you are leading.
- Realize you don't have to sing full volume all the time; pace yourself!
- When rehearsal is over, do a little vocal warm down. Remember the vocal athlete? So, just like a runner might walk a lap or two after a hard run, something simple, like doing a few sol-fa-mi-re-do scales while humming can help your voice relax after lots of use. Start in your middle range and work downward into your speaking voice range.

Differences between Men and Women's Voices

Both men and women have vocal folds, but men's vocal folds are longer and somewhat thicker than women's. This is part of why men's voices are lower (generally about an octave lower) and perhaps somewhat richer in quality than women's. The other reason is that because men are generally bigger overall than women (their necks are longer and mouths and throats are somewhat larger), this makes the resonator of their voice bigger; therefore, longer vocal folds and a bigger resonator mean a lower, somewhat richer sound for men. Despite these differences, both men and women can sing in classical and "belt" styles. Depending on the needs of the song, a well-trained singer can use either approach.

In the following paragraphs, when pitches are referred to, they are based on a system where middle C on the piano is called C4. Figure 3.2 shows a keyboard to help explain this.

For high-range singing in a more classical style (E5–C6, starting from the top space on the treble staff), women do best with open vowels like "ah" or "awh" and an open-mouth shape. Somewhat lower, in the upper part of their belt range (A4–D5), bright "ah" and "ae"—like in the English words "hat," "bat," and "rat"—also work really well if the female singer is belting. In this same range, however, if the singer wants to sing in a more classical type of production, a less spread open-mouth shape and more closed vowels are needed. As women sing lower in their range (C4–A4), close to middle C on a piano, a more closed-mouth shape works well. The vowels can be much more speech-like in this range.

For men, the main differences between the classical and belt approaches have to do with mouth shape and how high your larynx or voice box sits in your neck. A more classical approach to singing features a somewhat smaller mouth opening, with possibly some rounding

FIGURE 3.2 Diagram of a piano keyboard.

of mouth shape between about D4 and G4, and a more stable, low position of the larynx. Belting for men, on the other hand, features much the same mouth shape as seen in women belting in the same range: a more open, spread-mouth shape, bright vowels, and a larynx position that rises for higher notes.

GENERAL VOCAL EXERCISES FOR DAILY USE (MEN AND WOMEN)

1. *Tongue extensions.* Done without making any noise, this involves protruding the tongue out of the mouth to the right, straight out, and to the left for several seconds each. This helps free up the base of the tongue in speaking and singing.
2. *Lip buzzes; humming; singing vowels into a straw.* All of these help singers and speakers to discover "resonant voice" production. These exercises can also be performed as a lead-in/running start to speaking or singing in order to help transfer the resonant production.
3. *Yawn-sigh.* A descending slide featuring a low larynx position and releasing lots of air can improve speaking or singing.
4. *Ee—ah—ee—ah.* This rapid alternation of vowel positions can be used for developing freedom in the tongue and for better tongue/jaw movement independence, especially in higher-pitched speaking and singing. It can be performed in a spoken mode on a single pitch or a pitch slide or on various musical patterns when sung. Try to remain as easy and calm in your jaw as possible as you move between the two vowels.
5. *Bla bla.* This consonant/vowel combination can be used to promote an elevated palate position, a relaxed forward tongue position, and lip and jaw freedom. Like number 4, this can be performed in speech or sung mode. Do not worry about sounding funny—having a loose jaw is the goal.
6. *Pitch glides.* Done on any vowel, easy glides from high to low range promote a smooth transition of activity between registers.
7. *Agility work.* Agility exercises, or rapid wide jumps in pitch, promote quick adjustments in muscle activity inside and outside the larynx (use for singing voice only).
8. *Sustained singing.* This exercise requires stability of muscle function in the larynx, in the muscles that position the larynx, in the breathing system, and throughout the postural system.
9. *Onsets.* Requiring precise posturing of the vocal folds and breath management, this exercise can be explored first with easy laughter in a speech mode or as repeated vowel onsets on a single sung pitch, scale patterns, or arpeggios. Take care to not over-emphasize the initial "h" or use the so-called glottal onset.
10. *Long crescendo/decrescendo on a single vowel and pitch.* This exercise requires coordination of posturing of the vocal folds, breath pressure, breath management, and vowel adjustment.

VOCAL EXERCISES SPECIFICALLY FOR MEN

Male singers often "muscle" their way through songs, but it doesn't have to be that way. Moving around while practicing can be very helpful in heading off pushing habits. John Nix's

"The Hole in the Sky, Video 1" YouTube video (https://youtu.be/qL1-lqaulHE) shows him working with a young tenor to demonstrate this idea.

Falsetto can be used as a training device with male singers. It is important to state that the full upper voice is not some special kind of falsetto. Exercise patterns, which involve bridging out of falsetto into full voice, particularly on a "ooh" vowel, which tends to have a lower larynx position, can be very helpful. They also help singers experience approaching a high note while using lots of air and without hauling too much vocal weight into the note. John Nix's "The Hole in the Sky, Video 4" YouTube video (https://youtu.be/1w6-Tyd4RPc) shows him working with the same student as in Video 1 doing some other exercises, including coming out of falsetto in a full sound.

Patterns and phrases that touch upon, roll over, or sweep rapidly through higher notes help developing male singers to "sneak up" on singing higher without falling back on compensatory tensions/pushing. In other words, whether it is accomplished through using exercises or by using phrases excerpted from songs, the most successful means for developing high notes involves sweeping smoothly and briskly through high passages before attempting sustained notes.

Male singers need to be especially vigilant about overworking on consonants, particularly those placed at upward leaps in the melody. Falling back on "scoop and cover" as your trick for hitting high notes is a very easy habit to fall into, but it is not healthy in the long run. While it is exciting once in a while ("Gee, is he going to make it?"), such a production invites singing very heavily if done all the time.

VOCAL EXERCISES SPECIFICALLY FOR WOMEN

The best way to start a vocal warmup is to do a descending pattern in your middle range. So, starting around A4 if you are a mezzo or contralto, and around C5 if you are a soprano, sing easy five-note patterns (sol-fa-mi-re-do) on "yoo-yoo-yoo-yoo-yoo" or "wee-wee-wee-wee-wee." The idea is to begin the warmup in a light, head-voice mode on more closed or collected forward-sensation vowels. You can move this pattern around stepwise, upward and downward, seeking an easy start to the sound, and a smooth connection from one note to the next.

Next, try something for range extension upward. One good pattern is sol-do (high do)—sol-mi-do (low do), or 5-8-5-3-1. Starting in mid-range, this pattern can be done on open vowels like "ah" quite high—as high as you need to sing, moving the exercise steadily upward and back down. The goal is to allow your voice to sweep easily up and down.

Finally, something for the lower range. If you are doing more belt-type singing, you want to be sure that your belt singing still has good breathing patterns associated with it. So, using a calm, "proud" stance, breathe in and sing Do (high do)—do (low do) re mi fa sol fa mi re do, or 8-123454321. On a high top note, start on a light "ooh" vowel, and then slide down into "yahyahyahyahyahyahyahyahyah" for the scale portion. You can also do the "ae" vowel, like in "hat" or "cat," instead of "yah"—so the scale portion is very bright and brassy sounding. The slide down keeps the bottom notes from getting too heavy. Again, move the pattern around, starting in middle range, moving fairly low, then moving gradually higher.

ADDRESSING COMMON VOCAL PROBLEMS FACED BY MARIACHI SINGERS

Table 3.1 lists suggestions for troubleshooting common vocal issues.

TABLE 3.1 Suggestions for troubleshooting common vocal issues.

Vocal Technique Problem	Possible Causes	Possible Solutions
Throaty, tense tone quality	• Overall body tension • Neck tension • Tongue tension • Poor coordination of breathing with making a sound	• Body alignment work • General movement (turn head and sing) • Hum and chew at the same time • Doing exercises with consonants that front the tongue (like l, t, d, n) in front of the vowels • Alternate bright, forward vowels like "eee" and "ey" with darker vowels like "oh" or "ah" in exercises
Pinched, thin, metallic, shrill tone	• Vowels too closed • General tension in throat and mouth • Breath pressure too high (pushing too hard breathing-wise) • See pinched, thin tone above • Too much heavy production being brought too high • Soft palate lowered during singing • Muscles inside larynx not balanced well • Excess breath pressure—"supporting too much" • General body or neck tension	• Sigh down, pretending to yawn • Precede vowels in exercises with a "w" sound (rounds your mouth) • Alternate bright, forward vowels like "eee" and "ey" with darker vowels like "oh" or "ah" in exercises • Massage neck, shoulders • Reduce breath pressure; move around while singing; sit down and sing; intentionally try to be breathy
Singers keep singing sharper and sharper	• See pinched, thin tone above	• See above • Easy crescendo and decrescendo in comfortable range
Women cannot sing well above F5 (top line F)	• Too much heavy production being brought too high	• Descending exercises • Check vowels for appropriate modification for pitch and power (mouth open enough?) • Snore—loosens up your palate • Sirens (down first)
Nasal tone	• Soft palate lowered during singing	• Snort • Do a lip buzz • Check breath pressure—may be too high • Use plosive consonants (/b/, /d/, /g/) in front of the vowels in exercises

TABLE 3.1 Continued

Vocal Technique Problem	Possible Causes	Possible Solutions
Straight tone	• Muscles inside larynx not balanced well • Excess breath pressure—"supporting too much" • General body or neck tension	• Imitate a siren • Imitate a revival preacher • Endless movement ideas • Move around and watch movement • Fast-moving exercises and patterns
Singing flat all of the time	• Too heavy a production taken too high • Palate lowered • Tongue tension	• Descending exercises • Snort • Lip buzz
Tanking up and singing too pressured	• Too much breath for the musical phrase	• Sit down • Movement work • Bounced exercises • Start at end of phrase, work backward
Too many hard "glottal" attacks	• Habits from listening to pop music? • Wanting to be overly emotional when singing	• Use an intentional H before words with vowels • Unpitched-pitched-unpitched on lip buzz • Avoid taking too big of a breath before singing
No register coordination (can't go from high to low voice without breaks in sound)	• Influence of popular styles • Inside the larynx, muscle balance not good • Tensions in throat • Inexperienced	• Glide up and down without worrying about specific pitches • Descending exercises • Careful use of vowels to aid in register bridging
Problems with females around C5 (the C above middle C)	• Too heavy a production too high, and subsequent weakness in full head voice	• Descending exercises • Pair ascending and descending exercises • Check palate—snort to loosen it up

IF YOU ARE A TEACHER, BE A GOOD EXAMPLE

The actions of adult role models have a great influence on young learners. Nothing better reinforces visual, verbal, and textual messages about good singing technique and vocal health than a teacher who puts those messages into action. If you lead a mariachi ensemble, you should demonstrate that you practice what you preach, that is, that you vocalise daily, eat a balanced diet, maintain a stable body weight, exercise regularly, and do not abuse tobacco, caffeine, alcohol, and other drugs. Specific example behaviors should also include the use of a healthy start (no glottals) and release (no grunts or punched releases) when making a sound at all times, and the use of healthy breathing habits, including not speaking or singing too long on one breath.

Teachers should exhibit good body alignment when sitting, standing, and conducting. This may mean rearranging teaching spaces and placing mirrors around classrooms so that you do not have to compromise efficient, healthy body alignment in order to see and be seen by your students. As good body use is essential to coordinated breathing, sound making, resonation, and pronunciation, to say nothing about avoiding injuries, all music educators and students can benefit from this type of physical risk management.

The pitch, inflection, and dynamic range of vocal commands and the types of gestures used as non-verbal commands for leading individuals and ensembles should be healthy for both the educator to produce and should elicit healthy sounds from the students involved. It is essential that the vocal directions and gestures you use match the character of the music, yet not cause either you or your students to lose body awareness.

REINFORCE HEALTHY HABITS

In some school situations, you as the ensemble teacher may be the only person sensitive to un-healthy vocal and body use habits in students. This makes it even more important to reinforce healthy choices in lessons and classes early and often. Specific to the voice, you as a teacher can reinforce good habits being established in the singing voice by making sure these habits are also transferred into the speaking voice. This can be achieved by having your singers alternate speaking, then chanting (singing the text in rhythm but on a single pitch), then singing short phrases from their repertoire as well as short phrases from everyday speech. Such transference work can be incorporated into warm-up and warm-down portions of lessons.

As an ensemble leader, you must expect and encourage appropriate sounds from singers. There is no reason for teenage singers to sound like forty-year-old adults. You can help your students produce appropriate sounds through the selection of pieces you have them sing. Repertoire must build in success and be not only age and gender appropriate but also skill-level appropriate. Oftentimes, teachers/directors make repertoire choices based on musical aspects/values first. While they are important, these criteria must follow what is physically most beneficial for the student.

FINAL THOUGHTS

Getting a good technical foundation as a singer is an important investment of your time. If you establish good habits early, you will be able to sing more expressively, have a wider range, and have greater ease in performing different styles of songs. You will also be less likely to have vocal problems from acquired bad habits. Even if you have performed for years, it is never too late to learn how to sing better.

STAYING HEALTHY AS A SINGER EXERCISES

1. What is it that makes someone a good singer? Listen to some of your favorite performers, and identify what qualities are the hallmarks of good singing.
2. Mariachi performers often have to play an instrument in between singing verses of a song, or they have to play while singing. How does your posture while playing your instrument impact your singing? Are there things you can do with your instrumental playing posture to help the quality of your singing?

3. Being an exciting performer requires a singer to portray emotions while singing. How do emotions affect your singing voice? Can being too emotional affect the quality and health of your singing?

4. Another aspect of performing mariachi music is wearing a *traje de charro*. Does it interfere with your singing? If so, what are some ways in which you could slightly adjust your costume to not impede your singing?

5. What things will you do when *you* become a mariachi group leader to enhance the singing of the people in your group? How can you promote healthy, expressive singing?

A Voice Lesson: Alignment, Breath, and Vowel

Every voice teacher has a particular approach, method, or philosophy. The vocal concepts described in this section describe one approach that has greatly helped the author (as taught by my voice teacher) along with many professional singers and teachers. Reading fundamental concepts about the voice helps singers analyze their thinking about their own vocal production. Reading Giovanni Battista Lamperti's *Vocal Wisdom* can also stimulate new ideas for sound production, aid with practicing, and perhaps guide singers toward how to evaluate the right voice teacher for them.[3]

Singers study privately to build their sound because each one has their own unique body structure, particular vocal habits, and special sound. In a mariachi ensemble or choral setting the director can teach lyrics, tempo, and musical notes and group interpretation. The director does not build individual voices because directions for each singer vary greatly.

Before training the voice, both mariachi and opera singers tend to often go direct to sound, envisioning a rich mariachi or operatic sound. Going direct to the phonator actually puts pressure on the vocal cords and causes fatigue. Conversely, if one goes to breath and vowel first, the result is a big sound. Amazing sounds can be achieved when alignment, breath, and vowel are properly coordinated in conjunction with a relaxed jaw. Practicing voice *a cappella* (see Glossary) slow motion, without accompaniment first, also helps singers isolate and coordinate alignment, breath, and vowel for each song.

When singers first begin voice lessons they learn about posture or alignment. This helps singers become aware of the natural airflow we already use for speaking and to develop consciousness of air compression. Air is always moving if it is not obstructed by bad alignment or other false concepts misunderstanding how air works. Each one of us has our own natural alignment that encourages effortless but engaged air flow. Have you noticed how many mariachi instrumentalists lock their knees and lean slightly back to hold their instrument, especially the guitarrón player? They often balance backward against their instrument instead of visualizing the inside of their body as the central instrument with air flowing inside them. Lung air can often seem to lock without developing an inner consciousness of a proper balance of consistent exhale with the resisting intercostal muscles that sustain the bulk of the air in the lungs. Releasing the knees can often release air back into its natural flow as it realigns the body into alignment.

Perhaps you have also seen mariachi singers tilt their heads back when lengthening long, climactic notes? This pose may look dramatic, but it cuts off the airstream at the throat as they tilt backward, and the top notes may not last as long as the singer might like. Thinking

---

[3] Giovanni B. Lamperti, *Vocal Wisdom: Maxims of Giovanni Battista Lamperti*, is available online on Amazon. Lamperti was an important bel canto Italian voice teacher and trained many professional singers.

of keeping one's ears always aligned over their shoulders is a good starting place (those who tilt their heads forwards to read their phones, beware!). Think about a centered alignment and picture air in the base of their lungs before each inhale. Keep exhaling while you sing without losing your awareness of air at the base of your lungs.

There are six natural points of balance in the body that should always feel flexible and lined up from bottom to top: ankle joints, knee joints, hip joints, gleno-humeral joints, the cervical or neck joint, and the atlas-occipital joint between the ears (think of this last one as the A-O joint, or the one that allows your head to move when you say yes or no).[4] A simple way to think about alignment is to constantly check that your ears are over your shoulders, and your shoulders and hips are over your ankles.[5] Easy, continuous airflow comes from enough air pressure and constant small adjustments in alignment as one is singing.

Students train to build air pressure and consistency. The pressure allows the air in the lungs to not escape (breath support). This leads to a richer supported tone and a wider range. A teacher may ask a student to isolate and recite and then sing the vowels from a song one by one over the breath. With the correct air pressure, this keeps the alignment in place, gives the singer breath support, and smoothly connects the notes. The resulting notes will be immediate, impressive, voluminous, and inspiring. Trust it! Suddenly, the sound becomes an end result and not a first and only focus. With the correct breath, there is no pressure on the phonator where the sound originates. When singing is right it feels effortless even while belting or singing a big song. Feeling the air pressure as breath support at all times as one sings provides a foundation and actually enhances the volume and growth of the voice while also preventing fatigue.

Over time, singers learn to allow the breath to move the sound instead of moving to find where they think the sound is. Think about it: Does it really make sense to produce sound directly from your phonator without first activating your motor (the air) to carry and support the sound? Would you try and drive your car without its motor? Certainly not! Singers who lead with their phonator or sound are almost always vocally stressed and fatigued. By trusting the overall process of aligning the body, learning about inhale and air pressure, and then going to vowels, singers are sure to find the excellent, robust mariachi sounds that everybody loves.

Adopting healthy vocal habits often works well a step at a time. Singers with a solid technical foundation will share that learning to sing is a process that takes time. It is also a priceless gift no one can take away from you once you understand it. Singers with a strong foundation are able to adapt and make small adjustments to handle technical and life-changing challenges to the voice as they arise. If you love mariachi singing you'll definitely want to prepare for a long career with a solid foundation.

ALIGNMENT, BREATH, AND VOWEL EXERCISES

1. Take a moment to think about your body alignment. Are your ears over your shoulders when you look at your phone or computer?
2. Draw a human body and label the six points of balance. Tape it on a mirror or somewhere you look often to check in often with your alignment.

---

[4] The author learned the six points of balance with Dr. Melissa Malde. Students interested in anatomy may find her book useful: *What Every Singer Needs to Know About Their Body* (2016, Plural Publishing).

[5] Many students also benefit from vocal and instrumental alignment studies of Alexander Technique (www.alexandertechnique.com). Alexander specialists can be found worldwide.

Voice Teacher or Voice Coach—What Is the Difference?

Singers of many genres benefit from studying with both voice teachers and vocal coaches. Understanding the differences between the two can sometimes be confusing but also helpful. In this section, singers will get to know the similarities and differences between the two.

Generally, a voice teacher builds the voice technically, while a vocal coach focuses on the student's performance style and interpretation. These two terms are sometimes mistakenly interchanged. The terms voice coach and voice teacher can also be used differently depending upon what field one is singing in. To further confuse matters, it can also depend on the style of music, the background of the person involved, or the event itself. For example, when mariachi/orchestra directors, voice teachers, or celebrity singers offer voice master classes, they often take on the role of a voice coach. During these events they customarily focus on song presentation, lyrics, and interpretation with limited technical comments.

Voice teachers and vocal coaches have different functions, although there is some overlap. Some teachers also do both. Both teachers and coaches work on diction and choosing repertoire with singers. Aspiring singers and professionals will want to think about their own vocal needs, strategize, research, and decide how and when to consult with each. It is also important to always ask a teacher what their emphasis is and keep vigilant as to whether this indeed plays out.

In classical and musical theater worlds, the role of voice teachers and vocal coaches is well defined. This is not true in mariachi or commercial music styles. In popular music, vocalists and producers use the term vocal coach with a broad brush and do not distinguish between the two. When inquiring, singers should always ask specific questions as to what kind of material and work will be covered in private sessions. It can be helpful to try out a lesson, tape it, and bring a list of specific voice questions.

The mariachi tradition has many coaches but very few voice teachers. A voice teacher builds the voice. A vocal coach is not trained to build a voice from scratch, although they may have an intimate knowledge of mariachi style and song repertoire. When mariachi directors offer master classes, they most often work in a coaching capacity. This can be useful, as long as directors are fully trained singers themselves and avoid pushing singers into uncomfortable vocal keys to fit the needs of the instrumental ensemble.

Many top soloists at the height of ranchera music's Golden Age of charro musicals trained gradually and built their voices over time with voice teachers.[6] By contrast, in today's mariachi world ensembles have been largely unconnected to voice training. Voice teachers have also been unaware of the style. As an alternative, singers have been learning to sing through listening, song memorization, and limited coaching. This is understandable; nevertheless, singers who want a career with a voice they can depend on long term will want vocal technique sooner rather than later.

Voice teachers build the voice with private lessons because each singer sounds uniquely different and has a distinct body, or instrument. Without training, voices often show wear and tear with wide vibrato at early ages, and careers are generally short. Untrained singers can develop potentially challenging vocal problems (see Chapter 8 section: "Linda Ronstadt" and Chapter 3 section: "Vocal Pedagogy Exercises"). The past global success of solo singers Jorge Negrete and Pedro Vargas serves as a wonderful example. They took the time to gradually build their voices with José Pierson, master voice teacher (see Chapter 2 section: "José

---

[6] The author did not come across information on vocal coaches as distinct from voice teachers during Mexico's Golden Age of Cinema, although there may have been some. Arrangers, producers, and directors were actively involved with the films and recording and were probably active as coaches.

Pierson"). The relationship of the voice teacher to the student is often quite close because they invest several years building and maintaining the voice.

In the classical world, vocal coaches can also be piano accompanists, not simply voice teachers. The same is true of mariachi directors. They are often highly skilled and can be fantastic recital and/or concert collaborators. Many are also arrangers, conductors, or producers who specialize in repertoire, diction, and concert production for singers. The commitment to sessions with a coach can be by project or by lesson and is generally not as long term as that of a voice teacher. Coaches who work exclusively on diction or particular languages are called dialect coaches and can be contracted separately, as can stage directors or acting coaches for work in acting skills.

In commercial vocal styles, celebrity popular singers often take on the role of voice coaches, as seen on televised vocal competitions in both Spanish and English. These coaches are already successful commercial recording artists, and some are producers. Similar to academic voice coaches, they help choose commercial song repertoire, style and phrase interpretation, perhaps use of the microphone, and they might offer savvy commercial career advice. They will request effective diction, though usually limited to the language at hand and clarity of the story, without IPA or vowel analysis (see Chapter 6). Commercial voice coaches may have an array of diverse repertoire, contacts, and sometimes career promotion.

If in academia, students can search for a vocal specialist that will allow them to include mariachi songs within their overall plan of study. Strategize and look for compromise between what the program has to offer and your vocal passion for ranchera singing. Whatever the stylistic background of a teacher, everyone will agree that powerful expression, or "telling the story," is always an important goal. Some call it "selling the song." It is always easier to deliver when a singer loves the song deeply and can combine solid interpretation with vocal technique.

Female Mariachi Fach

Mariachi songs for the female voice sit significantly lower than female classical singing. The range corresponds to that of a contralto and part of the tenor range. The author has designated a special mariachi fach for women only in mariachi. The term fach draws from the German classical voice system commonly used in opera. Fach designates vocal repertoire based upon the range, weight, tessitura, and color of the voice. Adopting a female mariachi fach assists classical voice teachers in understanding how to stay true to the sound and style of mariachi by assigning songs in this range and vocal color for ranchera repertoire (see Glossary).

Once, the author had a well-known operatic lyric soprano from Mexico City's Bellas Artes opera house assure her that she also sang mariachi. After being invited to her house to watch a DVD recording of her singing in Mexico, I politely watched her singing the romantic bolero, "Vereda Tropical." Unfortunately, she kept the song in a very high classical key and style with a developed legato and vibrato, and had chosen a lyric soprano range for her key (f4–a5), all accompanied by a mariachi ensemble. The female voice does not employ any chest voice in this range. She never added mariachi heartfelt expression or adjust her vibrato, nor did she lessen her backspace. Above all, she never authenticated her sound by relocating the key into a lower female mariachi fach. While her singing had a technically beautiful legato, she continued to be an opera singer that happened to be accompanied by a mariachi ensemble, instead of at least mixing the styles a bit and honoring the style.

Female mariachi singers today can take pride and comfort in knowing that the fach system is an opera term that validates and describes the chest-based female fach as a non-negotiable part of mariachi singing. Singers are invited to communicate this to classical voice teachers, singers, and others unfamiliar with the style so that they can make appropriate adjustments. Otherwise, some will continue to teach women to perform mariachi and bolero songs in high keys that do not authentically represent the style.[7]

The female mariachi vocal center is based upon a dominant chest sound production (at least 60%) in the lower half of the regular female singing range. The range runs from approximately f3 to c5. The upper end of the chest range is most safely and authentically sung with a head-chest mix or belt voice, although many have not been trained for it. The upper mariachi chest tessitura (see Glossary) corresponds to what is called the middle voice in classical singing (c4–c5). Singers who train and solidify this middle classical range with a healthy chest-head mix and breath support will lose the need to push out sound.

While the main tessitura of the female mariachi fach goes up to b4 or c5, women also need portions of the octave above this range in head voice in order to sustain falsete (see Glossary). The full range for a trained professional singer with falsete is f3–a5 or even higher. Between c6 and g6 is another female range extension denominated whistle range. Not all women have this extension, and it is just being introduced in ranchera singing.[8] Linda Ronstadt does not explore the whistle upper range in huapangos in her two mariachi CDs "Canciones de mi Padre," but demonstrates her whistle register as she sings a high eb6 on the last climactic note of her aria "Poor Wandering One" in the operetta *Pirates of Penzance.* Listen to the unique color of her whistle range in this aria on YouTube: https://youtu.be/jmVivOLmsbs.

In the lower end of the female range, singers such as Lucha Villa have rich, tenor timbres hovering between e3 and a4. Listen to her sing in the "Lucha Villa "en Tren'" on YouTube (https://youtu.be/O_wSVyJMHtk) and "Lucha Villa 'Zenaida'" (https://youtu.be/7NJg ERKRNBo).

Female singers who learn to use mixed voice or belt above the lower *passaggio* (c#4–f# range) will gain access to increased power, breath support, and projection in this upper range (see Glossary). Technically advanced female singers will be able to switch to head voice in upper ranges of huapangos, purposely using a lighter flute-like head-voice vocal production as opposed to operatic singing when sustaining falsete. A chest-head mix or belt color is used as a springboard to the switch on the note prior to head voice, to provide as much color contrast as possible. The springboard note should fall into the upper female mariachi range with a dominant chest mix in the c4–c5 range (see section: "Finding the Right Key for Your Song" ahead in this chapter).

There is a somewhat standard "female key" for mariachi repertoire because of the expected chest dominant sound. It should fall in the female mariachi fach. The majority of the range of the song should emphasize the lower half of the female range in dominant chest-to-head mixed sound. Because of this, the key choices are semi-fixed. Women can generally vary a step up or down from the standard key, as long as the voice stays centered in the lower chest half of the female voice. If a singer is a soprano, they can highlight their soprano range when

---

[7] The author sings in an original *Operachi* style, always honoring the female mariachi lower fach but using a full upper extension. She adds additional notes in head voice when singing falsete and draws on mariachi classical vocal legato and rich vocal tone inspired by the teachings of José Pierson, master voice teacher for Jorge Negrete, Pedro Vargas, and many other mariachi singers in the first half of the twentieth century.

[8] Voice student of author, twenty-six-year-old Lidia Chávez, activated her whistle register on the last note of the huapango "El aguacero" to win first place in her Commercial Voice category in the 2022 National Association of Teacher's Voice Competition: Cal-Western Regional Finals. She was also the first to ever sing rancheras in this competition. Flor de Toloache used their head voice extensions as a duo in harmony when adding a cadenza at the end of La Cigarra when singing at the Kennedy Center.

singing falsete and even add notes or sustain them longer. Overall, women in ranchera singing do not fit neatly or comfortably into classical fachs of contralto, mezzo-soprano, tenor, or soprano, but, in fact, touch on partial aspects of all of them with a foundation within female mariachi fach.

In male mariachi singing, singers can choose keys more freely because the majority of the male voice range is naturally set in chest voice. The overall ranchera sound is chest-dominant based regardless of gender, however. Male vocal ranges in mariachi singing correspond with traditional classical training in tenor, bari-tenor, and baritone fachs. There are almost no basses, and this would introduce a new sound to the ranchera world. Many men in the bari-tenor range sing rancheras, similar to men in American musical theater.

Upon listening to top ranchera soloists, commercial voice teachers will note that the belt style in mariachi is considered a soft belt with darker vowels than musical theater. The sound quality is round and dark, not brassy nor forward. Contemporary commercial voice training helps with the belt sound and classical breathwork and exercises help students develop head voice and range for falsete singing and to keep healthy registration for the overall voice. Keeping the balance of head to chest voice throughout the full range is especially important for females since they sing primarily in the bottom half of their vocal range. Cross-training between classical and contemporary commercial voice belt techniques can build the voice quickly.

Students should feel free to openly share their mariachi goals with voice teachers. If the teacher isn't responsive or interested, don't give up. Search for another teacher. Singers can also cross-train with two teachers provided each teacher is in communication with the other. The teachers can communicate and interchange information, for example focusing on building middle and lower ranges first, always following the designations of the female mariachi fach. In this way, the singer builds technically while simultaneously learning to belt. The goal is to improve progressively while always honoring the authenticity and aesthetics of the mariachi style.

Mariachi *Falsete*: To Bridge or to Break

Falsete is a Mexican mariachi term for a sudden break or change in vocal register, not unlike a yodel. It is used as an expressive gesture. Singers in other styles also use yodel flips, although in ranchera singing the note can be sustained indefinitely. Yodeling highlights registration differences as singers jump from one note to a note in another register. The mariachi singer goes even further with a sudden accented switch of registration with a purposeful heightened color contrast, switching abruptly from one register in dominant chest sound to an isolated head voice range. The yodel flip in ranchera singing takes the song into a new and higher voice register, while also changing the color or timbre of the voice. While in mariachi it is called falsete, other music fields call it falsetto, literally meaning "false voice," although this term can mean different things in other fields.

The term falsete is used differently in the English language from Spanish. It is also perceived differently in Spain than in Mexico. To further complicate matters, mariachi singers speaking Spanish also incorrectly interchange the terms *voz de cabeza* (head voice) and falsete ("false voice"). Male singers have an upper head voice range (above the shift around c4–f4 to a4–b4), and above it lies the falsetto range. It has a unique color distinct from head voice. The falsetto range can vary greatly between individuals, but it is above a4 upward to a5. Falsetto can usually be discovered by men most easily on the vowels *u* or *e*. When women sustain falsete notes, as they switch into head voice they are actually imitating a falsetto sound in head voice. Women do not have a falsetto range, but some women have an additional whistle register above head voice between c6 and g6.

The falsete sound in mariachi has a unique expression from other ranchera vocal music. In classical music, the term falsete refers to a specific Italian Baroque singing style (1600–1750) whereby the male sings entire songs in a high falsetto voice, similar notes to a female range. At that time, women were not allowed to be professional singers. Men trained from puberty or earlier and performed full songs in falsetto voice. The movie *Farinelli* illustrates the classical cultivation of the falsete sound from one of the world's last and greatest Baroque male castrati singers. Mariachi singers, both men and women, sustain falsete notes for emotional expression in certain dramatic moments of a song but by no means keep entire songs in this range.

Country folk and commercial singers in the United States often stylize their songs with quick falsetto breaks, similar to yodeling. However, none of these styles cultivate mariachi falsete singing with both the sudden and quite long sustained high notes, with color contrasts, and register variations (see Chapter 5 section: "Huapangos").

In more contemporary stylized huapangos since the 1940s, skilled singers often choose specific emotive moments in the song and sustain falsete notes indefinitely. The hold or "fermata" (see Glossary) temporarily suspends the lyrics and forward motion of the song to highlight the singer's vocal prowess and beauty. Usually, the longer the note is held the more the audience gets excited and involved.[9] Instead of producing huge volume on high notes as is customary in operatic singing, ranchera singers in falsete shift into a sustained, almost floating sound on one vowel with continuous breath support but little vibrato. This "quieter and resonant" high note sounds like a flute and is a sharp contrast to earlier sections of the song in lower chest register. Read about singer Miguel Aceves Mejía, also known as the "King of Falsete" https://frontera.library.ucla.edu/tag/falsetto-king. Effective use of falsete is considered virtuosic in mariachi singing.

Falsete singers use vocal registers to enhance color changes. Registers change every five or six notes. Any intervallic jump up a fifth or sixth allows the voice to naturally change its color dramatically into a new vocal register, especially if the singer visualizes certain colors in addition to the register change. In the huapango song "Crucifijo de Piedra," sustained falsete is carefully evoked in dramatic, expressive moments and on specific words. Listen to "Crucifijo de Piedra" YouTube videos (https://youtu.be/HruOT8HOyYo and https://youtu.be/1GNq1zhNmyQ).

Falsete is a color change and often changes registers with a jump. Polished singers cultivate falsete on difficult mariachi songs such as Lola Beltrán's famous rendition of "Cucurrucucu Paloma." Note that in this song falsete is harder to sustain because the intervallic jumps of thirds and fourths are smaller. This song can be heard in two different YouTube videos (https://youtu.be/DHW-q8oD3gE or https://youtu.be/Yubu1cDqKEY).

CAN ANYONE SING FALSETE?

Some mariachi singers believe falsete is something you are simply born with—that some have it and some don't. False! Falsete is not difficult when singers take time to build their vocal range. Female mariachi belters often assume they have no falsete, without realizing it's only because they have not yet developed their full voice range. Some singers already sing falsete high notes and have some range, but they may not yet know how to sustain or control

---

[9] For more information on understanding falsetto read pp. 132–134 in Richard Miller's *The Structure of Singing.*

their head voice, nor be aware of all the emotive color choices available. In huapangos, the ranges for each song tend to be wider, including several vocal registers. Singing this style generally requires more vocal training (see Chapter 5). Huapangos are not easy for beginning singers.

WHERE DOES FALSETE COME FROM?

Falsete has rural folk roots connected to the huapango style in 6/8 meter (see Chapter 5 section: "Mariachi Rhythmic Styles"). The huapango comes from Mexico's eastern coastal state of Veracruz. During the nineteenth century, *huasteca* and huapango songs existed primarily in this region, huastecas in the north and huapangos from the city of Veracuz to the south. In rural huapango style, falsete flips are a constant with one or two flips per phrase. In rural huapangos the falsete notes are traditionally quick, and the second note is a throwaway note without phonating the vowel. It is not sustained.[10] The rural style often includes solos with call-and-response choral responses in harmony. The singers often accompany themselves instrumentally, alternate solos, and dance as well.

After the Mexican Revolution (1910–1921), singers from many Mexican regions, including Veracruz, began performing more often in Mexico City. A more stylized contemporary huapango singing style evolved with operatic influence.[11] The urban huapango style includes sustained long lines similar to bel canto legato lines (see Glossary). Rather than use falsete often, the flip is strategically placed in the song to color important words. Well-trained singers cultivate vocal virtuosity by indefinitely sustaining the higher second note in the falsete break. In ranchera music many honor the falsete of Miguela Aceves Mejía, nicknamed *El Rey del Falsete* (The King of Falsete). The huapango singing style remains a favorite today for trained singers (Miguel Aceves Mejía on YouTube: https://youtu.be/k23iUxmOZ78).

HOW DO I LEARN FALSETE?

Voice teachers are aware that voices have a natural and subtle register change every five to seven notes. Part of vocal training consists in learning to bridge rather than break between these register changes so they are seamless, smooth, and imperceptible. In mariachi-style voice training singers learn the same as above, but for huapango voice training they learn to purposely accentuate and dramatize register breaks for expressive color. Both techniques require building constant air pressure.

Learning falsete can include daily yodel warm-ups after initial hums and sirens, while adding in exercises specific to balancing voice production over a fuller range as the voice grows. Women also work to develop a mid-range blend in the required head/chest mix and a soft belt contrasting sound for notes f4–c4. As the range expands, singers can gradually add the "Falsete Exercises and Warm-ups, Vocalises, and Practicing" section in this chapter, as well as the "Final Exercises" in the "Understanding Your Vocal Instrument" by John Nix, also in this chapter.

Female mariachi singers in a university classical program should feel free to request that their voice teacher assign middle-range songs with exercises that use yodels and/or build air pressure if they know they do not want an opera career. A demonstration of falsete and some YouTube listening samples will give teachers context if they are unfamiliar with the style.

---

[10] Jean B. Johnson, "The Huapango: A Mexican Song Contest," *California Folklore Quarterly* 1, no. 3 (1942): 233–236.

[11] The author bases this on her own listening and comparisons regarding the singing style over time.

Otherwise, classical teachers tend to focus on head voice production for females, over 80 percent, as the majority of the female range naturally sits in head voice. This blend does not work for mariachi, but a well-trained singer can learn to do both styles with proper air pressure. By learning both a singer can expand their range and enjoy fantastic falsete. The overall goal is to have enough breath compression to support both bridging registrations in classical singing and/or sudden falsete breaks in mariachi singing.

When not using falsete, voice students will improve their smoothness in boleros and other styles by learning to seamlessly blend the various registers around their middle voice. Some singers even add hints of falsete in other singing styles, for example, Mexican pop singer Luis Miguel toward the end of the bolero "La barca" on YouTube (https://youtu.be/PzKieeZfPLs). Building bridges between registers is also an important vocal building block for all singers who wish to cross with ease between styles.

Over time, students will be able to both bridge and break. Learning to both break and bridge registers is an important long-range goal for aspiring professional singers.

PRACTICING FALSETE

For those new to falsete, yodeling is a starting place for practice. Listen and sing along to the following YouTube videos:

- *Sofia Shkidchenko* (https://youtu.be/5R9PbibXul8): A young female Russian fast yodeler singing in English in a song competition. She yodels primarily in intervals of sixths.
- *Jewel* (https://youtu.be/HqNe5Ugs0Qk): American singer-songwriter Jewel sings a folk song, yodeling intervals of sixths and accelerating the speed.
- *Juanita Ulloa* (https://youtu.be/ceMyG0r4TZA): In the Disney-winning recording *Canta mi son! Mariachi for Kids and Families*, she accelerates the second half of "Corazón de Chapulín," with flips at the end.
- *Frank Ifield* (https://youtu.be/LybSS4amIS0): He sings "She Taught Me to Yodel," one of Europe's most popular yodel tunes.

Falsete exercises are useful for a singer's daily practice after warm-ups as a vocalise (see the section: "Warm-Ups, Vocalises, and Practicing" ahead in this chapter). If working on building head-voice range, you can choose to practice descending head-voice exercises daily prior to the falsete vocalises. Daily yodels and jumps of a fifth or sixth on the same vowel are helpful if you speak and then sing each vowel in the same place over the breath. Can you do this without pushing air or changing the air as you continue to feel the air pressure below you? The note before the falsete break is usually in a head-chest mixed voice with a strong chest color. Try phonating the falsete vowel twice for the jump, once on the transition note and again on the second note of the jump. A different vowel may also be used for each of the two notes (see the "Time to Sing Falsete!" and "Warm-ups, Vocalises, and Exercises" sections within this chapter).

Steady practice will ultimately lead to dominion over sudden falsete shifts and the development of a full palette of colors. By giving the upper range of the voice equal access in training, falsetes are a natural outcome.

VOCAL YODELING EXERCISES

1. *Yodel:* For those new to falsete, begin with yodeling. Choose from a variety of notes on which to begin the yodel. Begin speaking in your normal speaking voice range for the

lower first note. Imitate yodelers from the mountains by putting your hands around your mouth and calling out "yo-de-lay-ee-oo." You should feel the natural register break into your upper register on "ee."

2. *Machete knife exercise:* Use your hands as if holding a machete and cutting something just as you shift from the lower note in one color to the higher note in the new color. Experiment with different vowels.

3. *Change vowels:* Larger interval jumps are easier to find the yodel on. Flips of a fifth or sixth are common in huapangos. Visualize the vowels before phonating them. Rephonate the "a" vowel on the second note, not just the first. Allow the voice to break freely as you alternate between the lower and higher notes. Production should feel gentle with no pushing of sound from the throat, despite the fact that the color change is dramatic. After working the vowel on "ah," try other vowels and discover which one works best for you.

BEGINNING FALSETE EXERCISES

Once you can yodel freely, listen to one of the songs below and read the matching sheet music for the song at the end of Chapter 6. Next, isolate the falsete phrases within the song, and slowly work them into your daily practice after warming up. Note that the quick falsete breaks are almost identical to yodeling. Also, you may choose to research and listen to *son huasteco* traditional folk style of singing and compare traditional to contemporary falsete flips. Have fun singing along! Below are additional exercises to build falsete.

1. *"Corazón de chapulín" (#7):* Listen to a recording of this song on YouTube (https://youtu.be/ceMyG0r4TZA). You'll hear falsetes on the word "canta" (sing) in the last half of the song. The falsete syllable appears below in quotation marks. Sing along until you can flip quickly on the accelerated section during the last thirty seconds of the song.

   Can-"ta"   ['kan ta]

2. *"Cuando canto" (#8):* Listen to a recording of this song on YouTube (https://youtu.be/cvdQDBYM5D8). Find the falsete words below, and try falsete on each of the different vowels. Be sure and phonate the vowel twice, once before the flip in chest range and again in head voice.

   Can "to"   ['kan t ɔ]
   Se-gui-"ré" can-"tan"-do   [sɛ ɣi'rɛ kan'tan'dɔ]
   Ar-mo-ní-"as"   [ar mɔ'ni as]
   Me-lo-dí-"as"   [mɛ lɔ'di as]
   di-vi-"no"   [di'βi nɔ]

ADVANCED FALSETE EXERCISES

Complete examples 1, 2, and 3. Once you can switch freely back and forth between them, work on these song examples with more difficult and sustained falsete breaks.

CHAPTER 3: MARIACHI VOICE PEDAGOGY   95

1. *"El Pastor" (#10):* Listen to a recording of Miguel Aceves Mejía, also known as the El rey del falsete (King of Falsete), on YouTube https://youtu.be/JvT8lbxH6yI. Listen to Mariachi Vargas de Tecatitlán soloist at https://youtu.be/F9WCTKZkPHo, or females Aida Cuevas at https://youtu.be/bui8pLRRF3g, or the Operachi singer Juanita Ulloa at https://youtu.be/JC0Rou4Dqog. Enjoy the different styles of singing of the same song, all with falsetes. The chorus has five falsete notes, but the entire line must be completely legato, that is, smoothly connected.

   El flau-"tin" del pas-"tor" al ar-"rear" "can"-ta a-"sí" [ɛl flau'tin dɛl pas'tɔr al a'rrear'kan ta a'si]

2. *"Malagueña salerosa":* Listen to a recording of this song on YouTube (https://youtu.be/RWZ05BcqgLU or https://youtu.be/f78xi1Czu20).

   | Ma-la- "gue-e" –ña | [ma la' ɣɛ ŋa] |
   | Que e-res "li-in"- da | [kɛ 'ɛ rɛs'lin da] |

3. *"Cielo rojo":* Listen to a recording of this song on YouTube (https://youtu.be/pG_1T_DbPwI, https://youtu.be/WPJva1H8NPw, or https://youtu.be/cd_yltbcWxQ). Listen to the falsete and vowels on the final climactic line.

   Ya no te a-"cuer"-des de aquel ayer [ja nɔ tɛ‿a'cwɛ' dɛs dɛ‿a'k ɛl a'i ɛr]

FALSETE QUIZ

1. How do you define the word falsete?
2. List two mariachi songs that sustain long falsete notes.
3. List two songs that do quick falsete switches.
4. Who is known as "El Rey del Falsete" (King of Falsete)?
5. Is the woman's whistle register the same as or different from falsete?

Yodeling is familiar to many voice teachers, especially those who work more in commercial voice (CM). These voice teachers may be of special assistance to mariachi singers in developing soft belt voice or chest-head mix with dark vowels, as they use it in other folk and popular styles.

What Is the Belt Voice?

Belt voice refers to a vocal timbre or color used often in popular singing styles, including mariachi. Ranchera singing uses a soft belt, not brassy or bright sound. It is especially useful for female singers in the ranchera style as it allows them to extend a chest mix into their head voice range with power but without sounding like head-voice color. Belt singing is not the same as chest voice; when singing in mariachi belt the voice should maintain a healthy mix of chest and head registers but the breath support, projection, and resonance have a more intense feel. Belters are actually singing on the edge of the vocal cords. The intensity of the air pressure creates acoustical projection. If supported correctly, the air pressure in the body underneath the throat feels strong. Both women and men can use belt voice to amplify their power and sound in expressive areas of any song. No one should belt all the time as it fatigues the voice to do it constantly. It is best saved for exciting moments, such as the final high notes in *Aires del Mayab*, *El Rey*, or sustained notes in *La charreada* or *Los Laureles* as in Linda Ronstadt's mixed voice with chest dominance with a touch of belt on YouTube https://youtu.be/R-k4eEStQa0 (see Chapter 2 section: "Lucha Reyes").[12]

Handling Vocal Fatigue and Developing Mindfulness

Great singers learn to handle vocal fatigue by developing healthy vocal habits and learning to depend on air pressure as their breath support. Singers regularly work on learning to not overuse their voice or over-sing in practice, rehearsals, and performances. Musical-theater singers have to maintain a grueling schedule of eight shows per week (see the Linda Ronstadt interview in Chapter 8 regarding her *Pirates of Penzance* schedule prior to recording mariachi) and mariachi professionals also have challenging situations (see "In Performance" in this chapter). Singers can avoid fatigue by learning to hammer out new songs on a separate instrument first before practicing vocally to get each phrase of the song on the breath. Memorizing a song by reading and/or listening with eyes and ears first is true vocal expediency. Singers can also avoid fatigue by knowing how to find the correct key for each song and learning to recognize when it feels and sounds comfortable (see "Finding the Right Key for Your Song" in this chapter).

DEVELOP MINDFULNESS AND PROTECT YOURSELF

Some singers practice mindfulness and meditation to develop more awareness of their inner body and breath while studying voice. Technically speaking, singers avoid fatigue by developing more awareness of the breath in the lungs as support and allowing the breath to move the sound instead of leading with loud sounds. This improves tone and averts vocal fatigue. Mentally and spiritually minded singers and athletes often meditate daily to balance and unite mental, spiritual, and physical thought.[13] Meditation encourages easy but constant breath flow. This practice can also be useful to combat anxiety for auditions, competitions, and big performances.

Learning to practice can also be a mindful activity. It takes time to create and sustain a consistent practice schedule. Practicing for short periods each day in a gentle way with frequent breaks is a solid way to build stamina and a healthy supported sound for longer rehearsals and performances (see the "Understanding Your Vocal Instrument" section for more tips). Successful singers often learn to avoid fatigue by first finding their own personal vocal limits while practicing. By trusting a relaxed vocal production in the private sessions, singers learn to use this same production in challenging situations. It can be applied to noisy places, performances without sound equipment, or rehearsals with fifteen instrumentalists. Discovering one's vocal limits, along with correct breath training, leads to heightened vocal mindfulness.

---

[12] Those interested in learning more about belt singing may consult Jeannie Gagne's *Belting, A Guide to Healthy, Powerful Singing* (Berkleepress.com).

[13] There are many meditation resources on Youtube. Some include Deepak Chopra: https://youtu.be/BiYWp6I-RcE and Sarah Mclain Meditation https://youtu.be/1x0YnLinwXc.

As you practice, pay attention to when you are feeling vocally tired. It may be different for you than someone else. Ask yourself, "Am I pushing to produce my sound, or did I get a good breath on that last phrase?" See if you can identify your own personal stopping point in practice sessions. Some signs are physical throat pain, numbness, hoarseness, wobble in the voice, wide vibrato, vocal fatigue, loss of high notes, and constant intonation problems. If your throat feels strange, it is best to stop singing. The best healers are vocal rest with absolutely no talking and continued vocal training to build better breath support. Unfortunately, there is no pill that cures faulty vocal production, overuse, or vocal misuse.

Singers cannot afford to be shy about addressing noise levels or balance problems in rehearsals or pre-performance sound-checks if they are uncomfortable. It is both reasonable and mindful to speak up regarding the use and balancing of microphones and stage monitors. If no microphone is available in rehearsals, purchase a small amplifier and microphone for a modest fee.

Each step taken above builds a stronger and healthier voice over time from both a physical and mental point of view. It is extremely rare for a performer to play or sing perfectly from one day to the next. As singers build their sound gradually, they also learn to set their own vocal limits and limits responding to outside situations. Meanwhile, begin observing and noting when you hear untrained mariachi singers pushing and straining their voices. They are unaware that protections exist and are probably wondering why their voices tire so easily. Be proactive; you don't have to be one of those singers!

IN PERFORMANCE

In concert performance, mariachi solo professionals are able to sing well during long concerts by alternating soloists and adding instrumentals within a forty-five minute set. Soloists on their own often alternate smaller groups of solos with the ensemble or with dancers taking part in the show. Touring professionals have concert schedules that can require two shows nightly back-to-back. In this situation, soloists should use their voices sparingly during the day, or be on complete vocal rest. Rehearsals are best scheduled on days off or for very brief periods the day of a show. Solo singers will do well when setting aside a quiet time for gentle warmups, eating well, and getting plenty of rest. In between shows, it is best to avoid speaking loudly, and use email and text messages instead of talking on the telephone (see the "Understanding your Vocal Instrument" section for more tips).

Professional mariachi ensemble musicians in non-concert settings often have a grueling full-time performance schedule each week. While the ensemble alternates the members taking solos, the group often performs continuously more than eight hours and sometimes up to twelve hours a day as they move from event to event. Their main break consists of traveling between locations. During this break talk should be avoided to rest the voice (especially over car noise). Mariachis often work non-stop from Thursdays to Mondays. Although mariachi singers alternate solos, these long hours tire the entire body including the vocal cords. This causes vocal fatigue in even the best of voices. Over time, even the best of singers can develop symptoms if they haven't adopted healthy vocal habits. Vocal rest for two days on Tuesdays and Wednesdays before returning to mid-week rehearsals is helpful. This can be especially difficult for the mariachi director who might be booking engagements on the telephone during free time; in this case, moving quickly from initial telephone contact to written agreement exchanges can be helpful.

Ranchera singers with daily performances are naturally thrust into learning to think preventively, taking on new habits of talking less and texting more, watching movies when resting the voice, and avoiding yelling or loud places (*see* the "Understanding Your Vocal Instrument" section for more tips). This is the process of developing healthy vocal habits.

Mariachi Directors Provide Vocal Leadership

Mariachi ensemble directors are in a unique position to demonstrate strong leadership regarding the voice. During weekly rehearsals, the director may ask secondary soloists to cover main solos. This allows lead singers to rest more mid-week while building confidence in singers who have less vocal experience. Every ensemble should plan to have two or three singers cover each vocal solo, hopefully in the same or similar keys. The director may also choose to motivate singers to improve by offering extra pay to those who solo the most alongside their instrumental work. The director might arrange more rehearsal time or sectionals to have weaker players work on solos or bring in a vocal specialist to offer group voice training sessions in a master-class format. Note that much can be learned when the focus is technical and not limited to memorization of lyrics, interpretation, or choreography.

Ensemble directors can develop awareness to tune in often to the health of their lead singers. Their leadership in recommending several days of mid-week vocal rest for particular singers on occasion will have the entire group pausing and self-evaluating. This is common practice for singers in general, but less so with ranchera groups.

The mariachi director also leads best by example and should plan to be proactive as a student of singing, thus setting a vocal standard for the ensemble. It will inspire the group. As a student of singing, the director, if male, should also know every vocal solo in the repertoire to cover for absences and emergencies and can designate a female understudy to cover all repertoire in female keys.

Soloists usually *mark* their singing in rehearsals by singing an octave lower or half as loud (always with breath support). Competing against trumpets or a large group will naturally tempt a singer to push. It is helpful to have a microphone handy no matter how small the room is (see the section: "Understanding Your Vocal Instrument" earlier in this chapter). If soloists already maintain a heavy weekend professional performance schedule, they will often schedule short thirty-minute voice lessons on Wednesdays and Thursdays to continue balancing the voice and building breath support to avoid fatigue.

Finally, in one's own practice sessions singing along to a new song, do you always match your singing volume equally to the singer's voice on the recording? Mariachi singers love singing along to learn stylistic traits and phrasing. If you do this, make sure you can hear your voice *more* than the singer you are emulating but without pushing your own voice.

Care lovingly for your voice; it is the only one you have! You may begin with the mindfulness exercise and lesson questions below.

MARIACHI MINDFULNESS EXERCISE

1. Have you tried listening to the recording first, then singing on your own line by line without the recording instead of "following" the recording all the time? It allows you to stop and prepare your awareness of breath underneath you. Get this habit solid and then proceed to sing along with the recording.
2. Tape yourself practicing a song a cappella. Sing the song entirely. Then, tape yourself again singing the same song again with the same breath support but gentler vocal production? Listen to the two tapes and compare them.

3. As you learn a new song, have you experimented with keeping the breath flowing and alternating one or two vowels without thinking first about making a big sound? This is a great exercise for balancing the breath with vocal sound.

4. Always sense the breath based in your lungs before you begin each new phrase. Tape several phrases and compare and analyze your breaths. Listen afterward.

5. As you sing along with the recording, make sure you always hear your sound louder than the artist. Tape yourself with an accompaniment track. If you are not in time with the track, practice using your hand to conduct the track while speaking the counts "1-2-3-4." Allow yourself time and space to grow into each track.

6. Sense your emotions for each song. How does this song make you feel? Why do you resonate with the song? Can you read the lyrics out loud as a poem and dramatize it? You are a singing athlete, and your body, mind, and emotions need to all work together.

MARIACHI MINDFULNESS CHECK-IN

1. Describe any time you have felt vocally tired. How many times have you experienced this? Was it a certain type of location with certain acoustics? Had you been practicing daily, gradually building up your stamina? Do you consistently feel breath supporting your sound? Was the mariachi's sound equipment not functioning? Do you see any patterns?

2. What positive habits are you already doing? Keep them!

3. What negative vocal habits can you personally identify and change?

4. Do you know your personal stopping point for singing? What might help you avoid getting to this point? Track this backward so you know to stop sooner.

5. List three ways mariachi directors can vocally help their ensemble.

6. Do you own a microphone and small amplifier you might use in rehearsals?

7. What is marking? Practice marking alone to an accompaniment track in a practice session. Check that you are supporting your voice at a lower volume than your typical singing whether on pitch or one octave below.

Similarities and Differences between Mariachi and Classical Voice Production

For those new to teaching the mariachi voice, it is encouraging to know that mariachi and classical singing share many technical similarities. Both styles demand strong breath support, a round tone, legato, long lines, and a voice that projects.

SIMILARITIES

The list below includes similarities between mariachi and classical singing often used by judges in vocal competitions:

- *Diction and language*: How well have you prepared your pronunciation for the song? Is the diction clear and easy to understand?
- *Alignment and posture*: Are your ears over your shoulders and your shoulders over your hips all the time when you sing? This will improve your airflow as well as overall sound.

- *Breath support*: Are you able to be completely still while inhaling as well as during your singing on the exhale? Is your throat still when you feel your body inhale? When you inhale, are you able to avoid lifting your shoulders and/or high chest shallow breathing? Shallow breathing can affect your intonation.
- *Tone and legato*: Is your tone pleasing, rich, and/or round? Whether belting or singing classically, the tone should sound relaxed and not pushed or strained. Are your notes linked together with vowels? This creates a legato line and avoids any separation, breaks, or stoppage of airflow within or between words.
- *Interpretation:* Are you expressive and emotionally connected to the song? True acting is about being genuine and allowing yourself to feel the song as you sing. If you don't feel it your audience won't either.
- *Awareness of performance context and/or performance space*: Have you analyzed how much physical space you plan to use for your song and how much is available in your upcoming performance? The lyrics of the song and music will often answer this question for you. Your movements will become bigger as your stage becomes larger. Conversely, if the room is small your expression will come from your heart to your eyes, with less physical movement.
- *General musicality*: Are you precise with your pitch, rhythms, and the rhythmic groove? Are you clear on where the song changes harmonies even though you are singing the melody? Strong musicians analyze this automatically before they perform a song in public. It adds depth and confidence to your overall presentation.
- *Song appropriateness*: Make sure the song you choose reflects who you are and your level of singing; for example, if you are a beginning singer you won't want to start with "Mexico lindo y querido," a long, multi-sectioned piece that requires a singer with vocal stamina, style, and a wide range (see Chapter 5 Graded Song Lists: Beginning, Young Beginners, Intermediate, Advanced Vocal Levels). We have included several children's songs in this book to provide shorter songs with an easier range for younger adults (see Chapter 6).
- Always be sure the music and lyrics fit your character and vocal level at this moment in time.

DIFFERENCES

The next list details important vocal differences between mariachi and classical singers. Many of them apply to the female voice. Classical training is important alongside contemporary commercial vocal production with cross-training for females. If you are a voice student with a classical voice teacher, they may welcome the guide below.

Vibrato and backspace: Overall there is much less vibrato and less backspace in mariachi singing.

Sound: The sound is warm and often robust except when singing falsete. While sound production should never be pushed, breathy, or strained in soft belt or classical voice production there is an earthy richness sound expectation for both men and women. This is based upon chest voice dominance (with 30–40% head voice mix maximum). In boleros, the sound production varies, contrasting robust singing in choruses with muted, intimate expression in many verses. Men, and sometimes women, often sing as crooners in the bolero style. Classical singers may choose slightly higher keys for boleros, but not as high as operatic keys. The goal in boleros is mid-range interpretive expression over virtuosic or impressive operatic sound, unless the bolero is being used in a classical setting with classical intent.

Vowels: Generally, vowels are more similar to classical voice production than other styles. Darker vowels are used in mariachi singing, especially when female singers use soft belt production. American musical theater belt vowels are much more forward and brassier. The darker mariachi vowels and tone color can be produced gently or more intensely in belt for bravío songs.

Female mariachi fach: The female mariachi fach is fixed between the contralto/tenor range. This is non-negotiable. Changing this more than a step up or a step down would be akin to asking a classical lyric soprano coloratura to perform a bass aria, or a tenor to sing with only his top five high notes. Natural mariachi fach range and the chest-head mix or use of belt leans toward approximately 70 percent to 30 percent chest-to-head vocal production. Much stylistic variety can be achieved within this fach. Female singers are encouraged to train and discover their full head and chest range. This helps them access falsete. It also keeps the overall vocal registration balanced and often extends singing careers. Female mariachi singers sometimes overblow their bottom range before getting training, but this can be remedied. Without training, those that push or overblow often later wonder why they lack gentle intimacy on boleros or falsete range and ease.

Falsete: Falsete or falsetto flips occur during register changes and always use contrasting tone color when flipping. Classical singers blend the registers instead of accentuating differences for color purposes. The second top note in the falsete break is usually sustained with a light, floating sound. By contrast, opera singers often sing top notes at full volume and intensity, always using backspace for roundness of tone. Mariachi "money" notes are sustained with a flute sound on the top but without the backspace of a classical high note.

Style and interpretation: Style and interpretation are important and separate for each mariachi rhythm.. Listening to other singers for style is traditionally recommended for mariachi as it is an oral folk tradition. Top singers in both styles learn to balance technique while all the time sensing style and interpretation. Ranchera and bolero interpreters often make minor rhythmic and melodic changes, while always feeling the rhythmic groove of the song. Generally, there is less emphasis on singing on the downbeat, especially beat number one. In classical singing, the singer sings exactly what is written, except for cadenzas. The folk roots of ranchera singing allow for freer variation once a singer knows the style.

Acting: Acting is often more active, physical, and passionate in mariachi as compared to classical singing. When students compete in classical voice competitions, their focus on technique is generally higher than the interpretation. In ranchera singing this is slightly reversed.

Wake-up Warm-ups, Vocalises, and Practicing

All singers benefit from warming up their voice before proceeding full steam into songs. Instrumentalists may already be familiar with lip buzzing, humming, and other gentle warm-ups that wake up our bodies and our mind-body connection. After you complete the warm-ups listed below, include some of the mariachi vocalises further ahead into your daily practice. The vocalises are standard mariachi song excerpts that can be repeated on different pitches. Teachers may also use these song suggestions as repertoire ideas. Those teaching music fundamentals may choose to make use of the melodic interval markings to the right of each song excerpt to teach aural skills and improve intonation for singers.

WAKE-UP WARM-UPS

The warm-ups listed in this section are designed to increase inner-body awareness and prepare you to sing. As you warm up, keep checking in often with your posture, always making small adjustments. Try warm-ups each morning before talking or singing. Warm downs with hums are also helpful. Work these simple exercises into your general daily routine. (For more exercises, see the "Understanding Your Vocal Instrument" section in this chapter.)

- *Hum:* Allow your lips and face to naturally buzz with gentle humming for a minute. Vary the pitch with gentle slides in a small range at first, without going too high or too low. You can build this into your daily routine by humming while brushing your teeth (standing straight up!).
- *Release jaw:* Take a moment to release your jaw by finding and releasing the hinge of your jaw. The hinge is located behind your cheeks and in front of your ears on the sides of your face. Locate a small indentation where the upper and lower jaw parts meet. You will find the hinge if you pretend to chew gum while searching for an indentation with your fingers. Notice how much space is in your mouth when your jaw releases from the full hinge instead of from the front of your mouth. Close your eyes and take several breaths while enjoying the relaxed feeling of your loosely hanging jaw (all the while keeping your hands on the jaw hinge). Your goal is to continue to feel free at the hinge while you sing, not just before you take a breath.
- *Loosen tongue:* The tongue is a large and long muscle. Loosen it up by wagging it around sideways and sticking it in and out of your mouth like a snake for thirty seconds. Repeat once again. Is it lying relaxed and flat alongside your side teeth? Now, check that both the tongue and jaw are relaxed and independent of each other. Can you move one and notice that the other is uninvolved? Try gently singing a particular mid-range phrase or two from a song, checking in with your relaxed concept of tongue and jaw before every inhaled breath and during your singing. Ask your teacher for more exercises to separate the tongue from the jaw and your voice will sound more relaxed.
- *Loosen lips/blubber lips:* Allow your voice to slide up and down in a comfortable speaking range. Gradually add higher and lower notes.
- *Posture*: Your inner body works as a wind instrument when you sing. If you keep your posture aligned as you sing (not just before taking a breath), you will feel a natural and constant flow of air. This air is your energy source or motor. Check in with your

FIGURE 3.3 Treble clef downward slides.

- body alignment throughout the day. Are your feet firmly planted like a tripod in the ground? Are your knees relaxed and unlocked? Mariachi guitarrón players tend to unconsciously lock their knees to balance their bodies against the large instrument. Unfortunately, this tightens other parts of the body and throws off alignment for singing. Are your ears over your shoulders? Are your shoulders over your hips? Is your neck lined up with your hips (not in front of them)? Check in with your alignment periodically as you sing. Do you throw your head backward or forward as you go to high notes? You might not be over the breath flow any longer. Your mindfulness and lessons on natural breath flow and alignment are sure to improve your posture, your singing, and your health overall.
- *"Popote"*: This word means straw in Spanish, and this breath exercise is practiced with a straw. Inhale a small amount of air quickly from a straw. Notice how your lower intercostal muscles respond immediately to support your body's request for air and breath support. You can also suck a small amount of air by joining your fingers together in front of your mouth and sucking. This creates air compression in the body. You should feel an immediate response from your intercostal muscles around your ribs, and all around your body. Next, inhale again with the straw, and sing a vowel. Allow the vowel to feel like it comes almost directly out of the straw immediately after inhaling. Don't wait to tank or tense up before you sing your vowel. It comes faster than you think.
- *Slides*: Begin in your mid to low range. Employ the straw exercise in between each breath for the following exercise. Gently slide from step 5 down to step 1 on a comfortable vowel. Downward slides are gentle on the voice. Note that most popular songs go upward. By exercising the voice in both directions with downward exercises and slides, the vocal cords stay limber.
- *Yoga Breath:* Bend your knees slightly and raise your hands vertically as you inhale. As you exhale very slowly, count to twenty. As you do this, allow your arms to gradually spread to a horizontal position from their previous vertical position. Notice you can slow down your exhale if your arms move slowly and gradually.

Keep the above-mentioned alignment and breath information in mind as you learn to sing the vocalises in the next section.

104 THE MARIACHI VOICE

FIGURE 3.4 Vocalises from mariachi songs—ascending.

FIGURE 3.4 Continued

MARIACHI VOCALISES

Another way to improve and master vocal technique while having some fun is to sing excerpts from mariachi songs. These vocalises can assist singers in developing range, tone, and breath support when the body is carefully aligned before each breath and during singing. It also prepares singers for the songs in each vocalise.

The song excerpts also contain melodic intervals listed on the right-hand side of each excerpt. The same vocalises can assist teachers and students with music interval recognition and aural skills. If a student likes the song, they will most likely remember the interval.

Begin singing the exercises in a natural talking range and not necessarily the key indicated. Repeat, going up or down by step. Once you know the notes and rhythms, try going a bit higher. Stop when uncomfortable. Here are some questions to ask yourself in the process:

- Am I singing smoothly?
- Am I allowing the breath to move notes with jumps without moving my body or jaw to "help"?
- Is my mind on posture, the air in my lungs, and the vowels I am singing, or am I moving to try and adjust pitches? Keep your mind on the breath as your anchor.

FIGURE 3.5 Vocalises from mariachi songs—descending.

PRACTICING

Contrary to some instrumentalists, singers do not actively sing all the time during their practice sessions. Some instrumentalists can practice all day. Singers have small and delicate vocal chords. They often progress better in twenty- to thirty- or sixty-minute segments with multiple breaks, depending on their age and vocal level. Singers should plan to rest often during practice as they build breath support and stamina. Resting often also refreshes the mind with new ideas.

Singers learn to rest their voice from actual singing by interspersing some (or all) of the following vocally related tasks in their practice sessions:

- Listen to recent or old practice tapes. Take notes for your next practice session.
- Listen to different renditions of particular songs, or study the vocal style of one artist, either from song to song or comparing early career songs to later ones.
- Write out and isolate the lyrics, translations, and/or IPA to the songs being studied (see Chapter 6).
- Look up unfamiliar words in Spanish and study the overall meaning of the song.
- Recite the lyrics out loud as a poem, paying attention to your breathing. Repeat slowly, lengthening the vowels (see Chapter 6 section: "Memorizing Lyrics"). When ready, speed it up, never losing awareness of the vowels.
- Sound out new IPA sounds and symbols and match to a song (see Chapter 6 section: "Important Mariachi words with IPA." Watch Youtube videos on Learning IPA https://youtu.be/IH0J-d0pWhE).
- Read the sheet music for songs or transcribe the melody and chords yourself to create a song sheet with melody and chords.
- Play the melodies of given songs on the piano or a string instrument. Playing the trumpet is not vocally restful, as both the voice and the trumpet are wind instruments and need separate rest times.
- Write lyrics in a journal or write down and collect musical ideas. Many singers also create their own song endings and write their own songs.
- Create slight variations on song repeats for certain styles or notice your own ideas emerging around the song. Tape or write out.
- Practice the rhythmic groove of different mariachi rhythms on the guitar or vihuela without singing out loud. Notice how the strumming downbeats coincide with or syncopate against the vocal line of the song (in your head).
- Write out your personal interpretation and any planned choreography for a song with diagrams.

Practice Location

Find a quiet space where you can sit and stand with a piano or musical instrument and a mirror nearby. The space should preferably be enclosed with no television or other sounds to disturb your practice. Turn off your telephone. Keep a separate recording device handy to tape and listen. If you are able, hang two mirrors, one for your profile alignment and one to observe a loose jaw and throat.

Day and Time

Identify a similar time to practice daily five days per week. Beginners should practice for twenty to thirty minutes maximum and then rest for at least five minutes or more. Advanced beginners can extend their practice session to thirty to forty-five minutes, but rest twice for five minutes or once for ten minutes. Intermediate singers might practice for forty-five to sixty minutes, resting twice or three times during a session as desired. Advanced singers practice for more hours per day, but not all at once. Note that resting can include listening to yourself on tape and writing down critiques, as well as writing out lyrics or listening on

YouTube. Be willing to commit to a schedule and consistency if you want to see progress and growth.

Advanced Growth in Practicing

Practicing is the art of self-discovery. Rote practicing of warm-ups, vocalises, and songs offers an important structure, but it can mean much more. Inspiration comes with establishing practice as a discipline. Practicing is the art of getting to know yourself—that is, discovering new body awareness with new sounds and interpretations, as well as figuring out what to discard.

We grow the most in practice by not always doing the same thing, being open to exploration, and trying out new things in practice. Do you really want to sing the same songs over and over again each day and call that practice? Have you noticed that there are some problem sections you might isolate and study in depth? One day every two weeks can be spent reviewing songs to change up the schedule. Don't wait to be inspired to practice. Just do it.

Voice Practice Schedule Ideas for Young Singers (under Thirteen)

These two private practice schedules can be followed to get youngsters started. Each session may also be split into two separate parts per day.

- *Schedule A:* First, practice warmups (ten minutes) and vocalises (ten minutes), and rest (10 minutes). Then, practice songs (ten minutes), locating and singing challenging individual song phrases for five minutes and reviewing one song you already know for five minutes.
- *Schedule B:* First, practice warmups (five minutes) and vocalises (ten minutes), and rest (ten minutes). Then, practice songs (fifteen minutes), focusing on isolated spots within songs for five minutes and reviewing three songs for ten minutes.

Practicing Quiz

1. How long should you practice singing every day?
2. Is it helpful to take breaks? How often and why?
3. How much time is spent singing full songs in a thirty-minute practice?
4. Is it good or bad to have your cellphone on and nearby when you practice? Why or why not?
5. Design your personal practice schedule. Label it A. Post your schedule in your room, kitchen, bathroom mirror, and share with your teacher or exchange with a music friend.

Finding the Right Key for Your Song

Finding the right key for a singer's voice is not as obvious as it seems. A starting place for ranchera songs is to work with "friendly" string-based mariachi keys. The most popular mariachi keys are C-G-D-A-F-Bb, and for minor keys, am, dm, and em (see Chapter 3 section: "Popular Mariachi Keys"). There are not as many as a classical singer might enjoy if singing with a piano or orchestra.

The mariachi style also dictates specific key choices for female singers to stay close to chest-voice production in the bottom half of the female range. Keys for women are semi-fixed in the female mariachi fach (approximately f3 to c4; see the "Female Mariachi Fac" section in this chapter).

CHAPTER 3: MARIACHI VOICE PEDAGOGY   109

For example, "Los Laureles" for women is usually in F, G, or possibly A Major. The range of the song in G Major is from g3 to a4. There is no reason a lower contralto could not sing it in F Major should she have extremely comfortable lower notes around f3. Singing it in Bb Major would have female singers pushing chest voice above a4 unless the singer has great support in belt or mixed head-chest voice production above f4. When the range sits above a4 (or above d4 for men) the sound gets too far away from the natural mariachi chest mixed sound for both men and women.

Within standard mariachi key choices, singers need to know enough about their own voice to select what best fits them. They should be aware of their *range, tessitura,* and *passaggio*. The word *range* refers to every note one can sing from top to bottom, including extremities. *Tessitura* refers to a zone within one's range where the singer sounds the best and feels most vocally at ease. *Passaggio* is a music term describing the transition area where the voice changes registers between chest and head voice. The overall goal is to choose a key in which most of the notes in the song coincide with the singer's range and tessitura, also considering comfortable shifts and color contrasts through the passaggio. The notes in Figure 3.6 give an approximate tessitura for each vocal range. Keep in mind that each voice is unique and not all voices fit perfectly into categories.

Some singers evaluate a song key by intuition and singing along with someone's rendition of the song. This can help identify possible high or low sections of the song to try in different keys. There are also other ways to do this more precisely. One method is to write out one's own range and tessitura and label the tessitura and passaggio with separate colors. With this in hand, singers can proceed to visually check the range of any future song melody against their personal voice color sheet.

In choosing a key, singers with music training often transcribe songs to inspect the melodic range visually. After identifying particular sections of the song in question, they circle it and practice it in various keys. It is helpful to visually check that the high points of the song coincide with areas of their range that show off their voice. When a singer's passaggio notes within the tessitura coincide with the opening up of the song's chorus, the song can powerfully match with the singer. Make sure the climax notes are equally powerful!

If undecided on the exact song key after trying the above ideas, it can be helpful to alternate singing the full song in each potential key until it becomes obvious. Recording it or getting feedback from musically trained friends or voice teachers helps. Sing the song at different times of the day as well. There is always a perfect key for every song, and songs can vary greatly in their own melodic movement and range. There is no need for singers to hurt their voices by squeezing them into the preferred instrumental ensemble key. Trust your intuition. If the key feels strange it may not be right for your voice. In summary, finding a perfect song key includes some trial and error, but with practice, the search for the perfect song key is often quick and easy.

KEY CHOICES FOR WOMEN

Music directors will be able to make quicker and easier decisions on key choices for female ensemble soloists by having their students chart out their own vocal range, tessitura, and passaggio. Separate each with distinct colors.

For example, many women naturally switch from chest to head voice or a mix in a given song anywhere between c4 and f#4. This natural switching area is generally part of the female passaggio. Higher female voices switch toward the higher notes Eb-E-F, while those who naturally sing in contralto or mezzo-soprano ranges may switch on the lower end of the passaggio between c4 and E. It can also depend on the song in question, particular vowels, the singer's voice, or how much training they have had. Those who switch higher than f4 in mariachi

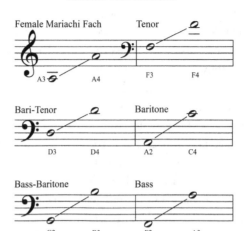

FIGURE 3.6 Mariachi voice tessituras for each vocal range. Note that tessitura is where the range of this voice part sounds best but does not indicate the full range of the voice. Natural female ranges, for example, run at least one octave above the mariachi fach.

singing will hopefully be mixing head and chest in a blended voice without ever resorting to pure chest. Women who have trained in belt voice or commercial styles begin mixing or switching between d4 and f4 or even c# and f#. They may have learned to gradually ascend melodically in a head-chest mix or belt color to b4–c5. If a director hears yelling or a tight or pushed voice, the song key should be lowered.

The keys chosen for women in mariachi or commercial singing are based upon a chest-head blended voice between c4 and c5 when no falsete is present. In classical singing, the keys chosen for women are completely different because women develop head-voice range from c4 to c6 or even further into the female whistle register for coloraturas. The head-chest blended voice in classical female singing might be 75 percent to 25 percent head-to-chest dominance between c4 and c5 as an optimum sound. Conversely, healthy mariachi female singers might prefer a 70 percent to 30 percent chest-to-head dominance for optimum sound.

Less-trained singers will always be most comfortable in the lowest key possible, resembling a natural speaking-voice range. Some directors push female singers into higher keys to accommodate a comfortable instrumental key. This hurts their voices and constricts their range.

Female singers with mixed voice or soft belt technique in their upper chest range are able to add excitement to mariachi songs because it adds power, volume, and projection. Vocal training opens up more key choices as the range expands, with easy falsete, and easier switches into a mixed-voice blend or belt. Women should check that the chorus or highest climactic notes of the song in question coincide with their strongest notes.

KEY CHOICES FOR MEN

Most of the male vocal range is already in chest voice, making key choices more straightforward. Men can sing as basses, baritones, bari-tenors, or tenors in both mariachi and classical singing styles; therefore, the passaggio and register changes stay the same. Similar to the female voice, the male passaggio generally lies between c4 and f#4.[14] Once again, lower voices tend to switch in the lower end of the passaggio while tenors switch on the high end (see the "Choosing a Key With Falsete" section in this chapter).

Soloists find more key choices as they develop their voices. This is especially true for women, who, upon building their upper range, find a sudden ease singing in their lower range. Keeping this balance helps singers avoid wide vibrato or going flat due to heavy pressure on the lower end of the voice. Healthy vocalists exercise their full range from top to bottom. This is especially important for women, even though they will not be performing rancheras that sit in the top of their range.

FINDING THE RIGHT KEY EXERCISES

- *Vocal Range Color Chart:* Use a musical instrument to calculate your range, tessitura, and passaggio. Write it down on a sheet of music paper and assign a separate color to each of the three areas.
- *Voice Chart Presentation:* Compare and contrast your sheet with a male and female music colleague. Test it out: have each colleague sing from each of the three areas of the voice to verify and contrast. Can you hear each other's color differences when they change to different parts of their range?

FINDING THE RIGHT KEY QUIZ

1. List the mariachi ensemble's most popular keys.
2. Define a singer's range.
3. Define a singer's tessitura.
4. Define a singer's passaggio. Is it the same for men as women?
5. How far away are typical male keys for songs as opposed to female keys?

Answers: (1) Major Keys: C-G-D-A-F-Bb. Minor Keys: am–em-dm. (2) Range refers to every note one can sing from their top not extremities to their bottom note extremities. (3) Tessitura refers to a zone somewhere within one's range where the singer sounds the best and feels most vocally at ease. (4) *Passaggio* is a music term describing the transition area where the voice changes registers between chest and head voice. (5) Four or even five full steps away.

---

[14] Basses often change as low as Bb3 and are relatively unknown in the mariachi world.

FIGURE 3.7 Young Ranchera Singer Jizelle Rodriguez singing at San Antonio's annual vocal competition, Mariachi Extravaganza. Photographed by Javier Vela.

CHOOSING A KEY WITH FALSETE

Special care should be taken when choosing a key for a mariachi song with sustained falsete tones. When long, sustained falsete register breaks are in a song, namely huapangos, singers can choose the key by measuring where the falsete transition and subsequent notes sit most comfortably. These notes usually fall in the singer's passaggio and upward (c4–f#4). The transition note with unwavering breath support is the key to a solid switch that includes the accentuated color contrast. Try these suggestions for testing out keys:

1. First, proceed through the steps listed in the preceding section for finding the best song key. Test several key choices by singing the transition note prior to the falsete note and then the note itself. Make sure both notes feel comfortable using the vowels from the lyrics despite the possibly different timbre, or color, of each.
2. Isolate the two notes where the switch in register activates. Sing several times on the indicated vowels of the song to make sure the falsete switch is comfortable. Try out one or two key choices until you are sure which is more comfortable. Sing it like a yodel as well. A singer's focus should be upon the transition note and its corresponding vowel.

It is best to start with easier huapangos with one falsete note and less range overall. They are "El Jinete," "Canta mi son!," and "Cielo rojo" (for more song choices, see Chapter 5).

Once a singer knows their key, it is helpful to find sheet music or a lyrics sheet and organize a binder of songs with a master list naming the keys to each song. Sheet-music books of ranchera music are just becoming available, although romantic bolero song books are published and not difficult to find.[15] Unfortunately, Latin American songs are currently published in male keys. Male song keys are generally located four to five keys away from female keys in any given song. The ranchera songs available in this book are in two contrasting keys (see Chapter 6).

Answer Keys to Quizzes

Vocal Cords Quiz Answer Key (Quiz on p. 12)

1. *False.* In women, vocal folds are typically half an inch long. Men's folds are somewhat longer—but never more than one inch long.
2. *True.*
3. *False.* The vocal folds separate for inhaling and come together to make a sound.
4. *True.*
5. *False.* See number 1 above.

Falsete Quiz Answer Key (Quiz on p. 47)

1. Falsete is a Mexican mariachi term for a sudden break or change in vocal register, not unlike a yodel. It is used as an expressive gesture and can switch abruptly and switch back immediately or be sustained indefinitely.
2. Many mariachi songs sustain long falsete notes. Some examples are: El Pastor, Cielo Rojo, Cuando Canto, El Preso No. 9, Malagueña Salerosa, El Jinete, Crucifijo de Piedra, and La Cigarra.
3. Many mariachi songs utilize quick falsete switches as a standard part of the style, especially those from Veracruz. Two examples are:
   "Y Andale" and "Cuando canto" (see Chapter 6).
4. The King of Falsete "El Rey del Falsete" is attributed to Miguel Aceves Mejía. https://frontera.library.ucla.edu/tag/falsetto-king.
5. The female whistle register is different from falsete, although it is imitated by women. Technically, this female register is called head voice. Women also have a very high whistle register above their head voice register.

Practicing Quiz Answer Key (Quiz on p. 67)

1. Please plan to begin practicing singing twenty to thirty minutes per day per week.
2. It is helpful to take breaks often, at least five minutes for every thirty minutes of practice in order to rest the vocal cords. It is similar to resting the body between repetitions in weight lifting.
3. A maximum of ten to fifteen minutes should be spent singing full songs per thirty-minute practice, in order to build pedagogical and linguistic elements alongside songs.
4. It is good to have a cell phone nearby when practicing to tape, replay, and transcribe practice sessions. It is not useful to keep a phone handy if listening to it ring with

---

[15] Hal Leonard has publications of commercial romantic boleros. The bolero tradition has always existed earlier and independently of ranchera music, although it is also linked to it through the bolero ranchero style. www.musicnotes.com also features many individual boleros and other styles with limited rancheras.

messages, calls, or any other interruption. If this is too tempting a separate taping device can be used in lieu of the telephone.

5. Design your personal practice schedule. Post your schedule in your room, kitchen, and bathroom mirror, and share with your teacher or exchange with a music friend.

Finding the Right Key Answer Key (Quiz on p. 73)

1. The most popular keys for mariachi ensembles are Major keys: C-G-D-A-F-Bb, and minor keys: am-em.
2. *Range* refers to every note a person can sing from top to bottom, not including extremities.
3. *Tessitura* refers to a zone somewhere within one's range where the singer sounds the best and feels most vocally at ease.
4. *Passaggio* is a music term describing the transition area where the voice changes registers between chest and head voice.
5. Four or even five full steps away.

CHAPTER 4

PREPARING TO BE A MARIACHI SINGER

FIGURE 4.1 *China Poblana* costume with gold brocade for a female mariachi solo singer. Traditional regional dress style from Puebla, Mexico. Image courtesy of Division of Culture and the Arts, National Museum of American History, Behring Center, Smithsonian Institution.

The Voice Is the Instrument Everybody Shares

The voice is actually a mariachi musician's most powerful vehicle of expression when one considers that performers always carry their vocal instrument inside them and can access it anytime. Strong singing adds electric presence to a show when the lyrics are thoughtfully delivered. Every performer is an important singer in the mariachi world. All will want to make plans to study singing because more than 80 percent of ranchera repertoire is vocal. Some terrific mariachi instrumentalists ignore or are disconnected from their voice. They forget that their very own bodies house a small, delicate, yet amazingly powerful wind instrument. The voice cannot be treated lightly, overblown, or forgotten as an afterthought. Unlike the trumpet, violin, or guitar, if the voice is mistreated or damaged, it can never be replaced. Even as an advanced beginning singer, performers can make a valuable contribution to the group. Read ahead to find out where you fit in as a ranchera singer, both now and down the line.

Group Singers, Ensemble Soloist, Mariachi Soloist: Where Do You Fit In?

Singers have various functions within the mariachi world. There are three basic categories, although they can overlap occasionally or change during the course of someone's long-term career. Each category emphasizes slightly different talents and musical preparation. See what you identify with and where you fit in.

GROUP SINGERS

Some singers are simply better instrumentalists or they are new to the voice; regardless, all mariachi performers are expected to provide rich choral vocal sound for the group while also covering some solos. If you are in your early stages of performing, don't necessarily assume you can only do one thing well. Give yourself time and space to explore and grow!

Ensembles distinguish themselves when they are able to show off both their soloists and choral power, while matching it to their instrumental delivery. When the group's overall choral vocal sound is developed over time, robust impressive sound, precision, and deep expression fill the room with electric and indescribable power and resonance. Singing unites all mariachi performers, and the voice is the one instrument everybody shares.

Instrumentally based mariachi singers should never underestimate themselves vocally. Group singers are often the most solid musicians. Their strong musicianship skills can help solidify the group's foundation in sustaining choral harmonies with a solid blend. Group singers typically learn about singing in mariachi voice sectionals, group voice classes, and choir singing, but rarely know how to practice to build their voices technically beyond learning lyrics and songs (see Chapter 3 section: "Warm-ups, Vocalises and Practicing").

ENSEMBLE SOLOIST

Ensemble soloists take solos from within the mariachi ensemble. The strongest group singers are assigned more solos, while still excelling at another instrument. Solo vocal technical levels can vary widely from ensemble to ensemble. While groups typically have everyone prepare solos, ensemble soloists tackle the more challenging song repertoire, and are given more solo opportunities. They usually begin their solo by walking to the front of the stage, although they can begin from anywhere on stage if planned. Many come forward standing in front of the microphone stand without employing stage choreography or extensive movement. Those with acting training know to leave their instrument behind on a stand to have free use of their hands for instrumentation, especially if planning to hold the microphone at some point during the song. Groups such as Flor de Toloache, Mariachi Vargas, Mariachi Sol de México, Mariachi Divas, and Mariachi Cobre feature world-class ensemble soloists (see Chapter 8 section: "Flor de Toloache").

FIGURE 4.2 Youth mariachi ensembles such as *Mariachi Juvenil Corazón Jalisciense* from Hollister, California, feature youth ranging from eight to eighteen years old. In California, groups lack academic programs with vocal study and gather in centers, churches, and lower schools, while Texas boasts mariachi degrees with limited vocal study at universities.

MARIACHI SOLO SINGER

Mariachi solo singers freelance with mariachi ensembles. They also perform with guitarists, bolero trios, and may perform other styles of music. Soloists are often versatile and typically work in different performance situations. Ranchera soloists are supposed to be the *crème de la crème* of mariachi singers and strive to represent the highest level of mariachi singing. They are expected to have vocal training with tonal beauty and power, style, entertainment talent, acting skills, and versatility. They are also expected to learn their music independently, and often book and produce their own events. These soloists often wear many kinds of Mexican regional costumes.

Top-level serious professional soloists typically cross vocally between huapangos, rancheras valseadas, polkas, ranchera lenta, bolero ranchero, and beyond into other styles. Jorge Negrete, Pedro Infante, Miguel Aceves Mejía, and Pedro Vargas are *Siglo de oro* examples of top-level solo singer-actors with vocal versatility in these different styles. Miguel Aceves Mejía achieved a more dramatic vocal career change between styles, shifting from Carribean salsa to Mexican ranchera huapangos. Jorge Negrete and Pedro Vargas were originally trained as opera singers but technically worked with teacher José Pierson to also cross into rancheras and bolero crooning with less backspace than is used in opera (see Chapter 2 sections: "Jorge Negrete," "Maestro José Pierson"; Chapter 8 section: "Jorge Negrete: Dispelling Myths about Legendary *ranchera* Singer, *El charro cantor*").

Linda Ronstadt might be considered the contemporary ranchera queen of crossover styles. She has been one of the world's greatest and most successful singers to date, precisely because of her vocal versatility. Before soloing on two different Grammy-winning ranchera recordings

FIGURE 4.3 Linda Ronstadt, queen of contemporary crossover styles, singing with her father in Arizona. Courtesy of Rick Wiley, editor of photography, *Arizona Daily Star*.

of "Canciones de mi Padre," she had already achieved world celebrity status for her work in rock and musical theater, and even tried opera (see Chapter 8 section: "Linda Ronstadt"). In Figure 4.3 she is singing live with her father in Tucson, Arizona.

Solo singers from within mariachi ensembles are also important role models today: Steve Carrillo is both a soloist and lead singer for the Mariachi Cobre ensemble. This ensemble has long represented Mexico at the Epcot Center in Florida. (Listen to Mariachi Cobre perform "Estrellita" by composer Manuel M. Ponce on YouTube: https://youtu.be/fXgfjMAg0Ps.) Steve Carrillo trained vocally, separate from the ensemble. He deftly shifts between presenting as a soloist/actor to being an ensemble member as an instrumentalist. Mariachi Vargas has done the same with many of their lead vocalists over their more than one-hundred-year existence. Three Vargas solo singers are pictured singing live on the culminating note of a song at the San Antonio Mariachi Extravaganza in San Antonio in Figure 4.4. In the picture, note the

FIGURE 4.4 Three main soloists from Mariachi Vargas performing in San Antonio, Texas, at the Annual Mariachi Extravaganza Concert. Note that they culminate the song sustaining a high note, not only raising their sombreros in tandem, but also keeping their posture aligned and knees unlocked and relaxed. Photograph by Javier Vela.

erect body alignment of each singer, the sense of timing of the trio as they work in tandem. They show strong interpretive style raising their sombreros together, while simultaneously keeping their alignment intact and knees slightly bent. They are slightly distanced from the microphone on purpose as they sustain a high note (see "Costumes, Make-up, Song Studies, and Singing with a Microphone" in this chapter).

To be a successful non-ensemble mariachi soloist one should be completely at home on the stage and prefer acting to instrumental accompaniment. Experienced soloists such as Lola Beltrán possessed impressive choreographic skills that always heightened the drama of each song she acted out. Her interpretation of "Huapango Torero," the story of a young boy who dies while secretly trying to fight a bull, illustrates this (https://youtu.be/KR3UcpAOYQI). Note that in this type of song she chooses to remain centered and still as a narrator telling a heart wrenching story, yet she acts dramatically from her heart. Her heart is seen through her eyes and heard through her voice. She uses minimal stage movement. This is one interpretative choice as a narrator that is truly powerful, although another interpretation might be to fully use the stage to act out the role of the child bullfighter, which can also be quite effective.

Another kind of ranchera soloist is that of the singer-songwriter. In this style the message of the song comes from deep within the singer because they wrote the song. In many cases with singer/songwriters the message overrides the beautiful tone and virtuosity of the voice. This singing style emerged in the ranchera world with the success of José Alfredo Jiménez (1926–1973) (see Chapter 2 section: "Singer/Songwriter: José Alfredo Jiménez"). He was a highly creative storyteller who strummed ranchera guitar rhythms to share the message and accompany himself. "José Alfredo," as he is often affectionately called, did not play regularly in a mariachi ensemble, nor did he seek to highly train his voice or take acting lessons;

nevertheless, his vision gave the ranchera world a new vocal perspective. José Alfredo's highly personal message about humanity and personal relationships was crafted into every song he wrote. José Alfredo's success opened up a new path for singers, a path that has yet to be seriously pursued or surpassed except by commercial and ranchera singer/songwriter, Juan Gabriel (1950–2016). (see Chapter 2 section: "José Alfredo Jiménez").

Some soloists are excellent singers but have never learned to play an instrument. It is never too late to learn! Just as instrumentalists are expected to sing, solo singers should at minimum learn basic accompaniment. This helps them learn songs more quickly and with ease and, if in an ensemble, will also support the group's overall instrumental sound of the group (see Linda Ronstadt's comments on this topic in Chapter 8 section: "Linda Ronstadt"). Solo singers experience more dominion in their singing upon learning solid musicianship skills. These skills assist them in correctly choosing keys for songs, arranging, directing rehearsals, writing lyrics and/or composing their own original songs (see Chapter 7).

When any mariachi singer commits to a song they take on the responsibility of honoring and transmitting the song's message as beautifully and effectively as possible. A singer is able to move their audience through their own expressive intentions and song preparation. A strong ensemble will pick up on this and follow the soloist's lead transmitting the same emotions in their own playing.

What kind of a ranchera singer do you think you are?

Costumes, Make-up, Song Studies, and Singing with a Microphone

Each of Mexico's many regions has beautifully crafted and brightly colored costumes typical to their area of origin. Figure 4.1 at the beginning of this chapter highlights one of Mexico's most beautiful China Poblana brocaded costumes from Puebla, Mexico. It is housed today in the Smithsonian Museum in Washington DC. Regional costumes are regularly featured by folkloric dance companies as well as solo singers and occasionally by mariachi ensembles. The varied costume choices, hairstyling, and make-up together demonstrate each performer's authenticity and elegance in representing Mexico's heritage. The costumes also add to a singer's presence and sound. Find your favorite costumes from Mexico's thirty-two states beginning with the broader regions pictured in the diagram in Figure 4.5.

While the black *traje de charro* or *vestido de charro* (see Glossary) is a current standard for mariachi ensembles, up until the early 1900s mariachi performers actually dressed quite simply. They wore off-white peasant clothes with *huaraches* (sandals). Today, singers or newly formed ensembles with budget constraints need not worry that they are missing out. It is not uncommon to see young groups united by the same-colored *moño* (Mexican bow tie) with a white shirt and dark pants or a skirt.

The *zarape* is a colorful blanket that can be effective when draped diagonally over one shoulder. It can be used over a shirt with a moño or over the *traje de charro*. The *zarape* blanket can hinder instrumentalists when playing if not properly secured. Solo singers may also consider draping it on or off between songs to vary their visual presentation. The *zarape* adds color to the stage. It is inexpensive and not difficult to purchase.

In hot weather, performers have been known to opt for lighter-weight, white folklórico costumes from Veracruz (Gulf of México) or the brightly colored lightweight huipil white flowered dresses and shirts from Yucatán (Eastern México) instead of the black *traje de charro*. The Yucatán huipil is also a convenient choice for female performers going through pregnancy

FIGURE 4.5 Mexico has a rich array of regional costumes for singers and dancers to choose from for ranchera solo singers. This diagram of dancers from different regions depicts some of Mexico's many beautiful costume choices for singers. Diagram illustrated by Juan Carlos Sánchez.

or anyone fitting costumes for new members of the group, as they are two piece with elastic waistlines and are easy to adjust.

Some of today's contemporary soloists and groups have deliberately invented newer and diverse versions of the *charro* outfit, for example, Latin Grammy-winning ensemble Flor de Toloache (see Chapter 8 section: "Flor de Toloache"). The contemporary costume depicted in Figure 4.6 represents their innovative style, much of it originally achieved on a budget.

FIGURE 4.6 Customized contemporary personalized costumes by Latin Grammy-winning group, *Flor de Toloache*. Photography and Permission from Andrei Paul Averbuch.

FIGURE 4.7 *Operachi* singer Juanita Ulloa in a customized charro evening gown designed by Zenón Barrón, dance director of the San Francisco–based Mexican folklórico group *Ensambles*. Photograph with permission by Patrick Johnson.

Likewise, many solo singers have formal mariachi evening gowns custom made for special events, as seen in Figure 4.7 with the author's *charro* evening gown designed by Zenón Barrón, dance director of *Ensembles* folklórico dance group based in San Francisco, California.

MAKE-UP AND HAIR

Performers accentuate their presence on stage with costumes, movement, hair, and make-up. These elements combine with the voice to add drama to performances. Experienced performers know they must carefully prepare their "look" before each show. These visual elements take time, practice, and planning. Much can be learned about stage make-up and costumes from consulting with Mexico's many folkloric dance companies.

Singers and dancers of Mexican music living in the United States might be unaware that Mexican women tend to wear heavier make-up in everyday life than do women in the United States. Performers on any stage for Mexican dance and music are also expected to accentuate make-up even further for a professional, dramatic look.

Most mariachi performers learn to apply theatrical make-up as part of their costume preparation. While male folklórico dancers often wear some blush and liner, male mariachi musicians generally do not wear much make-up, although they may choose to do so for large stages and television presentations.

The amount of make-up applied can vary just as performance venues vary widely in terms of stage size, lighting, and technicians. If the distance between the stage and the audience is large, even with good lighting a performer's face becomes less noticeable unless make-up is liberally used. In general, singers should plan to be dramatic in the application of make-up in order to be easily seen and appreciated from a distance.

Essential make-up for women on stage includes: primer, foundation, eyeliner, long eyelashes, eye shadow, and blush. Product purchasing needs to be planned and a make-up bag kept with their costume.

Large gold Mexican earrings are used with flowers and/or ribbons in the hair. Hairstyles can vary depending on the costume. The hair is generally pulled away from the woman's face in either a bun or braids. It is important that the hair not be loose. Notice how the eyes of a performer stand out after make-up is applied and hair is pulled back, as depicted in Figure 4.8.

FIGURE 4.8 Recommended make-up, jewelry, and pulled-back hairstyle for ranchera singers and dancers depicted by Laryssa Ramos, in Oaxacan costume. Courtesy of Larrysa Ramos.

CHAPTER 4: PREPARING TO BE A MARIACHI SINGER   125

Both singers and dancers gel their hair back, as it allows the audience to see the expression in their eyes throughout the song. Singers with acting skills know to convey the message of each song straight from their heart. The heart is revealed through the eyes and then out to the limbs of the body. The eyes are often considered "the windows of the soul." The sparkle of the eyes can illuminate full theaters, naturally transmitting the spirit, culture, and heart of ranchera music.

It is helpful for performers to practice applying make-up ahead of time and find a partner to work with. After a trial run applying make-up, be sure and time the application process. This provides performers with an estimate of how much time to allot on the day of each performance.

YouTube hosts many free tutorials with guidance on how to apply affordable make-up for ranchera performances. Thanks to the Mexican folklórico dance ensemble from the University of Santa Barbara, California, for the following make-up video on YouTube: https://youtu.be/qDhzbzGb7O8.

SONG STUDIES

In order to interpret well and sell a song to an audience, singers need to have studied that song thoroughly. See Chapter 6 for song study research and preparation of lyrics, along with other studies of artists and composers.

SINGING WITH A MICROPHONE

The microphone is something many people use daily but few know how to use correctly, especially when singing. Practice with the suggestions below to develop ease in singing solos with a microphone. Remember, your vocal cords are infinitely smaller than the instruments in a mariachi ensemble and using a microphone protects your vocal instrument.

1. *Hold the microphone very close to your lips.* Most people hold the microphone too far away and assume someone else will adjust the volume for them. You are in charge. Practice holding the microphone close to your mouth throughout the song as seen in Figures 4.9 and 4.10. Keep your lips within a centimeter of touching the microphone as if you are almost kissing the microphone. Video record yourself as you sing to check if you accidentally let the microphone drop or sag during certain moments of the song. The microphone shouldn't move, but it does take practice to master this. Check between phrases that you continue to hold the microphone steady and consistently close to the mouth. Singers tend to drop their focus and relax their bodies, letting the microphone sag either in between phrases or toward the end of phrases. While there is no substitute for practicing with a microphone stand and microphone cord, if you do not own one yet, a good substitute is a small (three- to five-pound) barbell. The weight of the barbell approximates the weight of a large, cordless microphone. It will be easier for you to interpret a song if you are used to holding something the same weight as the microphone while you practice. You don't want to be distracted by the sudden weight of holding a heavy microphone when under performance pressure.
2. *Check your alignment when setting up your microphone.* Set up the microphone on a stand, and carefully measure the stand to your height. Adjust the stand just below the level of your mouth but angle the microphone up toward your mouth without covering it. If you set it too high the audience cannot see your full face. Some singers accidentally incline their heads down or lean over into the microphone as they are singing.

FIGURE 4.9 Mariachi outdoor singer. Note he carefully keeps the microphone close to his mouth for consistent projection.

FIGURE 4.10 Jizelle Rodriguez performing at the Mariachi Extravaganza where she won first place. Note the proper use of the microphone close to the mouth and the musician's erect body alignment. Photograph by Javier Vela.

Others unconsciously angle their entire body forward, not realizing they are cutting off the airflow to a beautiful sound at the neck. Video record yourself practicing, and check your profile alignment.

3. *Set up the performance microphone ahead of time.* Have the vocal microphone stand set up and firmly adjusted prior to sound check before your performances (and rehearsals). Double check it during sound check. Get used to moving the knobs as some are stiff or too tight and some work better than others. Mark where you like to adjust the microphone to with a small piece of tape in case anyone else uses it.

4. *Always use a microphone during rehearsals with other performers.* It is important for singers to always use a microphone during rehearsals. If there is no sound system available, a small bass amplifier works well and is inexpensive.

5. *Practice singing hands-free.* If you are an ensemble performer, purchase a small instrumental stand and leave your instrument on the stand behind you when you step forward to take solos. To fully interpret a song, you need to have your hands free. Did you know that the audience gets distracted and worried when they see singers struggling to balance microphones, instruments, and possibly a violin bow all at the same time? When the audience gets distracted, they are no longer listening to your voice or the song. Be sure you practice singing with both hands free, even if they remain quietly at your sides by your thighs. As you learn acting skills your free hands are sure to be a strong asset.

6. *Practice with both boom and vertical microphone stands.* Do you know how to re-angle a boom stand, or adjust and take the microphone on and off the stand without assistance? Have you planned how and when you will take the microphone off the stand in a live

performance and practiced this way? You might choose an instrumental interlude, between the verses of a song, or just before an important chorus. Let the lyrics, mood, and music intuitively tell you where to switch from a fixed microphone position to walking with it in your hand. Strategize your song interpretation using the microphone and stand within your presentation.

You are now on a path towards professional ranchera singing!

PREPARATION TIPS FOR AUDITIONS AND PERFORMANCES (LIVE AND ONLINE)*

1. *Be prepared.* Learn your piece well many weeks or months prior to your deadline. Only perform what feels comfortable and easy. If you are unsure about answering some of the questions below, you'll score more points by waiting and improving your preparation.
   - Have you studied the song for several months with your teacher?
   - Is it in the best key for your voice?
   - Have you taped it, listened back, and made technical adjustments as you practice?
   - Have you performed it in front of anyone?
2. *Practice what you don't know and perform only what you know.* For auditions and performances only perform what you truly already know well.
3. *Memorize and Digest the Lyrics.* If you have to read lyrics from paper or a cellphone, then your lyrics are not performance ready. You cannot expect to transmit the intent behind the lyrics and share the song from your heart unless you know the lyrics inside and out. If you write them out each day and study them you will get creative interpretation ideas and memorize quickly.
4. *Introductions.* Be sure you have researched and written down information on your song: composer, history, artists, or whatever originally triggered your interest in learning this song. Be prepared to speak about it live. Practice your personal and song introductions out loud, tape yourself, and play it back. Have a short one ready for auditions and a longer one ready for performances. Adjust and redo as needed. Practice reading it to a friend and get feedback. You never know when you will be asked to speak about the song. Personal song connections are a beautiful way to connect with your audience.
5. *Dress as if it's a final performance,* no matter how small the audition or event. Take a picture of yourself fully dressed beforehand and self-evaluate as if you are a judge. Women are also expected to wear make-up with Mexican earrings and have their hair pulled back (see earlier in this Chapter: "Preparation for Mariachi Singers: Costumes and Make-up").
6. *Plan ahead for song video preparation.* Prepare online auditions via camera recording. Avoid the stress of setting up your camera too close to the day of your deadline or a live event by creating a permanent background space and camera weeks prior. Plan to record a test video first as well. If you need to occasionally move the camera, be sure and mark your permanent spots with tape to reset with ease or keep as is permanently. Use the following tips as a guide:
   - Do you have a professional and inviting "stage" backdrop behind you as you sing?
   - Upon listening to your test recording, does your voice shine through above the accompaniment? Remember, listeners want to hear your lyrics and voice.

FIGURE 4.11 Larrysa Ramos, Model and dancer in traditional Oaxacan dress. Courtesy of Larrysa Ramos.

- Do you move too much, or can you transmit the energy of the song by feeling it from your heart? Try being less physical and more centered from within.
- Set up lighting in front of you. How is the lighting around and behind your face? Does your face have light?
- Are you in a quiet space without interruptions?
- Does the camera picture your face and at least part of your costume down to your waist?
- Is the camera looking straight at you and not up at you? Be sure the camera is at the same level or above your face but never below you.

7. *Meditate through quiet breath preparation.* Take quiet time prior to event to set a vocal intention about performing your personal best. Visualize yourself at the event and running your song during this solo prep time. If you feel anxious, close your eyes, and practice some long, slow breaths for several minutes. If you regularly practice meditation or slow breaths it connects you to your breath and voice with ease. This practice is also useful just before a live audition or performance.

8. *Share the good news.* Consider ways to market your performances—invite all your friends and family, and post everywhere about all your events. Every presentation is a performance, even to your best friend, neighbor, mom, or your dog. When you practice in front of people you are sharing a beautiful tradition with your community. Music is meant to be shared. You can't share it if there is no one to share it with. Spread the good news. Your love for mariachi's expressive and upbeat energy will shine through. Learn to practice trusting your expression overall rather than how professional you sound or how well you sing every individual note. Let your inner childlike spirit be present and it will be a success.

CHAPTER 5

MARIACHI RHYTHMS AND CHOOSING SONG REPERTOIRE

FIGURE 5.1 *Tehuana* regional costume from Oaxaca, Mexico, featuring Larrysa Ramos. *Tehuanas* are from the region of Tehuantepec. Courtesy of Larrysa Ramos.

Overview of Mariachi Rhythmic Styles

It is no secret that rhythm is a strong part of what defines Latin American music, and Mexican ranchera music is no exception to this uniqueness. Ranchera rhythms offer great variety with thick textures that can interplay rhythmically between different mariachi instruments, not to mention strong rhythmic changes between different sections of songs. These rhythms are both fascinating and complex. The solo singer must sing over these rich expressions and at the same time be able to internalize how the instruments and voice work together. By learning the rhythmic styles and patterns in ranchera repertoire, singers will be able to immediately hear and identify the groove or groove choices for any given song. This groove is what keeps all the musicians united when performing.

In this chapter we introduce six of the most common ranchera styles used to accompany the solo voice. Each is based around a rhythmic pattern that has its own pattern, mood, tempo, and a special *sabor* or feel (see Glossary). All of the above factors interplay closely with the vocal melody and lyrics. Singers who strive for excellence in interpretation also deeply internalize both the rhythmic groove and vocal style. As singers learn to feel the rhythms and overall style, their own solo interpretations become more varied and interesting.

A good starting place for beginning singers or those new to ranchera and/or Latin American rhythms is the bolero ranchero in 4/4 meter, polka in 2/4 meter, and ranchera *valseada* or waltz in 3/4 meter[1] (see Chapter 2 section: "The Bolero in Mexico" or Chapter 6 section: "Songs" for a variety of song choices). Two traditional upbeat 2/4 polkas in ranchera style for beginning and intermediate singers are "Atotonilco," heard by female duo Hermanas Huerta in harmony on YouTube: https://youtu.be/-RyHnGzvdYM. The composer is Juan José Espinoza Guevara. He dedicated this song to Atotonilco El Alto, a city east of where he grew up in Guadalajara, Jalisco. Another polca is *Rancho alegre* by Felipe Bermejo (view on YouTube by Irma Vila (https://youtu.be/wY5KzFs1WiQ) or by Juanita Ulloa (https://youtu.be/6Xkv FmMqA0E)).

From a solo vocal point of view, the more complex rhythms of *son* and huapango (in 12/8 and 6/8 meters, respectively, see Glossary) are best added gradually to repertoire after mastering the aforementioned rhythms. While an experienced mariachi bravío solo singer can shake the concert hall with a great solo rendition of a *son*, the rhythms are challenging.[2] In the *son* "La Charreada," for example, expert singer Linda Ronstadt comments that she was always counting behind her back when recording "La Charreada" (The Rodeo) (see Chapter 8 section: "Linda Ronstadt"). She kept counting actively due to the complexity of the 12/8 rhythmic pattern against the voice. Professionals and advanced solo singers can often cover the wide range and variety of a son and steal the show. Listen to a more stylized solo vocal version of the son jaliscience "Guadalajara" by Mariachi de México on YouTube: https://youtu.be/efhiov_o8gI.

Many mariachi ensembles devote their time to perfecting the rhythmically complex *son* style instrumentally or opt for instrumentally based *sones* or *sones* that alternate instruments with choral group harmonies. One imperative standard is the *son* "La Negra." The ensemble can add great vocal power as a unit, and the power doubles in size when the instrumentalists have voice training. Besides feeling the groove rhythmically, the choral entrances of the famous *son* "La negra" require great rhythmic precision. When analyzing the vocal part against

---

[1] To study mariachi rhythms in more depth, consult Erick Mora, *La guitarra de Mariachi, Completa Aproximación Técnico-Estilística* (Secretaría de Cultura de Jalisco, 2016).

[2] Learn about the son jaliscience rhythmic variations (and others) with Fernando Briseño, director of the School of Mariachi in Guadalajara, Jalisco, in his YouTube video: https://youtu.be/_-GtOUZpo0o (in Spanish with English subtitles).

the 12/8 instrumental rhythmic groove, few ensembles do it perfectly (watch Mariachi sol de México performing "La negra" on YouTube: https://youtu.be/dDTgx61Mu-g).

Another example is the *son veracruzana* from Veracruz in Eastern Mexico near the Gulf of Mexico (*see* Glossary).[3] Similar to the bolero, this son is not originally from the mariachi tradition but is sometimes honored within it. Despite all *sones* having a thick textured 12/8 meter, each *son* has its own instrumental accompaniment pattern and overall feel. Listen to this *son veracruzana* medley featuring both instrumental solos and tight choral harmonies performed mariachi style by Mariachi Nuevo Tecatitlán: https://youtu.be/BzHM0E2g0p0 (see Chapter 5 sections: "Overview of Mariachi Rhythmic Styles" and "Six Basic Rhythms").

The huapango is a slower 6/8 rhythm that shows off the virtuosity of advanced and professional soloists. Huapangos usually have a wide vocal range and can be musically complex. The long, legato lines for each phrase require great breath control, with both short and sustained long falsete notes (see Chapter 2 section: "Miguel Aceves Mejía" and Chapter 3 section: "Falsete: To Bridge or to Break"). Listen to the modulations and drama in the story of a boy wanting to be a bullfighter, entitled "Huapango Torero" sung by Lola Beltrán on YouTube: https://youtu.be/KR3UcpAOYQI.

The corrido is a nineteenth-century Northern Mexico song style that narrates a story (see Chapter 2 sections: "Ranchera Rural Folk Origins" and "Pre-twentieth Century Vocal Roots"). It is idiomatic to Mexico and often patriotic although verses can also be improvised as is common in the famous corrido "La cucaracha". Contemporary corridos have even been written as narco-corrido stories. The more traditional corrido "Carabina 30-30" depicts the story of the Revolution, as sung by Francisco "El Charro" Avitia on YouTube: https://youtu.be/EO3YBFZ18F4.

The song *Cielito lindo* (well known for its *Ay, ay ay* chorus sung all over the world), is an example of a ranchera waltz, or *ranchera valseada*. The song was written just prior to the twentieth century in around 1882 by Quirino Mendoza y Cortés (c. 1859–1957).

Why Good Singers Listen to Rhythm

Song rhythms are at the heart of rancheras. Solo singers who do not yet play armonía, guitar, vihuela, or guitarrón can familiarize themselves by listening closely to the common two-bar repeating "clave" pattern in the instrumental parts. The repeating two-bar pattern of the guitarrón may be especially noticeable. This is the rhythmic groove.

The word "clave" is known for its use in Caribbean salsa music or Afro-Peruvian songs rather than in mariachi, but it is the same concept (see Glossary). Claves are the two wooden sticks that repeat a two-bar rhythmic pattern and unite Latin American or salsa ensembles. Clave patterns that lock in a two-bar repetitive rhythm are similar in mariachi instrumental parts. Singers in classical and commercial popular styles from outside of Latin America often tend to think from one bar to the next, not in two-bar patterns. The concept of clave helps singers feel the rhythm in a broader way and settle into the Latin American instrumental rhythmic groove. Singers should plan to match their vocal entrances and phrasing in two-bar groupings as well to match the instrumental phrasing.

Rhythmic expertise can also help singers form their own personal vocal style. Singers work best if in tandem with the instrumental groove. Once they are familiar with the rhythmic groove and style, they will learn songs more quickly and can proceed to create

---

[3] Veracruzan jaranas also have their own instrumentation from Veracruz, independent of the Western Mexico ranchera tradition.

their own personal phrasing by varying the melodic rhythm and/or notes. While the melody and rhythm should always resemble the original song and fit into the style, some notes, chords, and rhythms are often modified, reflecting the personal interpretation and style of the singer.

Some examples of originality that singers develop in through rhythmic and melodic phrasing can be appreciated through comparing two vocal versions of the same bolero "Cien años." Listen to this bolero, first sung by Pedro Infante (https://youtu.be/diSAz7xfpvE) and then Vicente Fernandez (https://youtu.be/REwG10CR0F4). Notice how Vicente often skips the downbeat rhythmically in his melodic interpretation. Both artists slow down the melodic rhythm a bit behind the regular beat, especially toward the end of each verse. Now, compare these two renditions to a third version of the same song, this time sung by Antonio Aguilar (https://youtu.be/KUSQPHZVVRQ). Note that Aguilar chooses more artistic rhythmic variety. Aguilar often sustains notes on vocal entrances, coming in prior to the typical entrance and syncopating the melodic line into something completely new and independent. None of these artists would be able to do this without constantly feeling the internal rhythmic heartbeat of the song as their home base.

The world of Mexican and Latin American folk rhythms is vast, and mariachi ensembles also play rhythms from other traditions. Singers who are successful are always listening to rhythms, identifying them, and studying the instrumental patterns to songs above and beyond their personal vocal melody and lyrics.

Rhythm Exercises and Learning Songs

Follow the steps below to become rhythmically savvy and develop more ease in learning your song melodies and lyrics:

1. *Learning a Song: Count!* Begin by clapping or tapping rhythms out loud, first for the melody, then for the harmonic rhythm flow. Imagine the melody in your head as you tap your hands or feet or pulse your body. Use a metronome or play an instrument to help you learn. Your goal is to never lose the beat while you sing the melody. Each time you get discouraged, listen to Grammy-winning singer Linda Ronstadt in a 2019 YouTube interview (https://youtu.be/YIeBfw85eWI), wishing she had learned a musical instrument, alluding to how easily María Callas dominated her musicianship and learned roles because she had been a concert pianist (see Chapter 8 section: "Linda Ronstadt"). It's often best to learn the melody verbatim inside and out first before trying to vary or create a personal version.

2. *Become Informed: Listen and Research.* Learn each style by listening to as many artist renditions as possible. Compare them to any sheet-music version you may have. Become familiar with each of mariachi's common rhythmic styles listed in this chapter. When practicing, sing the numbers of each beat with a metronome to keep a steady beat. Internalize the repetitive rhythm along with its mood. Be sure and listen to the "clave", that is, the repeating two-bar accompaniment patterns of each instrument. Memorize your entrances and keep them matched to the instrumental accompaniment. Learn to strum the rhythm on a guitar or vihuela. If you don't have an instrument you can imitate the strum on your chest or a table while practicing (see Glossary).

3. *Song Practice.* Keep listening and follow along with sheet music or transcribe the melody with correct rhythmic values. Read and listen to your favorite song version: once

CHAPTER 5: MARIACHI RHYTHMS AND CHOOSING SONG REPERTOIRE 135

for melody, once for rhythmic flow, and once to hear how often the harmonies change and where. Practice singing the melody on "la" without accompaniment first. Can you play the melody on a musical instrument? You may check your counting by practicing singing the melody to the steady beat of a metronome. Can you sing it with the metronome while you clap at the same time? When you know it well, try singing it against the harmony as you either play chords on an instrument or sing along with a music track.

4. *Tips for Memorizing Lyrics.* Recite song lyrics out loud at a slow pace as if you are reciting dramatic poetry but without a tempo. As you speak, focus on lengthening each vowel since vowels carry the sound with your breath (see Chapter 3). Read the lyrics a second time, this time with a very slow but regular metronome marking. Keep thinking about vowels as you recite. Repeat slightly faster but not up to tempo. When ready, recite a third time from memory if possible. Keep the lyric sheet nearby but avoid using it. Check your mistakes and recite a final time. As you memorize, gradually bring the song up to tempo, and you will feel your expression and the mood of the piece naturally take hold. Try writing out your lyrics by memory each night before you go to sleep. If you have memory blocks on certain sections, circle that section but keep writing. After copying out, check and recopy the missing sections.

5. *Interpretation Tip: Shape the melody and rhythm directly from the lyrics.* Both the lyrics and music separately offer interpretive ideas. In ranchera songs and boleros, rhythmic variation can be used to achieve this goal. Choose a strong word in each phrase to emphasize important ideas. You can vary by lengthening that word, change the rhythmic value assigned, or change the intonation very slightly if appropriate coming from a half step above or below and then resolving the note. Lengthening vowels within words helps emphasize certain syllables or the full word, while improving your diction. Try underlining the word or color code it. Adding commas for a gentle breath or dramatic pause, or consider using a fermata to hold out a note ("fermata"—see Glossary). Note how the melodic line takes on a unique shape when you do this line by line. They are perhaps the most important part of song interpretation. Keep checking in with the natural rhythmic flow of the lyrics and check the evolving flow against the groove. In 6/8 and 12/8 meters, the voice is often felt and/or written in 3/4 meter, while the accompaniment emphasizes dotted-quarter notes. There are many rhythmic choices for inflection or syncopation beyond the downbeats.

6. *Deeper Rhythmic Ideas for Interpretation.* In general, when building a unique interpretation for a ranchera song the rhythms of the melody itself is often varied more than the pitches themselves. On a deeper level, poetry and interpretive accents may purposely go against the rhythmic downbeats of the style if, for example, you want to describe a surprise or a conflict. By building a full rhythmic concept around the intent you want to express, some conflictive, some not, you will transmit your song interpretation from a deeper, and more meaningful place.

7. *Style.* Your interpretive style evolves gradually out of your feelings and knowledge of the song. Your technique will help you create breath flow with vowels, and this flow helps you lengthen any sound or word that you know is important while still feeling the breath support and flow. Your intonation will be strong if you get a solid breath; it will reveal your precision and evolving inner expression; your rhythmic training will allow you to syncopate when you feel it reflects the lyrics or music, for example a sob might be audible and briefly stop the sound. Sometimes a falsete note or a short higher note may be added at the end of a song depending on the style. If you practice composing

your own music melodies and lyrics, your personal style may emerge even more quickly. Some enjoy building ideas by writing a bit each day in a journal or on music paper.[4]

Some ranchera styles are easier to sing than others. Prowess can often depend on the natural voice production and training of the singer. For example, belters might find the gentleness of boleros challenging, although learning to regulate air flow in the studio can help for belt versus non-belt styles. Switching back and forth between the two genres with enough supported air pressure, but without pushing for the bravío belt production, actually improves both vocal styles (see Chapter 3 section: "Voice Production and Vocal Care: What Is Belt Voice"). This is the essence and importance of crossover vocal training.

Singers with classical training will find the wide vocal range and beauty of huapangos attractive but will be very new to rhythmic improvisation around the huapango song groove, or the aesthetic and technical aspects of falsete (see Chapter 3 section: "Falsete").

"Perform what you know-Practice what you don't know" is a useful slogan to keep in mind while developing a relationship with these rhythms and styles. Overall, it is best to perform rhythms one knows well first while working more gradually on the more challenging ones. Quality singers who can present a wide variety of song styles in concert are guaranteed to keep their audiences entertained.

Six Basic Rhythms

While ranchera singing today primarily leans on string ensembles for vocal accompaniment, the mariachi rhythmic examples depicted in Figure 5.2 offer both guitar chords and piano accompaniment. Music teachers may play these rhythms on any instrument. Almost all academic musicians have access to pianos for composing or teaching. Don't wait to practice until you find a mariachi ensemble. Bolero singers have always traditionally used piano, guitar, or orchestra since boleros first emerged in Cuba (see Chapter 2 section: "Bolero in Mexico"). The piano has also always played an important background role in ranchera composition. Many *charro* film composers of rancheras were classically trained and composed from the piano.

Choosing Mariachi Voice Repertoire

Mariachi ensemble directors tend to choose particular songs for beginning ensemble instrumentalists. Unfortunately, not all mariachi beginning classic songs are good singing choices for beginning singers; in fact, advanced vocal songs such as "Aires del Mayab" and "Malagueña salerosa" can harm young singers that have not found active breath support yet. While many young singers have an ear for the sound they want to produce, they may not have been shown how the breath supports the vowels with its resulting sound. Without vocal guidance, they tend to push the sound out, putting pressure on the larynx. This vocal pressure can keep the range limited, produce fatigue, and, over time, hurt voices. Younger singers also deserve special attention because of their smaller, developing vocal chords (see the "Graded Ranchera Song List" section in this chapter). In general, singers under age thirteen will perform consistently and in tune if the following is kept in mind:

- Sing shorter songs under three minutes. (Shorten the song or add a longer instrumental section.)
- Select songs with a small range of a fifth or sixth, and always less than an octave.

---

[4] Sheet music paper is available online for free download.

Common Mariachi Rhythms For Piano

FIGURE 5.2A Chart of mariachi rhythms, page 1 of 2.

- Choose songs with fewer linguistic and rhythmic complexities.
- Verify songs are age appropriate in topic.

Singers building song repertoire often seek unique songs that move them. Much can be learned from reviewing older recordings and song titles by prominent ranchera soloists. Figure 5.3 depicts an Orfeon 78 recording featuring ranchera singers, including Lola Beltrán. Although the recording has no date, Orfeon 78 recordings became extinct during the mid-1950s. The songs listed highlight female solo song choices of the day and can suggest wonderful titles for singers.

138 THE MARIACHI VOICE

FIGURE 5.2B Chart of mariachi rhythms, page 2.

One example is "Huapango torero" (Huapango of a Bullfighter), a dramatic and visual song with two complex modulations about a child matador who dies while fighting a bull. Those choosing this song should enjoy acting out the story and using the stage. This song is musically advanced, as it requires a high level of musicianship from both instrumentalists and the soloist. Many rancheras including this one, have become timeless classics. Lola Beltrán made this song part of her repertoire as imaged in Figure 5.3.

In summary, as a singer or director chooses songs, they will want to consider whether the vocal level is beginning, advanced beginning, intermediate, or advanced.

FIGURE 5.3 Mexican record cover from the 1950s to 1960s featuring Lola Beltrán and female vocalists with timeless classic rancheras. Orfeón was a popular record company run by Rogerio Lazcárraga, the son of Emilio Azcárraga, the founder of XEW Radio in Mexico City.

Graded Ranchera Song Lists: Beginner, Advanced Beginner, Intermediate, Advanced Vocal Levels

The list below of recommended songs is graded from easiest to most advanced in terms of vocal technique and ease. This list does not always correspond with the songs that are easy to play instrumentally, and a director will need to check and balance this issue delicately. The song list includes four levels of difficulty in alphabetical order with the rhythmic style listed after the title and occasional vocal comments. The list is not exhaustive as the ranchera canon is very deep (see Chapter 6).

Singers with limited vocal training will perform well from the beginner and advanced-beginner song levels. Intermediate and advanced songs require an octave or more range, switching in and out of belt voice, melodic jumps with breath support, linguistic issues, some acting skills, and falsete.

Mariachi directors will be tempted to use belt songs such as *Los Laureles* for beginning singers because of the small vocal range and easy instrumental accompaniment. Directors will protect students' voices if they refrain from assigning belt songs, unless the singer is already belting and cannot sing any other way. If the singer has an easy belt sound without tiring, this song is a wonderful choice. You can encourage them to continue exhaling air and take breaths often as they sing, which puts less pressure on the larynx. If the singer is going for a big chest-voice sound without much breath support, their voice will be undependable. They can become fatigued and bottom heavy, wondering why they have no upper notes. This problem can not only limit singers from finding their falsete range; it also keeps them from accessing gentle production to cross into soft bolero sounds.

Advanced singers will have achieved more breath support, range, and control. If a singer is able to switch between styles using the aforementioned technical elements, they are ready for advanced repertoire.

The songs below appear in alphabetical order. Songs marked with an asterisk are also available in sheet music and diction/translation formats within this book (see Chapter 6). Many boleros can also be found in commercial songbook publications.[5]

Those preparing a set of two to four songs or a concert will want to choose songs from different rhythmic styles within their vocal level to vary tempo and style. When building a concert the same applies. It is also helpful to feature instrumentalists as a contrast to the vocal songs. When building a concert set, check and vary mood changes from song to song by marking and separating songs with one of the three following adjectives: Hot, Warm, or Cold.

LEVEL 1: BEGINNING SOLO MARIACHI SONGS

Atotonilco (polca)
Bésame mucho (bolero)
Canta canta canta (polca)
Corrido de Chihuahua (ranchera valseada)
Cien años (bolero or ranchera valseada)
¡Canta mi son! (son jalisciense)*
De colores (ranchera valseada)
Devuélveme el corazón (bolero)
El herradero (polca)
El sol que tu eres (ranchera lenta)
Hay unos ojos (ranchera lenta)*
Hermoso cariño (ranchera valseada)
La barca de oro (ranchera valseada)*
La media vuelta (bolero)
La paloma (4/4 ballad)
La tequilera (polca)
Mucho corazón (bolero)
No volveré (ranchera valseada)
Perfidia (bolero)
Plegaria de una indita a la Virgencita morena (ranchera valseada)*
Por un amor (ranchera lenta)
Siempre hace frio (ranchera valseada)
Sin ti (bolero)
Solamente una vez (bolero)
Soy Mexicana (ranchera valseada or son)*
Tu, solo tu (ranchera valseada)
Vamos a la fiesta (children's polka)*
Y ándale (also known as Andale)

---

[5] Other online resources for Mexican songs include www.musicnotes.com, https://imslp.org/, www.classicalvocalrep.com, and www.sheetmusicplus.com.

CHAPTER 5: MARIACHI RHYTHMS AND CHOOSING SONG REPERTOIRE
141

LEVEL 2: ADVANCED-BEGINNER MARIACHI SONGS

Adoro (bolero)

Allá en el rancho grande (polca)

Camino de Guanajuato (ranchera valseada)

Canción Mixteca (ranchera valseada)

Cielito lindo (ranchera valseada; one falsete)*

Cielo rojo (huapango; one falsete)

Contigo aprendí (bolero)

Corazón de Chapulín (children's son; introduces falsete)*

El jinete (huapango; one falsete note at end)

El rey (ranchera lenta)

Guadalajara (son jaliscience; wide range; achievable with two advanced beginning
singers sharing the song)

Historia de un amor (bolero)

La cruz del olvido (bolero)

La mano de Dios (ranchera valseada)

La pajarera (ranchera valseada; builds female head voice)

Los laureles (ranchera valseada; small range but full belt)

Palomita de ojos negros (polca)

Rancho alegre (polca)*

Sabor a mi (bolero; watch vocal entrance)

Serenata Huasteca (son)

Usted (bolero)

Viva México (polca; belt in chorus)

Vivo añorando (ranchera valseada)*

LEVEL 3: INTERMEDIATE MARIACHI SONGS

Amor eterno (bolero; wide jump to chorus)

Ay Jalisco no te rajes (belted polca)

Carta a Eufemia (polca; acting and long lyrics; patter song)

Contigo aprendí (bolero)

Corrido de Higaditos (ranchera valseada or son; rhythmic changes)*

Cuando canto (huapango movida; uses belt in chorus)*

Cuatro caminos (ranchera valseada)

Deja que salga la luna (huapango; two falsete at end)

El mariachi (polca; son chorus)

La Adelita (corrido polca)*

La barca (bolero)

La charreada (son jalisciense; full belt)

Las mañanitas (multi-section ranchera lenta; valseada)*

María bonita (ranchera valseada)

Mil besos (bolero)

Mi ranchito (ranchera valseada; long lines)

Paloma negra (ranchera valseada; full belt)

Perdón (duet or solo; bolero)

Perfume de gardenia (bolero)

Quizás, quizás, quizás (bolero; wide jump to chorus)

Reloj (bolero; wide range in chorus)
Volver, volver (ranchera lenta)

LEVEL 4: ADVANCED MARIACHI SONGS (COMPETITION LEVEL)

Aires del Mayab (son; full belt in wide range)
La Borrachita (ranchera lenta)
Como quien pierde una estrella (bolero moruno; requires flexibility)
Crucifijo de piedra (huapango; falsete)*
Cu-cu-rru-cu-cu Paloma (huapango; falsete)
El aguacero (huapango)
El Pastor (huapango; full falsete, wide range)*
El aventurero (son jalisciense; acting and linguistic skills, multi-sectioned)
Estrellita (ranchera lenta; extensive range)
Flor de Azalea (bolero; extensive range)
Gorrioncillo de pecho amarillo (huapango)
Huapango torero (huapango; multi-sectioned with modulations, requires acting)
Júrame (bolero, ballad, or tango Argentino; extensive range)
La cigarra (huapango; many falsete notes)
La charreada (son; heavy belt, challenging counter-rhythms)
La golondrina (ranchera lenta; also called "Las golondrinas"; wide range)*
La negra noche (duet or solo; ranchera lenta; extensive range)*
Malagueña salerosa (huapango; full range and extensive falsete)

FIGURE 5.4 Three university female mariachi soloists from University of Texas at Rio Grande Valley. This program features a bachelor's degree in Mariachi and is run by Dr. Dahlia Guerrero, originally a classical pianist. Courtesy of Dr. Dahlia Guerra.

CHAPTER 5: MARIACHI RHYTHMS AND CHOOSING SONG REPERTOIRE 143

FIGURE 5.5 *La Chiapaneca* is the name for a singer or dancer in the traditional Chiapanecas regional costume from Chiapas in southwestern Mexico. Design by Marcia Cagandan.

Mexico lindo y querido (requires stamina, strong vocal legato and range, advanced musicianship; multi-section ranchera valseada-polka-huapango)
Noche de ronda (bolero; wide jump into chorus with sustained upper range)
Pelea de gallos (son; full constant belt throughout)
Por amor (ballad or bolero; wide range)
El Triste (ballad; wide range)

CHAPTER 6

SONGS, DICTION, LYRICS, IPA, AND TRANSLATIONS

Introduction to Mexican Spanish Lyric Diction

Diction isn't just about singing clearly, over-enunciating, breath supporting vowels, or moving one's mouth or jaw in a certain way. Singers with effective diction enjoy a better connection with their audience because the song is easily understood and, as a result, more quickly and deeply felt. It travels quickly to everyone's hearts.

Singers who think they don't need diction because they already know Spanish may unintentionally sacrifice depth in their technique-breath-to-vowel relationship-as well as opportunities to go deeper in their interpretation. Studying diction with its "secret" language of symbols called IPA (International Phonetic Alphabet) takes students on a journey well beyond the typical spelling of syllables into symbols.

Many levels of fluency exist in every language. This is quite noticeable if one compares first- to fourth-generation Hispanic families speaking Spanish within the United States, or fourth-generation Mexican Spanish speakers in the United States to speakers of their same age and regional location in Mexico. Take a moment to ask yourself some language-specific questions about yourself and your song as listed below.

- Do I speak or know Mexican Spanish from the region in Mexico where the lyrics and music of the song I'm singing are from? If not, do I know anyone from there I could talk to?
- Is my Spanish the same as the Spanish spoken when the song was first composed? Probably not.
- Am I aware of how to separate vowels from consonants when I sing and isolate and lengthen vowels? This study can lead to more effortless projection, clear words, and a richer sound.

For those seeking high-level authenticity in any language, diction studies are a must. Diction helps singers sound like native speakers even when they are not. Linda Ronstadt is a wonderful example of a world-class premiere Mexican American mariachi solo singer who recorded two Grammy-winning CDs in Spanish, despite not speaking fluent Spanish. Her interviews on Hispanic media were done with a Spanish interpreter (see Chapter 8 section: "Linda Ronstadt"). With IPA and/or diction practice most singers with a good ear will be able to proudly and authentically represent Mexico's music without needing to be fluent in Spanish. A few singers have extraordinary talent and naturally isolate vowels, but the vast majority take time to build diction skills.

When mariachi singers memorize song lyrics by ear from their favorite recording artist, they are assuming the diction of the artist is already precise. While listening is a very important stylistic aid, singers can unintentionally copy pronunciation mistakes. By

The Mariachi Voice. Dr. Juanita Ulloa, Oxford University Press. © Oxford University Press 2024. DOI: 10.1093/oso/9780190846244.003.0006

listening to recordings of different singers, comparing lyric sheets, studying the song's history, checking with directors, or even locating original sheet music or recording with lyrics, students can compare them and catch potential errors, thus avoiding passing them on unintentionally.

IPA (International Phonetic Alphabet) is a practical pronunciation learning tool for singers. It may be new to students in mariachi education and is sure to elevate every singer's connection to the Spanish language. IPA is a language of international symbols that allows singers, speakers, and linguists to isolate sounds so they may focus on the ones that carry real weight. Sound takes precedence over the spelling of words in IPA. IPA also facilitates switching smoothly between different languages. Singers learn to detect minute vocal differences in sound production between, say, English and Mexican Spanish or other languages, while also learning to modify their own personal vocal production habits.

IPA assists singers with sound authenticity when distinguishing between particular regions in Mexico/Southwestern United States. There are language details in English and Spanish that are sometimes unconsciously carried over and can be caught by studying and isolating sounds through IPA. IPA can also assist singers in distinguishing accents in any of the twenty-five or more countries where Spanish is spoken.[1] Writing out and reciting the Spanish IPA for songs out loud is also useful when leaning on ranchera rural or Indian dialectical accents. One example is the ranchera corrido, *La Chancla* (The Sandal) by Tomás Ponce Reyes:

"Amigos les contaré, una '*aición* particular . . . "

The literal meaning of these lyrics should literally translate as "Friends, let me tell you, a certain betrayal," meaning "Friends, let me tell you about a certain betrayal." The word "*aición*" is a contraction. It is short for the word *traición*, meaning betrayal. This contraction written by the lyricist alludes to pronunciation with a rural ranchera feel. Unfortunately, some singers change this word to "acción" meaning "action," without having researched the song. The IPA symbol for the first syllable should read [ai] and not [a]. This mistake changes both the pronunciation and the meaning of the lyrics. The correct word, *traición*, is a highly charged word that indicates the person singing is angry. Soloists can develop a strong character for their song based upon highly charged words such as these. Both IPA symbols and knowledge of Spanish pronunciation around contractions help build the natural rural ranchera Indian flavor of this important corrido.

The sound symbols for IPA are already found in most dictionaries. IPA symbols appear in parentheses after each word. This helps newcomers sound out new words. When using IPA symbols for sound, it gives singers a guide for pronouncing unknown words. They also free themselves of silent letters in any language. When focusing on symbols it is helpful to slow down the lyrics and sound the text out loud. A useful diction technique is to recite the lyrics dramatically as a poet might do with a focus on the rhythm of the words. Lyric recitation reading only the IPA symbols helps even more. Concentration on IPA symbols and diction elongates the vowels and gives singers technical tools to enhance meaning as they build their individual style.

Diction with IPA is a standard part of vocal study in universities. When the student doesn't see Spanish offered alongside Italian, English, French, and German diction, students can gently remind faculty that diction in Spanish is necessary, practical, and useful. Diction

---

[1] For those studying IPA wanting access to different types of Spanish, consult Nico Castel's book, *Lyric Spanish Diction*. He does not address Mexican Spanish. While YouTube has IPA tutorials, few, if any, specify Mexican Spanish.

classes in Spanish will continue to increase as many recognize that over twenty-five Spanish-speaking countries have strong vocal classical and folkloric traditions (see Chapter 1 section: "Growth of Mariachi Programs").

In this chapter IPA is introduced with individual mariachi words typically found in rancheras. A gentle way to start is to learn two symbols per week. All symbols can be accessed at the site https://ipa.typeit.org/. It is helpful to practice copying symbols often by hand, while also sounding them out. When students have pronunciation problem spots in songs, the corresponding IPA symbol can be added above problem words in the music or lyric sheet. This provides a visual to audio corrective aid for singers. For example, the IPA symbol [rr] above words that begin with a single letter r will remind students to always roll the single r when beginning a word, for example, RRápido ['rra pi dɔ]. One of many useful introductions to IPA on YouTube is: https://youtu.be/IH0J-d0pWhE.

Readers will note in this chapter that each song appears with sheet music as well as lyric sheets with IPA symbols and translations under the Spanish lyrics. Practice following the IPA symbols below the lyrics with a finger on each symbol while listening to a song or singing it to yourself, or just reciting the text. Next, isolate the lyrics and IPA symbols by copying them onto a separate page from the melody. Study, recite out loud, and record it. Have a native speaker friend or teacher provide feedback. Soon you will connect the vowels and melody more smoothly. This process is sure to help produce a crystal-clear message that magically projects without needing to over-enunciate the sounds physically or get into positions that interrupt natural air flow while singing.

MEXICAN SPANISH IS UNIQUE

Mexican Spanish has a singsong quality with forward placement as compared to accents in Castilian Spanish or those of South America. Native Spanish speakers from non-Mexican countries often comment that Mexican native speakers clearly pronounce all the letters in each word. By contrast, some South Americans and many Caribbean Spanish speakers often de-emphasize the middle and/or final -s at the end of words, as in the word *puesto*, which in English is the word for *job*. In Chile and Argentina, it would often sound as ['pwɛ: tɔ], while in Mexico it would be ['pwɛs tɔ].

Within Mexico's thirty-two states Spanish pronunciation can vary, although this may not be immediately noticeable to foreign speakers. Differences are especially notable, for example, when comparing accents from the Northern state of Chihuahua to the Indian influenced languages from Mexico's South and Southeastern states of Oaxaca, Chiapas, and Yucatán.

Nevertheless, Mexican Spanish lyric diction is somewhat standardized in rancheras. Mexico's western states have traditionally been the strongest linguistic mariachi center and general area of origin. Female Tex-Mex ranchera female duo singers also have their own unique sound with an extra twang as distinct from Western Mexico but equally authentic. Since the end of the Mexican Revolution in 1921, mariachi singers from around the country have also been centered in the more urban, cosmopolitan center of Mexico City, which can also change anyone's speech and accent. The international success of mariachi in film and radio in Mexico's urban capital between 1930 and 1970 served to amalgamate some regional accents into a more neutral Mexican urban accent with contrasting rural ones. If there are linguistic and cultural regional differences in any given song, accentuating one of these two emphases can add significant flavor to the interpretation.

Some linguistic features that are rather noticeable in Mexican Spanish are rancheras sung in various Northern Mexican states. Speakers from Chihuahua often pronounce the name of their state beginning with a sh sound [ʃ], while those from Mexico City pronounce the same word beginning with a harder ch sound [t͡ʃ]. Rancheras with corrido, polca, or waltz rhythms from Northern Mexico may sound more authentic if the softer *sh* sound is used, especially if the lyricist, theme, or composer is from the Northern Mexico border states of Sonora, Chihuahua, Tamaulipas, Coahuila, or Nuevo León (sometimes also Sinaloa and Durango). Nasalization is also emphasized in many North Mexican corridos when accompanied as mariachi rancheras. One Northern Mexico song example is *El Sinaloense* (12/8 son) written by Sinaloan composer Salvador Briseño in 1944, here on YouTube in a mariachi version (note the darker vowels when with mariachi) https://youtu.be/6h50WB0a3ms as compared to a northern Mexico banda arrangement https://youtu.be/TO-ZGNFwJ3o. For many mariachi songs, however, neutral Mexican Spanish is appropriate.

It is not uncommon for Mexican corridos from Northern states to also feature a melodic downward slide of a 3rd or 2nd interval at the end of certain music phrases, especially on the last note of any given line or verse. One example on YouTube is a recording of Vicente Fernández singing *Caballo bayo* (Bay Horse), a corrido in 3/4 ranchera valseada rhythm (see Glossary) https://youtu.be/ko3-z2A1xV8. Note the downward movement of each line, especially the phrase endings. The vowel is stretched as the phrase is lengthened. It should be re-phonated at the bottom note while fully supported by the breath to sound stylistically authentic. In essence, the vowel should be sung twice to carry forth the style and diction. This stylistic trait is similar to Mexican speech when, at the ends of phrases one often hears a strong upward or downward singsong lilt. For example, in the sentence below, the phrase ends with intonation tilting upward in a question with the word *no*, simply looking for agreement whether needed or not. In the English translation, it may also go up slightly but with much less lilt and tonal variation, and often stays quite neutral.

Vas a la casa, ¿no?   You're going home, right?   [ˈʙa sa la ˈka sa nɔ]

Mexican Spanish also avoids guttural sounds as compared to certain Spanish-speaking countries. As an example, the word for ham in Spanish is *jamón*. In Mexican Spanish, the j becomes an h [haˈmɔn]. A Spaniard speaking Castilian Spanish from Spain would pronounce the same word using a heavier h, with a guttural sound made in the throat. In IPA, we use the symbol [x] for the Castilian Spanish letter h, reflecting the throat sound [xaˈmɔn]. For those who have learned to sing Castilian Spanish or are familiar with Spanish zarzuela, a nationalistic operetta style from Spain (see Glossary), note that Mexican Spanish also does not imitate the Castilian th sound [θ] for the letter z. In neutral Mexican Spanish, both the letters s and z are pronounced as a hard s; hence, the English word zebra [ˈzi bra] begins in Spanish with a hard s sound [ˈsɛ bra]. In Castilian Spanish it would be pronounced [ˈθ bra].

Depicted below are ten pronunciation tips to perfect Mexican Spanish pronunciation. Sound out the words slowly, tape yourself and listen, or work with a partner. The IPA symbols appear below in brackets.

148 THE MARIACHI VOICE

Pronunciation Tips for Mexican Spanish

1. There are only five vowel sounds in Spanish: [a ɛ i ɔ u].
There is only one way to say each of these five vowels. This makes Spanish an easy language to learn! The five Spanish vowels are called pure vowels. Vowels with one sound per syllable are called pure vowels. English, by contrast, has over fourteen vowel sounds with many double sounds within one vowel sound, making it much more complicated. Double vowel sounds within one syllable are called diphthongs.

For those familiar with Italian, Spanish is much easier than Italian because the letters e and o are almost always pronounced as open vowels. In Italian, these two vowels can vary in pronunciation. For Spanish pronunciation we call these two vowels open vowels because when pronouncing them, one can feel the back of the throat open.

The open letter e in Spanish is written like this in IPA: [ɛ]. In English, it sounds like the e vowel in the words "set" or "head."

The open letter o in Spanish is written like this in IPA: [ɔ]. In English, it sounds like the o vowel in the first syllable of the word for the car "Volvo." The second o vowel sounds slightly different, as the back of the throat is closed.

Practice saying the following words aloud, paying attention to the open e and open o:

Volver, Habanera, Solamente una vez, Si nos dejan, Los Laureles, Morena, Volver, El Pastor, México

2. There are two r sounds, single or double rr.
The single r symbol for IPA is [r] and the double rr sound has either of two symbols: [ʀ] or [rr].

a. Single R is flipped and generally appears within the word, for example, tarántula, erupto.
b. Double R is rolled, for example, arroz, cigarro.
c. Single R beginning a word is also rolled, for example, radio, rancho, rabia.

Recite this popular tongue twister several times per day to distinguish your single and double rr:

R con R cigarro	[r kɔn r siˈga rrɔ]
R con R carril	[r kɔn r kaˈrril]
Rápido corren los carros	[ˈrra pi dɔ ˈkɔ rrɛn lɔsˈka rrɔs]
Bajo el ferrocarril.[2]	[ˈba hɔ ɛl fɛ rrɔ kaˈrril]

3. ñ=[ɲ] España, señor, jalapeño, año
4. All consonants are softer than English as in the following examples:

"d" softens to the IPA symbol [ð], for example, dedo [ˈdɛ ðɔ]

"b" softens to the IPA symbol [β], for example, baboso [baˈβɔ sɔ]

llevar [ʎɛ ˈβɑr] llave [ˈʎɑ βɛ]

5. The letter h is silent in Spanish.

hamburger [am burˈgɛ sa]

---

[2] This tongue twister is recorded as a song and can be downloaded from the author's *Canta conmigo* volume 1 CD (Sing With Me—Bilingual Songs for Children).

CHAPTER 6: SONGS, DICTION, LYRICS, IPA, AND TRANSLATIONS   149

6. The Spanish letter j is often pronounced like an h in English.
The letter h is actually an IPA symbol for the sound of rushing air. Some Mexican words with influence from various ethnic Indian language groups spell words with the letter x with various pronunciations, one of which can be with an h. One example is the word Oaxaca [ɔa'ha ka], one of Mexico's thirty-two states. Note that in the examples depicted below, the colon is used in IPA to indicate when one wishes to extend a vowel sound.

| Jalisco [ha'lis kɔ] | jalapeño [ha la'pɛ ɲɔ] | jamón [ha'mɔn] |
| jarra de jamaica | ['har ra dɛ ha'ma:i ka] | México ['mɛ hi kɔ] |

7. The letter l is forward.
The letter l has a forward placement with the tip of the tongue touching behind the front teeth or the gums just above it. By comparison, the consonant l in English is made focusing on the middle to back of the tongue.

El libro [ɛl 'li brɔ]   la langosta [la lan'gɔs ta]

8. In Mexican Spanish, the double "ll" sounds like "Y" =[ʎ].

| tortilla [tɔr'ti ʎa] | calle ['ka ʎɛ] |
| llama ['ʎa ma] | caballo [ka'ba ʎɔ] |

Note that in other countries such as Argentina or Uruguay, the same double ll might have another accent with a heavier sound [ʒ]. The word calle would sound like ['ka ʒɛ].

9. Elision marks are often used in Spanish to connect words that end in vowels when the next word also begins with a vowel. These are called diphthongs.
Listen extra closely for this. Sound out the vowels slowly and fully, carefully eliding from the end of one word to the beginning of the next. Be sure and give each vowel its full sound. An elision appears below between word one and word two. Note that in English two vowel sounds are also often used together, but instead of using two symbols, there is only one letter, for example, the letter I has two vowel sounds: I=[ai]. In both languages, two vowel sounds within one note or syllable is called a diphthong.

Ando allá   (I'm over there)   ['an dɔ̯a'ʎa]

10. When a syllable has an accent be sure and stress that syllable.

Corazón   (Heart)   [kɔ ra'sɔn]

If you enjoy sounding out IPA you will discover there are many more symbols to refine your pronunciation. You are sure to hear improvements in your singing!

Tips on Memorizing Lyrics

- Learn the music and lyrics separately first, then practice them together. Can you recite the lyrics as a poem in rhythm with your intended intonation? Can you recite and perform each separately?
- Write out the lyrics each morning and each evening until you have memorized them. Be sure to review and write them out again just before a performance. Leave blank each word or line that escapes you as you first copy out the lyrics. Then, check it, fill in, and recopy the lyrics.

150 THE MARIACHI VOICE

- Color-code your song according to different sections or the mood of the song. Do you have specific colors for different moods? Choose one color for the verses, one for the chorus, and another for the bridge if there is one. Think of the colors or mood as you practice reciting the lyrics.
- Recite the lyrics as a poet would recite a poem in front of an audience. If you lengthen each vowel, the sound carries more easily. Pretend you are a Latin American newscaster about to say what some like to call the longest word in the world: "GOOOOOL!"
- Look for rhymes and patterns in the lyrics as memory guides. Think also of the natural progression of the story when memorizing verse to verse.
- Do you have a special way you memorize lyrics?

Diction Lessons 1–5

DICTION LESSON 1: DRAW YOUR OWN IPA LETTERS AND SHORT WORDS

Practice copying the five Spanish vowel sounds using IPA [ɑ ɛ i ɔ u].

Spanish Term	IPA
A	ɑ
E	ɛ
I	i
O	ɔ
U	u

DICTION LESSON 2: IPA SHORT MARIACHI WORDS IN SPANISH

1. Practice studying and copying out IPA sounds for the short words below.
2. Remember to always use brackets for each word, phrase, or line of lyrics. Sound it out loud as you write.
3. Leave a space between each syllable.
4. Use an apostrophe before the stressed syllable in each word. Note that this is not necessary for short words of only one syllable.
5. Visit https://ipa.typeit.org/ and click "Full IPA" to learn more symbols or type them out.

Spanish Term	IPA	English Translation
Amor	[aˈmɔr]	Love
Hola	[ˈɔ la]	Hi
Canta	[ˈkan ta]	Sing
Jalapeño	[ha laˈpɛ ɲɔ]	Jalapeño pepper

CHAPTER 6: SONGS, DICTION, LYRICS, IPA, AND TRANSLATIONS 151

El Pastor	[ɛl pasˈtɔr]	The Shepherd
El Rey	[ɛl rrɛi]	The King
Ay Jalisco	[aːi haˈlis kɔ]	Oh, Jalisco
México	[ˈmɛ hi kɔ]	Mexico
Morena	[mɔˈrɛ na]	Dark skinned beloved
Toro	[ˈtɔ rɔ]	Bull

DICTION LESSON 3: IPA MARIACHI WORDS IN SPANISH

1. Read the words below out loud in Spanish. Study the meaning in the translation column.
2. Read the IPA slowly out loud. Copy one word at a time in IPA. Sound it out.
3. Look up new symbols, noting the following: consonants such as b, v, and d need to be softened in Spanish, especially within a word, and the ch sound in IPA is [tʃ].
4. Use the colon symbol when you hear a sound (usually a vowel) that needs to be lengthened.
5. Notice that many phrases below are the titles of standard rancheras or boleros from Mexico.
6. Note that punctuation marks are never used in IPA.
7. As homework, write out the words in Spanish, and copy them out in IPA looking only at the English translation. Tip: work on five words a day until you have the IPA memorized. Just fifteen minutes a day will make you an expert, and your singing is sure to improve!

Spanish Term	IPA	English Translation
Corazón	[kɔ rɑ ˈsɔn]	Heart
Día	[diːa]	Day
Los Laureles	[lɔs laːuˈrɛ lɛs]	The Laurels
Norte	[ˈnɔr tɛ]	North
Rancho	[ˈʀaːn tʃɔ]	Ranch
Si nos dejan	[si nɔsˈdɛ han]	If they let us
Torero	[tɔ ˈrɛ rɔ]	Bullfighter
¡Viva!	[ˈβi βa]	Live
Volver	[βɔl ˈβɛr]	Return

DICTION LESSON 4: IMPORTANT MARIACHI PHRASES AND SONG TITLES

1. Read the words out loud in Spanish and study translations.
2. Read the IPA slowly out loud. Write out one word at a time in IPA. Then sound it out.

THE MARIACHI VOICE

3. As homework, write out the words in Spanish, and copy them out in IPA looking only at the English translation. Work on five words a day until you have the IPA memorized. Just fifteen minutes a day will make you an expert, and your singing is sure to improve!

Spanish Term	IPA	English Translation
Caballo bayo	[kɑˈβɑ ʎɔ ˈbɑ ʎɔ]	Bay Horse
Canta mi son	[ˈkɑn tɑ mi sɔn]	Sing my Song
Cielito lindo	[sjɛˈli t ɔ ˈlin ðɔ]	Beautiful Darling
Hay unos ojos	[ˈɑi u nɔsˈɔ hɔs]	There are Some Eyes
Las Mañanitas	[las ma ɲaˈni tas]	The Morning Serenade
		(Mexican Birthday Song)
Mi felicidad	[mi fɛ li siˈ ða ð]	My Happiness
Norteña	[nɔr ˈtɛ ɲa]	Northern Mexican Woman
Norteño	[nɔr ˈtɛ ɲɔ]	Northern Mexican Man
Soy Mexicana	[sɔi mɛ hiˈkɑ nɑ]	I'm a Mexican Woman
¡Viva México!	[ˈβi βaˈmɛ hi kɔ]	Long live Mexico!

DICTION LESSON 5: MARIACHI LONGER SONG TITLES

1. Read the words out loud in Spanish, and study translations.
2. Read the IPA slowly out loud. Write out one word at a time in IPA, then sound it out.
3. Notice that some titles have an elision mark connecting the vowels from the end of one word to the beginning of another.
4. As homework, write out the words in Spanish, and copy them out in IPA looking only at the English translation. Work on five words a day until you have the IPA memorized. Just fifteen minutes a day will make you an expert, and your singing is sure to improve!

Spanish Term	IPA	English Translation
¡Ay Jalisco no te rajes!	[aːi haˈlisˈkɔ nɔ teˈrra hɛs]	Oh, Jalisco, don't give up!
Corazón de Chapúlin	[kɔ raˈsɔn ðɛ t͡ʃa puˈlin]	Grasshopper's Heart
Malagueña Salerosa	[ma la ˈɣɛ ɲa sa lɛ ˈrɔ sa]	Bewitching Women from Málaga
Piedras del campo	[ˈpjɛ ðras d̪ɛlˈkɑm pɔ]	Stones from the Country Field
Mexico lindo y querido	[ˈmɛ hi kɔˈlin d ɔI kɛˈri ðɔ]	Beautiful, Beloved Mexico
Mi ranchito	[mi ʀan ˈt͡ʃi tɔ]	My Little Ranch
Rancho alegre	[ˈʀaːn t͡ʃaˈlɛ ɣrɛ]	Happy Ranch
Siempre hace frío	[ˈsjɛːm prɛ ˈa sɛˈfri ɔ]	It's Always Cold
Solamente una vez	[sɔ laˈmɛn tɛˈu na βɛs]	Only Once

Lessons: Song Studies; History, Lyrics, and Translations, Guide; Acting; Performing Artist; Composer Studies

SONG STUDIES: HISTORY

Songs can have amazing histories. For example, few know that when Ema Elena Valdelamar wrote the bolero "Mucho corazón" she was only nineteen years old and upset with her older boyfriend because he had hired a detective to investigate everything about her and her family, including her previous boyfriends.[3] This information gives a specific context and new emotional depth to the lyrics, for example: "Di si encontraste en mi pasado una razón para olvidarme o para quererme?" [Tell me if you found something in my past that gives you a reason to forget me or to love me?].

Another example of illuminating song-study research is the story behind the ranchera farewell song "Las golondrinas" or "La golondrina" (The Swallow). The lyrics from Mexico's immortal song were taken from an Arab poem written by King Aben Humeya (1545–1569). The music was composed by Mexican musician and doctor Narciso Serradell (1843–1910) who found the Arab poem while forced to live in exile in France during the French invasion of Mexico (1862-1867). Serradell titled the song "La golondrina" in the singular, although publications exist with the title listed in both singular and plural forms. Finding out that the composer was forced to live in exile gives singers a fascinating clue on the specific history and original intent in the composer's mind.[4] This context often provides creative inspiration to singers when building possible interpretations for any given song.

Students often build deep relationships with songs when they research them first. Unfortunately, online sites often mistakenly list singers alongside song titles as if they were the songwriter. The composer frequently gets overlooked. Research for rancheras can be best conducted online if in both English and Spanish.[5] Singers can also analyze the vocal delivery of different artists all singing the same song. Teachers can then elicit students to ponder, compare, and try out their own vocal style ideas, interpretation, and sometimes improvisation. Studies also help students prepare more interesting and informative short song introductions for future performances. Specific examples and potential topics are provided in lessons (see further ahead in this chapter).

When singers choose more than one song to be studied, it is helpful if they compare and contrast songs from each of the three mariachi periods: pre-1950 *Siglo de oro* classics, after 1960 with the advent of new songs by singer-songwriter style of José Alfredo Jiménez, or current contemporary commercial favorites (see Chapter 5, Chapter 2 sections: "Media Expansion and Music Nationalism: *Ranchera* Singers become celebrities" until "Bravío *Ranchera* Singing-Lucha Reyes," and Resources for helpful links).

---

[3] Bolero songwriter Ema Elena Valdelamar and her son, DaríoValadelamar, have often shared this story personally with the author since their friendship began around 2002. Ms. Valdelamar passed on in 2012.

[4] https://frontera.library.ucla.edu/blog/2019/11/la-golondrina-song-soars-across-centuries-and-crosses-cultures.

[5] Many Mexican songs and composers are listed through Sociedad de autores y compositores de México (SACM) at https://www.sacm.org.mx/. This organization for songwriters is Mexico's equivalent to ASCAP and BMI in the United States. Google in Spanish also contains more resources for rancheras, including https://www.google.com.mx/.

Song Studies: Lyrics and Translations

Many Spanish-language heritage learners in the United States enjoy ranchera songs as the their main connection to Mexico. Some say rancheras are most appreciated from outside Mexico when one longs nostalgically for closeness to one's homeland. Singers often gain the confidence to communicate more fearlessly in Spanish or enjoy their bilingualism through explorations linking language, diction, and singing technique. Singing intonation added to lyrics often improves linguistic dexterity and memorization. Below are more song study topics that encourage singers to grow linguistically.

- *Write out your song translation.* Choose a favorite ranchera song. By hand, write out a literal translation from Spanish into English. Study the literal translation and rewrite it into a separate idiomatic or poetic translation (see Chapter 6 section: "Songs for Lyric Translation Samples").
- *Make a list and glossary of Mariachi terms.* Mariachi songs also have specialized terminology around topics such as horses, lost love, bullfighting, Mexican slang, and more. Language study is especially encouraged as an aid to newcomers to Spanish and will be as meaningful to Hispanic heritage learners as to fully bilingual singers. Collect a glossary of these words and reference which songs they come from. Can you also sound them out slowly and write them out using International Phonetic Alphabet (IPA) symbols (see Chapter 6)?[6]
- *Write out IPA words and full songs.* Singers learning the International Phonetic alphabet (IPA) can improve their sound and technique (see Chapter 6). If new to IPA, start with single ranchera word exercises in Chapter 6. Consult full songs in the same chapter and copy out the IPA already listed under the song lyrics on the translation sheet. Recite it aloud and slowly sound it out, always taking care to lengthen the vowels.

Language and song study are especially helpful for newcomers to Spanish. They are also meaningful to Hispanic heritage learners and fully bilingual singers. Language is an essential part of any song study, as lyric pronunciation affects vocal technique, diction, and ultimately the message.

CHECKLIST FOR SONG, LYRICS, AND TRANSLATION STUDIES

1. Can you translate the song you chose out loud from Spanish to English without looking at the English translation in this book? This is called a literal translation. To prepare, write out the literal translation on a notepad and begin a glossary list of words with their translation you think might come up often in ranchera music.
2. After you translate the song literally, can you speak each line of music out loud in English and reshape the individual words into poetic phrases that make better sense? This is called an idiomatic translation and is listed below the literal translation in italics.

---

[6] Hint: Common Mariachi song terminology with exercises is listed in Chapter 6 section: "International Phonetic Alphabet (IPA)."

CHAPTER 6: SONGS, DICTION, LYRICS, IPA, AND TRANSLATIONS 155

3. Describe the song content in one or two paragraph(s).
   What is the story or main point? Reduce your paragraph down to one or two sentences. Save the description on an index card and write out in both Spanish and English. This is your performance song introduction. Collect your song introductions in an index card box. You will always sound professional and well prepared.

5. Who are the characters in this song? How many are there? Is there a person narrating or is it in first person?

6. How might you interpret this song? Does it require great movement or quiet internal reflection? Your answer will directly tell you how much to move on stage during your performance.

7. What is the overall mood, rhythmic style, and tempo of the song? What do these musical factors tell you about your interpretation?

8. Listen to several recorded versions of this song if available. Identify the similarities and differences in interpretation between artists. Write down special features you enjoyed and try them out. Compare melodic and rhythmic changes, if any. Do they create a new, original ending?

ADVANCED FULL SONG STUDY PROJECT

Choose a song. Study and write out the following: Translations of lyrics (both literal and poetic similar to example sin songs below), IPA, song history and evolution of the song, lyric analysis, comparison of various artist interpretations performing the same song, choreography, and/or a list of artistic presentations of the song with commentary.

Some songs with a rich history and strong lyric message to get started are: "Ay Jalisco no te rajes," "El Pastor," "Media Vuelta," "Deja que salga la luna," "Mucho Corazón," "Estrellita," "Amorcito corazón," "La Golondrina," and "La Adelita."

Acting Study

If you love movement and interpretation, choose a song with visuals, and write out stage movement for each verse and chorus. Create a layout using the letters X for your position and arrows to indicate where you might be walking during different sections of the song. Write down where you will detach the microphone from the stand (if at all) and, if also an instrumentalist, where you will leave your instrument before singing. Begin your acting study choosing a song that has strong visual images or development. The following song examples have active visual messages: "El Mayor de los Dorados," "Huapango Torero," "Pelea de Gallo" [Fiesta de San Marcos], "La Adelita," or "Crucifijo de Piedra."

Performing Artist Study

Learn about the singers! You may study them biographically first, and then focus on the style and interpretation of one singer or a vocal duo.

- How often do they vary the standard melody or rhythm? Is their rhythmic syncopation only before the beat or also after the beat?
- Did they premiere a particular song, write the song themselves, or do they sing standard cover songs?

- Do they have other stylistic traits such as a particular sound that make them instantly recognizable? Does it remind you of anyone?
- What kinds of songs does the artist tend to choose and why do you believe they chose them? Are they stylistically similar or varied?
- What is their training and background? Did they have a support network?
- Listen to several songs by the artist on YouTube. Identify the similarities and differences in interpretation between songs. Write down special features you enjoyed and try them out in your singing.
- Compare any melodic changes the singer made to the main melody, if any.
- Do they create a new, original ending? How might you vary your ending?

Some artist choices to get you started include: Lucha Villa, leading female singer of *charro* musicals; Jorge Negrete; Lola Beltrán; Pedro Infante; and female mariachi singers or female duo singers such as Lucha Reyes, Sofía Álvarez, María Elena Sandoval, Lola Flores, Irma Vila, Hermanas Padilla, Hermanas Aguilar, Flore Silvestre, or operatic contralto Josefina "Cha Cha" Aguilar, who recorded rancheras and sang in the ranchera movie *Fantasía ranchera* (see Chapter 2 section: "Mariachi Singers and Their Songs—Crossover Singing in Rancheras and Opera"). Some may prefer studying contemporary singers such as Vicente and Alejandro Fernandez, Aída Cuevas, Alberto Aguilar, Linda Ronstadt, Flor de Toloache, Guadalupe Pineda, Aida Cuevas, Eugenia León, or solo singer Esteban Sandoval, originally from Mariachi Vargas. An advanced project might be a comparative style and life study of female or male vocalists in mariachi from a hundred years ago to those singing today.

Composer Study

As previously mentioned, the internet often makes mistakes and overlooks ranchera songwriters and composers when listing titles. They want you to recognize and purchase the song, believing you will recognize the artist first. Much can be learned about songs, songwriting, arranging, and producing by studying song composers.

Review this sample composer list as possible topics: Manuel Esperón, Ignacio "Tata" Nacho, Cuates Castilla, Hermanos Záizar, Ruben Fuentes, Bolero composers such as María Grever, Consuelo Velásquez, and Ema Elena Valdelamar, Agustín Lara, or José Alfredo Jiménez. Compile a song list and analyze the lyrics and song themes. If you are passionate about arranging or songwriting, you might research and even interview a composer online or contact their families directly. Families are often eager to honor the talents of the musicians in their families.

Ranchera Songs with IPA, Poetic, and Literal Translations

Note that each song is published two contrasting keys. The two keys are listed after the English translation in parenthesis.

1. "La Adelita" [Cute Adele], Traditional (C, F)
2. "La barca de oro" [The Golden Ship], Traditional (D, G)

CHAPTER 6: SONGS, DICTION, LYRICS, IPA, AND TRANSLATIONS 157

FIGURE 6.1 Singer Jizelle Rodriguez, winner of Mariachi Extravaganza solo voice competition led by Cynthia Muñoz in San Antonio, Texas. Photograph by Javier Vela.

3. "Cancion mixteca" [Mixteca Song], López Alavéz (A, D)
4. "¡Canta mi son!" [Sing my Song!], Juanita Ulloa (C, G)
5. "Cielito lindo" [Beautiful Darling], Quirino y Mendoza (F, C)
6. "Como México no hay dos" [There's Nothing Better Than Mexico], Juanita Ulloa (C, F)
7. "Corazón de Chapulín" [A Grasshopper's Heart], Juan Ortíz (A, D)
8. "Cuando canto" [When I Sing], Juanita Ulloa (Em, Am)
9. "El Corrido de Higaditos" [Ballad of Higaditos], Antonio Gomezanda (C, A)
10. "El Pastor" [The Shepherd], Los Cuates Castilla (Dm, Am)
11. "Hay unos ojos" [There are Eyes], Traditional (A, D)
12. "Las Gaviotas" [The Seagulls], Traditional (G, C)
13. "La Golondrina" [The Swallow], Narciso Serradell (Eb, Bb)
14. "La negra noche" [The Dark Night], Emilio Uranga (C, F)
15. "Las Mañanitas" [Little Morning Song], Traditional—Mexican Birthday Song (D, A)
16. "Plegaria de una indita morena a la virgencita Morena" [Prayer from an Indian Woman to the Dark-Skinned Virgin], Antonio Gomezanda (C, F)
17. "Por un amor" [For a Love], Gilberto Parra (F, C)
18. "Rancho alegre" [Happy Ranch], Traditional (A, C)
19. "Soy Mexicana" [I'm a Mexican Woman], Antonio Gomezanda (D, Bb)
20. "Vivo añorando" [I Live Longing], Juanita Ulloa (A, D)

158 THE MARIACHI VOICE

1. LA ADELITA [CUTE ADELE]

Traditional Mexican Song

CHAPTER 6: SONGS, DICTION, LYRICS, IPA, AND TRANSLATIONS 159

This lively polka is a corrido, or historical ballad. La Adelita is one of Mexico's most popular Mexican Revolutionary corridos.

CHAPTER 6: SONGS, DICTION, LYRICS, IPA, AND TRANSLATIONS 161

This lively polka is a corrido, or historical ballad. La Adelita is one of Mexico's most popular Mexican Revolutionary corridos.

En lo alto de la abrupta serranía

[ɛn lɔ ˈal tɔ dɛ la̯a ˈβɾup ta sɛ rraˈni: a]

In the high abrupt mountains

In the jagged mountainous landscape (of Mexico)

Acampado se encontraba un regimiento

[a kamˈpa ðɔ sɛ̯ɛn cɔnˈtra ba̯un rɛ hiˈmjɛn tɔ]

Camped was a regiment

A regiment was camped.

Y una moza que valiente los seguía

[i̯un aˈmɔ sa kɛ ʙaˈljɛn tɛ lɔs sɛˈgi:a]

And a woman who was brave followed them

And a brave and courageous woman was with them

Locamente enamorada de un sargento

[lɔ kaˈmɛn tɛ̯ɛn a mɔˈɾa da dɛ un sarˈhɛn tɔ]

Wildly in love with a sergeant

Wildly in love with a sergeant.

Popular entre la tropa era Adelita,

[pɔ puˈlarˈɛn tɾɛ laˈtrɔ pa̯ɛɾa̯að ɛˈli ta]

Popular within the troops was Adelita

Adelita was a favorite of the troops.

La mujer que el sargento idolatraba

[la muˈhɛr kɛ̯ɛl sarˈhɛn tɔ̯ið la̯ˈtra βa]

The woman who the sergeant adored

And the sergeant adored her.

Porque más de inteligente era valiente

[ˈpɔr kɛ mas ðɛ̯in tɛ liˈhɛn tɛ̯ɛra ʙaˈljɛn tɛ]

Because more than intelligent she was brave

Besides being smart, she was courageous.

Que hasta el mismo coronel la respetaba

[kɛ̯as ta ɛl ˈmis mɔ kɔ rɔˈnɛl la rɛs peˈta βa]

That even the coronel respected her

Even the colonel respected her.

Y se oía que decía aquel que tanto la quería—

[i sɛ̯ɔj:a kɛ dɛsˈi:a aˈkɛl kɛ ˈta:n tɔ la kɛˈɾi:a]

And one heard that the one said who so much loved her

And one would hear the colonel who loved her so much, tell everyone—

CHAPTER 6: SONGS, DICTION, LYRICS, IPA, AND TRANSLATIONS 163

Y si Adelita se fuera con otro

[i si a̯ ðɛˈli ta sɛ fwɛ ra kɔnˈɔt ɾɔ]

And if Adelita would leave with another

If Adelita left him for another

La seguiría por tierra y por mar

[la sɛ ɡiˈɾiːa pɔr ˈtjɛ rra i pɔr mar]

He would follow her by land and by sea

He would follow her over land and sea.

Si es por mar en un buque de guerra

[si̯ɛs pɔr mar ɛn un ˈʙu kɛ dɛ ˈɡe rra]

If by sea in a warship

If by sea, in a warship

Si es por tierra en un tren "melitar,"

[si̯ɛs pɔrˈtjɛ rra̯ ɛn un trɛn mɛ liˈtar]

If by land in a military train

If by land in a military train.

Y si Adelita quisiera ser mi novia

[i si̯a ðɛˈli ta kiˈsjɛ ɾa sɛr miˈnɔβ ia]

And if Adelita would like to be my girlfriend

And if Adelita wants to be my formal girlfriend,

Y si Adelita fuera mi mujer,

[i si̯að ɛˈli taˈfwɛ ra mi muˈhɛr]

and if Adelita was my woman

And if Adeita was my woman,

La compraria un vestido de seda

[la kɔmˈpɾa ɾiːa un βɛsˈti ðɔ ðɛˈsɛ ða]

I would buy her a dress of silk

I'd buy her a silk dress

para llevarla a pasear al cuartel.

[ˈpa ɾa jɛˈβar la̯ a pa sɛˈar al kwarˈtɛl]

To take her to walk around the military barracks

To take her on a strols through the military barracks.

2. LA BARCA DE ORO [THE GOLDEN SHIP]

Traditional Folk Song

Yo ya me voy al puerto donde se halla
[jɔ ja mɛ βoi al ˈpwɛr tɔ ˈðɔn dɛ sɛ ˈa ʎa]
I'm now leaving to the port where one can find
I'm on my way to the port where

La barca de oro que debe conducirme.
[la ˈβar ka ðɛ ˈɔ rɔ kɛ ˈðɛ βɛ kɔn du ˈsir mɛ]
the ship of gold that will lead me.
The golden ship awaits and will guide me.

Yo ya me voy solo vengo a despedirme
[jɔ ja mɛ βoi sɔlɔ ˈβɛŋ gɔ‿a ðɛspɛ'dirmɛ]
I'm now leaving only come to say goodbye
I am leaving now; I just came by to say good-bye.

Adiós mujer,* adiós para siempre, adiós.
[aðjɔs mu ˈhɛr a'ðjɔs ˈpara ˈsjɛm prɛ‿a ˈðjɔs]
Good-bye woman, good-bye forever, good-bye
Good-bye my love, good-bye forever, good-bye.

No volverán mis ojos a mirarte
[nɔ βɔl βɛ ˈran tus ˈɔ hɔs a mi ˈrar mɛ]
No return my eyes to see you
We won't be seeing each other again,

Ni tus oídos escucharán mi canto
[ni tus ɔˈI ðɔs ɛs ku tʃa ˈran mi ˈkan tɔ]
Nor your ear will hear my song
Neither will you hear my song

Voy a aumentar los mares con mi llanto.
[βɔi̯ a‿au mɛn ˈtar los ˈmar ɛs kɔn mi ˈʎan tɔ]
I will augment the oceans with my tears.
The ocean will swell with my tears.

Adiós mujer,* adiós para siempre, adios.
[a ˈðjɔs mu ˈhɛr a ˈðjɔs pa ra ˈsjɛm prɛ‿a ˈðjɔs]
Good-bye woman, goodbye forever, good-bye.
Good-bye my love, good-bye forever, good-bye,*

*The text "mi amor" [my love] may be inserted instead of "mujer" [woman] to make the song non-gender specific.

CHAPTER 6: SONGS, DICTION, LYRICS, IPA, AND TRANSLATIONS 167

3. CANCIÓN MIXTECA* [MIXTECA SONG]

Traditional Song from Oaxaca by José López Alavez, ca. 1918

Canción Mixteca
(Mixteca Song)
ranchera valseada

Mexican Folk Song from Oaxaca
by José López Alavéz ca. 1912
Vocal arr. by Noe Sánchez

Canción Mixteca

(Mixteca Song)

ranchera valseada

Mexican Folk Song from Oaxaca
by José López Alavéz ca. 1912
Vocal arr. by Noe Sánchez

Qué le-jos es-toy, del sue-lo don-de_he na-ci-do.

In-ten-sa nos-tal-gia_in-va-de mi pen-sa-mien-to.

Y_al ver-me tan so-lo_y tri-ste cual ho-ja_al vien-to.

Qui-sie-ra llo-rar, Qui-sie-re mo-rir de sen-ti-

mien-to. Oh tie-rra del sol Oh tie-rra del sol. sus-pi-ro por sus-

ver-te. A-ho-ra que le-jos A-ho-ra que le-jos Yo vi-vo sin
pi-ro por ver-te.

luz sin a-mor. Y_al ver-me tan so-lo_y tris-te cual

ho-ja_al vien-to. Qui-sie-ra llo-rar, Qui-sie-ra mo-

rir de sen-ti-mien-to.

CHAPTER 6: SONGS, DICTION, LYRICS, IPA, AND TRANSLATIONS   169

Que lejos estoy del suelo donde he nacido

[kɛ 'lɛ hɔs ɛs 'tɔi ðɛl 'swɛ lɔ 'ðɔn ðɛ ɛ na 'si ðɔ]

How far I am from the ground where I was born

I'm so far from my homeland.

Inmensa nostalgia invade mi pensamiento

[In 'mɛn sa nɔs 'talxja in 'βaðɛ mi pɛnsa 'mjɛn tɔ]

Immense nostalgia invades my thoughts

Immense nostalgia overwhelms me

Y al verme tan solo* y triste cual hoja al viento

[j̥al 'βɛr mɛ tan 'sɔ lɔ i 'tris tɛ kwal 'ɔ xa al 'βjɛn tɔ]

And seeing myself so alone and sad which leaf in the wind

And seeing myself so lonely and sad like a leaf in the wind

Quisiera llorar quisiera morir de sentimiento.

[ki 'sjɛ ra ʎɔ 'rar ki 'sjɛ ra mɔ 'rir ðɛ sɛn ti 'mjɛn tɔ]

I want to cry I want to die of my feelings

I want to cry, I want to die of grief.

*"Sola," if the singer is a woman.

Oh! Tierra del sol suspiro por verte

[ɔ 'tjɛr a ðɛl sɔl sus 'pi rɔ pɔr 'βɛr tɛ]

Oh! Land of sun I breathe to see you

Oh! Land of the sun I live to see you.

Ahora que lejos yo vivo sin luz, sin amor

[a 'ɔra kɛ 'lɛ hɔs jɔ 'βi βɔ sin lu̯ sin a 'mɔr]

Now how far I live without light, without love

Now so far away I live without light, without love.

*This song describes the composer's homesick feelings after leaving his homeland state of Oaxaca to live in Mexico City.

4. CANTA MI SON!* [SING MY SONG]

From the CD Canta mi son!; *lyrics and Music by Juanita Ulloa*

Copyright 2009 ASCAP All Rights Reserved
Please do not post, print or take pictures with without permission of book author from
www.juanitamusic.com, www.voicetrainerdr.com, or email: juanitavoicetrainer@gmail.com

CHAPTER 6: SONGS, DICTION, LYRICS, IPA, AND TRANSLATIONS   171

¡Canta Mi Son!
(Sing my Song!)
son jaliscience

Lyrics and Music by
Juanita Ulloa

Copyright 2009 ASCAP All Rights Reserved
Please do not post, print or take pictures with without permission of book author from
www.juanitamusic.com, www.voicetrainerdr.com, or email: juanitavoicetrainer@gmail.com

Se canta con mariachi

[sɛ 'kan ta kɔn ma' rja tʃi]

It is sung with mariachi

It's sung with mariachi.

la fiesta ya se armó

[la 'fjɛ sta ja sɛ aɾ' mɔ]

The party is already together

The party is already in full swing.

y juntos celebramos

[i 'xun tɔs sɛ lɛ β'ɾa mɔs]

and together we celebrate

We'll celebrate together.

¡Ven, canta mi son, que si!

[bɛn 'kan ta mi sɔn kɛ si]

Come, sing my song—Oh, yes!

Come, sing my song—Oh, yes!

Canta conmigo tilín tilón

['kan ta kɔm'mi ɣɔ ti'lin ti'lɔn]

Sing with me tilin tilon.

Sing with me, tilín tilón.

Baila conmigo

['bai la kɔm'mi ɣɔ]

Dance with me

Dance with me.

¡Ven, canta mi son!

[bɛn'kan ta mi sɔn]

Come, sing my song!

Come, sing my song!

Se canta con mariachi

[sɛ 'kan ta kɔn ma' rja tʃi]

It's sung with mariachi

It's sung with mariachi.

CHAPTER 6: SONGS, DICTION, LYRICS, IPA, AND TRANSLATIONS

Se canta con vigor

[sɛ 'kan ta kɔn bi' ɣɔr]

It is sung with vigor.

Sing it with energy.

Estamos bien vestidos

[ɛs' ta mɔs βjen bɛs' ti ðɔs]

We are well dressed

We're all dressed up.

¡Ven, canta mi son, que si!

[bɛn 'kan ta mi sɔn kɛ si]

Come, sing my song—yes

Come, sing my song—yes!

Canta conmigo tilín tilón.

['kan ta kɔm'mi ɣɔ ti' lin ti' lɔn]]

Sing with me tilin tilon

Sing with me tilín tilón.

Rezumba y rezumbando

[rɛ'sum ba̯ i rɛ sum' ban dɔ]

It's sounding and sounding

It sounds like it sings.

¡Ven, canta mi son-canta mi son!

[bɛn 'kan ta mi sɔn'kan ta mi sɔn]

Come, sing my song—sing my song!

Come, sing my song—sing my song!

*The term "son" means both a song and refers to an important 12/8 rhythm in mariachi repertoire (see Chapter 5 "Six Basic Rhythms and Accompaniment).

5. CIELITO LINDO [BEAUTIFUL DARLING]

Traditional Song by Quirino y Mendoza

Additional lyrics:

Ese lunar que tienes, cielito lindo, junto a la boca
No se lo des a nadie cielito lindo que a mí me toca.
Ese lunar que tienes, cielito lindo, junto a la boca
No se lo des a nadie cielito lindo que a mí me toca.

Cielito Lindo
(Beautiful Darling)
ranchera valseada

Traditional Mexican Folk Song by
Quirino and Mendoza

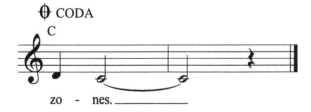

Additional lyrics:

Ese lunar que tienes, cielito lindo, junto a la boca
No se lo des a nadie cielito lindo que a mí me toca.
Ese lunar que tienes, cielito lindo, junto a la boca
No se lo des a nadie cielito lindo que a mí me toca.

De la Sierra Morena cielito lindo vienen bajando

[dɛ la ˈsjɛ ra mɔ ˈrɛ na sjɛ ˈli tɔ ˈlin ðɔ ˈbjɛ nɛn ba ˈhan ðɔ]

From the Sierra Morena, my beautiful darling is coming down

A pair of cute black eyes are on their way down from the Sierra Morena mountains,

Un par de ojitos negros cielito lindo de contrabando

[un par dɛ̯ˈɔ hi tɔs ˈnɛ ɣrɔs sjɛ ˈli tɔ ˈlin ðɔ dɛ kɔn tra ˈβan ðɔ]

A pair of cute black eyes, my beautiful darling is smuggling

My beloved, to smuggle away my heart.

Ay, ay, ay, ay canta y no llores

[aj aj aj aj ˈkan taːi nɔ ˈʎɔ rɛs]

Ay, ay, ay, ay sing and don't cry.

Ay, ay, ay, ay sing and don't cry.

porque cantando se alegran cielito lindo los corazones.

[por ˈkɛ kan ˈtan ðɔ sɛ̯a'lɛ ɣran sjɛ ˈli tɔ ˈlin ðɔ lɔs kɔ ra ˈsɔn ɛs]

Because singing makes happy my beautiful darling the hearts.

Because, my beloved, singing makes our hearts happy.

Ese lunar que tienes cielito lindo junto a la boca

[ˈɛ sɛ lu ˈnar kɛ ˈtjɛ nɛs sjɛ ˈli tɔ ˈlin ðɔ ˈhun tɔ̯a la ˈbɔ ka]

That mole that you have, my beautiful darling next to your mouth

My beloved, that mole that you have right next to your mouth.

No se lo des a nadie cielito lindo que a mi me toca

[nɔ sɛ lɔ dɛs a ˈna ðjɛ sjɛ ˈli tɔ ˈlin dɔ kɛ̯a mi mɛ ˈtɔ ka]

No don't give it to anyone my beautiful darling that it is mine

Don't offer it to anyone, my beloved, because it is meant for me.

CHAPTER 6: SONGS, DICTION, LYRICS, IPA, AND TRANSLATIONS   177

6. COMO MEXICO NO HAY DOS [THERE'S NOTHING LIKE MEXICO]

By Juanita Ulloa

This song teaches parts of the *traje de charro* (mariachi outfit) and wearing it with pride.

Copyright © 2009 ASCAP All Rights Reserved
Please do not post, print or take pictures with without permission of book author from
www.juanitamusic.com, www.voicetrainerdr.com, or email: juanitavoicetrainer@gmail.com

2   Como México No Hay Dos

Additional lyrics:

Tengo traje de charro y me gusta cantar.
Con mi moño y botanadura yo me se arreglar.
Aunque me cuesta limpiarlo yo no se como planchar.
Me gusta sentirme charra como buen charro no hay dos.
Que grande la tradición. ¡Como México no hay dos!
Que grande la tradición. ¡Como México no hay dos!

En Tejas hay buen mariachi y el canto es esencial.
Hay charros tambien hay charras y todo saben tocar.
y al tocar se grita "¡Vámanos!" "¡Vámos ya!"
Que grande la tradición. ¡Como México no hay dos!
Que grande la tradición. ¡Como México no hay dos!
Que grande la tradición. ¡Como México no hay dos!

* This song and its karaoke track is available on Canta mi son!
GrIndy-Disney prize winning CD through CDBaby, Spotify or iTunes.

CHAPTER 6: SONGS, DICTION, LYRICS, IPA, AND TRANSLATIONS   179

Copyright © 2009 ASCAP All Rights Reserved
Please do not post, print or take pictures with without permission of book author from
www.juanitamusic.com, www.voicetrainerdr.com, or email: juanitavoicetrainer@gmail.com

Como México No Hay Dos

Additional lyrics:

Tengo traje de charro y me gusta cantar.
Con mi moño y botanadura yo me se arreglar.
Aunque me cuesta limpiarlo yo no se como planchar.
Me gusta sentirme charra como buen charro no hay dos.
Que grande la tradición. ¡Como México no hay dos!
Que grande la tradición. ¡Como México no hay dos!

En Tejas hay buen mariachi y el canto es esencial.
Hay charros tambien hay charras y todo saben tocar.
y al tocar se grita "¡Vámanos!" "¡Vámos ya!"
Que grande la tradición. ¡Como México no hay dos!
Que grande la tradición. ¡Como México no hay dos!
Que grande la tradición. ¡Como México no hay dos!

* This song and its karaoke track is available on Canta mi son!
GrIndy-Disney prize winning CD through CDBaby, Spotify or iTunes.

CHAPTER 6: SONGS, DICTION, LYRICS, IPA, AND TRANSLATIONS

Con mi caballo bayo me gusta andar

[kɔn mi ka'ba jɔ'ʙa jɔ mɛ'ɢus ta an'ðar]

With my bay horse I like to go

I like to go riding on my bay horse.

Con mi caballo bayo siempre salgo a pasear

[kɔn mi ka'ba jɔ'ʙa jɔ 'sjɛm prɛ'sal gɔ a pa'sɛar]

With my bay horse I always go out

I always go for rides with my horse.

Sin mi caballo bayo no soy nadie, nada soy

[sin mi ka'ba jɔ'ʙa jɔ nɔ sɔi'na ðjɛ'na ða sɔi]

Without my bay horse I am nothing, nothing I am

I'm nothing without my bay horse, nothing at all.

Es noble es orgulloso como caballo no hay dos

[ɛs'nɔ βlɛ ɛs ɔr ɣu ʎɔ sɔ'kɔ mɔ ka'βa ɣɔ nɔ ai dɔs]

It's noble it's proud like horse there is not another

He's noble and proud. There's no better horse.

Que grande la tradición. ¡Como México no hay dos!

[kɛ'gran dɛ la tra ði'sjɔn 'kɔ mɔ'mɛ hi kɔ nɔ ai dɔs]

How big the tradition like Mexico there is not a second

What a huge tradition. There's nothing better than Mexico!

Tengo traje de charra* y me gusta cantar

['tɛŋɣɔ'tra hɛ dɛ'tʃa rrɔa̯ i mɛ'ɣus ta'kan tar]

I have an outfit of a charra and I like to sing

I have my charra outfit and love to sing.

Con moño** y botanadura** yo me sé arreglar

[kɔn'mɔ ŋɔ̯ i bɔ tɔ na'ðu ra jɔ mɛ sɛ a rrɛ'ɣlar]

I have the tie and silver buttons on I know how to dress

With my tie and silver buttons I know how to shine in this outfit.

Aunque me cuesta limpiarlo y no sé cómo planchar

['aun kɛ mɛ'kwɛs ta lim'pjar lɔ i nɔ sɛ'kɔ mɔ plan' tʃar]

Even though it's hard to keep clean and I don't know how to iron

Even though it's hard for me to keep it clean and I have no idea how to iron,

Me gusta sentirme charra como buen charra no hay dos

[mɛ'gus ta sɛn'tir mɛ'tʃa rra'kɔ mɔ bwɛn' tʃa rra nɔ ai dɔs]

I like to feel like a charra like a good charro there's not another

There's nothing better in the world than being a great charra. I like it!

Que grande la tradición ¡Como México no hay dos!

[kɛ'gran dɛ la tra ði'sjɔn 'kɔ mɔ'mɛ hi kɔ nɔ ai dɔs]

How big is the tradition like Mexico there is not a second

What a huge tradition. There's nothing better than Mexico!

En Téjas*** hay buen mariachi y el canto es esencial

[ɛn'tɛ has ai ʙɯɛn ma'rja t͡ʃi i̯ ɛl'kan tɔ‿es ɛn'sja:l]

In Texas is good mariachi and singing is essential

Texas*** has great mariachi and singing is essential

Hay charros también hay charras y todos saben tocar

[ai' t͡ʃa rrɔs tam'βjɛn ai't͡ʃa rras i 'tɔ ðɔs'sa βɛn tɔ'kar]

There are charros also charras and all know to play

There are charros, also charras and everyone knows how to play,

y al cantar se grita "¡Vámonos!" "¡Vámos ya!"

[i̯ al kan'tar sɛ'gri'ta'ʙa mɔ nɔs'ʙa mɔs ja]

and to sing, yells Let's go. Let's go now.

and while singing when they yell "Let's go!" Let's go now!

Que grande la tradición ¡Como México no hay dos!

[kɛ'gran dɛ la tra ði'sjɔn 'kɔ mɔ'mɛ hi kɔ nɔ ai dɔs]

How big the tradition like Mexico there is not a second

What a huge tradition. There's nothing better than Mexico!

*Charra/charro is a mariachi performer with a specific outfit (*see* Glossary).

**Moño (tie) and botonadura [silver buttons down the side of the charro pants] are part of the charro outfit (see Glossary).

***Singers may choose to celebrate where they live by inserting the name of their own city or state.

CHAPTER 6: SONGS, DICTION, LYRICS, IPA, AND TRANSLATIONS

7. CORAZÓN DE CHAPULÍN [HEART OF CHAPULÍN]*

By Juan Ortíz; Written for the ¡Canta mi son! *CD by Dr. Juanita Ulloa*

2   Corazón de Chapulín*

CHAPTER 6: SONGS, DICTION, LYRICS, IPA, AND TRANSLATIONS 185

* Juan Ortíz living composed this song winner, arrangements and accompaniment for Juanita Ulloa's GrIndy-Disney prize winning CD "Canta mi son!", available on iTunes, Spotify and CDbaby.

**"This is an excellent song section to practice falsete (falsetto yodel flips with color contrast) from here to the end of the song. Earlier duo section may practice light head voice on top line.

*** "The first recitative section is optional."

CHAPTER 6: SONGS, DICTION, LYRICS, IPA, AND TRANSLATIONS 187

Corazón de Chapulín*

* Juan Ortíz living composed this song winner, arrangements and accompaniment for Juanita Ulloa's GrInzdy-Disney prize winning CD "Canta mi son!", available on iTunes, Spotify and CDbaby.

**"This is an excellent song section to practice falsete (falsetto yodel flips with color contrast) from here to the end of the song. Earlier duo section may practice light head voice on top line.

*** "The first recitative section is optional."

Yo soy Santiago el saltamonte y me dicen el chapulín
[jo 'sɔi san'tja yɔ ɛl sal ta'mɔn tɛ i mɛ 'ði sɛn ɛl tʃa pu'lin]
I am Santiago the grasshopper and they say to me chapulín
I am Santiago the grasshopper and they call me chapulín.*

Mi color es verde amarillento y canto así: rin, rin, rin, rin.

[mi kɔˈlɔr ezˈβɛɾ ðɛ a ma ɾiˈʎɛn tɔ iˈkan to aˈsi rrin rrin rrin rrin]

My color is green yellowish and I sing this: rin, rin, rin, rin

I am yellowish green in color and I sing like this: rin, rin, rin, rin.

Ya nació el chapulín. Ya salió el chapulín.

[ɟa naˈsjɔ ɛl tʃa puˈlin ɟa saˈljɔ ɛl tʃa puˈlin]

Now was born the chapulín now has come out the chapulín

Chapulín was born. Chapulín has emerged.

Y salió con una canción.

[i saˈljɔ kɔnˈu na kanˈsjɔn]

And he came out with a song

And he was born already singing a song.

Canta, brinca, corazón de chapulín

[ˈkan taˈbriŋ ka kɔ ɾaˈsɔn dɛ tʃa puˈlin]

Sing, jump, heart of chapulín

Chapulín's heart sings {and} jumps.

Salta, brinca corazón de chapulín (2x)

[ˈsal taˈbriŋ ka kɔ ɾaˈsɔn dɛ tʃa puˈlin]

Hop, jump, heart of chapulín

Chapulín's heart hops {and} jumps.

Brinca, brinca el chapulín. Canta, canta el chapulín.

[ˈbriŋ kaˈbriŋ ka ɛl tʃa puˈlin ˈkan ta ˈkan ta ɛl tʃa puˈlin]

Jump, jump Chapulín. Sing, sing, Chapulín

Chapulín jumps {and} jumps. Chapulín sings {and} sings.

Salta y brinca mi corazón.

[ˈsal ta i βˈriŋ ka mi ko ɾaˈsɔn]

Hope and jumps my heart

My heart hops and jumps.

Dime, dime, dime mi bien.

[ˈdi mɛˈdi mɛˈdi mɛˈdi mɛ mi βjɛn]

Tell me, tell me, tell me my love

Tell me, tell me, tell me my love.

Si es que tu me quieres también

[si ɛs kɛ tu mɛ ˈkje ɾɛs tamˈbjen]

If you like me, too

If you also like me.

Quiero ser tu gran amor.

[ˈkjɛ rɔ sɛɾ tu ɣran aˈmɔɾ]

I want to be your big love

I would like to be your greatest love.

Descant**: **Salta con amor. Brinca con amor.**

  [ˈsal ta kɔn aˈmɔr ˈbɾiŋ ka kɔn aˈmɔɾ]

  Hop with love. Jump with love.

  Hop in love. Jump in love.

Falsete***: **Can-ta, Brin-ca, corazón de Chapulín.**

  [ˈkan ta ˈbɾiŋ ka kɔ ɾaˈsɔn dɛ tʃa puˈlin]

  Sing, jump, heart of Chapulín.

  Chapulin's heart jumps and sings.

*"Chapulín" is the Mexican Nahuatl language word for "grasshopper".

***Descant* refers to a counter melody that sounds simultaneously to the main melody.

****Falsete* refers to a yodel sounding flip of the voice when jumping between two notes that are in different registers. (see Chapter 3 section: "Falsete: To Bridge or to Break").

CHAPTER 6: SONGS, DICTION, LYRICS, IPA, AND TRANSLATIONS

8. **CUANDO CANTO [WHEN I SING]**

By Juanita Ulloa

Copyright © 2002 ASCAP All Rights Reserved
Please do not post, print or take pictures with without permission of book author from
www.juanitamusic.com, www.voicetrainerdr.com, or email: juanitavoicetrainer@gmail.com

Cuando Canto

2

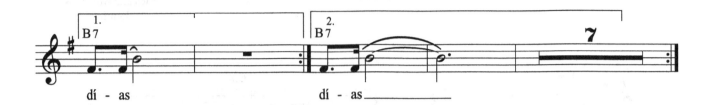

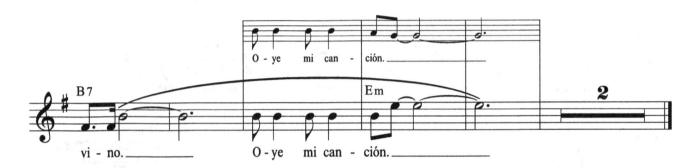

Additional lyrics:

[3rd Chorus]
Es por eso que canto
porque es mi pasión.
Cuando te sientes triste
oye mi canción.
Seguiré cantando
inventando amonías
Se que el canto es mi vida
Se que el canto es divino
Oye mi canción.
Sé que el canto es mi vida.
Sé que el canto es divino.
Oye mi canción.

Song Winner of Festival de la canción latinoamericana

From Mujeres & Mariachi Cd available on iTunes, Spotify and CDBaby

CHAPTER 6: SONGS, DICTION, LYRICS, IPA, AND TRANSLATIONS   193

Cuando Canto
(When I Sing)
huapango furioso

Lyrics and Music by
Juanita Ulloa

Copyright © 2002 ASCAP All Rights Reserved
Please do not post, print or take pictures with without permission of book author from
www.juanitamusic.com, www.voicetrainerdr.com, or email: juanitavoicetrainer@gmail.com

Cuando Canto

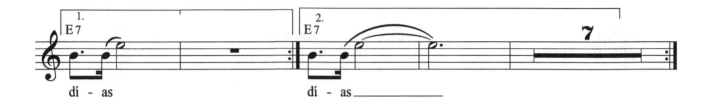

Additional lyrics:

[3rd Chorus]
Es por eso que canto
porque es mi pasión.
Cuando te sientes triste
oye mi canción.
Seguiré cantando
inventando amonías
Se que el canto es mi vida
Se que el canto es divino
Oye mi canción.
Sé que el canto es mi vida.
Sé que el canto es divino.
Oye mi canción.

Song Winner of Festival de la canción latinoamericana

From Mujeres & Mariachi Cd available on iTunes, Spotify and CDBaby

Cuando canto veo el cielo y es más bello su color

[ˈkwan ðɔ ˈkan tɔˈβɛɔ‿ɛlˈsjɛ lɔ jɛs masˈβɛ ʎɔ su kɔˈlɔr]

When I sing I see the sky and is more beautiful its color

When I sing I can see the most beautiful color in the sky

Cuando canto me emociono y en mi alma hay solo amor.

[ˈkwan ðɔˈkan tɔ mɛ‿ɛ mɔˈsjɔ nɔ i‿ɛn miˈal ma‿ai ˈsɔ lɔ‿aˈmɔr]

When I sing I get excited and in my soul is only love
When I sing I become excited and my soul brims with love.

Cuando canto vuelo alto y mis alas son de luz
['kwan ðɔ'kan tɔ'βwɛ lɔ‿'al tɔ i mis‿'a las sɔn dɛ lus]
When I sing I fly high and my wings are of light
When I sing I fly high with wings as light as a feather.

Yo me siento inspirada* cuando canto con amor.
[jɔ mɛ sjɛn tɔ in spi'ra ða kwan ðɔ 'kan tɔ kɔn‿a'mɔr]
I feel inspired when sing with love
I am inspired when I sing with love.

Es por eso que canto porque es mi pasión
[ɛs pɔr'ɛs ɔ kɛ 'kan tɔ 'pɔr kɛ‿ɛs mi pa'sjɔn]
That is why I sing because is my passion
That is why I sing because it's my passion.

Cuando te sientes triste oye mi canción
['kwan ðɔ tɛ sjɛn tɛs'tris tɛ'ɔ jɛ mi kan'sjɔn]
When you feel sad hear my song
When you're feeling sad listen to my song.
Ending 1.

Seguiré cantando inventando armonías
[sɛ ɣi'rɛ kan'tan dɔ in βɛn'tan ðɔ‿ar mɔ'ni:as]
I will follow singing inventing harmonies
I will continue singing creating new harmonies.

Esperando y soñando con nuevas melodías
[ɛs pɛ'ran ðɔ‿i sɔ'ɲan ðɔ kɔn'nwɛ βas mɛ lɔ'ði:as]
Hoping and dreaming with new melodies
Hoping and dreaming with new melodies.

Ending 2.
Se que el canto es mi vida
[sɛ kɛ‿ɛl 'kan tɔ‿ɛs mi'βi ða
I know that song is my life
I know singing is my life.

Sé que el canto es divino- oye mi canción!
[sɛ kɛ‿ɛl 'kan tɔ‿ɛs di'βi nɔ 'ɔi jɛ mi kan'sj ɔn]
I know that song is divine—listen to my song!
I know singing is divine—listen to my song!

9. EL CORRIDO DE HIGADITOS [THE BALLAD OF HIGADITOS]

Text and Music by Antonio Gomezanda

This song is dedicated to Gomezanda's colleague and personal friend, German scenic designer Richard Hasse-Held, who immigrated to Mexico with Gomezanda when he returned from Berlin. Hasse never left Mexico. He nationalized as a Mexican citizen and formed part of the Gomezanda family. Higaditos is an imaginary name.

El Corrido de Higaditos

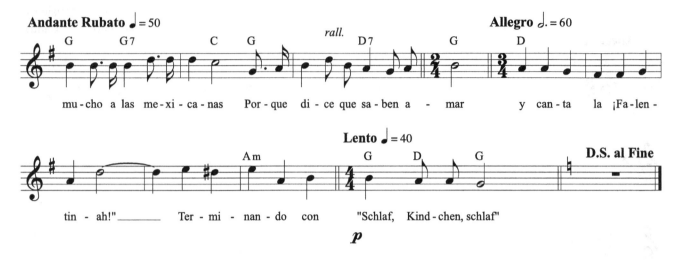

Additional lyrics:

Se quemó con el sol de A-ca-pul-co,
Se espinó por subir se al no-pal
Y quedó lleno de mataduras
Por querer presumir de charrear
Con todo esto el buen Higaditos
Muy contento en México está

Y no pien-sa vol-ver a A-le-ma-nia

Porque tiene un amor por acá.

* Full vocal/piano versions of these songs are available with Classical Vocal Reprints.

CHAPTER 6: SONGS, DICTION, LYRICS, IPA, AND TRANSLATIONS   199

Copyright 2017 ASCAP All Rights Reserved
Used with permission of Gomezanda Family
Please do not post, print or take pictures with without permission of book author from
www.juanitamusic.com, www.voicetrainerdr.com, or email: juanitavoicetrainer@gmail.com

El Corrido de Higaditos

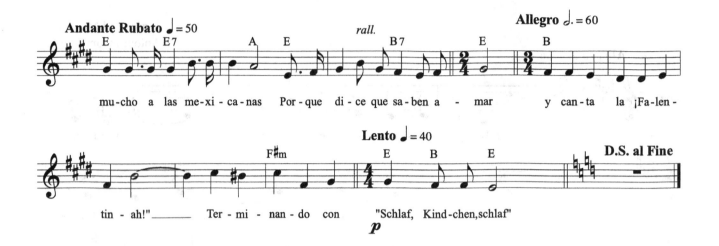

Additional lyrics:

Se quemó con el sol de A-ca-pul-co,
Se espinó por subir se al no-pal
Y quedó lleno de mataduras
Por querer presumir de charrear
Con todo esto el buen Higaditos
Muy contento en México está

Y no pien-sa vol-ver a A-le-ma-nia

Porque tiene un amor por acá.

* Full vocal/piano versions of these songs are available with Classical Vocal Reprints.

CHAPTER 6: SONGS, DICTION, LYRICS, IPA, AND TRANSLATIONS   201

Higaditos salió de Alemania

[i ʎaˈði tɔs sa ˈljɔ ðɛ̯a lɛˈma ɲja]

Higaditos left Germany

Higaditos left Germany

y hasta México vino a parar.

[i̯ˀ as taˈmɛ xi kɔˈβi nɔ̯a paˈrar]

and to Mexico came to stop.

and came to live in Mexico.

Entendió muy prontito el idioma

[ɛn tɛnˈdjɔˈmui prɔnˈti to̯ ɛl iˈðjɔ ma]

He understood very quickly the language

He learned the language quickly

Y en un mes aprendió a gritar.

[i̯ ɛn un mɛs a prɛnˈðjɔ a griˈtar]

and in a month learned to yell.

and within a month could do the Mexican yell.*

Si en la mesa le sirven *kartoffel*

[si̯ ɛn laˈmɛ sa lɛˈsir βɛn karˈto fɛl]

If at the table they serve him *kartoffel*

If they serve him a meal with Kartoffel [German: Potato]

Pumpernickel y vino del Rhin,

[pum pɛrˈni kɛl iˈβi nɔ ðɛl rin]

Pumpernickel and Rhine wine,

Pumpernickel and Rhine wine,

Le dan nauseas y grita indignado

[lɛ ðanˈnau sɛas iˈgri tajn digˈna ðɔ]

It gives him nausea and he indignantly yells

he gets nauseous and, yells indignantly.

"¡Que me manden tortilla con sal!"

[kɛ mɛˈman dɛn torˈti ɣa kɔn sal]

That they send me tortilla with salt.

"Send me over tortillas with salt!"

Festejando el grito del quince,

[fɛs tɛˈxan ðɔ ɛlˈʎri tɔ ðɛlˈkin sɛ]

Celebrating the yell on the fifteenth,

Celebrating the Independence Holiday on September 15th,

Fin del año y la Navidad
[fin dɛl'a ɲɔ i la na βi'ðað]
end of the year and Christmas
the end of the year and Christmas.

Canta y baila los "Lieder" de Prusia
['kan ta̯ i'baj̯ la lɔs 'li ðɛr dɛ 'pru sja]
he sings and dances Lieder from Prussia
he sings and dances Lieder from Prussia.

entre estrofas del himno de acá.
['ɛn tre̯ ɛs'trɔ fas del̯ 'iɱ nɔ ðɛ a'ka]
between verses of our anthem from here
In between verses of our anthem here.

Quiere mucho a las mexicanas
['kje̯ rɛ'mu t͡ʃɔ a las mɛ xi'ka nas]*
He loves a lot Mexican women
He really loves Mexican women

porque dice que saben amar
[pɔr kɛ 'ði sɛ kɛ 'sa βɛn a'mar]
because he says they know how to love
because he says they know how to love.

Y canta la "¡Falentina!"
[i 'kan ta la fa lɛn'ti na]
And he sings La "F"alentina
*And he sings La "F"alentina***

terminando con "Schalf, Kindchen, Schlaf."
[tɛr mi'nan dɔ kɔn ʃlaf 'kin t͡ʃɛn ʃlaf]
finishing with *Schlaf, Kindchen, Schlaf* [German: Sleep, Children, Sleep]
finishing with Schlaf, Kindchen, Schlaf [German: Sleep, Children, Sleep]

Se quemó con el sol de Acapulco
[sɛ kɛ'mɔ kɔn el sɔl de̯ a ka'pul kɔ]
He burned himself in the sun from *Acapulco*
He burned himself in the Acapulco sun

Se espinó por subirse al *nopal*
[se̯ ɛs pi'nɔ pɔr su'βir se̯ al no'pal]
He pricked himself trying to climb a *nopal* [cactus]
He pricked himself climbing a cactus.

CHAPTER 6: SONGS, DICTION, LYRICS, IPA, AND TRANSLATIONS 203

Y quedó lleno de mataduras

[i kɛˈdɔ ˈɣɛ nɔ ðɛ ma taˈðu ras]

and was left filled with bruises

And he covered himself with bruises

Por querer presumir de charrear.

[por kɛˈrɛr prɛ su mir ðɛ t͡ʃaˈrrɛar]

For trying to be a charro.

pretending to be charro.

Con todo esto el buen Higaditos

[kɔnˈtɔ dɔ‿ɛs tɔ ɛl bwɛn‿i gaˈði tɔs]

With all this good Higaditos

Despite all this good Higaditos.

Muy contento en México está

[muj kɔnˈtɛn tɔ ɛnˈmɛ xi kɔ‿ɛsˈta]

is very happy in Mexico

is very happy in Mexico

Y no piensa volver a Alemania

[i noˈpjɛn sa βɔlˈβɛɾ‿a‿a lɛˈma nja]

And he's thinking of not returning to Germany

And he has no plans at all to return to Germany .

Porque tiene un amor por acá.

[pɔr kɛˈtjɛ nɛ‿un aˈmɔr pɔr aˈka]

because he has a love over here.

because he has a girlfriend over here.

*Mexican yells are called *gritos* and both performers and audiences participate with gritos during songs.

**Here we use a guttural [x] sound to imitate Higaditos speaking Spanish with a German accent.

***Valentina* is a famous Mexican corrido; here a strong "F" sound was inserted by the composers to emphasize the German accent in Spanish.

10. EL PASTOR [THE SHEPHERD]

Los Cuates Castilla, ca. 1955

Additional lyrics:

El pastor ya está de vuelta
Pues, el sol se está ocultando
Va subiendo por la cuesta a guardar su rebaño

Con su flautín va llamando
Uno a uno sus ovejas
Y les va comunicando
Sus gozes y sus tristezas

El Pastor

(The Shepherd)
huapango

Words and Music by
Cuates Castilla

Additional lyrics:

El pastor ya está de vuelta
Pues, el sol se está ocultando
Va subiendo por la cuesta a guardar su rebaño

Con su flautín va llamando
Uno a uno sus ovejas
Y les va comunicando
Sus gozes y sus tristezas

Va el pastor con su rebaño

[ʙa̯ ɛl pas'tɔr kɔn su rrɛ'βa ɲɔ]

Going the shepherd with his flock

The shepherd is moving with his flock.

A despuntar la mañana

[a dɛs pun'tar la ma'ɲa na]

Breaking the morning

Morning is breaking.

Bajando por el sendero

[ʙa'han ðɔ pɔr ɛl sɛn'ðɛ rɔ]

Coming down by the path

[He is]coming down the path

De la sierra a la pradera.

[dɛ la'sje rra̯ a la pra'ðɛ ra]

From the mountains to the plains

From the mountains to the plains.

Va musicando sus quejas

[ʙa mu si'kan ðɔ sus'kɛ has]

He goes musicalizing his complaints

He moves, expressing his problems through music

Con su flautín de carrizo

[kɔn su fla:u'tin dɛ ka'rri sɔ]

With his flute of bamboo

With his bamboo flute,

Seguido por sus ovejas

[sɛ'ɣi ðɔ pɔr sus ɔ'βɛ has]

Followed by his sheep.

Followed by his sheep,

Como si fuera un hechizo.

['kɔ mɔ si'fwɛ ra̯ unɛ'tʃi sɔ]

As if was a spell

As if in an enchanted spell.

CHAPTER 6: SONGS, DICTION, LYRICS, IPA, AND TRANSLATIONS

El pastor ya va de vuelta

[ɛl pas'tɔr ja βa ðɛ 'βwɛl ta]

The shepherd is returning

The shepherd is now going back

Pues, el sol se está ocultando

[pwɛs ɛl sɔl sɛ ɛs'ta͜ ɔ kul'tan ðɔ]

Because the sun is hiding

Because the sun is going down.

Va subiendo por la cuesta

[ʙa su'βjɛn dɔ pɔr la'kwɛs ta]

Going upwards the hill

He climbs the slope

Para guardar su rebaño

['pa ra ɢwar'dar su rrɛ'βa ɲɔ]

To take back his flock

To take his flock back.

Con su flautín va llamando

[kɔn su fla:u'tin ʙa ja'man dɔ]

With his flute he goes calling

With his flute he calls out

Uno a uno a sus ovejas

['u nɔ͜a'u nɔ͜a sus ɔ'βɛ has]

One by one to his sheep

Each sheep, one by one.

Y les va comunicando

[i lɛs ʙa kɔ mu ni'kan dɔ]

And he goes communicating

And he shares his sorrow

Sus penas y sus tristezas.

[sus'pɛ nas i sus tris'tɛ sas]

his happiness and sadness

and sadness to them.

11. HAY UNOS OJOS [THERE ARE EYES]

Traditional Mexican Folk Song

2 HAY UNOS OJOS

ti. _____

Additional lyrics:

2. Ay quien pudiera mirarse en ellos
   Ay, quien pudiera besarlos más.
   Gozando siempre de sus destellos
   y no ol-vidarlos nunca ja -más.

3. Y todos dicen que no te quiero
   que no te quiero con frenesí
   y yo les digo que mienten, mienten
   Que has- ta la vida daría por tí.

HAY UNOS OJOS

ti._____

Additional lyrics:

2. Ay quien pudiera mirarse en ellos
   Ay, quien pudiera besarlos más.
   Gozando siempre de sus destellos
   y no ol-vidarlos nunca ja -más.

3. Y todos dicen que no te quiero
   que no te quiero con frenesí
   y yo les digo que mienten, mienten
   Que has- ta la vida daría por tí.

Hay unos ojos que si me miran

[ai'u nɔs'ɔ hɔs kɛ si mɛ'mi ran]

There are eyes that if they see me

There are these eyes. When they look at me

Hacen que mi alma tiemble de amor

['a sɛn kɛ mi̯ 'al ma tjɛm βlɛ dɛ̯ a'mɔr]

they make my soul tremble with love

they make my inner soul tremble with love.

Son unos ojos tan primorosos

[sɔn'u nɔs'ɔ hɔs tan pri mɔ'rɔ sɔs]

They are some eyes so enchanting

Those eyes are so enchanting.

Ojos tan lindos no he visto yo.

['ɔ hɔːs tan'lin ðɔs nɔ̯ɛ 'βis tɔ jɔ]

Eyes so beautiful I see not

I've never seen such beautiful eyes.

Hay quienes dicen que no te quiero

[ai 'kjɛ nɛs'di sɛn kɛ nɔ tɛ'kjɛ rɔ]

There are those saying I don't love you

There are some that say I don't love you,

Que no te adoro con frenesí

[kɛ nɔ tɛ̯ a'ðɔ rɔ kɔn frɛ nɛ'si]

That I don't adore you with frenesí

That I don't adore you with unbridled passion.

Y yo les digo que mienten, mienten

[i jɔ lɛs'di ɣɔ kɛ'mjɛn tɛn'mjɛn tɛn]

And I tell them that lies, lies

And I respond that no, they're lying.

Que hasta la vida daría por ti.

[kɛ̯ 'as taː la'βi ða'riːa pɔr ti]

That even life I would give for you

That I would give up my life for you.

CHAPTER 6: SONGS, DICTION, LYRICS, IPA, AND TRANSLATIONS   213

12. LAS GAVIOTAS [THE SEAGULLS]

Traditional Mexican Folk Song

Las Gaviotas

"from Prize winning CD "Canta mi son!" available online at iTunes and Spotify.""

Additional lyrics:

Ya las gaviotas se detuvieron
se enamoraron dos de verdad
Y las otras siguen buscando
a su pareja pa'jugetear.

Gaviotas leves y muy felices
como aprecian su libertad
Gaviotas leves, gaviotas libres
celebran vida y amistad.

Coro:
Gaviotas leves, Gaviotas libres
y muy felices deben estar
Viven del mar viven del sol
y del mariachi, si señor
Ay como vuelan
llevando nuestro amor.

Ya las gaviotas tienden su vuelo
[ja las ga'βjɔ tas'tjɛn dɛn su'ʙwɛ lɔ]
Now the seagulls stretch their flight
The seagulls have stretched open in flight

y abren sus alas para volar
[j'aβrɛn sus'a las'pa ra ʙɔ'lar]
and opened their wings to fly
and spread their wings to fly.

Andan buscando nidos de amores
['an ðan ʙus'kan ðɔ'ni ðɔs dɛ̞ a'mɔ rɛs]

CHAPTER 6: SONGS, DICTION, LYRICS, IPA, AND TRANSLATIONS   215

They go looking nests of lovers
They seek nests of love.

nidos de amores encontrarán
[ˈni ðɔs dɛ̯ a'mɔ res ɛn kɔn tra'ran]
nests of lovers they will find
They will find their nests of love.

Si quieres vamos a mi barquilla
[si kjɛ' rɛs 'ʙa mɔs a mi ʙar'ki ʎa]
If you want let's go to my little boat
If you like we can go to my little boat.

no está muy lejos te llevaré
[nɔ̯ ɛs' ta mu:i'lɛ hɔs tɛ ʎje βa'rɛ]
it's not far away I'll take you
It's not far. I'll take you there.

Y cuando estemos en la otra orilla
[i'kwan ðɔ ɛs'tɛ mɔs ɛn la̯ ɔ tra̯ ɔ'ri ʎa]
And when we are on the other edge
And when we reach the other side

con mis canciones te arrullaré.
[kɔn mis kan'sjɔ nɛs tɛ̯ a'rru ʎa'rɛ]
with my songs I will lullaby you
I will croon lullabies to you.

Gaviotas leves gaviotas libres
[ga'vjɔ tas'lɛ βɛs ga'vjɔ tas'li βrɛs]
Light seagulls free seagulls
Seagulls, so light and free.

y muy felices deben estar
[i mu:i fɛ'li sɛs'dɛ βɛn ɛs'tar]
and very happy they should be
they must be very happy.

Viven del mar viven del sol y del mariachi si señor
[ˈʙi βɛn dɛl mar 'βi βɛn dɛl sɔl i dɛl ma'rja ʧi si sɛ'ŋɔr]
Living of the sea, living of sun and mariachi, yes sir.
They live off of the sea, the sun, and mariachi, yes sir

Ay, cómo vuelan llevando nuestro amor.

[ai' kɔ mɔ'βwɛ'lan ʎɛ'βan ðɔ'nwɛs trɔ‿a'mɔr]

Oh, how fly carrying our love.

Oh, how they fly, carrying our love with them.

Ya las gaviotas se detuvieron

[ja las ga' βjɔ tas sɛ dɛ tu'βjɛ rɔn]

Now the seagulls have stopped

The seagulls have now stopped.

Se enamoraron dos de verdad

[sɛ ɛ na mɔ'ra rɔn dɔs dɛ ʙɛɾ'ðað]

they are in love two really

Two of them have fallen in love for real,

Y los otros siguen buscando

[i lɔs'ɔ trɔs'si ɣɛn ʙus'kan ðɔ]

and the others keep looking

and the others continue searching

A su pareja pa'jugetear

[a su pa'rɛ ha pa hu gɛ'tɛar]

their partners to play

for their perfect partner to play with.

Gaviotas leves gaviotas libres

[ga'vjɔ tas'lɛ βɛs ga'vjɔ tas'li βrɛs]

Light seagulls, free seagulls

Seagulls, so light and free.

Celebran vida y amistad

[cɛ'lɛ βran'ʙi ða i a mis'tað]

They celebrate life and friendship

Celebrating life and friendship.

Gaviotas leves, gaviotas libres y muy felices . . .

[ga'vjɔ tas'lɛ βɛs ga'vjɔ tas'li βrɛs i mu:i fɛ'li sɛs]

Light seagulls, free seagulls

Seagulls, so light and free.

CHAPTER 6: SONGS, DICTION, LYRICS, IPA, AND TRANSLATIONS 217

13. LA GOLONDRINA [THE SWALLOW]*

By Narciso Serradell (1843–1910)

La Golondrina

CHAPTER 6: SONGS, DICTION, LYRICS, IPA, AND TRANSLATIONS 219

* Despite the wide range of this song, it has been extremely popular for many generations. It is most often sung at farewells and funerals.

** If the singer wishes, they may add a falsete flip and sustain a top note on this last word of the song.

*** A harmony part has been added for those wanting to sing a duet.

La Golondrina*
(The Swallow)
Ranchera lenta

Lyrics and Music by
Narciso Serradel

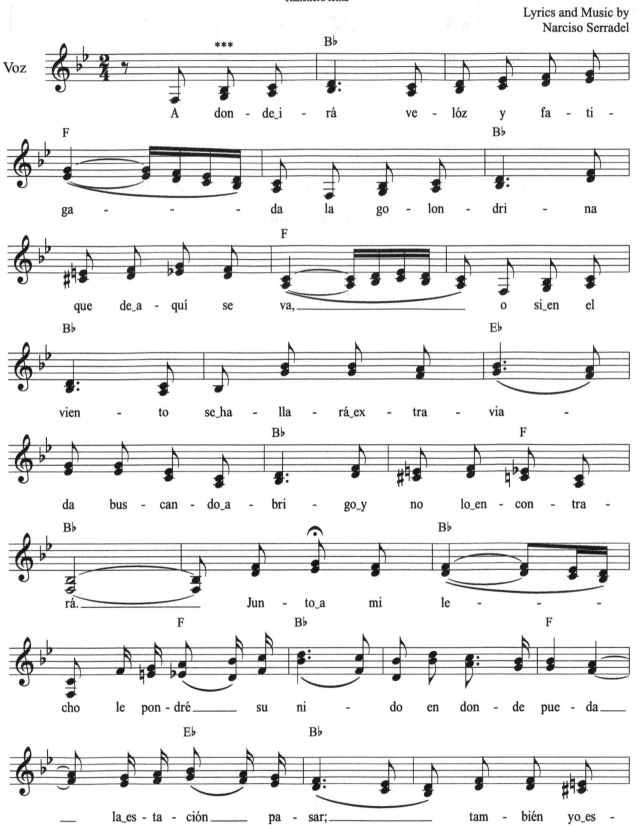

CHAPTER 6: SONGS, DICTION, LYRICS, IPA, AND TRANSLATIONS 221

222 THE MARIACHI VOICE

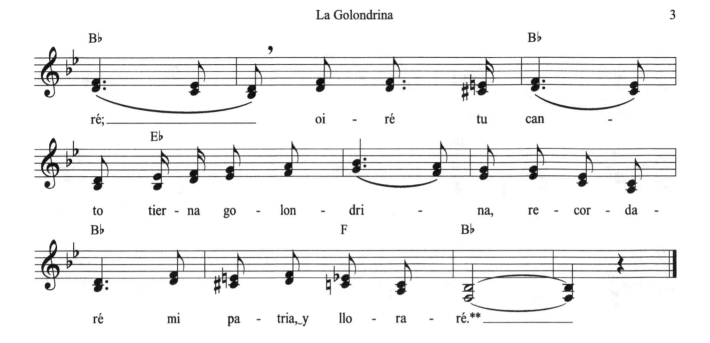

* Despite the wide range of this song, it has been extremely popular for many generations. It is most often sung at farewells and funerals.

** If the singer wishes, they may add a falsete flip and sustain a top note on this last word of the song.

*** A harmony part has been added for those wanting to sing a duet.

CHAPTER 6: SONGS, DICTION, LYRICS, IPA, AND TRANSLATIONS   223

¿A dónde irá veloz y fatigada la golondrina que de aquí se va?
[a dɔn dɛ̠ iɾ'a vɛ'lɔz i fa ti'ga da la gɔ lɔn'dɾi na 'kɛ dɛ̠ a'ki sɛ va]
Where will go fast and tired the swallow from here going
The swallow is leaving. Where will he go, so quick, yet tired?

O si en el viento se hallará extraviada buscando alivio y no lo encontrará.
[ɔ si̠ ɛn ɛl 'vjɛn tɔ sɛ̠ aʎa'ɾa̠ ɛk stɾa'vja da bus'kan dɔ̠ a'li'vjɔ i nɔ lɔ̠ ɛn kɔn tɾa'ɾa]
O if in the wind they find him lost, looking for help without finding it.
Maybe he'll be found lost in the wind, looking in vain for help.

Junto a mi lecho le pondré su nido en donde pueda la estación pasar
['hun tɔ̠ a mi lɛ tʃɔ lɛ pɔn'dɾɛ su 'ni dɔ ɛn 'dɔn dɛ 'pwɛ da la̠ ɛs ta'sjɔn pa'sar]
Next to my bed I'll put his nest where the season can pass
Next to my bed I'll make him his nest where he can spend the season.

También yo estoy en la región perdida buscando alivio y sin poder volar.
[tam'bjɛn jɔ̠ ɛs'toj ɛn la ɾe'hjɔn pɛɾ'di da bus'can'dɔ̠ a'li vjɔ i sin pɔ'dɛr vɔ̠ 'lar]
Also I am in the lost region looking for help and without being able to fly.
I'm also lost, looking for help without being able to fly.

Dejé también mi patria idolatrada esa nación que me vió nacer
[dɛ'hɛ tam'bjɛn mi 'pa trja̠ i dɔ la'tra da 'ɛ sa nas'jɔn kɛ mɛ'viɔ na'sɛr]
I left also my beloved country that country that saw me born
I also left my beloved country, the same nation I was born in.

Mi vida es hoy errante y angustiada y ya no puedo a mi nación volver.
[mi 'vi da̠ ɛs ɔj ɛ'rran tɛ̠ i an gus'tja da i ja nɔ 'pwɛ dɔ a mi man'sjɔn vɔl'vɛr]
My life today is drifting and anguished and I cannot to my nation return.
My life now is anguished and drifting, and I cannot return to my country.

Ave querida amada peregrina mi corazón al tuyo estrecharé
['a vɛ kɛ'ri da a'ma da pɛ ɾɛ'gri na mi kɔ ra'son al 'tu jɔ̠ ɛs trɛ tʃa'ɾɛ]
Bird, beautiful beloved pilgrim my heart to yours will be stretched
Beloved bird and beautiful pilgrim, I will stretch out my heart to you.

Oiré tu canto tierna golondrina. Recordaré mi patria y lloraré.
[ɔi'ɾɛ tu 'kan tɔ 'tjɛɾ na gɔ lɔn'dɾi na ɾɛ kor da'ɾɛ mi 'pa trja̠ i jɔ ɾa'ɾɛ]
I'll hear your song tender swallow. I'll remember my homeland and cry.
Tender swallow, I'll hear your song and cry remembering my homeland.

La golondrina is a very important farewell song in Mexico. Mariachi ensembles often call this song *Las golondrinas.*

14. LA NEGRA NOCHE [THE DARK NIGHT]

By Emilio Uranga

CHAPTER 6: SONGS, DICTION, LYRICS, IPA, AND TRANSLATIONS 225

2   La Negra Noche

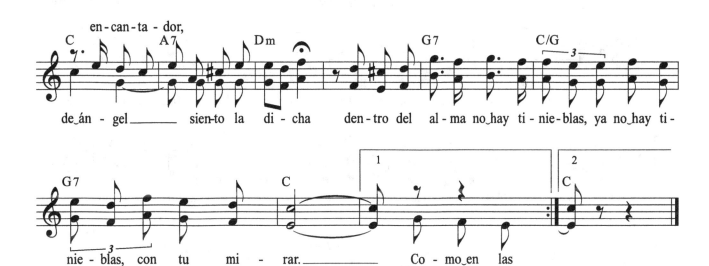

* "Classical singers may also enjoy a habanera dotted accompaniment."

** A harmony part has been added for those wanting to sing a duet.

La Negra Noche

2

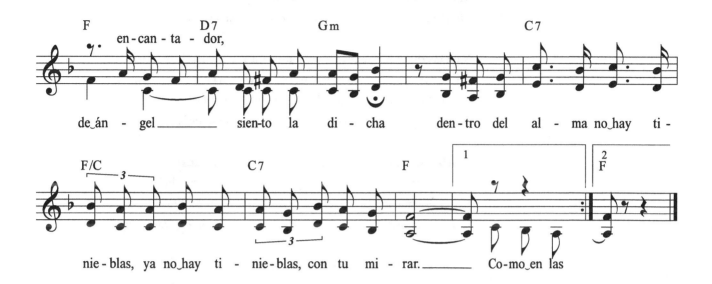

* "Classical singers may also enjoy a habanera dotted accompaniment."

** A harmony part has been added for those wanting to sing a duet.

La negra noche tendió su manto surgió la niebla murió la luz

[la 'nɛ ɣra 'nɔ tʃɛ tɛn 'djɔ su 'man tɔ sur 'hjɔ la 'njɛ bla mu 'rjɔ la lus]

The black night extended its cloak came up the fog died the light

The dark night spread its veil, the fog emerged, all light disappeared,

Y en las tinieblas de mi alma triste como una estrella brotaste tu.

[i̯ ɛn las ti 'ɲɛ blas dɛ mi 'al ma 'tri stɛ 'kɔ mɔ 'u na ɛ 'strɛ ʎa brɔ 'tas tɛ tu]

And in the fog of my soul sad like a star blossomed you.

And in the gloomy darkness of my sad soul you blossomed forth like a star.

Ven ilumina la árida senda por donde vaga loca ilusión

[bɛn i lu 'mi na la:'a ri ða 'sɛn da pɔr dɔn dɛ 'βa ɣa 'lɔ ka̯ i lu 'sjɔn]

Come, illuminate the dry path by where wander wild illusion

Come, light up the arid pathway where my wild dreams are wandering.

Dame tan solo una esperanza que fortifique mi corazón.

['da mɛ tan 'sɔ lɔ 'u na̯ ɛs pe 'ran sa kɛ fɔr ti 'fi kɛ mi kɔ ra 'sɔn]

Give me just one hope to fortify my heart.

Give me just a little hope so I may strengthen my heart.

Como en las noches y en los jardines

[' kɔ mɔ̯ ɛn las 'nɔ tʃes i̯ ɛn lɔs har 'din ɛs]

Like in the nights and in the gardens

Just like at nighttime and in the gardens.

Así en mi alma, adorada niña nació mi amor.

[a 'si̯ ɛn mi̯ 'al ma:a ðɔ 'ra ða 'ni ɲa na 'sjɔ mi̯ a 'mɔr]

Like that in my soul adored girl was born my love

That, my adorable beloved, is how my love was born.

Ya veo que asoma tu rostro de ángel

[ja 'bɛ ɔ kɛ̯ a 'sɔ ma tu 'rɔ strɔ dɛ̯ 'aŋ hɛl]

I can see showing your face of angel

I see your angel face appear.

Siento la dicha dentro del alma

['sjɛn tɔ la 'di tʃa 'dɛn trɔ dɛl 'al ma]

I feel joy in my soul

I feel bliss within my soul

No hay tinieblas, ya no hay tinieblas con tu mirar.

[nɔ̯ aj ti 'ɲɛ blas ja nɔ̯ aj ti 'ɲɛ blas kɔn tu mi 'rar]

There's no fog anymore, no fog with your gaze.

There's no longer any darkness, everything clears when looking at you.

CHAPTER 6: SONGS, DICTION, LYRICS, IPA, AND TRANSLATIONS 229

15. LAS MAÑANITAS [LITTLE MORNING SONG]

Traditional Mexican Birthday Song, most often sung as a serenade as the sun comes up.

Additional lyrics:

El día que tu naciste nacieron todas las flores.
Y en las pila de bautizo cantaron los ruiseñores.

* There are many versions and additional verses, but this is the version that is most commonly sung.

CHAPTER 6: SONGS, DICTION, LYRICS, IPA, AND TRANSLATIONS   231

Las Mañanitas*
(Birthday Song)
ranchera valseada

Traditional Mexican Folk Song

Additional lyrics:

El día que tu naciste nacieron todas las flores.
Y en las pila de bautizo cantaron los ruiseñores.

* There are many versions and additional verses, but this is the version that is most commonly sung.

CHAPTER 6: SONGS, DICTION, LYRICS, IPA, AND TRANSLATIONS 233

Estas son las mañanitas que cantaba el Rey David

['ɛs tas̪ sɔn las ma ɲja 'ni tas kɛ kan 'ta βa̯ɛl rrɛi da 'við]

This the little mornings that King David sang

This is the little morning song that King David sang,

Hoy por ser día de tu santo te las cantamos aquí

[ɔj pɔr sɛr 'dia dɛ tu 'san tɔ tɛ las kan 'ta mɔs a 'ki]

Today because it's your birthday we sing it here to you.

Because it's your birthday today, we sing it to you here.

Despierta mi bien despierta mira que ya amaneció

[dɛs 'pjɛr ta mi bjɛn dɛs 'pjɛr ta mi 'ɾa kɛ ja̯ama nɛ 'sjɔ]

Wake up my love wake up see that the sun has come up

Wake up my love, wake up. Look, the sun is up.

Ya los pajaritos cantan la luna ya se metió.

[ja lɔs pa ha 'ri tɔs 'kan tan la 'lu na ja sɛ mɛ 'tjɔ]

Now the birds are singing and the moon has gone away.

The birds are now singing and the moon has disappeared.

Que linda está la mañana en que vengo a saludarte

[kɛ 'lin da̯ɛs 'ta la ma 'ɲja na̯ɛn kɛ 'βɛn gɔ̯a sa lu 'ðar tɛ]

How beautiful is the morning that I come to greet you

What a beautiful morning we have today that I've come to greet you.

Venimos todos con gusto y placer a felicitarte

[βɛ 'ni mɔs 'tɔ dɔs kɔn 'gu stɔ i pla 'sɛr a fɛ li si 'tar tɛ]

We came all with gusto and pleasure to greet you

We've all come together with great pleasure to greet you.

El día en que tu naciste nacieron todas las flores

[ɛl 'di:a̯ɛn kɛ tu na 'si stɛ na 'sjɛ ɾɔn 'tɔ ðas las 'flɔ ɾɛs]

The day you were born were born all the flowers

The day you were born all the flowers began to bloom.

Y en la pila del bautismo cantaron los ruiseñores.

[i̯ɛn la 'pi la dɛl bau 'tis mɔ kan 'ta ɾɔn lɔs rwi sɛ 'ɲjɔɾɛs]

And the basin of baptism will sing the nightingales.

And the nightingales sang from the baptismal font.

Ya viene amaneciendo ya la luz del día nos dió

[ja 'vjɛ nɛ̯ama nɛ 'sjɛn dɔ ja la lus dɛl 'di:a nɔs djo]

It comes the dawn and already the light of day gave us

The sun is coming up and the light of day is with us

Levántate de mañana mira que ya amaneció.

[lɛ 'βan ta tɛ dɛ ma 'ɲja na mi ɾa kɛ ja̯a man ɛ 'sjɔ]

Get up tomorrow. Look, it's already dawn.

Get up! It's already morning. Look! The day awaits.

234 THE MARIACHI VOICE

16. PLEGARIA DE UNA INDITA MORENA A LA VIRGENCITA MORENA
[PRAYER FROM AN INDIAN WOMAN TO THE DARK-SKINNED VIRGIN]

Music and Lyrics by Antonio Gomezanda

Copyright © 2017 ASCAP All Rights Reserved
Used with full permission of Gomezanda Family
Please do not post, print or take pictures with without permission of book author from
www.juanitamusic.com, www.voicetrainerdr.com, or email: juanitavoicetrainer@gmail.com

CHAPTER 6: SONGS, DICTION, LYRICS, IPA, AND TRANSLATIONS 235

Plegaria
De Una Indita A La Virgencita Morena
(Prayer from an Indian Woman to the Dark-skinned Virgin)

Lyrics and Music by
Antonio Gomezanda

Copyright © 2017 ASCAP All Rights Reserved
Used with full permission of Gomezanda Family
Please do not post, print or take pictures with without permission of book author from
www.juanitamusic.com, www.voicetrainerdr.com, or email: juanitavoicetrainer@gmail.com

Ay, Virgencita de Guadalupe
[aj ʙir xɛnˈsi ta dɛ ɣwa daˈlu pɛ]
Oh, Virgin of Guadalupe
Oh, Virgin of Guadalupe.

Ay, ¡cuanto sufro por culpa d'el!
[ajˈkwan tɔˈsu frɔ pɔrˈkul pa dɛl]
Oh, how much I suffer because of him!
Oh, how I suffer because of him!

Haz que s'enmiende y que sea bueno
[ˈas kɛ sɛnˈmjen dɛ i kɛˈsɛ a ˈʙwɛ nɔ]
Make him well again and that he be good
Heal him and make him be good,

y que no quiera a otra mujer.
[i kɛ nɔ ˈkjɛ ra aˈo tra muˈxɛr]
and that he not love another woman.
and don't let him love another woman.

Ya que le diste tamaños ojos
[ja kɛ lɛ ˈðis tɛ taˈa ɲɔsˈɔ xɔs]
Since you gave him those big eyes
Since you gave him those big eyes

y esas fuerzotas y ese querer.
[iˈɛ sas fwɛrˈsɔ tas iˈ‿ɛ sɛ kɛˈrer]
And that big strength and that love.
And that awesome strength and that special love.

'hora lo cuidas y lo acompañas
[ˈɔ ra lɔˈkwi das i lɔ‿a kɔɱˈpa ɲas]
Now take care of him and accompany him
Now you take care of him and accompany him,

para que me ame como yo a él.
[ˈpa ra kɛ mɛˈ a mɛˈkɔ mɔ jɔ‿a ɛl]
so that he will love me like I do him.
so that he'll love me the way I love him.

CHAPTER 6: SONGS, DICTION, LYRICS, IPA, AND TRANSLATIONS

17. POR UN AMOR [FOR A LOVE]

2 Por un Amor

Additional lyrics:

Por un amor he llorado gotitas de sangre del corazón
Me has dejado con el alma herida sin compasión
Pobre de mi. Esta vida es mejor que se acabe no es para mi
Pobre de mi, pobre de mi
Cuánto sufre mi pecho que late tan solo por ti.

CHAPTER 6: SONGS, DICTION, LYRICS, IPA, AND TRANSLATIONS 239

Por un Amor
(For a Love)
Ranchera lenta

Lyrics and Music by
Gilberto Parra

Por un Amor

Additional lyrics:

Por un amor he llorado gotitas de sangre del corazón
Me has dejado con el alma herida sin compasión
Pobre de mi. Esta vida es mejor que se acabe no es para mi
Pobre de mi, pobre de mi
Cuánto sufre mi pecho que late tan solo por ti

Por un amor me desvelo y vivo apasionado*

[pɔr un a 'mɔr mɛ ðɛs 'βɛ lɔ i 'βi βɔ a pas jɔ 'na dɔ]

For a love I don't sleep and live passionately

Because of love I'm sleepless at night and live in a state of passion.

Tengo un amor

[tɛŋgɔ un a 'mɔr]

I have a love

I have a love.

Que en mi vida dejó para siempre amargo dolor

[kɛ ɛn mi 'βi ða ðɛ 'xɔ para 'sjɛm prɛ a 'marɣɔ ðɔ 'lɔr]

Who in my life left forever, bitter pain
Who has left my life with bitter pain.

Pobre de mí. Esta vida es mejor que se acabe, no es para mi.
['pɔ βɾɛ ðɛ mi 'ɛs ta 'βi ða es mɛ 'xɔr ke se̯a 'ka βɛ no̯ɛs 'pa ra mi]
Poor me. This life is better if it ends it's not for me
Poor me. It's better to end my life, it's not worth living like this.

*Possible author, Gilberto Parra.
**A female singer would sing the word *apasionada* instead of *apasionado*.

Pobre de mí, pobre de mí
['pɔ βɾɛ ðɛ mi 'pɔ βɾɛ ðɛ mi]
Poor me, poor me
poor me, poor me.

Cuánto sufre mi pecho que late tan solo por ti
['kwan tɔ 'su fɾɛ mi 'petʃɔ ke 'la tɛ tan 'sɔ lɔ pɔr ti]
How much suffers my chest that beats only for you
I'm suffering and my heart beats only for you.

Por un amor he llorado gotitas de sangre del corazón
[pɔr un a 'mɔr ɛ ʎɔ 'ra ðɔ ɣɔ 'ti tas ðɛ 'saŋ gɾɛ ðɛl kɔ ra 'sɔn]
For a love I've cried little drops of blood from my heart
Because of love, I have cried blood drops from my heart.

Me has dejado con el alma herida sin compasión.
[me̯a ðɛ 'xa ðɔ kɔn ɛl 'al ma ɛ 'ri ða sin kɔm pas 'jɔn]
You've left me with a soul wounded with no compassion
With no compassion at all you've wounded my soul.

Pobre de mí. Esta vida es mejor que se acabe, no es para mi.
['pɔ βɾɛ ðɛ mi 'ɛs ta 'βi ða es mɛ 'xɔr ke se̯a 'ka βɛ no ɛs 'pa ra mi]
Poor me. This life is better if it ends, this is not for me.
Poor me. It's better to end my life, it's not worth living like this.

Pobre de mí, pobre de mí
['pɔ βɾɛ ðɛ mi 'pɔ βɾɛ ðɛ mi]
Poor me, poor me
poor me, poor me.

Cuánto sufre mi pecho que late tan solo por ti.
['kwan tɔ 'su fɾɛ mi 'petʃɔ ke 'la tɛ tan 'sɔ lɔ pɔr ti]
How much suffers my chest, it beats only for you
My heart grieves so much because it beats only for you.

242 THE MARIACHI VOICE

18. RANCHO ALEGRE [HAPPY RANCH]

Traditional Mexican Folk Song

CHAPTER 6: SONGS, DICTION, LYRICS, IPA, AND TRANSLATIONS 243

2 Rancho Alegre

Additional lyrics:

En mi rancho tengo todo
Animales, agua y sol
Y una tierra prieta y buena
Que trabajo con ardor.

Cuando acabo mis labores
Ya que se ha metido el sol
A la luz de las estrellas
Canto alegre mi canción.

CHAPTER 6: SONGS, DICTION, LYRICS, IPA, AND TRANSLATIONS   245

Rancho Alegre
(Happy Ranch)
Polca

Mexican Folk Song

Rancho Alegre

Don - de guar - do ___ Mi a - mor - ci -

to. ___ Tie - ne o - jos de lu - ce - ro y ca - pu -

lín. ___ En mi lín. ___

So - lo fal - ta a - llí u - na co - sa Que muy

pron - to yo ten - dré. Co - mo soy re - cién ca -

sa - da A - di - ví - nen lo que ___ es. Ha de

ser un ___ chil - pa - ya - te Gran - de y fuer - te a no du -

dar Que tra - ba - ja ___ de la - brie - go Ma - yor -

CHAPTER 6: SONGS, DICTION, LYRICS, IPA, AND TRANSLATIONS 247

Rancho Alegre 3

Additional lyrics:

En mi rancho tengo todo
Animales, agua y sol
Y una tierra prieta y buena
Que trabajo con ardor.

Cuando acabo mis labores
Ya que se ha metido el sol
A la luz de las estrellas
Canto alegre mi canción.

Soy del mero rancho alegre

[sɔːi dɛl'mɛ rɔ'rran t͡ʃɔ̯a'lɛ ɣrɛ]

I'm from the real ranch happy

I'm from a truly happy ranch.

Soy ranchera* de verdad

[sɔːi rran't͡ʃɛ ra dɛ βɛr'ðað]

I'm a rancher the truth

I'm a real rancher.

Que trabaja* de labriego

[kɛ tra'βa ha ðɛ la'βrjɛ ɣɔ]

that works as a laborer

I'm the farmer,

Mayordomo y caporal.

[ma jɔr'dɔ mɔ̯i ka pɔ'ral]

foreman, and the boss.

The foreman, and also the boss.

Mi querencia es este rancho

[mi kɛ'rɛn sja̯ɛs'es tɛ'rran t͡ʃɔ]

My heart is this ranch

My love and heart are in this ranch.

Donde vivo muy felíz

['dɔn ðɛ'βi βɔ muːi fɛ'liz]

where I live very happy

Where I happily live.

Escondido entre montañas

[ɛs kɔn'ði ð͡ɔ̯ɛn trɛ mɔn'ta njas]

Hidden between mountains

[It's]hidden away in the mountains,

De color azul añil.

[dɛ kɔ'lɔr a'sul a'ɲil]

Of color blue indigo

Blue indigo mountains.

CHAPTER 6: SONGS, DICTION, LYRICS, IPA, AND TRANSLATIONS   249

Rancho alegre mi nidito

[rran t͡ʃ‿a'lɛ grɛ mi ni'ði tɔ]

Ranch happy my little nest

Happy ranch, my cute, little nest.

Mi nidito perfumado de jazmín.

[mi ni'ði tɔ pɛr fu'ma ðɔ ðɛ has'min]

My little nest, perfumed with jasmine

My cute, little nest, perfumed with jasmine.

Donde guardo mi amorcito

['dɔn ðɛ'gwar ðɔ mi‿a mɔr'si tɔ]

Where I keep my little lover

Where my love, my beloved lives with me.

Tiene ojos de lucero y capulín.

['tjɛ nɛ'ɔ hɔs dɛ lu'sɛ rɔ‿i ka pu'lin]

She has eyes of light and and cherry flowers

She has starry, cherry blossom eyes.

Solo falta allí una cosa

['sɔ lɔ'fal ta‿a'ʎi‿'u na 'kɔ sa]

Only missing there is one thing

Only one thing is missing,

Que muy pronto yo tendré.

[kɛ mu:i'prɔn tɔ jɔ tɛn'ðrɛ]

That very soon will have

And soon I will have it.

Como soy recien casada*

['kɔ mɔ sɔ:i rrɛ'sjɛn ka'sa ða]

Since I'm recently married

Since I've just gotten married,

Adivinen lo que es.

[a ði'βi nɛn lɔ kɛ ɛs]

Guess what it is

Guess what it is.

Ha de ser un chilpayate
[a dɛ sɛr un t͡ʃil pa'ja tɛ]
Should to be a little kid
He will surely be a cute little kid.

Grande y fuerte a no dudar
['gran dɛ i'fwɛr tɛ̯ a nɔ ðu'ðar]
Big and strong no doubt
Big and strong without a doubt.

Que trabaja de labriego
[kɛ tra'ba ha dɛ la'brjɛ ɣɔ]
That will work as a farmer
He will work the land as a farmer,

Mayordomo y caporal.
[ma ɣɔr'ðɔ mɔːi ka pɔ'ral]
a foreman and boss
a foreman, and a boss.

Rancho alegre . . .
[rran t͡ʃɔ̯ a'lɛ grɛ]
Ranch happy
Happy ranch . . .

*Word endings for the female gender usually end in the letter a. Those choosing male gender identification would end the same words with the letter o.

CHAPTER 6: SONGS, DICTION, LYRICS, IPA, AND TRANSLATIONS   251

19. SOY MEXICANA [I AM A MEXICAN WOMAN]

Ranchera ca. 1950–1951

Lyrics and Music by Antonio Gomezanda

Additional lyrics:

Tengo pasión por las flores
mucho me gusta reír
Se comprender los amores
Las penas huyen de mí.

[Chorus]
Puerto Rico me gusta de veras
y allá voy a parar
A ver si hay un valiente
¡Que me quiera acompañar!

2. El hombre que a mi me ama, ha de ser fuerte y formal
Para que haga conmigo un calientito hogar
Quiero tener mi casita, cerca muy cerca del mar
bajo esbeltas palmeras en un país tropical.

Copyright 2017 ASCAP All Rights Reserved
Used with full permission of Gomezanda Family
Please do not post, print or take pictures with without permission of book author from
www.juanitamusic.com, www.voicetrainerdr.com, or email: juanitavoicetrainer@gmail.com

Soy Mexicana
(I'm a Mexican Woman)
son jalisciense or ranchera valseada

Lyrics and Music by
Antonio Gomezanda

Additional lyrics:

Tengo pasión por las flores
mucho me gusta reír
Se comprender los amores
Las penas huyen de mí.

[Chorus]
Puerto Rico me gusta de veras
y allá voy a parar
A ver si hay un valiente
¡Que me quiera acompañar!

2. El hombre que a mi me ama, ha de ser fuerte y formal
Para que haga conmigo un calientito hogar
Quiero tener mi casita, cerca muy cerca del mar
bajo esbeltas palmeras en un país tropical.

Copyright 2017 ASCAP All Rights Reserved
Used with full permission of Gomezanda Family
Please do not post, print or take pictures with without permission of book author from
www.juanitamusic.com, www.voicetrainerdr.com, or email: juanitavoicetrainer@gmail.com

CHAPTER 6: SONGS, DICTION, LYRICS, IPA, AND TRANSLATIONS   253

Soy mexicana y libre con alas para volar.

[sɔi mɛ xiˈka na̯ i'li βrɛ kɔn̯ˈa lasˈpa ra βɔˈlar]

I am a Mexican woman and free with wings to fly

I am a free Mexican woman with wings to fly.

Canto y bailo jarabe más yo también sé rezar.

[ˈkan tɔ iˈʙaj lɔ xaˈra βɛ mas jɔ tamˈbjɛn sɛ rrɛˈsar]

I sing and dance the jarabe but I also know how to pray

I sing and dance the jarabe but I also know how to pray.

Tengo pasión por las flores. Mucho me gusta reír.

[ˈtɛɲ gɔ paˈsjɔn pɔr lasˈflɔ rɛs ˈmu͡ tʃɔ mɛˈgus ta rrɛˈir]

I have passion for flowers. A lot I like to laugh

I'm passionate about flowers. I love to laugh.

Sé comprender los amores. Las penas huyen de mí.

[sɛ kɔm prɛnˈder lɔs aˈmɔ rɛs lasˈpɛ nasˈui jɛn dɛ mi]

I understand about love. Sorrow runs away from me

I understand about love. Sorrow runs away from me.

Golondrina que voy por los aires desde el Norte hasta el Sur.

[gɔ lɔnˈdri na kɛ ʙɔi pɔr lɔsˈaj rɛsˈdɛz de̯ɛlˈnɔr te̯ˈas ta̯ɛl sur]

Golondrina, I am flying through the air from the North to the South

*Golondrina, I am flying through the air from North to South.***

Ando buscando un campito donde poder anidar.

[ˈan dɔ ʙusˈkaɲ dɔ kamˈpi tɔˈdɔn dɛ pɔˈðɛr a niˈðar]

I'm looking for a little camping place where I can nest

I'm searching for a little place to nest and call my own.

El hombre que a mí me ame ha de ser fuerte y formal

[ɛlˈɔm βrɛ kɛ̯ˈa mi mɛˈa mɛ a dɛ sɛr ˈfwɛr tɛ i fɔrˈmal]

The man who loves me should be strong and courteous

The man who loves me should be strong and courteous,

para que haga conmigo un calientito hogar.

[ˈpa ra kɛ̯ˈa ga kɔɲˈmi gɔ un ka ljɛnˈti tɔ̯ ɔˈgar]

So that he can make with me a really warm home

So that together, we can create a warm, cozy home.

Quiero tener mi casita cerca muy cerca del mar

[ˈkjɛ rɔ tɛˈnɛr mi kaˈsi taˈsɛr ka mujˈsɛr ka ðɛl mar]

I want to have my own little house close, very close to the sea

I want to have my own little house close, very close to the sea.

bajo esbeltas palmeras en un país tropical.

['ba hɔ ɛs'bɛl tas pal'mɛ ras ɛn un pa'is trɔ pi'kal]

Under slender palm trees in a tropical country

Under slender palm trees in a tropical country.

Puerto Rico me gusta de veras y allá voy a parar.***

[pwɛr tɔ'rri kɔ mɛ'gus ta ðɛ'ʙɛ ras i̯ a'ʎa βɔi̯ a pa'rar]

Puerto Rico I like truly and over there I will stop

I really like Puerto Rico and I'm going to go there.

A ver si hay un valiente ¡Qué me quiera acompañar!

[a βɛr si ai̯ un ʙa'lįɛn tɛ kɛ mɛ'kįɛ ra̯ ɑ kɔŋ pa'ɲar]

Let's see if they have a courageous man who wants to go with me!

Let's see if there's a brave man who wants to go with me!

Jarabe is a popular Mexican national folk dance and rhythmic genre dating back to the nineteenth century.

**Golondrina* is a swallow. In Mexican songs one commonly recurs to swallows or doves to solve problems related to love. Two examples are the songs *Cu-cu-rru-cu-cu Paloma* and *Paloma negra*.

****The author writes in his original manuscript when he composed this song ca. 1951 that any location may substituted for Puerto Rico.*

CHAPTER 6: SONGS, DICTION, LYRICS, IPA, AND TRANSLATIONS   255

20. VIVO AÑORANDO [I LIVE LONGING]

By Dr. Juanita Ulloa (Ranchera valseada)*

Copyright © 1995 ASCAP All Rights Reserved
Please do not post, print or take pictures with without permission of author.
www.juanitamusic.com.
email: juanitavoicetrainer@gmail.com

Vivo Añorando

Additional lyrics:

Vivo añorando una tierra
donde haya sonrisas y felicidad.
Es un oasis de tranquilidad
donde existe la paz y bondad.

Esa nación no conoce el temor
allí se vive mejor.
En ese tierra que añoro yo
todo es belleza y color.

Todo es belleza paz y amor.

"This song was one of Top Winners at *Festival de la canción latinoamericana* and is on CD "Mujeres & Mariachi". Available on iTunes and Spotify. Chart Available upon request."

CHAPTER 6: SONGS, DICTION, LYRICS, IPA, AND TRANSLATIONS

Vivo Añorando
(I Live Longing)
Ranchera valseada

Lyrics and Music by Juanita Ulloa

Copyright © 1995 ASCAP All Rights Reserved
Please do not post, print or take pictures with without permission of author.
www.juanitamusic.com. email: juanitavoicetrainer@gmail.com

Vivo Añorando

Additional lyrics:

Vivo añorando una tierra
donde haya sonrisas y felicidad.
Es un oasis de tranquilidad
donde existe la paz y bondad.

Esa nación no conoce el temor
allí se vive mejor.
En ese tierra que añoro yo
todo es belleza y color.

Todo es belleza paz y amor.

"This song was one of Top Winners at *Festival de la canción latinoamericana* and is on CD "Mujeres & Mariachi". Available on iTunes and Spotify. Charts available upon request"

CHAPTER 6: SONGS, DICTION, LYRICS, IPA, AND TRANSLATIONS

Vivo añorando una tierra

['βi βɔaɲɔ'ran ðɔ̯u na 'tjɛr ra]

I live longing for a land

I'm longing for a land

que yo no conozco ni sé donde está

[kɛ jɔ nɔ kɔ'nɔs kɔ ni sɛ 'ðɔn ðɛɛs'ta]

that I don't know neither do I know where it is

I've never seen and I don't know where it is.

una nación sin fronteras con mil primaveras

['u na na'sjɔn sin frɔn'tɛ ras kɔn mil pri ma 'βɛ ras]

a nation with no boundaries with a thousand springs

a nation without boundaries with a thousand springtimes.

un cielo ideal

[un 'sjɛ lɔ̯i dɛal]

a sky ideal

An ideal heaven.

En esa tierra la gente comparte riquezas

[ɛn 'ɛsa 'tjɛ rra la hɛn 'tɛ kɔm 'par tɛ ri 'kɛ sas]

In that land people share their riches

In that place people share their wealth

y vive en paz

[i 'βi βɛ ɛn pas]

and live in peace

and live in peace.

Es un oasis de tranquilidad

[ɛs un ɔ'a sis dɛ tran 'ki li ðað]

It's an oasis of tranquility

It's an oasis of peace.

esa tierra en mis sueños está

['ɛ sa 'tjɛ rraɛn mis 'suɛ ɲɔs ɛs'ta]

that land in my dreams is there

That's the land in my dreams.

una nación donde réina el amor

['u na na 'cjɔn 'ðɔn ðɛ 'rrɛːi naɛl a 'mɔr]

a nation where reigns love

A nation where love reigns supreme.

donde no existe el dolor

['dɔn ðɛ nɔɛ'sis tɛɛl ðɔ'lðr]

where no exists pain

Where there is no pain.

en esa tierra que añoro yo

[ɛn'ɛ sa'tje rra kɛa̯ 'ɲɔ rɔ yɔ]

in the land that I long for

That's the land I long for.

todo es belleza y calor

['tɔ ðɔes 'βɛ ʎɛ sai̯ ka 'lɔr]

all is beauty and warmth.

Everything is beautiful and warm.

Esa nación no conoce el temor

['ɛ sa na 'sjɔn nɔ kɔ 'nɔ cɛɛ̯l 'tɛ mɔr]

that land knows no fear

In that land there is no fear

allí se vive mejor

[a:i sɛ 'βɛ βɛ mɛ'hɔr]

there living is better

One can live better there.

en esa tierra que añoro yo

[ɛn 'ɛ sa tjɛ 'rra kɛ a'ɲɔ rɔ yɔ]

in that land that I long for

That's the land I long for.

todo es bondad y color.

['tɔ ðɔes βɔn 'ðað i ka'lɔr]

all is generous and colorful

Everything is rich and full of color.

Vivo añorando una tierra

['βi βɔaɲɔ'ran ðɔ'una'tjɛ rra]

I live longing for a land

I'm longing for a land

donde haya sonrisas y felicidad.

[dɔn'dɛ 'a:i ja sɔn 'ri sas i fɛ li si 'ðað]

where there are smiles and happiness

where people smile and are happy.

Es un oasis de tranquilidad

[ɛs un ɔ'a sis dɛ tran ki li 'ðað]

It's an oasis of tranquility

It's an oasis of peace.

esa tierra en mi sueños está
[ɛsa 'tjɛ rra ɛn mi 'suɛ ɲɔs ɛs'ta]
that land in my dreams is
That's the land I dream of.

todo es bondad paz y amor.
['tɔ ðɔɛs βɔn 'ðað pas i a'mɔr]
all is generous and colorful
everything is rich with peace and love.

*This song won top honors at the Festival de la canción latinoamericana for song composition and song interpretation.

FIGURE 6.2 Ranchera singing in duet dressed in traditional black *traje de charro* from Jalisco, Western Mexico. Design by Marcia Cagandahan.

CHAPTER 7

MARIACHI MUSIC FUNDAMENTALS

FIGURE 7.1 Santa Fe, New Mexico, dancers in live performance.

Sheet Music in Mariachi's Urban Period

While ranchera music has its roots in an oral folk tradition, mariachi performers came into contact with sheet music and song charts upon flocking to Mexico City to seek work, sometime after the Mexican Revolution (1910–1921). This period is often called the urban or contemporary mariachi period, as compared to mariachi's earlier rural ranch roots (see Chapter 2 sections: "Mexico's Golden Age of Cinema, Singers, and Songs" and "Crossover Singing: Jorge Negrete and *Operas rancheras*").

Beginning around 1913, the composer and pedagogue Manuel M. Ponce spearheaded a movement to collect, transpose, arrange, publish, and compose Mexican folk songs, also creating precedence to preserve Mexico's folksong heritage. Ponce's arrangements, folksong collection, and pioneering vision for Mexico inspired and encouraged future generations of musicians to appreciate and write down folk music (see Chapter 2 sections: "Manuel M. Ponce, 'The Father of Mexican Song'").

Beginning in the 1930s, many composers, arrangers, performers, and solo singers were hired to write, arrange, sing, and record in hugely popular *charro* musical films. Singers and songwriters had to turn around songs rapidly for back-to-back movies, performances, and studio recordings. Timelines were demanding for everyone involved. Musicians with written music skills and more vocal training not only learned quickly and sounded better; they were offered more jobs and overcame whatever technical challenges each song might present for the

CHAPTER 7: MARIACHI MUSIC FUNDAMENTALS   263

voice with more ease (see Chapter 2: History: Mariachi Singers and Their Songs: "Early and Mid-Twentieth Century: Rural to Urban Contemporary Rancheras").

Ranchera Composers and Arrangers Use Sheet Music: Manuel Esperón, Ruben Fuentes, Mariachi Vargas, Jorge Negrete

Manuel Esperón was one of the leading producers during the *Epoca de oro del cine mexicano* (Golden Age of Mexican Cinema) with over 300 *charro* music films. Esperón and most classical musicians used sheet music to compose and arrange music for the films (see Chapter 2: History: Mariachi Singers and Their Songs: "Mexico's Golden Age of Cinema, Singers, and Songs"). Esperón had a high level of musicianship and knew how to work quickly under pressure.

Between 1943 and 1947, Esperón also directed and produced the *Opera ranchera* entitled *Fantasía ranchera* together with Jalisco composer and pianist, Antonio Gomezanda (see Chapter 1: Introduction: "Terminology: *Mariache*," and Chapter 2: History: Mariachi Singers and Their Songs, "*Operas rancheras*"). In the film, Esperón featured Gomezanda's personal story as a composer honoring his ranchera musical roots in a small rural town towards the end of the Mexican Revolution (Gomezanda is played by Ricardo Montalbán). The *Fantasía ranchera* film includes segments of what has turned out to be the world's first opera ranchera, entitled *Mariache*. Trained opera singers with music reading skills performed leading roles in the movie alongside actor Ricardo Montalbán. The following singers crossed over into ranchera singing: Tenor, Pedro Vargas, contralto Josefina "Cha Cha" Aguilar, and, from Chile, the baritone Ramón Viñay. Lead soprano, Manolita Saval, sings in operatic style.

Manuel Esperón trained violinist Ruben Fuentes, who later followed Esperón's lead as an arranger. In the recording studio, Ruben Fuentes surprised Mariachi Vargas by using music charts. The ensemble then discovered they could record songs more quickly and efficiently, increasing their marketability and income.[1]

Crossover ranchera and opera singers were trained to read music. This is true, for example, for José Mojica, Jorge Negrete, and Pedro Vargas. In his autobiography, Mariachi Vargas trumpeter Miguel Martinez noted the talents of Pedro Vargas and Jorge Negrete. He mentions a specific experience in the recording studio with Negrete. Martinez admired Negrete's focus, discipline, quick learning, and ability to sing for long periods of time while recording, all of which reflect both solid voice training and a high level of musicianship.[2]

Unlike Vargas and Negrete, however, many singers did not and some still do not read music or music charts. Strong music readers with musicianship skills have a solid advantage, especially if they are planning long-term careers.

Music Fundamentals in Schools

In United States mariachi programs today, mariachi singers and instrumentalists commonly read music in preparation for rehearsals. The music is either written on a song sheet with melody and chord symbols, chord charts with no melody, or fully written out note for note. The notes and rhythms are intended as a guide and not always read note for note as one might

---

[1] Martinez, *Mi vida, mis viajes, mis vivencias,* 89–91.

[2] Martinez, *Mi vida, mis viajes, mis vivencias,* 89–91.

expect in classical singing; in fact, some son and huapango rhythms are notoriously difficult to notate, feel, and read even for the best-trained singers and instrumentalists. They nevertheless serve as important memory guides.

Singers with music training usually perform in better tune. Musicianship skills also enable singers to work independently to identify the specific range, key, and best *tessitura*, or vocal comfort zone (see Glossary), for any given song that best fits their particular voice. It is important to define one's tessitura and key choices prior to group rehearsals, not during. It helps singers know how to choose and specify desired tempos, key changes, and counting entrances in rehearsals. Music skills tend to open up new creative ideas for songwriting, better collaboration with instrumentalists, and general confidence.

Advanced singers should note that mariachi arrangers often forget and leave the solo singer's line out of mariachi arrangements. This can and should always be requested when available. Awareness of how the voice fits in with the mariachi ensemble leads to higher-quality performances and better communication overall.

Bilingual Theory and Solfege versus Letter Note Reading

Mariachi and classical musicians describe music theory differently. In the United States, it is important to "speak" the theoretical language of music in both Spanish and English. Many performers already move with ease between mariachi and classical music, speaking both Spanish and English. Both languages are used in mariachi rehearsals depending on the make-up of the group, where they live, and where they are from. The music-theory system in Latin America is also based upon a non-movable solfege system, not letter names. It is advantageous to learn both systems—and both languages—to be prepared for all options.

FIGURE 7.2 Children's Mariachi, *Ayudando Latinos a Soñar* (ALAS—Helping Latin Americans Dream) celebrates Mexico's heritage and culture through mariachi classes in Half Moon Bay, California. **Courtesy of Founder Dr. Belinda Arreaga.**

If the music fundamentals explained in this chapter seem rudimentary for advanced music students or professionals, please skip ahead to the Spanish music-theory section to work on bilingual linguistic music skills. Students may sign up for music-theory courses at local community colleges, search on YouTube, or work independently using theory applications (see Glossary). Weekly meetings with a music study partner whose strength is the opposite language and/or culture can also be quite helpful. A singer's long-term goal is to learn from both listening and reading music in both languages and styles.

SOLFEGE-SOLFEGIO

Music note reading is also often called *solfege*. In Spanish, the term is *solfegio*. In Latin America and the mariachi world, however, *solfege* is based upon a fixed and not often movable *do*, contrary to the musical system taught in the United States. Therefore, *do* is always the letter C. The C scale from *do* to *do* would therefore appear as seen in Figure 7.3 from C4 to C5. In mariachi and many Latin American music settings, the *solfege* system prevails. Remember, the *do* is almost always fixed as the letter C.

REVIEW QUESTIONS: SHEET MUSIC IN MARIACHI'S URBAN PERIOD, MANUEL M. PONCE, MANUEL ESPERÓN, AND SOLFEGE

1. How and when did Manuel Ponce contribute to the writing down and publishing of Mexican folk songs?
2. Who is Manuel Esperón, and how did he use his music talents in the ranchera music world?
3. Why is it advantageous for a singer to read music and train in music fundamentals or theory?
4. In Latin America, what is solfege or *solfegio*? In Latin America is the solfege musical system based upon a movable or unmovable *do*?
5. Write down two steps you can take to improve your music fundamental skills.

Answers:

1. In 1913, Manuel M. Ponce, Father of Mexican Song, collected folk songs and spearheaded a movement to establish Mexico's song heritage.
2. Manuel Esperón was a prolific composer, arranger, and producer of over 300 *charro* musicals. His training allowed him to produce quick, top-notch musical results. He also led the direction of *Fantasía ranchera*, featuring part of the world's first opera ranchera, *Mariache* by Antonio Gomezanda (see Chapter 2: Mariachi Voice History).
3. Singers who are familiar with music theory learn music more quickly, sing in better tune, make stronger creative choices, find their own keys for songs, and communicate better with the ensemble.
4. In Latin America the solfege system uses do-re-mi rather than letter names, but the note *do* is always for the letter C and does not transpose or change.
5. Find a study partner, download theory applications, or take a community-college music class.

Bilingual Music Fundamentals

The following is a music staff for note reading. Notice there are five lines and four spaces, that is, between the five lines are four spaces. Each note is positioned on a line or in a space and has

DO, RE, MI, FA, SO, LA, SI, DO

FIGURE 7.3 Treble clef do scale—*Escala de do.*

Space 4	Line 5
Space 3	Line 4
Space 2	Line 3
Space 1	Line 2
	Line 1

FIGURE 7.4 Treble clef music staff.

a letter name or *solfege* name (e.g., A, B, C or do, re, mi). Always count from the bottom note up. Figure 7.3 shows a treble clef symbol on the left with the lines and spaces.

Figures 7.4 and 7.5 are treble-clef music staffs for note reading. Notice in Figure 7.4, there are five lines and four spaces. Between the five lines are four spaces. Each note is positioned on a line or in a space and has a letter name or *solfege* name (e.g., A, B, C or do, re, mi). Always count from the bottom note up. Note the treble-clef symbol to the left of the lines and spaces.

When playing the piano, the right hand plays *treble-clef* notes on the right half of the piano (Clave de sol, also called G clef). The *bass-clef* notes are located on the left-hand side of the piano and are played with the left hand (bass clef is also called Clave de fa, or F clef).

Melodies and ranges for female singers are located mostly in the treble clef. The baritone and bass male ranges are located primarily in the bass clef. The higher male tenor voice falls between the two clefs and can be written in either treble or bass clef depending on the range of the song.

TREBLE CLEF (CLAVE DE SOL)

Lines: The five lines, E, G, B, D, F, spell the phrase, "Every Girl, Boy Deserves Fudge."
In *solfege* they are called mi, sol, si, re, fa.

Spaces: The four spaces, F, A, C, E spell the word "Face." In *solfege*, they are called fa, la, do, mi.

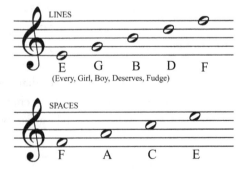

FIGURE 7.5 Treble clef letter names.

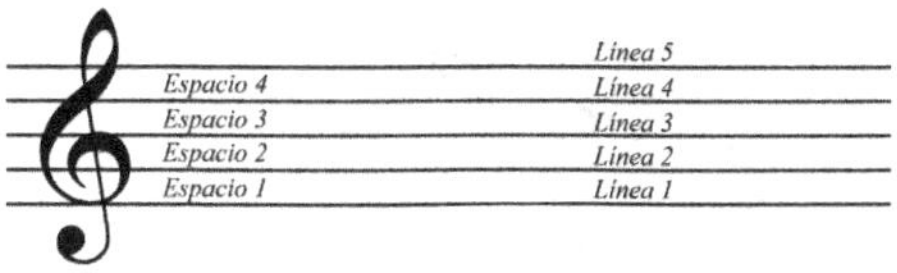

FIGURE 7.6 *Pentagrama* means staff and *Clave de sol* is treble clef.

E G B D F   F A C E
(Este guacamole bárbaro da fuerza)   (Franciso así come enchiladas)

FIGURE 7.7 Letter names in Spanish for treble clef.

Note that the lines and spaces in treble clef have to do with people. Be sure and always count from the bottom line or space upwards. Memory hint: You can call this clef the "people" clef.

TREBLE CLEF IN SPANISH—CLAVE DE SOL EN ESPAÑOL

If you already read music, begin learning the same notes in Spanish in the next section. Memory hints for remembering the note names in Spanish are listed in Figures 7.6 and 7.7.

In Spanish, the staff is called a *pentagrama*, and it also has five *líneas* (lines) and four *espacios* (spaces). Memorize the lines and spaces.

CLAVE DE SOL

Líneas: Las cinco líneas, E, G, B, D, F, deletrean la frase, "Este guacamole bárbaro da fuerza" (This amazing guacamole makes one strong).[3] *En solfegio se llaman mi, sol, si, re, fa.*

Espacios: Los cuatro espacios F, A, C, E deletrean la frase, "Franciso así come enchiladas" (This is how Francisco eats enchiladas). *En solfegio se llaman fa, la, do, mi.*

Note that the lines and spaces for the treble clef in Spanish have to do with Mexican food. Memory hint: You can call this clef the "food" clef (Figure 7.8).[4]

BASS CLEF (CLAVE DE FA)

Similar to the treble clef, the bass clef also has five lines and four spaces (Figure 7.9). The clef symbol designates lower notes, however, and a different set of notes.

---

[3] Thanks to Peruvian musician Nayo Ulloa for his collaboration creating fun memory hints in Spanish. Thanks also to the Community Music Center and MelBay Publications for grants supporting the publication of the author's *Beginner Latin American Piano Book* with bilingual solfege and children's Mexican and Latin American songs.

[4] Students can practice their music fundamentals online for free on free apps, including UCLA Music Theory, Music Theory, Music Tutor, teoria.com, and others.

FIGURE 7.8 MMF memory hints in Spanish for treble clef.

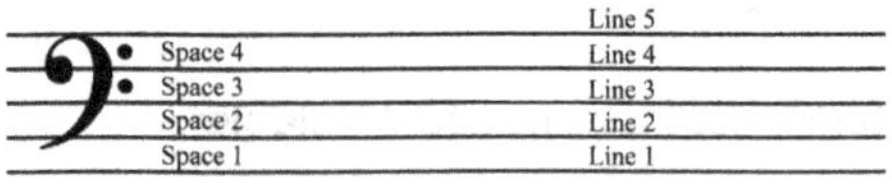

FIGURE 7.9 Bass clef lines and spaces.

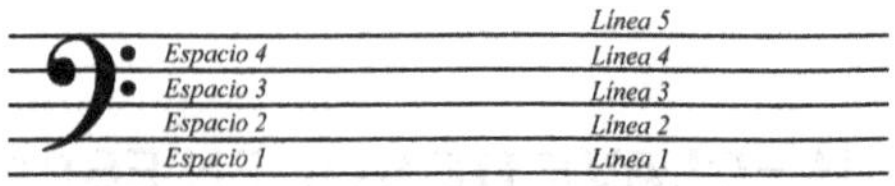

FIGURE 7.10 Letter names for bass clef lines and spaces in Spanish.

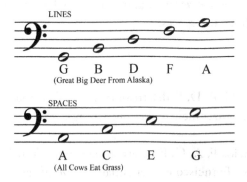

FIGURE 7.11 MMF memory hints in Spanish for bass clef.

Figure 7.10 shows the letter names for the Bass Clef lines and spaces in Spanish.

Bass Clef

Lines: The five lines, G, B, D, F, A, spell the phrase, "Great Big Deer From Alaska."
In *solfege*, they are called sol, si, re, fa, la.
Spaces: The four spaces, A, C, E, G, spell the phrase, "All Cows Eat Grass." In *solfege* they are called fa, la, do, mi.

Note that the lines and spaces in bass clef use animal topics. Memory Hint: call it the "animal" clef. The letters appear below.

FIGURE 7.12 Bass clef—*Clave de fa* names.

BASS CLEF IN SPANISH—CLAVE DE FA

Líneas: Las cinco líneas, G, B, D, F, A, deletrean la frase, "Gran burro de fuerza animal" (Big Burro with Brute Strength). En *solfegio*, se llaman sol, si, re, fa, la.

Espacios: Los cuatro espacios A, C, E, G, deletrean la frase, "Allá corren elefantes gordos" (Fat Elephants Run Over There). En *solfegio*, se llaman la, do, mi, sol.

Note that the lines and spaces for the Bass Clef in Spanish also have animal topics. Memory hint: You can call it the "animal" clef in either English or Spanish. The names are depicted below in Figure 7.12.

Meter and Rhythmic Note Values

Singers will learn songs efficiently if they practice counting and conducting the meter for each song being studied. Meter is the overall measurement of time throughout the song. The meter is intrinsically linked to the rhythmic genre or style. For example, the polka is always in 2/4 meter and is conducted by repeatedly counting 1, 2 throughout the song. The ranchera valseada is in 3/4, and singers should count 1, 2, 3 throughout the song. The huapango is in 6/8, which can be felt in either 1, 2, 3 or 1, 2, or both simultaneously. As singers learn each new song, they should first identify the rhythmic style by listening to identify the meter. Daily practice should include conducting while singing. Advanced singers will know where to improvise new rhythms and melodic notes if they have learned to always feel the meter's groove and can count with ease (see Rhythmic Styles).

To learn a song, students must identify the melody with pitch as well as rhythmic values. They must know how long to hold each note. Rhythmic values appear in Figure 7.13 in Spanish and English.

NOTES VALUES IN SPANISH

Redonda is a Whole Note
Blanca con puntilla is a Dotted Half Note
Blanca is a Half Note
Negra is a Quarter Note
Corchea is an Eighth Note
Semicorchea is a Sixteenth Note

270 THE MARIACHI VOICE

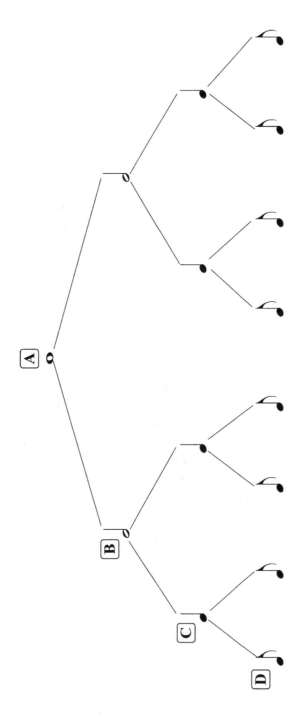

A. 1 Whole note is equal to / 1 Redonda es igual a
B. 2 Half notes is equal to / 2 Blancas es igual a
C. 4 Quarter notes is equal 2 / 4 Negras es igual a
D. 8 Eighth notes / 8 Corcheas

FIGURE 7.13 Rhythmic values in English and Spanish.

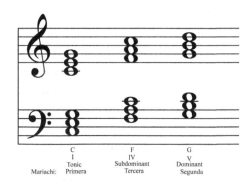

FIGURE 7.14 I IV V Chords in C.

TRANSCRIPTION OF MELODIES AND RHYTHMS

Singers who learn to write down their melodies along with matching lyrics will process songs on a deeper level. This process is called music transcription. Audiences are moved when a performer transmits intention and depth of feeling through a song. When a singer isolates song melodies by playing them on an instrument, this can trigger valuable ideas for varying the melody or improvising rhythmic variations. Building this process often leads to the emergence of a singer's personal style.

Play and write out the melody to your song. If you are unable to begin, have a teacher help you find the key of the song or start you off with the first two to five notes of the song. Then add rhythmic values. Some feel more comfortable counting out the meter and writing out rhythm values first, and then finding the pitches. Your next step is to combine the melody with the rhythm. Are you steady against a metronome? Can you count out loud in both languages? Advanced singers will later also be able to add the left-hand chords on piano or a strum on vihuela or guitar. Can you quickly recite the names with both letters and solfegio as you play? Mastering these ideas a step at a time will allow singers to integrate the many steps above while they separately work their vocal technique through breath, alignment, and vowels. The goal is to integrate all of this with movement and song interpretation.

THREE BASIC CHORDS

Three basic chords are the harmonic foundation of ranchera folk songs. Why is this important to a singer? In the words of Lamperti, famed voice pedagogue from the 1800s, "Pitch of tones should be associated with harmonies, not melodies," and "the tones of the underlying harmony and not the passing notes keep the trueness of tonality."[5] In order to be completely in tune and in a groove, a singer must "hear" and "sense" the harmony beneath their sung melody. For this reason, singers benefit from learning to accompany themselves with at least three basic mariachi chords in each tonality, even if just for practice.

In classical music theory, Roman numerals are often used to describe the three chords: I, IV, and V. They are also known as the tonic (also called root), subdominant, and dominant, respectively. These three chords are the main chords used in polka, ranchera lenta, and ranchera valseada rhythmic styles. Mariachi musicians often name these chords do, fa, sol, or C, F, G. While this is fine, working with Roman numerals can make it much easier to transpose to new keys. Explore them all! See the various labels for I, IV, and V chords below.

---

[5] Giovanni Battista Lamperti, "Vocal Wisdom, Writings of Lamperti" (2010 reprint of 1931 edition), 56.

In the mariachi world, I, V, and V chords have a different nomenclature and are assigned different numbers. It is commonly used in rehearsals and needs to be memorized. The three most common chords are known as *Primero* (I-First), *Segundo* (V7-Second), and *Tercero* (IV-Third). This refers to the first, second, and third most important chords in each song. Note that the most important chord is the tonic or I chord in both systems. The second most important chord, however, is the dominant or V chord. The third most important chord is the subdominant or IV chord.

It is helpful to accompany oneself and call out the chords on the downbeats (skipping a word or two to call out the chord), once in English and once in Spanish. Repeat the song again using classical terms and repeat a final time using mariachi terms. Once regularity and speed are achieved with a metronome, the full singing voice can be added.

Some ranchera songs (especially boleros) have more complex chords, and many have extremely complicated rhythms; nevertheless, the above foundation must be firm before moving into more complex harmonies or rhythms and 6/8 huapangos or 12/8 sones. Even those well attuned to challenging rhythms such as the *son* in "El son de la negra" will improve by slowing down the song and isolating the vocal lines with a metronome to isolate the rhythms of the vocal entrances. Vocal harmonies or singing with the group can be added after this is mastered.

While counting a song, singers do well when visualizing themselves within the larger context of the full arrangement. Counting is what keeps everyone united. It is also helpful to practice with a metronome to build consistency, whether with or without accompaniment.

If a singer in a live bilingual performance calls out a song title and needs to name the key out loud, please be aware of the following when calling out key names: the pronunciation of the letter C in English sounds identical to the pronunciation of the note B in Spanish. B is pronounced *si* instead of *ti* in Spanish. It is helpful to call out, saying "*C in English,*" "*C en inglés,*" "Do" (for C in English) or "*si en español*" (B).

Practice in C Major: Practice strumming the three main chords on the guitar, vihuela, guitarrón, and/or piano on downbeats. Practice with block chords first with no particular rhythm. Repeat saying the names of the chords in various systems as listed below. Once mastered, sing the melody as you play and find where the chords change within your song. As you improve, add different rhythmic strums. This prepares you for learning melodies while you feel the harmony simultaneously. This can also be practiced on the piano.

POPULAR MARIACHI KEYS

While classical singers benefit from being able to adapt their vocal range into any chromatic key for an orchestra, pianist, or chamber ensemble unless singing opera arias, in the mariachi ensemble there are more specific keys with fewer chromatic choices. Mariachi ensembles use predominantly string instruments, and beginning and intermediate mariachi ensembles will sound better using as many open strings as possible. Open strings provide more resonance and easier sound projection. In order for pre-professional ensembles to sound terrific and enjoy working with any given singer, it is often better to adapt a singer's best vocal key into one of the following keys: C, D, F, G, A (sometimes Bb).

When choosing a key, mariachi instrumentalists know that the trumpet reads music written one step below other instruments. For example, the key of F Major may be perfect for the singer and simple for the strings, but the trumpet has to play a step down in Eb with three flats. This may not be a good key selection for the ensemble unless the arrangement does not

CHAPTER 7: MARIACHI MUSIC FUNDAMENTALS 273

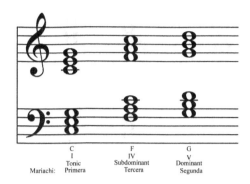

FIGURE 7.15 Chords in C Major.

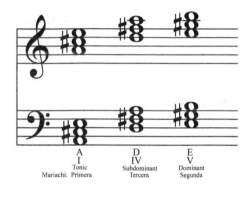

FIGURE 7.16 Chords in A Major.

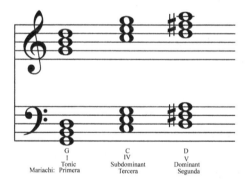

FIGURE 7.17 Chords in G Major.

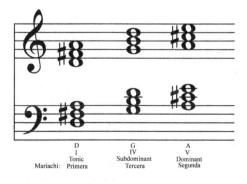

FIGURE 7.18 Chords in D Major.

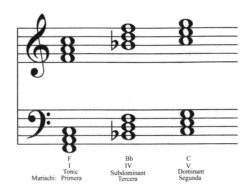

FIGURE 7.19 Chords in F Major.

include the trumpet or the trumpeter is highly trained. Advanced ensembles add more keys when able.

Practice the three basic chords for the mariachi friendly keys listed in Figures 7.15–7.19.

FINDING A SINGER'S BEST KEY

As discussed in the previous section, singers do well when honoring mariachi-friendly keys upon choosing a key. Before considering this, a singer will first want to find their own best key by analyzing the given song's range and movement. This should be compared to the singer's own personal singing *range* and *tessitura*. The word *range* refers to every note one can sing from bottom to top extremities. *Tessitura* refers to a zone somewhere in the middle of the range where the singer feels vocal ease and sounds the best (see Glossary). Singers often call their tessitura "money notes." Most of the melodic range within any song should highlight one's tessitura.

As an example, the general tessitura of many female mariachi singers is a3–f4. This is fairly consistent because the female mariachi fach is semi-fixed to highlight female chest range. While some higher notes may be used in belt and falsete mariachi singing, the upper half of the female vocal range is not as actively cultivated as in classical singing (see Chapter 3: Mariachi Voice Pedagogy: "Female Mariachi Fach"). The female key for a ranchera should generally begin in the lower end of a3–f4 and travel to higher notes for the chorus.

Women who have trained in mixed or belt voice will be able to go higher by activating a head-chest mix or soft belt up to between g4 and c5. In choosing a key the singer will want the chorus of the song to show off their best high notes. As an example, the high note c5 is often used on the last culminating note of the song *Aires de Mayab*. This song is a popular showpiece for women often performed in F Major. Because of the extended high belted range of this song with a low range section as well, it is considered an advanced vocal piece. The upper belt range offers more power, volume, and projection for the climax of the song when the belt voice is supported. Untrained singers quickly lose their voices if they yell in this section. If unsure how to support a belt sound or achieve a head-chest mix, one can try the song in a lower key if the low notes project, or change songs until belt voice production is more secure. To avoid vocal fatigue, the mixed voice and especially belt timbre should be used for climactic moments and not throughout the song. (see Chapter 3: Mariachi Voice Pedagogy: "What Is Belt Voice?").

Most of the male vocal range is already in chest voice; therefore, men can sing as basses, baritones, bari-tenors, or tenors without changing their tessitura for crossing between classical and mariachi vocal styles. If a particular singer has ease with high notes or a strong

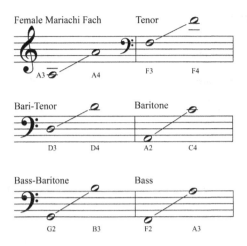

FIGURE 7.20 Voice tessituras. Note that tessitura is where the range of this voice part sounds naturally best but does not indicate the full range of the voice. Natural female ranges, for example, run at least one octave above the female mariachi fach.

falsete range, they will want the climax or highest notes of the song to fall within the upper part of their tessitura (see Chapter 3: Mariachi Voice Pedagogy: "Understanding Your Vocal Instrument").

With additional vocal training, both the range and the tessitura of virtually all voices can be extended with richer sounds. This opens up new key choices. Older singers who have worked this out avoid symptoms such as going flat, wide vibrato, or overheavy registration in the bottom half of the voice. Well-trained, healthy singers continue to exercise their full upper vocal range in order to keep the voice balanced from top to bottom, even when they do not use the top range in performance (see Chapter 3: Mariachi Voice Pedagogy, Warm-ups, Vocalises, and Practicing: "Vocalises: Mariachi Song Excerpts"). Figure 7.20 gives an approximate tessitura for each vocal range, keeping in mind that each voice is unique and not all voices fit perfectly into categories.

Special care should be applied to choosing a key for a mariachi song that has sustained falsete tones. This happens most often when singing huapangos in 6/8 rhythm:

1. Proceed through the steps already listed above.
2. Test several key choices by singing the transition note prior to the falsete note then the note itself. Make sure both feel comfortable despite the different timbre or color of each.
3. Isolate the two notes where the falsete switch activates a change in register. Sing several times on the indicated vowels to make sure the falsete switch is comfortable. Try several key choices until you are sure which one is more comfortable. A singer's focus should be upon the transition note and its corresponding vowel. Isolate the notes, but then focus on the vowels for each of the notes to create a solid falsete. The second falsete vowel should be sung where the last vowel was, that is, over the breath in the back of the mouth. The transition note usually falls within a two- or three-note transitional range where chest register begins transitioning into either female mariachi belt range or male upper register (for women approximately d4–g5 and for men c4–f#4). Good beginning huapangos with one or two falsete notes are *El Jinete, Canta mi son!, Corazón de Chapulín,* and *Cielo rojo.*

TABLE 7.1 Musical Terms for dynamic range and tempi in Italian, Spanish, and English.

Italian Italiano	Spanish Español	English Inglés
Forte (F)	Fuerte	Loud
Piano (P)	Suave	Soft
Accento (^)	Acento	Accent
Crescendo	Creciendo	Growing Louder
Decrescendo	Disminuendo	Growing Softer
Diminuendo	Disminuendo	Growing Softer
Accelerando	Acelerando	Accelerating
Ritardando	Ralentirar	Gradually Slower
Rallentando	Atardando	Gradually Slower
Con Moto	Con Moción (Animado)	With Motion (Animated)
Staccato	Stacato (Nota Breve)	Short Unconnected Note
Legato	Ligado (Notas Ligadas)	Smooth Connected Notes

Finally, in choosing a perfect song key singers will want to check that the high points of the song coincide with areas of their range that best show off their voice. If unsure, it helps to record oneself and listen back. Asking for feedback from musically trained friends or teachers helps as well. There is always a perfect key for every singer in every song!

DYNAMICS AND TEMPO TERMS IN SPANISH, ITALIAN, AND ENGLISH

In Table 7.1, a list of common *tempi* or rate of speed is provided in Italian. Italian is the typical tempo language for classical music. Tempo terms are translated into both Spanish and English below so students may see how closely related the Spanish and Italian *tempi* indications are (see Glossary). In mariachi, Spanish is most often used for tempo indications.

Establishing a slower tempo is particularly useful for practicing, with a faster speed for the song in performance. Once a singer has found their perfect performance tempo, they may label it with one of the appropriate tempo terms in Table 7.1. Some assign a number and others use terms. Both numbers and tempi terms are marked on metronomes. Once this is established, it is important for singers to practice melodies with a metronome. Always begin with the slower tempo, gradually increasing the speed once the vowels are smoothly connected and the song feels connected to the body. The metronome keeps singers honest with their counting.

For more complex studies of rhythms and music training, seek out tutorials on YouTube and online resources for mariachi rhythms and music theory. Full Voice Music (www.thefullvoice.com) from Canada also has useful ear training and theory exercises for young singers.

FIGURE 7.21 Solo singer at San Antonio's annual Mariachi Extravaganza. Photograph by Javier Vela.

Ten Lesson Plans

Lesson Plan 1 - Why Study Mariachi Music Fundamentals?

1. After the Mexican Revolution (1910 – 1921) in what city did many Mexican mariachi singers and musicians come into contact with written out classical sheet music and charts?

   _____

2. Why and how did singers and songwriters between the 1930's and 1950's benefit from reading and writing music?

   _____

3. Who was Manuel M. Ponce and why is he important to Mexican song? What was he often called? (see Chapter 2 Mexican Vocal History for more details on Ponce)

   _____

4. Who was Manuel Esperón and what was he known for?

   _____

5. Why is reading music useful to both mariachi singers and instrumentalists?

   _____

Circle true (T) or false (F):

T \ F   6. Charro musicals became popular in Mexico, Latin America, and Spain.

T \ F   7. Those with the most training and talent often got more work

T \ F   8. Mariachi Vargas learned that reading music helped speed up their ability to learn new songs and make recordings.

T \ F   9. Pedro Vargas and Jorge Negrete were both operatically trained before becoming celebrity ranchera singers.

T \ F   10. The written out notes, rhythmic patterns, and chords are intended as a guide and not always read note for note as in classical singing.

T \ F   11. Son and huapango rhythms are notoriously easy to read.

T \ F   12. Tessitura is a mariachi singer's favorite type of salsa.

T \ F   13. By defining one's vocal tessitura through voice lessons, a singer can efficiently choose the best key for each song prior to group rehearsals.

Lesson Plan 2 - Staff, Lines, and Spaces
  El pentagrama, líneas, y espacios

The staff (*pentagrama*) is made of 5 lines (*líneas*) and 4 spaces (*espacios*).

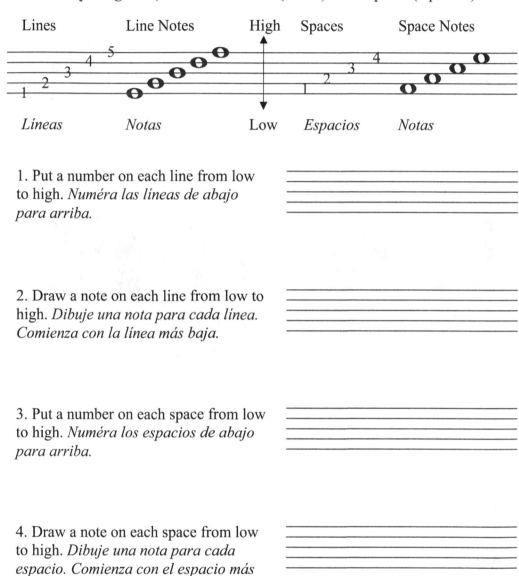

1. Put a number on each line from low to high. *Numéra las líneas de abajo para arriba.*

2. Draw a note on each line from low to high. *Dibuje una nota para cada línea. Comienza con la línea más baja.*

3. Put a number on each space from low to high. *Numéra los espacios de abajo para arriba.*

4. Draw a note on each space from low to high. *Dibuje una nota para cada espacio. Comienza con el espacio más bajo.*

5. Label (S) for each space note or (L) for each line note. *Indique si la nota se encuentra en un espacio (E) o sobre una línea (L) con la letra indicada.*

Lesson Plan 3 - Treble Clef (G Clef)
Clave de sol

Melodies and ranges for female singers, violin, trumpet, vihuela, and guitar are on the treble clef.

Reminder: Treble clef notes on the piano are located to the right of middle C.

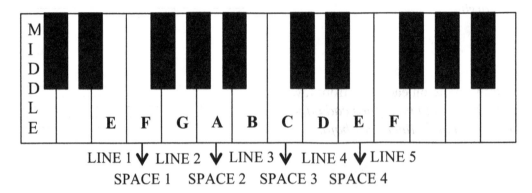

1. Practice drawing eight treble clefs on the staff below.
   Dibuje la clave de sol ocho veces en el pentagrama a continuación.

2. Label the letter name for each note. *Llene la letra correcta para cada nota.*

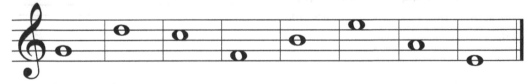

3. Draw a note on the staff indicated by the letter below.
   Según la letra, dibuje la nota en el pentagrama.

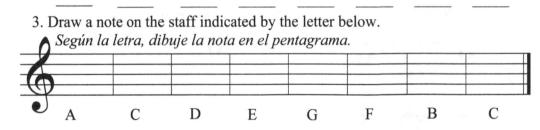

Spanish - *Español*
Reminder: In Spanish, the treble clef is known as the food clef. *En castellano uno puede memorizar los espacios y líneas pensando en la comida mexicana.*

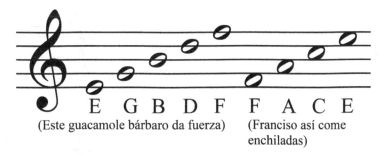

E G B D F   F A C E
(Este guacamole bárbaro da fuerza)   (Francisco así come enchiladas)

Solfege in Latin America uses a fixed Do, or C. *En solfegio estilo latinoamericano se trata a do como la letra C.*

DO, RE, MI, FA, SO, LA, SI, DO

4. Label the *solfege* letter under each note. *Llene el nombre de la letra debajo de cada nota.*

5. Draw the note on the staff indicated by the *solfege* name. *Según la nota en solféo, dibuje la nota en el pentagrama.*

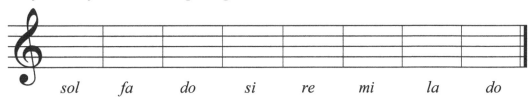

sol   fa   do   si   re   mi   la   do

6. Label the letter name **and** the *solfege* for each note on the line below. *Indique la nota en solféo así como la letra en las dos líneas debajo de las notas.*

282 THE MARIACHI VOICE

7. Draw a line matching the letters or *solfege* on the left to the notes on the right. *Dibuje una línea y conecta las letras o solfegio a mano izquierda con las notas del pentagrama al lado derecho.*

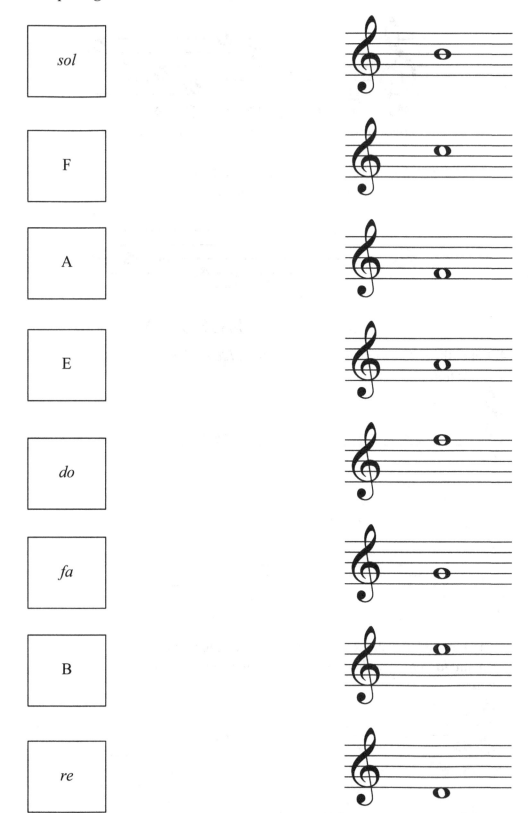

Lesson Plan 4 - Bass Clef (F Clef)
Clave de fa

Ranges for male singers are lower than women. They are located on the bass clef along with guitarrón patterns. *El registro para voces masculinas así como para el guitarrón se anota principalmente en clave de fa.*

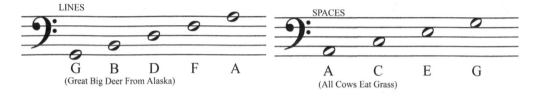

Reminder: Bass clef notes on the piano are located to the left of middle C.
Las notas del clave de fa se localizan a la izquierda de do central en el piano.

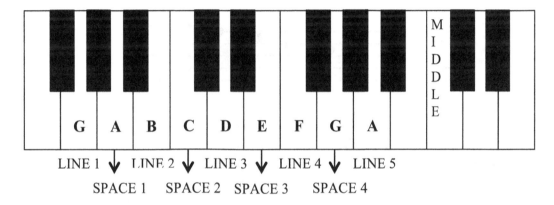

1. Draw eight bass clefs on the staff below.
Dibuje la clave de fa ocho veces en el pentagrama a continuación.

2. Label the letter name for each note.
Llene el nombre de cada letra debajo de cada nota.

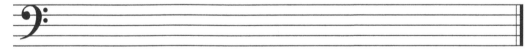

3. Draw a note on the staff indicated by the letter below.
Según la letra, dibuje la nota en el pentagrama.

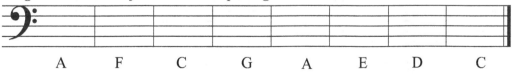

Spanish - *Español*

Reminder: In Spanish and English, the bass clef is known as the animal clef. *En castellano uno puede memorizar los espacios y líneas pensando en los animales.*

In *solfege*, Do is the same as C. *En solfegio se trata a la nota do como la letra C.* Important Reminder for Bilingual Learners: The note Si in Spanish means the letter B in English, not the letter C.

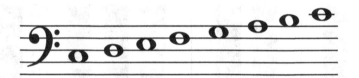

DO, RE, MI, FA, SOL, LA, SI, DO

4. Label the *solfege* letter under each note. *Llene el nombre de la letra debajo de cada nota.*

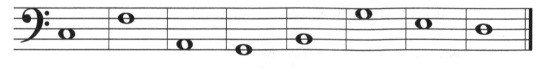

5. Draw the note on the staff indicated by the *solfege* name. *Según la nota indicada en solféo, dibuje la nota en el pentagrama.*

la   re   mi   do   si   fa   sol   do

6. Label the letter name and the *solfege* for each note on the line below. *Primero indique cada nota de solfeo y luego cada letra.*

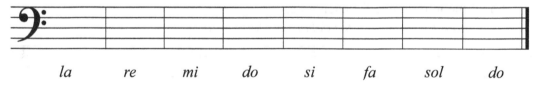

7. Draw a line matching the letters or *solfege* on the left to the notes on the right. *Dibuje una línea y conecta las letras o solfegio a mano izquierda con las notas del pentagrama al lado derecho.*

Lesson Plan 5 – Note Values
La duración de cada nota

Notes	Beats	English	Español
o	4	Whole note	Redondo
○.	3	Dotted-half note	Blanca con puntilla
○	2	Half note	Blanca
♩	1	Quarter note	Negra
♪	$\frac{1}{2}$	Eighth note	Corchea
♬	$\frac{1}{4}$	Sixteenth note	Semicorchea

1. Draw 3 more whole notes, then draw a measure line after each one.
Dibuje tres redondas y una linea marcando cada compás despues cada nota.

2. Draw 6 more half notes, then draw a measure line after every 2 notes.
Dibuje seis blancas y una linea marcanado cada compás despues cada dos notas.

3. Draw 12 more quarter notes, then draw a measure line after every 4 notes.
Dibuje doce negras y una linea marcando cada compás despues cada cuatro notas.

4. Draw 24 more eighth notes, then draw a measure line after every 8 notes.
Dibuje veinticuatro corcheas y una linea marcando cada compás despues cada ocho notas.

#5 – 8: Label the note letter in the box above and its value on the line below.
Llene el nombre de la nota arriba en la caja y la duración de bajo en la línea.

9. Under each line, write the sum value of the two notes above. *De bajo de cada línea, escribe las suma de las dos notas indicadas.*

Lesson 6 – Rhythm and Time Signatures
El compás y los marcadores de diferentes tiempos

Remember, the top note of the time signature indicates the number of beats per measure. *Acuérdense que el número superior del marcador de tiempo es el que indica cuantos pulsos hay total por compás.*

Notes	Beats	English	Español
o	4	Whole note	Redondo
◯.	3	Dotted-half note	Blanca con puntilla
◯	2	Half note	Blanca
♩	1	Quarter note	Negra
♪	$\frac{1}{2}$	Eighth note	Corchea
♬	$\frac{1}{4}$	Sixteenth note	Semicorchea

Directions/*Instrucciones*: #1 - 5

A. Fill in the missing bar with any mixture of notes adding up to the right amount of beats per measure. *Llene el compás vacío con una mezcla de notas que suman la cantidad correspondiente al marcador de tiempo.*

B. Write out the numbers for each beat under the notes. Ex. 1 & 2 & 3 & 4 & *Escriba el número de cada pulso debajo de cada nota.*

C. Can you conduct the time signature with your hand? Then try conducting while tapping the rhythm of each exercise with your foot. *¿Puedes dirigir cada ejercicio cantando como si fuera director? Al lograr eso, dirige siguiendo el valor de cada nota a la vez que marcas el ritmo de cada nota.*

Example/*Ejemplo*:

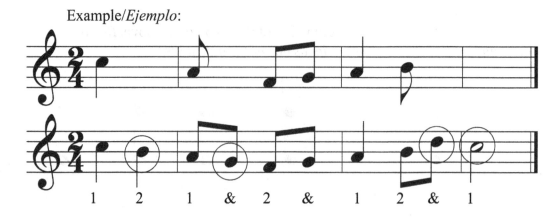

CHAPTER 7: MARIACHI MUSIC FUNDAMENTALS 289

1.

2.

3.

4.

5.

Lesson 7 – Mariachi Basic Rhythmic Patterns
Géneros rítmicos de mariachi

Bolero	Ranchera lenta	Polca
Son	Ranchera valseada	Huapango

#1 – 7: Identify and write in the name of the rhythm pattern for each music pattern below. *A mano izquierda anota el nombre del ritmo correcto. Las respuestas aparecen en las cuadras de arriba.*

1. ____________________

Vihuela
Guitarrón

2. ____________________

Vihuela
Guitarrón

3. ____________________

Vihuela
Guitarrón

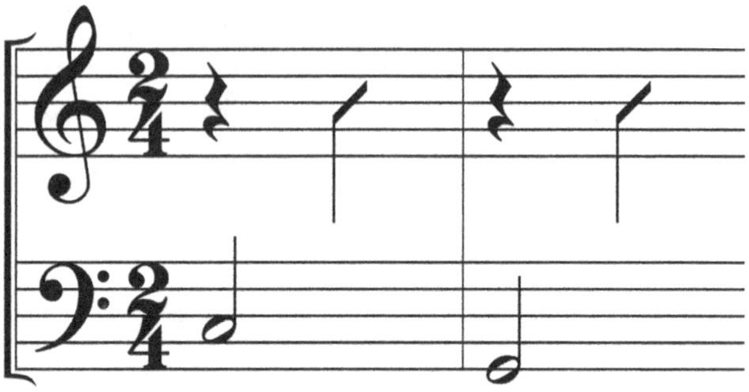

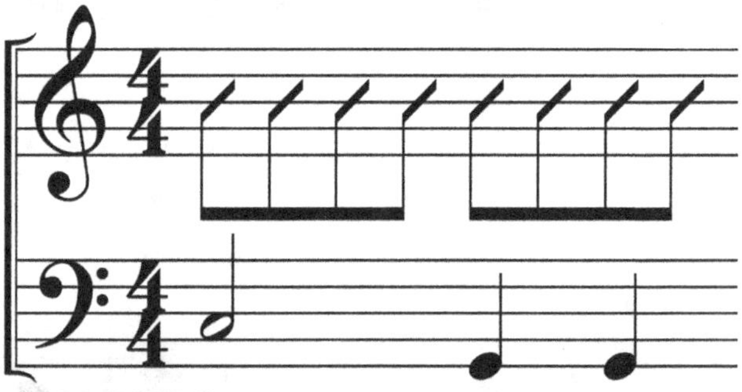

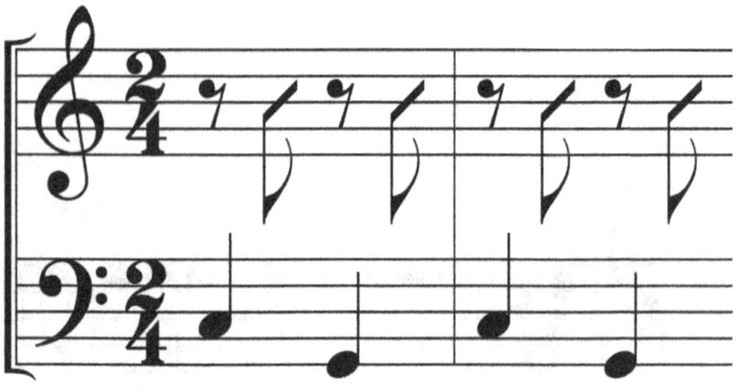

CHAPTER 7: MARIACHI MUSIC FUNDAMENTALS 291

4. _____

Vihuela

Guitarrón

5. _____

Vihuela

Guitarrón

6. _____

Vihuela

Guitarrón

7. _____

Vihuela

Guitarrón

Lesson Plan 8 – Chords
Acordes

1. Fill in the blanks on the table below.
Llene las cuadras vacías con la respuesta correcta.

Roman Numeral	I	IV	V
English	Tonic	Sub-dominant	
Español			Segunda

#2 – 5: Fill in the blanks in the tables below. Remember, the tonic chord (*la primera*) is always the same as the key (*el tono*) or tonic.
Llene las cuadras vacías con la respuesta correcta. No se olvide que la primera (do) también es el nombre del tono de la canción.

Example/*Ejemplo*: Key of C / *Tono de do*

Roman Numeral	I	IV	V
Letter Name			
Solfeo			

2. Key of A / *Tono de la*

Roman Numeral	I	IV	V
Letter Name			
Solfeo			

3. Key of G / *Tono de sol*

Roman Numeral	I	IV	V
Letter Name			
Solfeo			

4. Key of F / *Tono de fa*

Roman Numeral	I	IV	V
Letter Name			
Solfeo			

5. Key of D / *Tono de re*

Roman Numeral	I	IV	V
Letter Name			
Solfeo			

Directions/*Instrucciones*: #6-11
Draw the stack of 3 notes for every chord according to the given key.
Dibuje un pila de 3 notas para cada acorde de acuerdo con la clave dada.

Lesson Plan 9 a. – Musical Terminology
Terminología musical

1. **Draw a line connecting the symbols on the left to their Italian name on the right.** *Conecta los símbolos del lado izquierdo con el nombre correspondiente en italiano, ligándolos con una línea.*

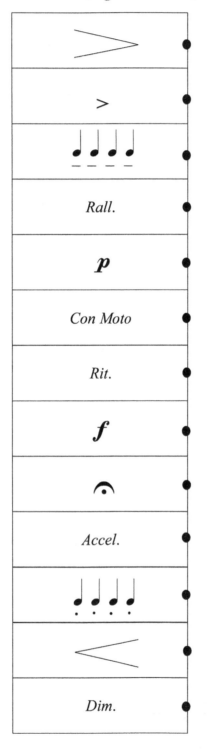

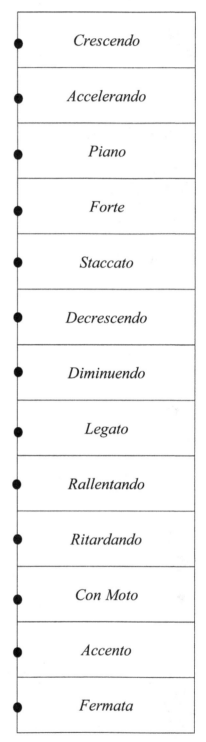

2. Draw a line connecting the Italian terms on the left to their English name on the right. *Conecta los terminlogía musicales en italiano del lado izquierdo con el nombre correspondiente en ingles, lígándolos con una línea.*

Italian		English
Ritardando	• •	Gradually slower
Diminuendo	• •	Growing softer
Fermata	• •	Short unconnected notes
Piano	• •	Loud
Staccato	• •	Accelerating
Accento	• •	With motion
Legato	• •	Smooth connected notes
Rallentando	• •	Gradually louder
Forte	• •	Soft
Con Moto	• •	Hold note
Crescendo	• •	Accent
Decrescendo	• •	Growing softer
Accelerando	• •	Gradually slower

Lesson Plan 9 b. – Musical Terminology
Terminología musical

1. Draw a line connecting the symbols on the left to their Spanish name on the right. *Conecta los símbolos del lado izquierdo con el nombre correspondiente en español, ligándolos con una línea.*

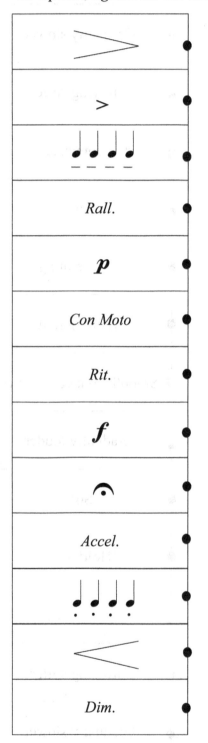

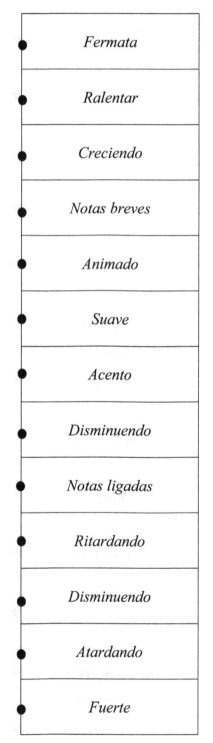

2. Draw a line connecting the English terms on the left to their Spanish name on the right. *Conecta los terminlogía musicales en ingles del lado izquierdo con el nombre correspondiente en español a mano derecha con una línea.*

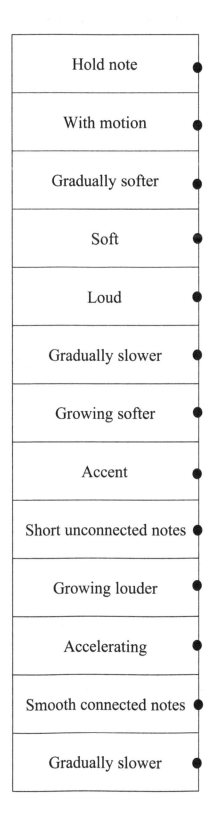

Lesson Plan 10 – Musical Terms in English and Spanish
Términos musicales básicas en inglés y español

Directions/*Instrucciones*: Translate the following phrases from English to Spanish. *Traduce las siguientes frases de inglés a español.*

1. Listen.

   _____

2. Find the steady beat.

   _____

3. Sing with me.

   _____

4. Please be quiet.

   _____

5. Please stand up.

   _____

6. Please sit down.

   _____

7. Please raise your hand.

   _____

8. Thank you for being a good listener.

   _____

9. Please line up.

   _____

10. Please make a circle.

   _____

Directions/*Instrucciones*: Translate the following phrases from Spanish to English. *Traduce las siguientes frases de español a inglés.*

11. Tocan con buen ánimo.

12. ¡Que bien suena el canto!

13. ¡Ensayaron bien!

14. No ensayaron (lo suficiente).

15. Sube el volumen.

16. Bajar el volumen.

17. ¿Lo pueden tocar más rápidamente?

18. ¿Lo pueden tocar más lentamente?

19. ¡Está perfecto!

20. Nota aguda/grave

MMF – Answer Key

Lesson Plan 1:

1. Mexico City

2. Singers and songwriters benefitted from reading and writing music between 1930's and 1950's by being able to learn new music quickly and therefore take on more work. Their high quality of musicianship also helped them stand out among the competition.

3. Manuel M. Ponce, often called "The Father of Mexican Song," advocated for the collection of folk music in order to write down, identify, and preserve Mexico's song traditions.

4. He was a prolific arranger, composer, and producer of over 300 movies.

5. Singers and instrumentalist can learn large amounts of music quickly and still lean on the oral flavor indigenous to the tradition.

6. T   7. T   8. T   9. T   10. T   11. F   12. F   13. T

Lesson Plan 2:

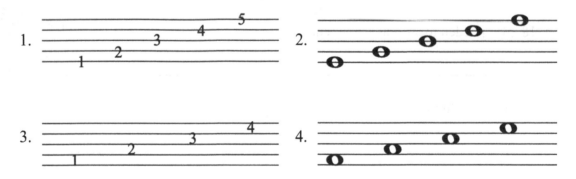

5. SLLSLLSSLS or ELLELLEELE

CHAPTER 7: MARIACHI MUSIC FUNDAMENTALS

Lesson Plan 3:

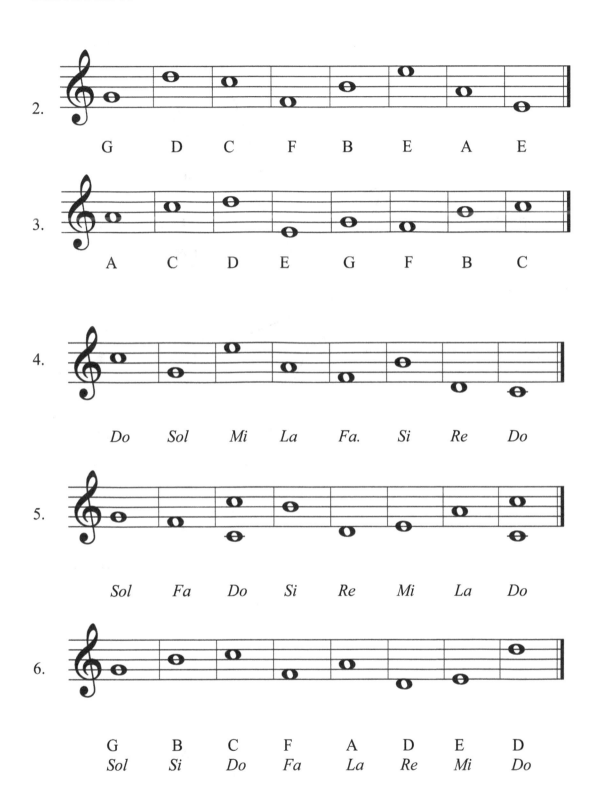

7.

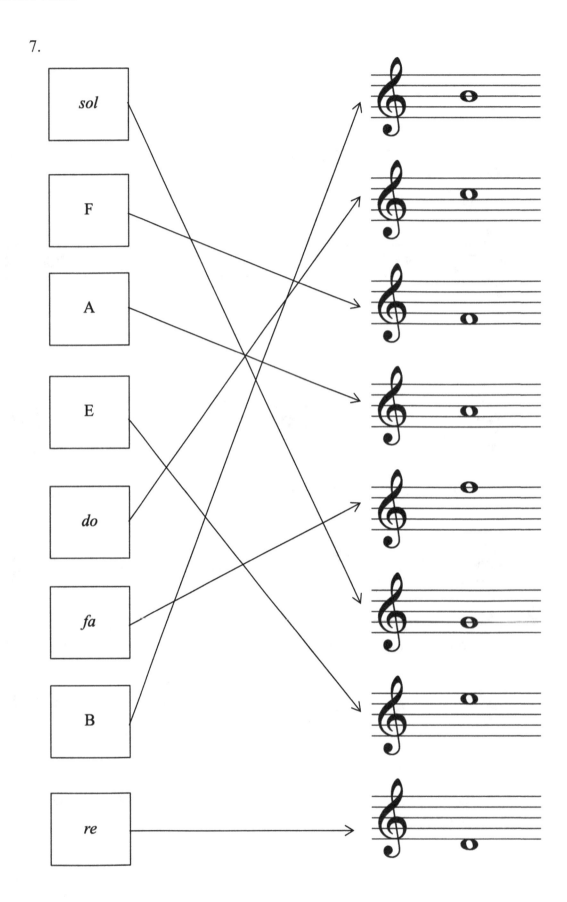

Lesson Plan 4:

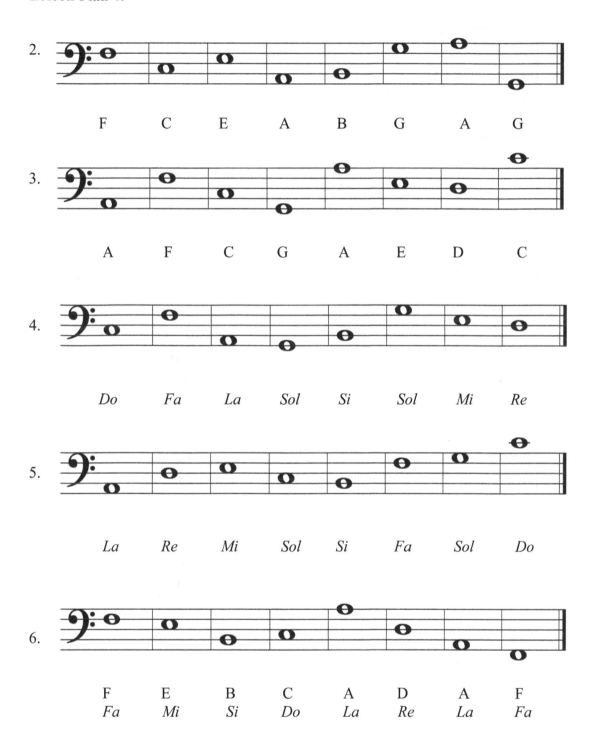

304   THE MARIACHI VOICE

7.

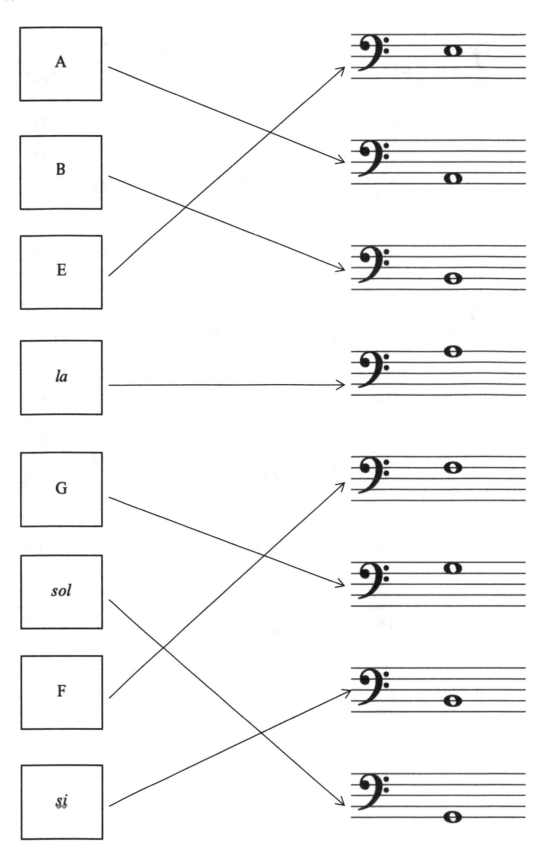

CHAPTER 7: MARIACHI MUSIC FUNDAMENTALS 305

Lesson Plan 5:

1.

2.

3.

4.

5.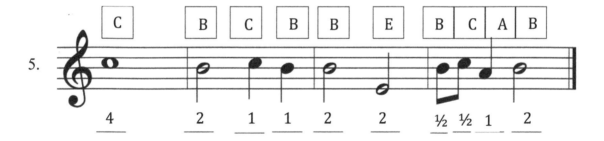

6.

306 THE MARIACHI VOICE

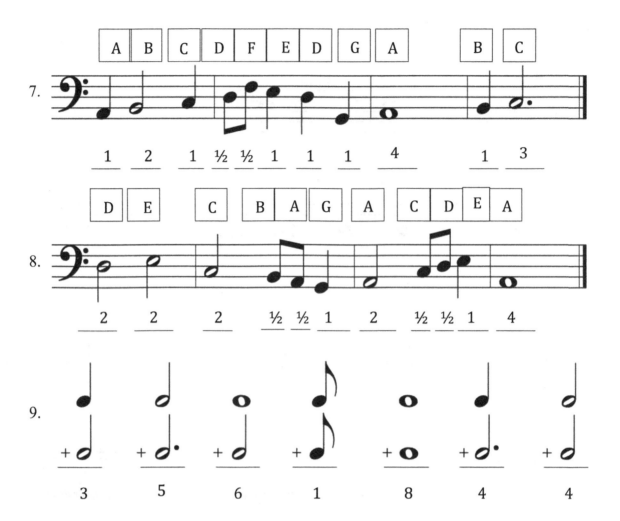

Lesson Plan 6:

1.

2.

3.

4.

5.

Lesson Plan 7:

1. Ranchera lenta   2. Bolero   3. Polca   4. Son

5. Ranchera valseada   6. Polca   7. Huapango

Lesson Plan 8:

1.

Roman Numeral	I	IV	V
English	Tonic	Sub-dominant	Dominant
Español	Primera	Tercera	Segunda

2. Key of A / *Tono de la*

Roman Numeral	I	IV	V
Letter Name	A	D	E
Solfeo	la	re	mi

3. Key of G / *Tono de sol*

Roman Numeral	I	IV	V
Letter Name	G	C	D
Solfeo	sol	do	re

4. Key of F / *Tono de fa*

Roman Numeral	I	IV	V
Letter Name	F	Bb	C
Solfeo	fa	Si bemol	do

5. Key of D / *Tono de re*

Roman Numeral	I	IV	V
Letter Name	D	G	A
Solfeo	re	sol	la

6. Key of G / *Tono de sol*

Tonic   Sub-dominant   Dominant

7. Key of F / *Tono de fa*

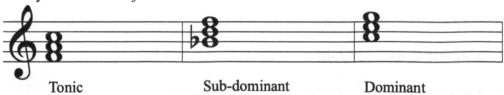

Tonic   Sub-dominant   Dominant

310 THE MARIACHI VOICE

Lesson Plan 9a:

1.

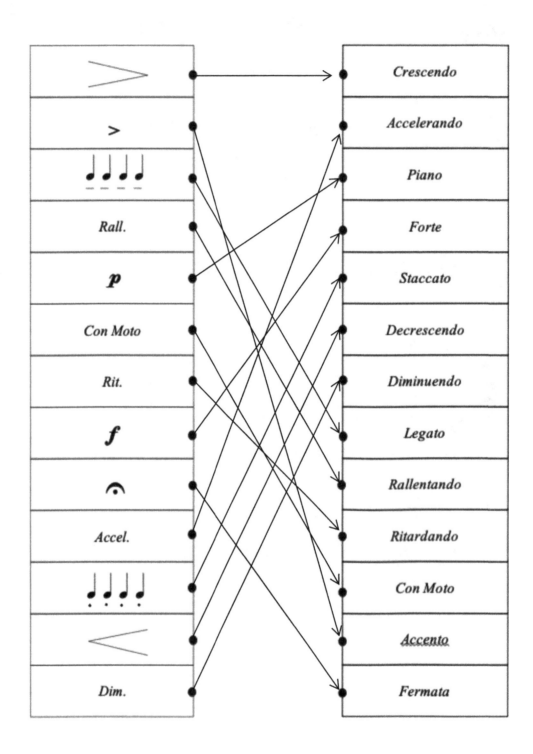

2.

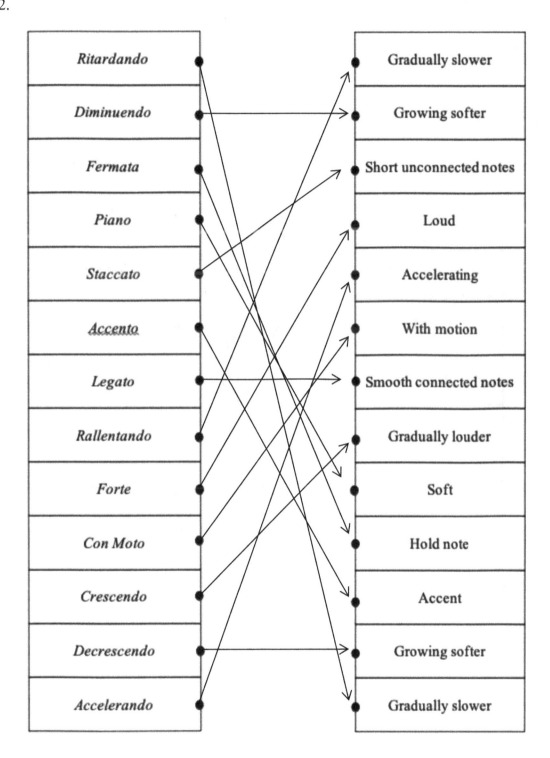

Lesson Plan 9b:

1.

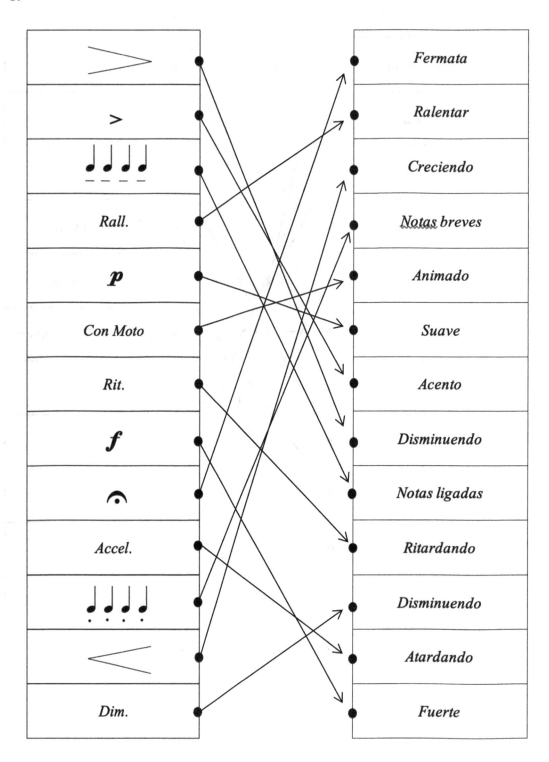

2.

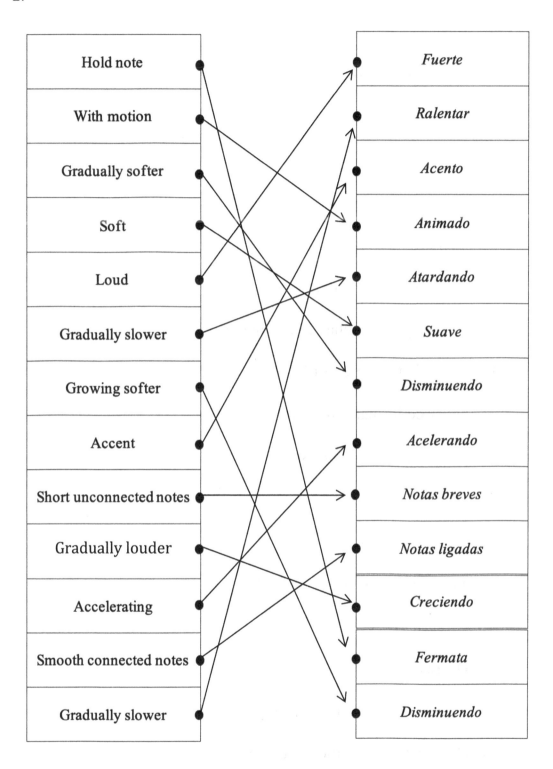

Lesson Plan 10:

1. Escuchen

2. Busquen el pulso

3. Canta conmigo

4. Silencio, por favor

5. Pónganse de pie

6. Siéntense, por favor

7. Por favor, levanten la mano

8. Gracias por escuchar con atención

9. Favor de formar una fila

10. Favor de formar un círculo

11. You play with a lot of spirit

12. Great singing!

13. You practiced well!

14. You didn't practice (enough)!

15. Crescendo

16. Decrescendo

17. Could you play it more fast, please?

18. Could you play it more slow, please?

19. That perfect!

20. High note/ low note

CHAPTER 8

FOUR INTERVIEWS WITH MARIACHI ARTISTS ON VOICE

FIGURE 8.1 Linda Ronstadt, Grammy- and Emmy-winning singer and queen of crossover singing, including mariachi. Courtesy of Rick Wiley, editor of photography, *Arizona Daily Star*.

Linda Ronstadt

Interview by Dr. Juanita Ulloa, April 19, 2018, San Francisco, California
"I think of music as dreaming in sound."

—Linda Ronstadt, *Sweet Dreams*

Mariachi soloist Linda Ronstadt has toured the world and sold more than 100 million records. She deserves huge accolades for bringing mariachi songs into so many US homes. Ronstadt's credits include recordings, twelve Grammys, two Academy of Country Music Awards, the Recording Academy's Lifetime Achievement Award in 2016, one Emmy Award, both Tony and Emmy nominations, the award-winning 2019 documentary "The Sound of my Voice," and a book autobiography, *Simple Dreams: A Musical Memoir*, in September 2013. In 2014, she was inducted into the Rock and Roll Hall of Fame, and in 2019 was a recipient of a Kennedy Center Honor. She is one of the most diverse female singers on the planet.

Despite Linda Ronstadt's incredible success, during the interview she explains her regrets at having waited until her mid-thirties to study voice. She reached out when faced with vocal challenges, as do many. Linda's subsequent vocal training, along with her own resourcefulness, discipline, and incredible talent, helped her continue singing until 2010.

It was a personal thrill to interview Linda because she was a singing role model, as the author had not grown up hearing women sing mariachi in Mexico City. Linda's pioneering success in the United States unconsciously gave her, and perhaps many other women, "permission" to move ahead. It opened doors. During the interview, the author also discovered they shared mutual interests in songs from all over the world, from mariachi and classical music to Bulgarian song and Aztec poetry. Linda's critical self-listening skills, talent, drive, and awareness helped her polish, refresh, refine, and keep improving her craft from a very early age. She prepared her songs thoroughly and never let fear or self-judgment keep her from trying out new musical directions, even when she wasn't sure it was good enough. Linda credits her success in mariachi singing to learning from her father's singing. She also listened to recordings of Mexican ranchera singer Lola Beltrán and opera singer, Maria Callas. Ronstadt believes her mariachi listening actually helped her define her own unique, original rock and roll vocal sound, not just her ranchera sound.

HERITAGE AND VOCAL BACKGROUND

Juanita: Tell us about your family and early music influences. I know you are Mexican American.
Linda: I was born Mexican-American with German blood, raised in Tucson, Arizona, and baptized Linda Maria Ronstadt Coleman. There was no Catholic saint for Linda so my parents added the name Maria. The grandparents on my father's side were born in Sonora, Mexico. My grandfather was a *ranchero* [rancher] that worked as a *mayordomo* [boss] on a *hacienda* [ranch]. They came to Tucson after moving from California around 1869. My grandfather was Coronel Pesqueira who took part in the military overthrow of Maximilian.

All my family was musical. They brought us up singing freely. My father and mother's family all played, although not professionally. My mom played banjo and voice as well as piano, with voice. My father had a rich baritone voice and played a little guitar. His voice was a cross between Frank Sinatra and Pedro Infante [Mexican bolero crooner]. They weren't professional musicians but they all did it and we sang together using harmonies.

I remember going to first grade and we were supposed to sing hymns. I sang anything as long as it was music. So, I started singing and all the kids would look at me like, why are you singing?

Juanita: They didn't know how to sing yet.

Linda: They couldn't sing harmony either! I thought there was something wrong with them. Each time we drove to Mexico, it was 110,000 degrees in the back seat of the car. We didn't have air conditioning, but we sang commercials, Mexican songs, Rhythm and Blues, and standards. We'd sing whatever we liked and did it all in harmony.

Juanita: Were your parents able to come enjoy your mariachi shows?

Linda: My dad came. My mom had already died. I would get him right up on the stage to sing, then my brother, my sister, and even my fifteen-year-old niece. We sang "Y Andale." My dad's father used to say to him "Now that you have a guitar, you'll never need to go hungry." That's what he later said to me when I left our family home in Tucson for Los Angeles.

Juanita: That's beautiful. When you left Tucson with your guitar, where did you go?

Linda: I went to Los Angeles in 1965 with no money and no car. East Los Angeles was the moon. I had a friend, Bobby, who played blues guitar and folk-type fingerpicking songs. We rehearsed so that we could get a job anywhere. Our rent was $80 a month and we split it three ways.

VOICE BACKGROUND AND TEACHERS

Juanita: How long have you studied voice? I hear training, a rich sound, and also gutsiness.

Linda: I didn't get an ounce of vocal training until I was well into my thirties, believe me! Listening to Lola Beltrán or Lucha Reyes was a better deal for me at the time. I was a kamikaze singer and would shout because I didn't know about singing in a mix. When I sang *Pirates of Penzance* on Broadway, I said to them "I have no idea how to do this." I tried to copy opera singers. I love María Callas and tried to copy her. I also began studying with a voice teacher working with the show.

I would also hear my little brother's boy soprano classical voice [in my mind], but with no muscle under it. Even though it's a wonderful singing atmosphere created for boys, it is an eerie, strange sound. For a little girl's voice it's a non-energized sound, but there I was in my thirties singing like a boy soprano, which I had done since age two.

Juanita: So, you sang with a lot of head voice when you were growing up.

Linda: Yes, I didn't have any chest voice until I was fourteen. Then the folk music thing came in. My brother, sister, and I were singing a song called "Columbus Stockade Blues." I came in with the top harmony in a belt voice. I had listened to Ella Fitzgerald and she sings in a heady mix. I would sing-a-long with her using my boy soprano imitation but I didn't know how to put that bottom end in.

THE MARIACHI VOICE

Later, after I went to Broadway I learned a little bit about voice mix but I never completely figured it out.

Juanita: What helped you in your voice training? Did you have a voice teacher or vocal coach?

Linda: Later in my career I had at least three voice teachers: The first one was the one working the *Pirates of Penzance* Show, "Magic" Marge Rivingston in New York City. I was 33 years old. She was classically trained but knew Broadway singing. She introduced me to mixed "vox mix" [mixed voice]. I needed to learn that. She tried to teach me how to sing classically, too, but I couldn't do it. I tried to free my throat but it was so tight. I could never completely figure it out.[1]

I had never had any formal voice training and the show's vocal demands were considerable.

The girls' chorus was being trained by Margaret to safely belt high notes that a soprano sings in her high range. It sounded funnier that way in a contemporary pop style. That was the vision for the show. Eight performances a week of belting high notes could have created serious vocal problems for the chorus were it not for Marge's careful guidance.

My problem was the opposite. I had an overdeveloped belt range and an underdeveloped upper extension from all my years of screaming Rock and Roll. Marge went to work to unravel these problems. The Broadway schedule allows only one day a week to rest, and that is not enough for vocal recovery. My new muscles were trying to gain strength but did not have enough time to rest. With Marge's coaching, my voice eventually gained enough strength to carry me through the grueling schedule.[2]

Working in the show developed my head voice. Singing [American] standards gave me a way to marry my head voice to my chest voice to form what voice teachers call singing in a "mix." This gave me tremendous flexibility that I hadn't had before. I could tell a richer and more nuanced story.[3]

Another voice teacher who helped me was Nolan Van Way. He taught natural authentic singing that works for any style. I can also recommend warm-ups by a great singer, Arnold Mc Culler, on an app called *Vocal Ease*. He inherited Nolan Van Way's vocal tradition and was one of the best singers I ever heard.

I worked a short time with one other voice teacher, Manny Lujan, but it was long after releasing my mariachi records. Manny trained all the Disney singers. He gave me a tape of exercises that were all falsetto like [she does a little tune in head voice]. He would just sit for half an hour. We worked on falsetto.[4] It was a heady, breathy sound. It was boring as hell. Steve Carrillo was working with him at the time when we recorded together.

Juanita: Did he ever show you the mariachi machete technique? [Vocal demonstration accentuating the break in the voice]

Linda: No, but that's very good. Your crack is very good.

---

[1] Author's note: Ronstadt was working under performance pressure and would have surely better understood her voice technically at an earlier age had she had non-performance time to gradually build a mix.

[2] Linda Ronstadt, *Sweet Dreams* (New York: Simon & Schuster), 141.

[3] Ronstadt, *Sweet Dreams*, 157–158.

[4] Author's note: This is known as falsete in the mariachi world.

CHAPTER 8: FOUR INTERVIEWS WITH MARIACHI ARTISTS ON VOICE 319

Juanita: I have young students that imitate that without thinking twice about it once they are shown how. They cross registers with ease using falsete. Did you have more voice teachers?

Linda: Yes, while touring with Nelson Riddle I found an amazing teacher but can't remember his name. I wish I had found him early on. It would have made a huge difference in my singing. He worked in Los Angeles with Popular and Rhythm and Blues singers I knew. He had flawless technique and pulled all of it together for me. Unfortunately, I had only a few years to work with him before I lost my voice.

LISTENING

Juanita: What music do you like to listen to?

Linda: I love both mariachi and classical. I've been drowning myself in classical, lately. I like Grieg, Brahms, Beethoven, Faure, Ravel, Debussy, Ralph Vaughan-Williams, all from the turn of the [twentieth-] century composers. I'm not a fan of Mozart or Bach. Have you ever listened to Robert Burns? He has great melodies, beautiful songs, and ballads. "Ye Banks in Bray" is my favorite.

As a little girl, early in the morning before school I used to set up my parents' record player with the songs I planned to hear after returning home. During school I would think about the songs waiting for me on the Victrola. I sang Mexican songs when I was little but was incomplete with the lyrics because I don't speak Spanish. I would sing along with Lola Beltrán often on la, la, la. That was the foundation of my Rock and Roll style because she [Lola] sang using high belt style and I tried to copy that. Listening to mariachi singers gave me my belt sound for my Rock & Roll singing—even for my falsetto.

Other American singers were more influenced by Blues, Rhythm and Blues, and Gospel, but I didn't have that in my basement. I had only heard it on the radio. It was also a bit confusing singing Rock and Roll, because I was copying people in my own style. I didn't realize that my style also counted for something. I thought it wasn't very good.

Juanita: When we are doing something that's different we sometimes think it must not be right, but it's unique.

Linda: Right, because it didn't sound like them. Listening to Lola was my favorite resource, though. I saw her sing live at the 1983 Tucson Mariachi Festival. Lola was magnificent. She commanded the stage, her beautiful hands, moving so gracefully that they were a show in themselves. Her voice was as powerful as an opera singer's, but she used it in a completely different way. She sang mostly in her huge belt voice, but would crack into a soaring falsetto, purposely emphasizing the break in the voice that classical singers try to conceal. She had a tremendous dynamic range, from a whispered caressing murmur, to an anguished wail that could blow down the walls. . . . Her voice hurdled over the language barrier to rip your heart out.[5] I loved Lola because she sang everything. I didn't hear Lucha Reyes until I was older. My four pillars are Lola, Lucha, Chavela Vargas, Amalia Mendoza is in another corner, she's less emotionally complex than the others but she's so musical, such musicianship. She's right on it, being one of the Tariacuris. When I hear the other three though, I am on the ground wanting to eat pieces of the carpet and pull my hair out.

---

[5] Ronstadt, *Sweet Dreams*, 163.

BREATH AND HARMONIZING

Linda: Did you know that for some, spirit means breath? Spirit is breath, so when you sing you are using your spirit. *Conspirare* means to breathe together. When you are singing together you are conspiring and breathing together.

My favorite thing is to lean in and sing harmony with somebody. Listening to what they're doing and fitting your voice right into what they're singing. It folds right into their voice.

Juanita: That is one of your big gifts. I clearly hear it in your duo of "La negra noche" [The Dark Night] with Steve Carrillo of Mariachi Cobre. I hear you folding into him while he was singing the melody. You matched him beautifully.

VOCAL PRODUCTION

Juanita: What are you thinking about when you produce sound?

Linda: Lip buzzes get your vocal cords relaxed in a way that singing can't do. I never had any help with breathing, but I do it right unconsciously. I didn't understand and didn't have much help with that darn "mixed voice," but I understand it now. I also never had time to develop much falsetto. To the end, it was always more of an energized falsetto, but I was getting better at it.

Juanita: A lot of the men in the mariachi style are doing that or just floating it lightly.

Linda: The feel of a belt vocal style is when you have all of your abdominal strength underneath it and you're singing it almost, on the edge of your chest voice. Then you pull in the high. I learned it finally for standards. I finally understood it. Brian Wilson from the Beach Boys also sings like that.

Juanita: Belting uses the edges of the vocal folds instead of all the folds. Those without breath support underneath end up yelling instead. Unfortunately, many mariachi women have not received belt or mixed voice training and not every teacher teaches it. How do you feel the difference between yelling versus belting?

Linda: I did a lot of yelling in my early singing. I would go all the way up to E flat. I could have finessed a lot better if I had known more early on. I made a record called *Winter Light.* It was one of my last films. At that point, I had learned how to feel my head voice down in my chest voice. I could go very smoothly in between and could pull it in without cracking. With *falsete* singing on *huapangos* you want to emphasize the break, but in the style I was singing I didn't. I could float in and out of it.

Singers can do anything with the right kind of singing production and cross between styles.

FALSETTO/FALSETE, LISTENING, FAVORITE SINGERS, AND FAVORITE SONGS

Linda: In the Rock and Roll song "Blue Bayou," I consciously tried to get in the falsetto and tried to make it sound Mexican. [at the end]. I was trying to be Lola Beltrán. When she cracked into falsetto she had a really strong voice. I didn't have that kind of support under me [yet] so my voice dropped away. My dad also wrote lyrics [Blue Bayou] in Spanish, so I would sing the last part in Spanish.

In the songs "Crucifijo de Piedra" and "Tata Dios," I was starting to use falsetto. I worked on it for the record but it wasn't loose, free, and strong until I had been doing it on stage for ten months. I always heard that falsetto originates with Indians called out to each other across canyons in mountainous areas. What moves me the most about mariachi singing are huapangos [Slow, rhythmic songs in 6/8 meter using a wide vocal range and falsetto flips]. They are magical, mystical, like praying, and are made for singers.

Juanita: What have been your top favorite songs over the span of your career and where were you vocally most at home?

Linda: I felt my truest, authentic voice in mariachi singing and Nelson Riddle songs. I loved singing "Mi ranchito." My whole heart was in "Ay Corazón que te vas." I also like the duet I recorded with Pepe [Martinez] in the Cuco Sánchez song "Sol que tu eres." In English, I liked "Cry Like a Rainstorm" and "Anyone Who Had a Heart" by Burt Bacharach. I never listen to my own work and am going by memory. I did what I set out to do and I felt like my whole heart was in certain songs. I hardly ever did anything perfectly. Once in a while, I would accept having sung a phrase or a verse decently.

Juanita: It is hard to listen to oneself and we can be tough on ourselves.

Linda: It's a slippery slope and you want to slit your throat and never sing again. "I can't believe I made that stupid choice. Why did I sing that I should have sung this other thing."

Juanita: It's nice to share with aspiring singers that even great singers like yourself have had doubts. You've made a lot of great choices. What makes you a star is that you figured out your technique, and then were able to cross between many styles, even though, as you said, it wasn't easy. I believe all this is what makes you so great.

MUSICIANSHIP, MUSICAL PREPARATION, AND MEXICAN RHYTHMS

Juanita: Could you comment on musicianship and singers finding an instrument for young singers?

Linda: I think everyone should enjoy singing. I don't mind if even tone-deaf people sing, as long as they don't do it in front of me. There are choirs that sing with tone-deaf people and it's soulful. It's amazing because they are learning to pour out their stories. American children are often tone deaf because they don't hear enough music and don't sing. They hear it on the radio but that's passive. One has to practice it live in order to be able to do it. Chinese choirs have perfect pitch because they have a tonal language. Their choirs are amazing. Many Chinese people have perfect pitch as well. American kids can't sing happy birthday in tune. Music used to be taught in school.

Everyone should learn piano if they can. The piano is the gateway to it all. I wanted to play it so badly. My brother and sister were taking piano lessons and I wanted to play their pieces. When my mother sent me to Catholic school a nun yelled and hit me on the hand. My mother didn't take me back. She was afraid that it would make me lose interest in music. So, I learned piano pieces by writing down all the names of the notes. I taught myself *Fur Elise, Moonlight Sonata,* and others. I played them as best I could until I started listening to them on my dad's classical recordings. It's so beautiful and smooth when played right. I've never gotten tired of it.

Also, to learn Mexican songs you've got to have the right instrument. If I could live my life over again, I would learn the *vihuela* or *jarana* [small string instruments in mariachi and Veracruzan music traditions]. Those two instruments represent a whole rhythm section in Mexican music. From that foundation you add in the melody and harmonies. Learn this and you're solid. I couldn't play the instruments but loved the rhythms.

Once 6/8 rhythms are fully understood singers can sing any mariachi song. I first learned American standards and then worked on Mexican songs. When I returned to American popular music the rhythms were easy. Also, I always thought my phrasing was terrible until about 1980. At that time, I did the record of standards. That made it possible for me to sing Mexican recordings with stronger phrasing and rhythm. I heard Mexican rhythms growing up, thank God, but that didn't mean that I understood them. I had to figure out a way to count music. I had to keep my hands behind my back and count with my fingers. It was my own way. I had to work it out. What's that song that had the real long note in the beginning?

Juanita: ¿La Charreada? [The Rodeo]

Linda: Yes, that one! I was counting one-two-three-four all the time. I'd count with my hand. I had to do it like that. After a while I didn't have to think about it, but for thirty years I had to have my hands behind my back counting away.

Juanita: That song is a killer for any singer, rhythmically speaking. Could you share how you practiced?

Linda: It wasn't easy. I was up every morning at 6 o'clock with a tape, going over my songs and over and over. I had to rehearse songs in a different key because I couldn't play them. I always encourage singers to learn how to play an instrument well and learn to accompany their singing. It is uncomfortable learning songs without it. Singers often give up studying the accompaniment instrument too early. Take Maria Callas, the opera singer. She was also a great concert pianist and could rehearse and learn her songs at home. Her musicianship was flawless.

GRAMMY-WINNING MARIACHI RECORDINGS: *CANCIONES DE MI PADRE* [SONGS OF MY FATHER]

Juanita: How did the idea of a mariachi recording come up?

Linda: I had always wanted to record mariachi. People often ask me who I am. I tell them I am Mexican. They ask, "You mean Spanish?" I responded, "No, not Spanish, Mexican! I'm a Mexican-German raised in the United States." When younger I would always search for Mexican music to listen to. We used to eat and connect at a particular restaurant with a good jukebox. Solo singers, duos, and a particular trio would also come in. The trio members were patient and kind. They taught me so much.

Later on, after moving to Los Angeles, I flew to Tucson from Los Angeles to hear Lola Beltrán sing at the newly organized Tucson Mariachi Festival. Not long afterwards, the Festival Conference committee approached me about singing with Mariachi Vargas at the next conference. I knew Vargas had never heard of me but was dying for an opportunity. I was determined to get there and just to do it. The songs were really hard but I didn't care. The first performance wasn't very good, but I felt confident about the style and invited them to make a record with me. They asked for a list of songs, and I sent them a long list with *huapangos* I had learned with my family. They commented that the songs were very old and helped me find old recordings of the songs.

Juanita: By any chance was one of the songs "La Paloma" [The Dove]? That's an old one that really makes me cry.

Linda: Oh, my God, that's a beautiful song. If it's not making you cry, then the song is not doing its job. I didn't suggest that song for the first mariachi record. I did record it eventually after my voice had gone. My family sings it much better than me. My brother and two cousins have a beautiful version, and my dad sang a version with all of us singing harmony to him. That's a really old song, right?

Juanita: The composer is a Spaniard, Narciso Serradell. I'm not sure how it got to Mexico, probably through Cuba because of the reference to La Habana, but it's one of the oldest songs on the continent. One can't go anywhere in Mexico without hearing it.

Linda: It got to Mexico, all right. My aunt wrote and published a little booklet about songs from Spain in 1946. She sang and was a scholar of Spanish folk songs. She spent time in Spain studying regional folk songs and later traveled to Mexico and wrote another booklet about northern Mexican songs. She heard that song [La Paloma] in the mountains of Mexico.

When I was singing pop music in Los Angeles. I was enthusiastic about the songs I was singing, but I always knew that Mexican songs are better. The compositions, harmonic, and rhythmic structure were far more interesting. It wasn't just the same old first chorus, first chorus, bridge, and chorus. There were many different forms of expression.

GENDER DIFFERENCES ON TOUR

Juanita: Did you ever encounter male-female issues while on tour since Mariachi Vargas is an all-male group?

Linda: People used to say to me, "It must be interesting comparing Mexican culture to American culture." "No," I answered, "it's interesting comparing American culture to both Mexican American AND Mexican culture." The boys [Mariachi Vargas] couldn't believe that women get to do what they want in United States culture, that they didn't have chaperones or a man's permission to do what they wanted. The men were astonished that women are free agents, but we all got along well and liked each other. We had great fun on that tour and it lasted months and months.

A CROSSOVER CONTRAST: OPERA: PUCCINI'S *LA BOHEME*

Linda: Puccini wasn't one of my successful crossovers. If I had been a trained opera singer I would have sung it better. But he wanted the whole thing in chest voice. I said I wouldn't do it.

Juanita: That's smart. How could you do the whole thing in chest voice, it goes so high? That's crazy.

Linda: Well, he saw that right away. I did one of the songs in chest voice in the beginning. I had no clue of what I was doing. First of all, I saw all these notes on the sheet music that were tiny little fly specs. I didn't think that I was supposed to sing that, until I asked, and he said "Yes, sing that." I thought, "Are you crazy?" I learned it, not knowing that if I'd been in the real opera, I would've been expected to improvise it.

Juanita: Yes, Mozart expected singers to improvise the final cadenzas and he didn't write them out. I found singing opera very challenging coming from Mexican lower register singing. How was it for you?

Linda: I thought I could do Puccini by copying the sound because I had done that with other styles. I heard it as a child and thought I could sing it, but I couldn't. It was too hard. My grandmother had been a huge opera fan. I used to go over to her house on Saturdays and listen to opera with her on the radio. In Puccini's *La Boheme* I got the high C. That was the only thing I had no problem with, but not the rest of it. I love when they go offstage singing into the night. The entire first and third acts are so beautiful.

The best part, however, was that I learned it so well. Now, when I hear it, my listening is very advanced. I know every little note and detail of the orchestration and everybody's parts. I love the fact that I got the opportunity to delve into that degree even though I couldn't sing it as well as I had liked.

It's so fun to talk to you. You can only talk to other singers about this stuff because they are the only ones who know what you are talking about.

BREATHING AND VOCAL ISSUES IN LATE CAREER

Linda: The problems started in 2000. My voice was just gone but I sang for another ten years. Suddenly it became difficult, and I was yelling. It became intimidating for me and was not fair to the audience. They came to see me sing.

Juanita: You found out later you were ill?

Linda: I knew something was wrong. I didn't know it was connected to my voice, but I knew it wasn't an age issue. It was different. I could tell I no longer had the ability to shade for pitch and was missing the glossy harmonics on the top of my voice. That's where I find the pitch to get the texture. I stir around in there and grab onto this and that texture. I didn't have that anymore; my toolbox was gone.

Juanita: Did you feel like you'd lost breath support?

Linda: With Parkinson's, I only use a third of my lungs most of the time. I used to be able to hold a note until the middle of tomorrow. Suddenly, I couldn't do that. Suddenly, I couldn't breathe when I used to breathe for a living. I couldn't get my lungs filled up. The number of repetitions that I have to make per second of the vibrations is huge, and with Parkinson's, one can't do repetitive movements.

Juanita: So, when you would inhale—

Linda: There are 75 to 1,500 cycles per single second from a signal in the brain to speaking. The vocal cords clap together 100 times per second for men and 200 times for women. For women singers, our vocal cords are hitting each other 1,000 times per second. If you have Parkinson's, the vocal cords won't do repetitive motions that require 1,000 times per second. They just stop repeating.

Juanita: Before that happened, how did you normally breathe? What worked for you, or did you not just think about it?

Linda: I didn't think about it, I just breathe. Somebody said to me "breathe in your back." Get it from your back. When I get stuck on stage or scared, I would say that to myself, then breathe and sing. Then my voice would come screaming at me.

Juanita: I know what it feels like to feel held back. It's hard.

Linda: It's really hard.

Juanita: Yet, sometimes that's when we're growing the most.

Linda: I always say you learn more from failures than from success. I always learn from my failures. So much more than what I'd learn from any success.

SINGING IS MAGIC

Linda: I really believe that singing, music, and art are the most spiritual things one can do. It's magic, and magic is spirituality. I don't believe in "abracadabra" magic but I believe music is magical. I am a great believer in prayer. Prayer is very good especially for the person who is praying but I think it affects others as well.

Juanita: They say singing is praying twice.

Linda: We should all be playing music or doing our own art. The heroes can stand up on stage and inspire people. That's fine. There's music for the public and there's music for people to play in the dead of the night when no one is around. That's when you can really pour your heart out. The music you make for yourself is some of the most important music you'll ever hear. Everything starts from that.

FIGURE 8.2 Jorge Negrete, *El Charro Cantor*, legendary ranchera singer trained by Maestro José Pierson during Mexico's Golden Age of Cinema.

Dispelling Myths about Legendary Ranchera Singer Jorge Negrete (1911–1953), *El Charro Cantor*

An interview with two of his grandchildren, both singers: Rafael Jorge and Diana Irene Negrete
By Dr. Juanita Ulloa, Mexico City, 2018

I had the honor of interviewing two of Jorge Negrete's grandchildren, Rafael Jorge and Diana Negrete. Both are singers involved in the music business, Diana with boleros and promotion, and Rafael as both an opera and mariachi singer. I wanted to learn more about the vocal training and life of their grandfather. Although they were born after his death in 1953, both shared valuable family knowledge. They also wanted to correct some of the myths and misinformation published about their grandfather. We met in Mexico City during the summer of 2018.[6]

Jorge Negrete is also known as *El charro cantor* [The Singing Cowboy]. He is still revered today as perhaps Mexico's very top celebrity singer. Although he trained as an opera singer, he achieved much deserved fame as a ranchera singer/actor. Negrete's rich, baritone voice and long, legato lines reflect extensive and consistent vocal training. According to his grandson Rafael, Jorge studied steadily with voice teacher José Pierson before and during his rise to fame. He continued studying voice with him in between tours as well until the year he died.

Negrete is perhaps the ranchera world's most disciplined vocal technician. He rose to fame in the 1930s until his untimely death at the height of his career. Jorge's good looks and strong work ethic combined perfectly with solid singing technique and a unique and personal vocal style. This led to a global career with over thirty-five movies, recordings, concerts, and about 200 songs. Jorge Negrete also advocated for artists as one of the co-founders and directors of Asociación Nacional de Actores (ANDA), Mexico's first actor's union.

WHAT REALLY HAPPENED WHEN JORGE NEGRETE FIRST ARRIVED BEFORE A HUGE NUMBER OF FEMALE FANS IN MADRID, SPAIN (1946–1947)

Juanita: I know this is one of the stories you've talked about, and you mentioned problems with some biographies about your grandfather. I have your mother's, Diana Negrete, 1987 biography, titled Jorge Negrete.

Rafael: Overall, my mother's biography is good although there are some small errors. She based it on a radio novel that was briefly broadcasted after my grandfather died. There is some misinformation, however, concerning my grandfather's arrival on tour in Spain in the 1940s. When he first arrived at the Madrid station, he was apparently greeted by a tumult of women. This was unheard of in 1946–1947. Fans became more common later in the sixties after the Beatles and the sexual revolution. At the time, Spain had a dictator, and both the police and Spanish Civil Guard were unprepared for the frenzy of female fans. My grandfather was not surprised, as he was already used to greeting enthusiastic crowds in Venezuela, Chile, and Cuba, but the Spaniards were unprepared. Back in Mexico, the sponsoring radio station would sometimes have to hide him in an ambulance to get him away from the crowds.

---

[6] The author translated this interview from Spanish to English.

Well, someone decided to create a fake media story about the excitement of the fans in response to my grandfather's arrival in Madrid. The published comment reported that upon seeing the screaming women, he supposedly said, "Aren't there any men here?" This comment does not reflect my grandfather's good-natured personality. The feigned arrogance insinuated with the comment was really a macho statement from the *macho charro* [cowboy] character he was playing at the time in a movie role. It was a ploy. Apart from this story, my mother's biography is for the most part accurate.

NOT ALL BIOGRAPHIES GET THE FACTS RIGHT.

Rafael: Unfortunately, I cannot recommend Enrique Serna's biography of my grandfather. One correction, for example, has to do with a well-known movie, *Escuela de vagabundos* [School of Bums]. It features well-known singer Pedro Infante and is a remake of an older movie, *Gallo en un corral ageno* [Rooster in an Unknown Coop], featuring my grandfather. The author incorrectly says that the Negrete movie was made afterwards because Negrete wanted to copy the movie version with Pedro Infante. In fact, the Negrete version was made years before. There are other mistakes.

Juanita: My research shows that the Infante movie was made in 1955 and the Negrete movie in 1952. Thank you for the opportunity to correct this.

WHAT REALLY HAPPENED AT JORGE NEGRETE'S AUDITION AT THE METROPOLITAN OPERA

Rafael: There is misinformation about my grandfather and the Metropolitan Opera. There are published reports saying he was offered an understudy opera role at the Met in New York and that he refused the offer out of pride.

Juanita: Is that true?

Rafael: It's false. I read this in a Barcelona newspaper interview. The truth is, my grandfather arrived in New York with eight dollars in his pocket and one wrinkled suit. He worked washing dishes in Latin American bars while also translating American songs into Spanish, like "Begin the Beguine."

Juanita: By Cole Porter?

Rafael: Yes, by Cole Porter! He translated from English to Spanish and sang at the restaurant. Another song he translated is Rose Medilo's "Amor indio" [Indian Love], setting the song in Canada [audio demonstration]. This is how my grandfather earned his initial income. [Some interviews have mentioned Negrete translated songs from English to Spanish for Southern Publishing, which published many hit songs during this time.]

At one point during his stay in New York, he was offered an audition date and time at the Metropolitan Opera. At that time, one had to have an agent. [This is still true today.] To get an agent, one needed a bond deposit of $1,000–2,000. My grandfather did not have that kind of money. This is the true reason he could not follow through with the Metropolitan Opera, not even as an alternate. Later, a new and different opportunity arose to make a movie in Mexico, *Ay, Jalisco no te rajes* [Oh, Jalisco don't give up]. This movie is the one that catapulted him to fame as a ranchera singer.

Some biographies get this information right, but not others.

Juanita: Regarding the Met, are you saying he never auditioned?

RAFAEL: He did audition, but without the proper agent or money. Then, while he continued to work and save money, the first charro movie in Mexico came up, and he forgot about New York and the Met. The rest is history.

THE REAL TRUTH ABOUT WHAT HAPPENED WHEN NEGRETE MADE THE MOVIE *AY, JALISCO NO TE RAJES* [OH, JALISCO DON'T GIVE UP]

Rafael: There are several myths surrounding the famous movie, *Ay, Jalisco no te rajes.* First of all, it was not his first movie. *Ay, Jalisco no te rajes* is the movie that made him famous, but by 1941, he had already appeared in three movies dressed as an elegant charro, singing rancheras. The three movies are: *El Fanfarrón* [The Braggart], *Cual sin miedo* [Without Fear], and *La Valentina* [The Valentina]. In this last one, he met my grandmother, Elisa Crochet. Her last name is spelled with only one "T" because it's a Catalán name from Northern Spain. She used her artistic name, Alisa Cristi.

Diana: Did you know my grandfather crumpled up Manuel Esperón's score for the movie?

Rafael: It's true. This is a second point. He did not immediately take to the song. As he started to listen, though, he changed his mind and then said, "Ah, it's not that bad." That is all he said. Gossip grows quickly, however, and negative versions of this story abound.

Juanita: Wasn't the main theme song, "Ay, Jalisco no te rajes," written by the composer/arranger/ producer, Manuel Esperón? According to Esperón's widow, he wrote the song especially for your father among his many other movie songs and arrangements.[7]

Rafael: The song was written in 1941 by two brothers working together as director and producer of the film, Ismael and Joselito Rodriguez. They were in charge and entrusted Manuel Esperón with all the music for the movie.

More misinformation has to do with the *charro* [Mexican cowboy] theme and costuming in the movie. When my grandfather first met with the costume crew, they handed him a *chinaco* outfit. This costume is rural peasant, white, loose cotton clothing with *huaraches* [sandals] and was used by mariachis prior to the more elegant, twentieth-century, black *traje de charro*. Besides the chinaco clothes, they actually added a tap dancer's hat into the costume! My grandfather protested. His family was from Guanajuato and Jalisco, and he knew what a real *traje de charro* was supposed to look like; however, the media made up a story about this, suggesting that he had not wanted to dress as a charro for other reasons.

Diana: The story they invented was that because he sang opera, he had protested wearing the outfit saying—"No, how could I dress like a charro?"—as if he was refusing to belittle himself.

Juanita: Oh, no!

---

[7] Author's Note: Only a week prior to this interview in Mexico City, the author spoke by telephone to Manuel Esperón's widow in Cuernavaca, Mexico.

Rafael: I don't know which rumor is sillier, this one, or the one in Spain where the media claimed he said, "Do you not have men here?"

Juanita: Tell me about your grandfather's voice teacher, José Pierson.

Rafael: My grandfather studied with him until the year he died. Pierson had students who trained only in opera, but he also trained successful lighter vocal acts such as the female trio "Las Tres Conchitas" and singer/actor Francisco Avitia Tapia, also known as "El Charro Avitia." Pierson's teaching was very good. He had many students and was an older man, but his vocalises were spot on. When I want to return to the basics, I try to remember his exercises, and they work well for me.

CONCLUSION

Rafael: I believe that when someone has relatives like my grandfather, we have the duty to be informed. He's not just anyone; he made a great contribution as a human being and as an artist. He has not been given his rightful place.

Juanita: He's important! His vocal discipline offers a vocal role model for all.

Diana: People think primarily about the stars, but little attention and support goes to the crew, makeup artists, extras, and supporting roles. My grandfather cared about the needs of all his artistic colleagues; at that time, even great stars were not receiving basic medical services and extras. He was dedicated to everyone and was a great man.

Flor de Toloache

Vocalists Mireya Ramos and Shea Fiol with Julie Acosta, French/Mexican violinist, Fox Theater, Oakland, CA March 9, 2018
Bilingual interview by Dr. Juanita Ulloa

Mariachi Flor de Toloache is a pioneering all-female contemporary mariachi fusion group. They were founded in 2008 in New York City by lead vocalists, Mireya Ramos and Shea Fiol. The group began as a trio with voice, harp, violin, and vihuela, reminiscent of early-day combos in mariachi history. Their group members hail from diverse cultural backgrounds including Mexico, Puerto Rico, Dominican Republic, Cuba, Australia, Colombia, Germany, Italy, France, and the United States. The group enjoys stretching boundaries and taking risks with a vision of new female sounds, chords and arrangements. They express using their cultural, linguistic and musical mix to create an edgy, versatile, and fresh approach, which led them to their first Latin Grammy award in 2017 and has kept them on steady tours ever since.

MUSICAL BACKGROUNDS, EVOLUTION OF STYLE AND FUSION

Juanita: How did your style evolve? Was it always Spanish and English? Was it a short or long process? Did your style reveal itself song by song?

Shea: In our style, we mix Spanish and English. Our style has definitely evolved over a long time and is still evolving. We like the instrumental *ranchera* sound, but over it we often change things up vocally. It depends on the song. For example, on the song "Let Down" we maintain a bluesy, jazzy feel, but treat the voices differently. We like contrasts. The original version of the song was a more pop style. Our first rendition of the song mixed

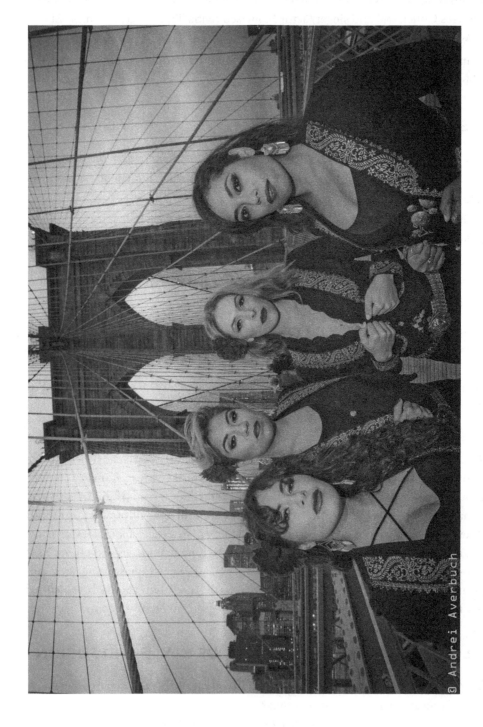

FIGURE 8.3 Flor de Toloache, Latin Grammy-winning duo led by vocalists Mireya Ramos and Shea Fiol, with Julie Acosta, French/Mexican violinist. Photograph by Andrei Paul Averbuch.

in both English and Spanish, but was not very jazzy or bluesy. The next time we recorded it, we made it jazzier—totally stretched Gypsy Jazz.

Juanita: Your father was a traditional Mariachi, right? What did he think when he saw you playing with so many new ideas?

Mireya: He loved it. We were raised in Puerto Rico where he opened a Mexican restaurant with his Mexican mariachi. He was married to a Dominican and was open to other cultures. He's originally from Los Angeles, and it was not the norm for a Mexican man, in his time, to marry a Dominican girl. He was already open to that. When they moved to Puerto Rico, he was surrounded with salsa and merengue styles [Caribbean rhythms].

Juanita: Was he already taking these steps in his own way?

Mireya: Yes, mentally. He didn't do it in his music but he loved the fact that we did all kinds of stuff. He was excited that we are keeping the mariachi tradition alive in our own way. Many people are similar to us, either mixed, third generation in the United States, or have been in the US for a long time. They can relate to this kind of music more than a traditional piece. It's a reflection of what is happening now and is also a reflection of New York, stylistically. My mother is also open-minded about music. She would always say: "Music doesn't belong to anybody, it's to share with everybody. There's beauty in all kinds of music."

She exposed me to all kinds of music. My approach to mariachi is different than a person who grows up in Mexico or someone coming through a US mariachi program.

Juanita: Yes, there's a traditional way to sound, dress, and move . . .

Mireya: Yes, exactly, especially for women. I don't come from that. My approach was all about making beautiful music. It brings me back home to my dad. I learned about my Mexican heritage through the music. I was fascinated by it. We all feel that way because we have different backgrounds.

Juanita: Growing up in New York with your special style has set you both up as female mariachi pioneers. It's an honor. One doesn't always realize they are in that role as it is happening, but I sense you ladies are conscious of that.

Mireya: Yes, we didn't realize it until we saw the effect that it had and we were like "Wow."

Juanita: I've seen mariachi ladies with wonderful solo and/or group vocals. In the past, they have not always been able to simultaneously accompany with the same strength. You are both quite beyond that. For those reading this article and not watching you live, both of you lead and carry the show with accompanists. Where and how did you learn the rhythms to develop this?

Mireya: Shea is half-Cuban. She is all rhythm.

Shea: I listen to more salsa and Cuban music. I didn't listen to mariachi. I am definitely a rhythm girl. Learning mariachi has been a long process. I am very new to the genre and its community. We trained informally with a local mariachi group, Angeles de Puebla.

Juanita: ¿Es mixto? [Was it a mixed group?]

Mireya: No, eran todos hombres y yo era la única mujer. [No, it was all male, and I was the only woman.]

Shea: There are few mariachi groups in New York, not as many as California, and the scene was new to me, I couldn't wrap my head around it rhythmically on the *vihuela*. There was a lot to learn.

Juanita: What were you playing before learning the vihuela? [The vihuela is a small mariachi guitar.]

Shea: I was playing rhythm guitar. Full rock, pop, R&B stuff, basic accompaniment for myself with salsa and world music influences. The *vihuela* was trailing behind because I was learning to sing the style and learning the whole repertoire. It was a massive thing to bite off of and chew. The mariachi rhythms came later. I was basic on *vihuela* rhythms for a long time. Once I could digest the song, the cultural context and the importance of the music, the lyrics, and its repertoire, sixty songs later, I could envision what the *vihuela's* role truly is.

Juanita: So important.

Shea: So important. Mariachi is very recent for me, within the last five years. I've been investigating, watching you tube videos, asking questions. Luckily, I already had the rhythms in in my head in general meter.

We had to go through all standard mariachi repertoire and styles to find our fusion. It wasn't cut and dry. We had to immerse ourselves completely in traditional mariachi. We performed at weddings and *quinceañeras* [a Mexican fifteen-year-old birthday celebration for girls]. We performed in traditional *charro* outfits for six years at church for masses, funerals, including the day of Guadalupe and Santa Cecilia.

Mireya: I am the only one who has been performing mariachi all along. You can't have a band without everyone experiencing it. We also played with other mariachi ensembles that I had previously worked with. It was a live workshop in real time! Many people don't know that about us. They assume we haven't lived the traditional mariachi experience.

Juanita: Tell me about your musical vision.

Mireya: Mi visión era lo que estamos haciendo ahora desde un comienzo. Era un sueño que mezcláramos géneros, nuestros arreglos, nuestras propias canciones, pero tomó mucho más tiempo y trabajo que uno piensa.

[My vision from the start was what we are now doing. Our vision was to mix genres with our own arrangements and original songs. It takes much more work and time than one thinks.]

LEARNING AND BALANCING RHYTHMS WITH VOCALS

Juanita: Mexican ranchera rhythms must have felt a little easier than the salsa rhythms you knew, correct?

Shea: Yes, the 6/8 feeling. It wasn't easy at first to get the feeling of 6/8 *huapangos*.

Juanita: You are both extraordinary with your rhythms. I thought we would focus the interview on your vocals, but it's important to explain how both of you cover the main rhythm section while singing lead solos.

Shea: It's really rare. I spoke to Gloria, our bass player, about the typical instruments for women in mariachi. If you see a mariachi with a woman in it, what is she playing?

Juanita: Violin.

Shea: Exactly. In most cases, it's violin probably 90 percent of the time. In traditional mariachi, there are less female *armonía* players [guitar, vihuela, guitarrón rhythmic accompaniment section]. It's cool that in tonight's performance Mireya is singing lead voice while playing and leading from the *guitarrón*.

Juanita: I know of many mariachis whose guitarrón player doesn't even attempt to sing, because of the rhythmic complexity.

SHEA: We're also very different in our presentation because there's no one lead singer, which can be fun and exciting; it's part of our tradition. We're both playing and singing the whole, entire time. It's very different.

ARRANGING

Juanita: I noticed that in the song "Guadalajara," you both shared the solo vocal at different points during the song. The result was different vocal colors overall for the solo. Did you always intend to share the lead?

Mireya: Yes, we have done this quite often from the beginning. We were both lead singers when previously working as soloists. After working together, our voices blended nicely but we each continued with our own solo vocal style. It's a signature of our band.

Shea: I had originally moved to New York to follow my dream to be a solo artist. I began to lean away from my personal solo style towards mariachi, when my mom saw me play basic *rancheras* with Mireya, with the two of us on only *vihuela* and violin. My mother is also a musician with insane hearing. She knows my solo music well, and very honestly said: "When you guys are together, it is just magical." That's what we kept hearing, particularly with the vocals, our focal point. At that point, I became more dedicated to the project.

At first, it seemed to be a detour, a U turn, or a whole new thing, but I was totally open to it. We would do full shows featuring our voices. Mireya was on voice and *guitarrón*, while I sang while playing the *vihuela*. We had no other instruments.

VOICE TRAINING

Juanita: Do either of you think that classical training helps? I incorporate it in my teaching, but many of my classical voice colleagues are unfamiliar with mariachi.

Mireya: I think it helps for breath support. It feels natural to me because I began lessons when I was very young. Voice training helps me avoid hurting my voice.

Shea: I had a handful of classical voice lessons in high school, and they were awful. The teacher was very strictly classical, and I was not there stylistically. I love classical music and opera, but it wasn't the way I wanted to sing. I loved Mariah Carey and Whitney Houston. I learned the song "Ave María," which I love, but the classical experience turned me off. I felt pushed to sing a certain way, so I stopped, and I stopped for fifteen years. I didn't even study voice in college. I can see how someone young can internalize vocal technique and how automatic some of those things can be, such as centeredness, especially through watching Mireya. I appreciate the studious part.

I also feel I might not have my own particular raw, unfiltered, untrained voice if I had started young. There's also beauty in that. It's like being a wild horse versus one that can do tricks. I learned to follow my instincts. That is how I envision the voice (not that trained vocalists don't follow their instincts, though). When we were on Junior's show, he gave a little lecture about studying: "Don't fool yourself into believing you are going to maintain your uniqueness by not studying voice, because vocal training gives you even more tools and options."

I can see that. It doesn't always work out that way for everyone. I began connecting with my voice as I started performing. As I gained experience, I began working on voice technique to avoid hurting my voice. Otherwise, I probably would have.

Juanita: If your voice teacher had allowed you to do a Mariah Carey song or "Ave María" in a low key in the female mariachi register with vertical alignment would that have helped you? Would it have helped you to have someone teaching you about register shifts and how to shift technically between styles?

Shea: The issue wasn't the low key or the register. It was the classical voice teacher's approach. She did not have the tools to teach me. She could have said less about the tone or sound, and more about the principles of breathing, principles of support, what the breath is for. I really needed the basics. My later teacher solved this for me. She was stylistically versatile, which helped. I had to drop my whole breathing technique of high breathing from years of being an athlete. It took years to make the shift to thinking low. We broke it down with exercises and did stylized call and response. I preferred exercises to songs and would actually lose interest with songs. I was a sponge with technique working in head voice, through the *passagio* (between registers), chest, etc.

Juanita: Thank you for sharing this important information for classical voice teachers. Have any of you worked in musical theater or been exposed to belt vocal technique? In the voice world it is part of CCM-Contemporary Commercial Music teaching.

Shea: I did not sing using belt voice until I began singing mariachi with Mireya. I really couldn't, not that way. I could do a nasal type of sound between head and chest voice, like Chaka Khan but not full belting. I learned belting next to Mireya. I heard her do it effortlessly, projecting her voice without the need for amplification.

Juanita: That last one can be good and bad.

Shea: Right! It also helped that I was taking lessons while I listened to Mireya as an example. I could see, hear, and then practice.

Mireya: I had to learn how to project as I sang live within the style.

SUGGESTIONS FOR STUDENTS

Juanita: Do you have suggestions for young singers based upon your experience? Are there things you received, missed, or especially value that might help or guide them?

Mireya: It is important to listen to all kinds of music, not just one kind. Find a singer you like, listening to their style without copying because you want to find your own voice.

Shea: Start that way. Little by little you will mold your own sound. I listened to more than one singer growing up: Joni Mitchell, Stevie Wonder, Chaka Khan. I have one compilation opera album I listen to. Listen to everything, every genre.

Juanita: Good advice!

One the other hand, I have a young student that recently sang "La Llorona" [The Weeping Woman] in my voice studio. He changed the melody before having learned the song, based upon listening to only one particular version on YouTube.

Julie (from France) on Violin: It's good that students have exposure to so many different things, but it can also be tough. I am sometimes overwhelmed by all the information available. One can be impressed by an artist and think "Wow, they are great." It makes you want to copy them, but that can also hinder your deeper internal growth as a musician. You have to explore things by yourself, practice alone and with other musicians, and listen to and work with your teachers. That's the real deal. Youtube is extra. It's great for inspiration but it will not teach you how to be a great musician.

Juanita: Yes, your inner voice.

¿Y, de dónde es usted? [And where are you from, Julie?]

Julie: Mi madre es Mexicana, de Baja California, mi papa es italiano y yo crecí en Francia. [My mother is Mexican from Baja California, my father is Italian, and I grew up in France.]

Juanita: Thank you ladies, for your incredible diversity, excellence, and contributions to the mariachi world of music.

LESSON PLAN FOR INTERVIEW WITH FLOR DE TOLOACHE

Students: Read article and listen to a song by Flor de Toloache on YouTube. Hand in answered questions below and/or write an essay on your own future mariachi music style, using the idea of new creativity from Flor de Toloache.

Teachers: Have students read the interview for homework, to be followed by classroom discussion. What makes these ladies different from traditional female singers? Compare them to soloists such as Lola Beltrán, Amalia Mendoza (she performed with her family as well as solo), and the duo Las Hermanas Padilla. Hone in on two to three major points that struck the students with a short, two-paragraph essay for subsequent homework.

DISCUSSION QUESTIONS

1. What makes Flor de Toloache's music unique?
2. Do you believe they are making an important part of the *ranchera* tradition?
3. Name all the group's vocal stylistic influences. What are yours? What do you like to listen to?
4. Have you heard mariachi singing in both English and Spanish, either alternating songs or within a song?
5. Did the group follow voice lessons and how did they find what they wanted?
6. How important is learning the standard tradition before innovating with something new?

FIGURE 8.4 Photo of San Antonio–raised Raul Cuellar, Jr., singer, and violinist with Los Camperos de Nati Cano and Mariachi Vargas.

Raul Cuellar, Jr.

Mariachi Soloist with Los Camperos de Nati Cano and Mariachi Vargas
Interview Conducted by Mariachi Historian Jonathan Clark, 2019 (voice questions from Dr. Ulloa)

Raul Cuellar has been a member of Mariachi Los Camperos de Nati Cano since approximately 2002 and more recently with Mariachi Vargas. Raul was raised in San Antonio, Texas, where he performed for many years with mariachi groups, including Mariachi Los Caporales, Mariachi Azteca, and Campanas de América. Before moving to Los Angeles in 2002, he also taught mariachi education at various middle and high schools in Southern Texas.

INTRODUCTION—EARLY SINGING, REPERTOIRE FOR YOUTH, OVERCOMING SHYNESS

Jonathan: Have you ever taken voice lessons?

Raul: Unfortunately, no. I wish I did.

Jonathan: How did you learn to sing?

Raul: That's a great question. When I first started in mariachi, I was too embarrassed to sing in front of a lot of people. I played the violin. My biggest fear was: "If I don't know *how* to sing, how do I do it?" The mariachi director at the church finally said, "You're going to sing."

Jonathan: How old were you then?

Raul: I was ten years old. At first, I didn't know what to do, what to expect, or what was going to happen. He said to listen and copy the singers. I already did that in my violin playing. I copied singers and matched the notes. What helped me the most is that I asked a lot of questions. They would answer, "No, just take a breath, or do it with more air, or this or that."

I sang in the church from about age ten to twelve or thirteen. When the cousin who involved me in the church mariachi began a new group, we branched off into a small, professional mariachi group for kids. By that time, I was singing more openly.

Jonathan: You didn't sing along with records?

Raul: I didn't at first. I was still embarrassed to sing. When the church director said, "We're all going to sing, so you're going to sing too," I became more interested and began listening to other artists. I copied or sang along with recordings and simultaneously held out notes with them.

Jonathan: Do you remember any early mariachi songs at the church that especially fit your voice between ages ten to thirteen? Were there any songs that were easy to pick up rather than difficult songs?

Raul: I started with church songs "Alleluia" and "Señor ten piedad" [Lord, have mercy]. [Audio demonstration] Looking back, the songs from the mass were easy for me. They were not easy at the time, but I could pick them up because they were not difficult.

Jonathan: Your group did the whole Misa Panamericana [The Panamerican Mass]?

Raul: Si, la Misa Panamericana, exactly.

Jonathan: What about like Pescador de hombres [Fisher of Men]?

Raul: No, I began that one when I was a little older. There was one song that I had heard our director sing, and at the time, it sounded amazing. I didn't get to sing it until I was a little older, but it was a church standard titled, *Yo te amo mucho*. It was not too difficult. [Audio demonstration]

Jonathan: What experiences formed you as a singer?

Raul: Watching other singers, including performing mariachis as in Mariachi Vargas.

Jonathan: Are there any events that influenced you?

Raul: We had several church festivals. The biggest experience I had was performing for Pope John Paul II when he came to San Antonio.

Jonathan: You got to sing a solo for the Pope?

Raul: Not a solo. I was part of a *coro* [choral group].

338 THE MARIACHI VOICE

LEARNING MARIACHI RHYTHMS AND EVOLVING A VOCAL STYLE

Jonathan: That was an unforgettable moment. Do you perform other vocal styles?

Raul: I've never sung anything other than mariachi.

Jonathan: You've never sung for banda or norteño or conjunto modern styles? [Conjunto moderno refers to a modern combo or orchestra with or without electric instrumentation. *Norteño* music includes folk and commercial styles from northern Mexico. *Banda* music is a commercial *norteño* style with combo instrumentation featuring brass instruments, syncopated rhythms, and voice.]

Raul: Karaoke, yes, but nothing professional.

Jonathan: Within mariachi are there different musical genres or styles that you perform?

Raul: Yes, of course. I sing only mariachi. Within mariachi, I can sing a *ranchera* the way it's supposed to be sung, or I can adjust my voice into a bolero style. I can make my voice fit into a more rustic style in the *huastecos* or the *sones*, or for the *huapango*, I can sound a little more like a true *huasteco* [style of singing from the Huasteco region of Mexico]. I can change my voice into the style required. If it's a *ranchera, voy a cantar más bravío, más ranchera* [I will sing it more belt style, like a rustic ranchera]. If it's a *bolero*, I'm going to soften it into something more romantic.

Jonathan: What about the balada [ballad]?

Raul: A *balada* for me is like a *bolero*, more romantic.

Jonathan: Are there specific singers that you copied? For the huapango, did you copy Miguel Aceves Mejia?

Raul: I researched singers in *huapangos*, in *boleros*, and in *sones*. I listened to Miguel Aceves and thought, "Oh nice, I like the way he did this." I listened to Cuco Sanchez and groups that performed *sones*, as in Mariachi Vargas or *los de antes, como cantaba Mario De Santiago los sones* [or those from earlier times, Mario De Santiago really knew how to sing *sones*]. He was amazing. I wanted to imitate him. I would imitate everyone that I thought was awesome. For *baladas* or *boleros*, I listened to bolero singers, Luis Miguel or Cristian Castro and José José, not just strict mariachi music. I practiced applying the artistic singing styles of these different singers to my own mariachi singing.

EXPRESSING FEELING AND INTERPRETATION

Jonathan: Do you freely use the stage to express the feelings of the song?

Raul: Oh, of course. This is a must, especially in a professional group, but it doesn't have to be a professional group. I've always believed interpreting is much more important than just singing. If you can relate the message to the audience and they can feel exactly what you are feeling, then you are really singing. A perfect example is José Alfredo Jiménez. He didn't have a great voice, but his interpretation was amazing.

Jonathan: Were you encouraged or trained to use the stage to express your feelings?

Raul: I watched how performers used the stage and how they told the song story with their hands or more. Obviously, it depends on what song I'm singing. With a *bolero*, a love

CHAPTER 8: FOUR INTERVIEWS WITH MARIACHI ARTISTS ON VOICE

song, I communicate who I'm in love with or whomever I'm singing to. If it's a heartache *ranchera*, you try to interpret expressing a heartache. Nati Cano [leader of *Mariachi Los Camperos de Nati Cano*] is the only one that came close to giving me advice. He would say:

"You can tell a lot about the song by doing little simple things with your hands. If you point to your heart, you're saying *corazón*. Put your hands on your heart and they know what you are talking about."

Nati was the only one who actually told me how small things go a long way.

Jonathan: As a soloist, how do you recommend interpreting a song?

Raul: If you have not gone through heartbreak, it's a little difficult, especially with young kids. The best advice I can give anyone is to act it out. First, find out what you're singing about, what the song means, and what the words mean. Once you understand the song, you can become an actor. Would you just sing words or just sing notes? No, you interpret *how*. You get into the song, *o que te quiere dar un beso* [oh, I want to give you a kiss], and you point to your lips. All this goes a long way when you are interpreting the song.

ADVICE TO YOUNG SINGERS, WARM-UPS, AND STAYING IN VOCAL SHAPE

Jonathan: When you see young aspiring mariachi singers, what are the biggest mistakes you see them making?

Raul: Two of the biggest mistakes I see is that they don't warm up and they don't take singing as seriously as they should. This means keeping their voices in shape. Also, many just belt everything out, no dynamics, no real interpretation. I like to share with them: "You don't have to be a great voice, but if you can interpret the song for me, I'll take that over a great voice any day."

Youngsters *se desvelan* [they stay up all night]. They don't warm up and assume they will sing well no matter what. I tell them to warm up. "If you warm up your voice, ten or fifteen years down the road your voice will be used to it. Your singing will be more consistent."

I try to have them stop taking their voices for granted, to think about the dynamics of the song, and not to forget about the interpretation of the song. I wish I had had someone tell me these things.

Jonathan: What is your own personal warm-up routine?

Raul: I wake up and start doing the little motorboat (lip trill) in the shower. I lubricate the vocal chords to start them off. It doesn't matter if it's a concert, bachelorette party, or trio gig. I warm up and try to achieve the same level of singing whether it's for two people or thousands. I sing warm-up scales; I hum and also warm up with yodeling.

The yodeling is for the *falsetes* [audio demonstration]. Try them out. They may help. If they do, awesome. If not, let's look for other warm-ups.

Jonathan: What vocal challenges have you faced?

Raul: All the songs are a challenge for me! I love singing, though, and do fine. Every time I sing, I try to do it better. The songs that really were challenging for me were "Júrame" and "Estrellita" [classically based mariachi crossover boleros and ballads]. Those are less common in mariachi, and they're more for classical, for opera, and those types of voices. Those two were a challenge for me.

Jonathan: Is it because of the extended range?

Raul: I don't think it's the range as much as the interpretation. I couldn't make it sound too *ranchera*, too mariachi, or fake sounding. I didn't want to try to imitate opera singers because that's not my training. I think you can make it sound great with your own personal voice.

Jonathan: Some people try to force the ranchera style on everything, on every type of song.

Raul: Exactly. I think it is a challenge in and of itself just singing whatever the style dictates. If I have a big *ranchera* voice, I'm not going to sing the same way in *sones* as I do in *huapangos* or as I do in *boleros*. It would still sound okay, but it won't be great.

Jonathan: How did you deal with vocal challenges?

Raul: When I first found out I was selected to sing *Júrame*, I thought, "wow!" I had never sung it before. I learned the words and had heard the song from the previous soloist in *Camperos* [*Mariachi Los Camperos de Nati Cano*]. His name is Arturo Palacios. He had been in *Camperos* for six years and had a huge voice. He was also the guitarist. I knew I couldn't sing it like him because his voice is so big. I listened to other singers, including Plácido Domingo. I tried out ideas, as in extending or cutting notes short. I played with dynamics and added little things. I sang it over and over until I was content. When I sang it in rehearsal, Nati liked it. I'm still singing that solo but not like Arturo.

Jonathan: Would it have helped you to have a mariachi voice teacher help you train your voice specific to mariachi as you became involved in the style?

Raul: It would have been cool to have someone introduce me to all the styles, play them for me, and tell me the differences. For example, in *ranchera* singing style, how to listen to certain singers, such as Vicente [Fernandez] or José Alfredo [Jiménez]. I had to learn it all on my own and research. This also did help me, though.

In mariachi, the most important thing is to transmit the feel. Even if I have an awesome vocal instructor tell me how to sing the notes like this or like that, they can't teach me how to feel or interpret the song.

When young mariachi players and school groups play fancy songs, they often play the notes without feeling the song. You can't teach that until they figure it out for themselves. I relay, "I feel it like this," or "try bowing like this." Less bow here, more dynamics, all within the overall feel of the song. That makes a mariachi sound better. Once they have the feel, they never lose it. I share with kids that they need to be willing to crawl before they walk.

Jonathan: How have you handled periods of not being able to sing, any problems with nodes, vocal fatigue, or related issues?

Raul: With fatigue, sometimes I don't have a voice because I'm sick. There have also been times where my voice is hoarse from us working a lot. Luckily, I've never had nodes. I've had my voice checked, and it is fine, thank God.

CHAPTER 8: FOUR INTERVIEWS WITH MARIACHI ARTISTS ON VOICE   341

I recommend lots of rest, sleep, and water. That keeps my voice intact. When you're sick and cough, it hurts the vocal cords. I try to pass saliva or drink water if I have to cough. When sick or fatigued, I drink more water than usual.

Jonathan: So, you don't go out, party all night and try to sing the next day.

Raul: When I was in my twenties, we would stay up all night talking, jamming, singing, often not even drinking, and I was fine. Now that I am older, I have to keep my voice intact. I've experienced moments of not being able to sing or not being able to even speak because of lack of sleep, tiredness, or being sick. It all affects your voice. It is crucial for me to care for my voice as much as possible. I do have an occasional drink but know my limits, especially if I know I'm going to perform that same day or the next.

Jonathan: Would you benefit from a teacher now? In the opera world, professionals often study until the day they die. They consider technical work a way to protect the voice and keep it in shape. Could we benefit from more protection and a higher standard in mariachi? I am differentiating the work of a voice professor (technical development) from a coach (interpretation and style).

Raul: Right. I would definitely benefit from a vocal teacher. We never stop learning. I feel I'm at my best singing right now. One can always get better! Yes, I want to keep singing until the day I die.

If someone can teach me how to keep singing as long as I can until I'm sixty, seventy, eighty years old, I would love that. I would also love to have someone tell me what I'm doing wrong, or if I'm doing something right, how I can keep that up, or how to maintain what I am doing. That would really help.

FIGURE 8.5 Ranchera singing in duet dressed in traditional black *traje de charro* from Jalisco, Western Mexico. Design by Marcia Cagandan.

GLOSSARY

Mariachi Voice Resources

Word	Definition
AABA	AABA and AABB are organizational structures commonly used for writing songs. They consist of thirty-two measures of song lyrics and melody with eight measures in each section. There are four sections, starting with two verses (AA), followed by a contrasting bridge (B). Section A repeats afterward concluding the song with a similar initial melodic idea (A), or section B can repeat twice. Songs organized in AABB structure, for example, are the ranchera "El Pastor" or the bolero "Sabor a mi."
a cappella	[in the church] In Italian, a cappella refers to singing without any accompaniment. A cappella song has long been sung in folk music and European churches beginning in the Middle Ages with Gregorian chant. Today, it refers to any performance by a singer or a duo or choir without instrumental accompaniment.
accelerando	[accelerating] *Acelerando* in Spanish. To speed up.
accompaniment	Instruments or voices providing harmonic musical support to the solo voice. The opposite of a cappella (see **a cappella**).
accento	[accent] *Acento* in Spanish. An accent mark (^) over or under a note is a symbol asking the performer to emphasize the pitch.
AFI	[International Phonetic Alphabet/IPA] AFI is the acronym in Spanish for *alfabeto fonético internacional*. This alphabet designates special symbols for each sound and crosses among all languages. (see **IPA**)
agudo	[sharp] *Agudo/aguda* is a musical and separate vocal term in Spanish. When a singer is singing sharp, they are not perfectly in tune and are slightly higher or lower than the desired pitch but not necessarily a full half step (see **sharp**).

¡ajua!	A spirited, expressive exclamation common to mariachi singers within a song. It is an onomatopoetic expressive sound pronounced [aʻhu-ah] without a particular meaning, as with "yaba-daba-do" in English.
allegro	[fast speed] A tempo marking indicating speed or a happy mood (or both). *Alegre* in Spanish.
alto	The lowest of the female voice ranges in standard classical singing. The term used in opera is contralto, which can be slightly lower or similar in range to alto. The term alto is used more in choral singing. Besides designating a range the term also infers a certain timbre or vocal color. The mariachi female range sits even slightly lower, between alto and male tenor ranges. Mariachi female singer Lucha Villa has a contralto/tenor range, one of the lowest solo voices of all female mariachi singers.
andante	[walking] A tempo marking asking for a regular walking speed. *Andar* is "to go/move" in Spanish.
appoggio	[support] This Italian term refers to breath support. In Spanish the corresponding term is *apoyar*to lean or support Appoggio also refers in singing to the compressed breath in the lungs which support sounds from the vocal cords. Correct *appoggio* allows singers to support a rich tone, long vocal lines, and high levels of virtuosity, with the breath doing much of the work. The study of appoggio is part of bel canto vocal training (see **bel canto**).
aretes	[earrings] One of many important female accessories used to complement the traditional mariachi look, with either *vestido de charro* or regional costumes.
aria	A solo vocal piece with instrumental accompaniment from a larger work, usually an opera. Arias are often more difficult to sing than songs. They can also be longer and often include recitative sections in which recited dialogue is sung. Double arias include a faster second section that is often virtuosic for the singer. Double arias were common during Italy's Romantic bel canto period during the 1800s. Lupe's aria for soprano from Antonio Gomezanda's *Mariache: Primera opera ranchera mexicana* is a double aria. This mariachi opera was first written in Mexico ca. 1929 (see Chapter 2: Jorge Negrete and mariachi operas).
armadura	[key signature] The key signature designates what key a song is written in. It is indicated by certain sharps or flats grouped together at the beginning of the song and at the beginning of each line of music. The key signature can be found on the left side of each staff after the clef sign and before the time signature. Singers who learn all the key signatures are able to identify song keys (*clave* or *tono*) that fit their voice with more ease (see ***clave***; ***tono***).

armonía	[harmony] In music theory, this word signifies the vertical placement of notes as chords. In *mariachi* the meaning is different, referring to the rhythmic string section within the mariachi ensemble. These instruments hold the rhythm and the chordal harmony. The *armonía* section of a *mariachi* ensemble includes guitar, *vihuela*, and *guitarrón*.
arpeggio	From the Italian word *arpa*, meaning harp. An arpeggio is a broken chord where individual notes are rolled one by one, rather than sounding all together simultaneously. Arpeggios are common on the harp.
arrangement	[*arreglo*] An arrangement of a song organizes notes and chords for each instrument in the mariachi ensemble. It is often written out if the song(s) are complex or long and should include the vocal part as well.
arreglo	[arrangement] A musical arrangement combining various voices and instruments with designated harmonies. Ruben Fuentes was a respected arranger of ranchera songs with Mariachi Vargas (see **arrangement**).
¡arriba!	[up] A typical exclamation used by singers or an ensemble within a song to express excitement and add energy.
"¡así se hace!"	["yes, that's it!"; "yes, that's how you do it!"] A vocal exclamation often used by singers or ensembles within a song in a performance..
atlas-occipital joint	[AO joint] One of the body's six natural points of balance and alignment. The atlas-occipital joint is an articulation between the top of the cervical spine and the base of the skull, roughly between the ears but below the brain. It is often simplified with the term AO joint. When this top joint is in alignment with five other joints, breath flows effortlessly through the air column for singers.
aural skills	This skill is part of musicianship training in music theory. Aural skills are also known as ear training. Aural skills help musicians identify pitches, rhythms, chords, and music intervals.
balada	[ballad] in Spanish (see **ballad**).
ballad	French word (*ballade*) from the same root in Spanish (*bailar*) meaning "to dance." These songs were originally danced. Today, they are usually slow songs, usually in 4/4 meter, that portray a story of love and loss. One of Mexico's most famous ballads sung by high-level singers in a mariachi ensemble is "El Triste" by Roberto Cantoral. A well-known English commercial ballad is "I Can't Help Falling in Love With You" by Elvis Presley. Ballads can be similar to Latin American boleros but do not have to be romantic nor set with the bolero's typical groove of 1/6th note accompaniment (see **bolero**; **bolero ranchero**).

346 GLOSSARY

banda

[band] Banda is a Spanish word designating a group, gang, or band of musicians. In Mexican music, *banda* is a commercial Northern Mexican or *norteño* musical style with solo singers that is often danced. The style features brass instruments, wind, and percussion. Although different from ranchera music and mariachi instrumentation, some songs overlap and also falls under the umbrella of *musica regional Mexicana*.

baritenor

This term indicates the range for a male singer above the baritone and below the tenor. Many male mariachi singers are comfortable singing in this range, including Pedro Infante, Jorge Negrete (baritone, sometimes baritenor), and Javier Solis. Legendary ranchera singer Vicente Fernández (father of Alejandro) has a tenor timbre or color but sang in baritenor range. In the United States there are also many baritenor voice roles in musical theater.

baritone

Medium range for the male voice, falling between tenor and bass ranges. Pedro Vargas is a celebrated baritone from the mariachi and bolero traditions, as is full-voiced Francisco "Charro" Avitia, also known as "El Ranchero Afamado" (The Famous Ranchero). Alejandro Fernández (son of Vicente Fernández) is a lyric or lighter baritone who sings in ranchera and commercial popular song styles.

bar lines

Bar lines are lines between the written-out notes that are used to separate each measure of music. This allows musicians to count regularly according to the indicated time signature. For example, if the time signature is 3/4, a bar line will appear in the music after every three beats (see **measure**).

Baroque

[*Barroco*] The term Baroque describes an artistic movement from Italy. The Baroque style was expressed beyond music in architecture, dance, painting, sculpture, and poetry. Baroque's musical history covers musicians between 1600 and 1750. During this period male countertenors often sang in the high "falsetto" range for female roles, because at the time women were prohibited from singing opera. "Falsete" in ranchera songs accesses the same range when accenting yodel-like register changes in a higher range and sustaining long high notes in huapango songs.

bass

[*bajo*] The lowest male range and darkest timbre, or color, for men. This voice range has not yet been featured in mariachi. Men with bass voices in opera often sing the roles of kings or sinister characters of the underworld.

bass clef

[*clave de fa*] A curved symbol with two dots around the fourth line from the bottom of the bass staff. This line indicates the note "F." In Spanish, the bass clef is called the F clef [*clave de fa*]. The *guitarrón*, string bass, and the bottom left side of the piano are all written in bass clef.

baton

The stick used by conductors to lead the orchestra or symphony (see **conducting**).

GLOSSARY 347

bel canto [beautiful singing] This famous Italian phrase refers to an operatic singing style and technique of singing. *Bel canto* became popular in early Romantic Italian operas between 1800 and the 1860s. The bel canto singing style uses *appoggio* or breath support system. With vocal training and air compression, singers perform with superior tone, long *legato* lines, and virtuosic melismatic lines. Voice pedagogues had various schools of bel canto singing such as Lamperti, Vaccai, Canzone, and García. Examples of Italian bel canto composers are Rossini, Bellini, Donizetti, and Verdi. Rossini's favorite bel canto tenor was Spaniard Manuel García, who performed many times in Mexico City during the first half of the 1800s (see **appoggio**).

belt A timbre, or color used in bravío, or gutsy mariachi singing. With adequate breath compression, the singer uses a "twang", singing on the edge of the vocal folds, while also adding a higher percentage of chest mixed with head resonance. There is more emphasis (but not exclusively so) on the thyroid arytenoid muscle (chest-voice sound). Mariachi bravío belt makes use of darker vowels than the US American belt voice used in musical theater. It is closer to American blues belters. Bravío belt is best expressed in the high-energy song "Pelea de Gallos." A slightly softer version of belt-voice color can also be used in mariachi singing with a mixed chest/head voice on often in the chorus of a bolero (see **mixed voice**).

bemol [flat] Spanish for flat, or a half step lower than the designated note; for example, Bb is a half step lower than B (see **flat**).

blanca [half note] Spanish for half note. This note value sustains for two beats.

blanca con puntilla [dotted half note] Spanish. The dotted half note sustains a note for three beats.

bolero In Mexico, the bolero is a slow couple's dance with a regular beat to it. It is usually a romantic song in 4/4 meter. The term has no relationship to the musical term "bolero" in classical music. The Latin American romantic bolero is first documented on the American continent in several Caribbean Islands and Cuba in the late 1800s. It spread to Mexico via the Yucatán Peninsula in a trio guitar-and-vocals format during the early to mid-1900s. Thanks to radio transmission in the 1930s–1950s, the bolero spread throughout Latin America and remains popular today. Boleros are a flexible genre that can be sung and accompanied in any key, with any number of voices or solo, and with any accompanying instrumental combination, including mariachi. During the 1940s–1950s, the bolero morphed into a new style—"bolero ranchero"—in mariachi recordings and movies that featured the sensational, crooning voices of Pedro Vargas, Pedro Infante, and Javier Solis There is also a strong twentieth-century tradition of Mexican female bolero songwriters (see **bolero ranchero**).

bolero moruno	This type of bolero is a subgenre of the bolero from Andalucía in southern Spain. It has a very specific *armonía* strumming pattern and harmonic structure including four descending chords in a row (see ***armonía***). Examples of this style are the songs "Como quien pierde a una estrella" made famous by singer Alejandro Fernández, and "Suerte Loca" sung by Javier Solis.
bolero ranchero	The bolero ranchero style was born in the 1940s when Mexican producers merged the Cuban romantic intimate bolero with Mexican ranchera style accompaniment and singing style (see **bolero**). Mariachi recordings and movies featured the sensational, crooning voices of Pedro Vargas, Pedro Infante, and Javier Solis, all singing boleros rancheros. Maria Elena Sandoval sang beautiful boleros as well. In the 1990s, commercial singer Luis Miguel re-popularized the bolero with Grammy-winning discs of boleros called "Romance." In mariachi instrumentation for the bolero ranchero, the *armonía*, or rhythm section, accompanies the vocalist by strumming an eighth note pattern against the bass line. The *guitarrón* (bass guitar) plays a half note followed by two quarter notes per measure a separate pattern.
botas	[boots] The distinguished mariachi *traje* (outfit) is always accompanied by leather or suede boots.
botines	[small boots] Ankle-high boots for charros. There are three common types: leather, *charol* (high-gloss finish), and *escaramuza* (fitted for females).
botonadura	[buttons] A set of silver, gold, or chrome-plated buttons worn lengthwise along the outside of pant legs on a *traje de charro* (black charro mariachi outfit). The buttons can be decorated with numerous designs.
bravío **style**	[brave, courageous] A ranchera belted vocal style of singing that has strong, gutsy, and fiery energy in a low female vocal range between tenor and contralto. Lucha Reyes was the first to sing in bravío style in mostly outdoor performances as early as 1913–1915. Female ranchera singers use her singing style as a model in mariachi, and men often model José Alfredo Jiménez's bravío compositions. Several typical bravío ranchera songs are: "Los Laureles," "El Herradero," "El Rey," and "La Charreada." Mexican ranchera belt singing uses darker vowels than many other belt singing styles, vaguely resembling the darker vowels used by American blues singers.

GLOSSARY   349

breath support	Breath support is an equal balance between a constant flow of air and the resistance of intercostal and abdominal muscles against the flow in *appoggio*, an Italian word meaning "leaning" or "supporting." With *appoggio*, singers become aware of the air already within the body and develop air compression. Good breath support frees singers, opening up the range and tone, allowing them to interpret, act, and play instruments simultaneously (see ***appoggio***).
bridge	The bridge is a contrasting section of a song that does not resemble the melody or the chorus.
cadenza	*Cadenza* is the Italian word for a musical cadence. Arias from the Italian Romantic period often feature a semi-improvised ornamental passage at the end of the song, without accompaniment. They are rhythmically free, that is, totally *rubato*, without meter. In ranchera songs, there are no fully improvised long cadenzas showing off the voice at the end of a song; however, the melody and the rhythm of the melody is often varied individually by singers during the song as it progresses. Changes in mariachi are planned or improvised within the same rhythmic groove and the song rarely stops, unless the last line of a song is repeated and re-interpreted by a singer out of time for dramatic emphasis.
calderón	[stop/halt] When a fermata symbol appears over or under a note, the note can be held for at least two beats longer than normal or an indefinite amount, rather than its written value. It is called fermata in both Italian and English (see **fermata**).
canción	[song] A song is an organized collection of notes that have melody, harmony, and/or rhythm, sung with lyrics.
canon	Composition technique that develops a melody with one or more imitations of the main melody line following each other. Canon also refers to a body of songs, as in the mariachi canon, or standard songs that identify mariachi.
cantar	Sing in Spanish.
canto a mi tierra	[I sing to my homeland] These songs are dedicated to one's homeland, a nostalgic and popular Mexican topic.
carpas	[tents] Beginning in the 1900s, Mexican performance entertainment was often held outdoors under tents, or *carpas*. Programs included ranchera singers, orchestras, comics, and a wide assortment of entertainers. Ranchera singer Lucha Reyes and the comic and film star Cantinflas often toured Mexico in *carpas*.

castrati	[castrated] Italian plural word for castrato. This voice type developed during the Baroque period (1600–1750), a time when women were not allowed to be professional singers in opera. Men were trained from puberty or earlier to perform full songs in a high falsetto voice. The movie *Farinelli* illustrates the classical cultivation of the falsete sound from one of the world's last and greatest Baroque male castrati singers. In Mexican mariachi, falsete singing does not include using falsete in entire songs, but rather select lines for dramatic emphasis. The mariachi world has never cultivated castrati (see **falsete**).
chamber	This term refers to a chamber or room. Chamber music originated with small groups of performers offering performances in small rooms or halls. Today, it still refers to music written specifically for small ensembles, generally one person per part. String instruments violin, viola, cello, double bass, and piano are showcased in chamber music, although other combinations exist. If a fifteen-piece mariachi has only one player per part they might be termed a chamber mariachi.
charreada	[rodeo] A *charreada* is a rodeo usually held outdoors in a bullring. The event highlights equestrian and musical virtuosity of many types in show and competitions. Singers and mariachi ensembles typically perform. Many mariachi songs describe charreadas and include equestrian terms. "El toro relajo," "La Charreada," and "huapango torero" are examples of well-known equestrian-related mariachi songs.
charrería	This term describes the Mexican equestrian world, including the typical equestrian and *charro* outfits.
charro	[Mexican cowboy] In a music setting, this term refers to the mariachi singer or player, or to the *traje de charro* —black attire with gold or silver *botonadura* worn by mariachi solo singers and ensembles. It is more elegant than US cowboy outfits. The *traje* or *vestido de charro* includes a large matching sombrero. *Charros* have a strong and charismatic presence.
charts	Charts are song guides or song sheets with chord symbols, a simplified form of written-out sheet music for songs. Musical notation in charts usually include t the melody with chord progressions, although in its most basic form consists of chords only.
chest voice	The thyroid-arytenoid muscle in the vocal cords produce a chest-voice sound, as opposed to the head-voice muscle, the crico-thyroid. Singers often feel their chest-voice resonate in their chest after they activate the thyroid-arytenoid muscle (often called TA muscle). In ranchera singing, the chest voice dominates over the head voice to create an authentic sound, although both should always mix to some degree in training to keep the voice healthy.

chinaco	This costume is a rural peasant's white, loose cotton clothing with *huaraches* (sandals) and was used by mariachis prior to the more elegant, black *traje de charro* of the twentieth century.
chords	Chords are multiple pitches played simultaneously to create harmony. The C Major chord has C-E-G notes played together at the same time.
chorus	A chorus within a song refers to the part of a song that is repeated after the main verse or verses. A chorus also refers to a group of singers singing jointly, whether a cappella or with accompaniment. Most operas usually f have a chorus. In mariachi ensembles the most frequent choral singing occurs in songs from ranchera music's highly rhythmic *jarabes* and *sones*. One of the ranchera world's most famous choruses begins with the famous line "Y volver, volver, volver" from the song "Volver, volver" written by Fernando Maldonado in 1972. It popularized by singer Vicente Fernández.
chromatic	[color] From the Greek word *chrôma*. Chromatic melodies are based on half-step movements and can change the color of a song with small unexpected changes from the diatonic scale. A chromatic scale is C, C#/Db, D, D#/Eb, E, F, F#/Gb, G, G#/Ab, A, A#/Bb, B.
classical	Classical music was originally from Europe but has spread all over the world over many generations. In this style, form and structure are stressed and music is written out. Opera falls within classical music The term classical also refers to a musical period that started approximately from 1750 to 1820. Well-known composers of the period are Haydn, Mozart, and Beethoven.
clave	[musical key, clef, Cuban rhythmic pattern] The term *clave* has many musical meanings. In Spanish, it can signify the musical key (*tono*, *llave*) of a song. As a music-theory term, *clave* can also refer to the clef symbols designating treble or bass clefs. In a Caribbean musical context, *claves* are two rhythm sticks that keep time in the salsa orchestra with a two-bar repeating syncopated pattern. In Mexican mariachi, the *guitarrón* and *armonía* instruments also have a two-bar repeating pattern in a locked-in groove that can be called a *clave*. The pattern changes depending on the rhythmic style being played.
clave de fa	[bass clef/F clef] Music symbol for the bass clef, which designates the lowest-sounding musical instruments and the left half of the piano's keys. The symbol itself describes the "F" pitch located on the fourth line counting up from the bottom of the staff. This symbol is used to write out music for *bass*-pitched instruments such as the *guitarrón*.

352   GLOSSARY

clave de sol [treble clef/G clef] Symbol notating that the second line from the bottom of the staff is the "G" pitch line. This symbol indicates notes for treble-pitched instruments such as the trumpet, violin, *vihuela*, and guitar, and it includes all the keys on the right-hand side of the piano.

coloratura Singing with fast-moving notes, ornamentation, leaps, and melodic trills. Coloratura sopranos are a common voice type for this kind of movement specializing in agility. In ranchera singing, ornaments such a triplets are occasionally used and quick falsete breaks sound like ornaments, but constant melodic agility and trills are not culti-vated. (see **ornamentation**).

comedias musicales [musical comedies] Spanish one-act *zarzuelas*, also called *sainetes*, *tonadillas*. The mariachi world's *comedias rancheras* drew from *comedias musicales* upon creating charro films during the 1930s. This structure was a dramatic structural model, but all references to Spain were abolished, and Mexican nationalistic themes, plots, scripts, and singing style were added instead (see ***comedias rancheras***).

comedias rancheras [ranch comedies/*charro* musicals] Ranchera *charro* musicals were popular during The Golden Age of Cinema, Singers, and Songs be-tween the 1930s and 1950s. The mariachi solo-singing tradition and many ranchera songs became world famous through *charro* musicals. One example is "Ay, Jalisco no te rajes" from 1937. Singers had to develop acting skills and were often the main feature for each movie. Singers Jorge Negrete, Pedro Vargas, and Lola Beltrán were among the celebrity singers during this period.

compose To compose is to write an original song or piece of music. An indi-vidual who writes music is called a songwriter or composer.

conducting The task of conducting, that is, directing the ensemble, falls to the conductor. Cues can be given with hand gestures or a baton (stick). Conductors keep track of entrances, dynamics, and tempo and lead the mariachi or orchestra. Mariachi leaders are called directors. "Director" is also the name for conductor in Spanish.

conjunto [musical ensemble] A group joined together to create music. In Mexico and the Southwestern United States, this term applies directly to Northern Mexican commercial music. It is called *con-junto norteño.* . In Mexico, the *conjunto* style differs from mariachi in its use of the accordion and/or Mexican bass guitar (*bajo sexto*) in lieu of the Mexican *guitarrón*. The vocal style is also different with a constant nasal twang in the singing and little, if any, bel canto classical vocal influences as has been documented in mari-achi vocal history.

con moto	[with motion] A tempo marking that indicates a fast-moving speed. *Con moción* in Spanish.
conservatory	A conservatory of music is a school that specializes in music.
conspirare	"To breathe together " in Latin. When ensembles or choirs learn to breathe together, it often unifies their sound and performance.
contemporary	Contemporary music generally refers to music of the present time. In classical music the term describes music of the twentieth century. In vocal teaching, the acronym CCM stands for contemporary commercial music. This term is also shortened to CM, meaning commercial vocal music. Commercial vocal music is a fast-growing vocal umbrella in voice competitions that encompasses many styles(including mariachi) that do not fit into classical or musical theater singing.
contralto	Typically, the lowest register of the female voice in operatic singing, although the female mariachi fach is slightly lower. Lucha Villa has one of the lowest female voices in mariachi singing and falls between contralto and tenor ranges. Also referred to as alto in choirs (see **alto**).
corazón	[heart] A common lyric used in ranchera songs.
corchea	[eighth note] An eighth note gets half of a beat. Two eighth notes equal one quarter note, or one beat.
coro	[choir/chorus] Spanish word for group singing (see **chorus**). The *coro* of a song also refers to the chorus or hook of a song.
corrida de toros	[bullfight] In Spanish, the term literally means "running of the bulls." Bullfights were brought to Mexico from Spain as sporting events and remain popular today. Bullfighting, or charreria, has always been a part of ranchera lifestyle in Mexico as competition and entertainment, and mariachi performances can be included. In modern times, mariachi performances are an integral performance element of most *charreadas* and *jaripeos* (rodeos and celebrations).
corrido	Popular narrative song and poetry or ballad. Corridos typically tell stories that comment on oppression, history, peasant life, and lost love. Corridos date back to at least the beginning of the eighteenth century during Mexico's independence from Spain. They gained popularity during the Mexican Revolution (1910–1921). Perhaps the most important corrido is "La cucaracha," which has political and historical origins. "El mayor de los dorados" or "La Chancla," "La Valentina," "Carabina 30-30," and "La Adelita" are examples of corridos sung within ranchera repertoire.

countertenor	The countertenor is the highest male range using the falsetto voice above the range of a tenor. Classical countertenors traditionally sing entire songs in falsetto voice with virtuosic fast runs (coloratura). This style of singing was especially popular in opera during the Baroque period (1600–1750). World renowned Italian countertenor, Farinelli, lived during this period (1705–1782). His real name was Carlo Maria Michelangelo Nicola Broschi. In mariachi singing, both men and women make use of falsetto range and color contrast the different registers. It is called falsete in Spanish. While countertenor sings in a different range in classical music, falsete in mariachi is only used for specific dramatic moments, sustaining long notes. Mariachi singers would never stay in countertenor range throughout the song or their repertoire as do countertenors.. The song "El Pastor" sung by lyric tenor Miguel Aceves Mejía ("El Rey del Falsete"/The King of falsete) is a famous example of falsete singing in countertenor range during part of the verses and the entire chorus of the song (see **falsete**).
crescendo	[to grow] This Italian term expresses dynamics. In this case "crecer" refers to gradually increasing volume. The musical symbol resembles the "less than" math symbol. Its opposite is decrescendo, to decrease in volume with a "more than" math symbol.
cricothyroid muscle	This muscle is the muscle within the vocal cords responsible for the upper part of the vocal range, often termed head voice. It is often called the CT muscle.
crooner	One who sings softly without imposing a great sound while still using breath support. Crooning sounds relaxed but with a resonant tone and is louder and fuller than *sotto voce* (very soft but supported pianissimo) in operatic singing. This vocal production is especially effective when singing boleros or in bolero ranchero style, but can be applied to other ranchera song styles as well. Crooning in mariachi was incorporated into male vocal sound by male singers Jorge Negrete, Pedro Infante, Javier Solis, and others. The softer mariachi vocal production with support is an important stylistic difference from full operatic vocal sound. Mexican singers during the 1940s were perhaps influenced by crooners popular in the United States and internationally at the time, most notably Bing Crosby and Frank Sinatra.
cross-training	The practice of learning how to switch between different singing styles. By cross-training with a voice teacher in both classical and mariachi style, students can progress in both areas simultaneously and classical exercises open up range for better mariachi singing. Singers today are often expected to address diversity by performing multiple styles, as it opens up their marketability. Voice teachers versed in contemporary commercial singing (CCM) are often helpful with non-classical styles, and those who teach both can assist singers by switching styles back and forth within the same studio.

GLOSSARY 355

danzón	This musical genre is the official name for a traditional Cuban intimate couple's dance used in many Latin American songs. It is felt in 2/4 meter with a dotted rhythm. *Danzón* originated from the popular Spanish *danza* and French *contredanse* that is similar to the *habanera* rhythm. Elements from some *danzones* prior to 1930 are still a part of ranchera repertoire today, including "La negra noche," "La barca de oro" (see Chapter 6: songs) and the ubiquitous "La Paloma."
decrescendo	[decrease] An Italian term used to express lowering the volume in dynamics. Opposite of crescendo. Decrescendo refers to gradually decreasing volume. The musical symbol resembles the "greater than" math symbol.
diction	Enunciation and clarity of pronunciation as one sings. Singers study International Phonetic Alphabet (**IPA**) to focus on sound over spelling, which helps clarify diction (see Chapter 6).
diminuendo	[growing softer] *Disminuyendo* in Spanish and diminishing volume in English. Also known as *decrescendo*, gradually getting softer.
diphthong	Double vowel sounds within one syllable.
Doce canciones mexicanas	[Twelve Mexican songs] Important early twentieth-century publication of Mexican folk songs collected by Manuel M. Ponce, known by many as the "Father of Mexican Song." Many of the songs have ranchera valseada accompaniments in 3/4 meter.
dominant	The dominant is the fifth note of the scale. In the mariachi world it is known as *segundo* (V7-Second). In sheet music it is represented by the Roman numeral (V7). The dominant is known in ranchera music as the second most important chord after the tonic (I), which is called *primera*.
dotted half note	Dotted half notes sustain for three beats. In Spanish this note value is called *blanca con puntilla*.
downbeat	A downbeat is the strongest beat of the measure. Typically, it is the first beat of each measure. It can change if the music has a syncopated rhythm.
dynamics	This term refers to musical symbols that indicate the volume level. Two examples are crescendo, to grow, and decrescendo, to decrease.
ear training	Learning to recognize melodies and harmonic intervals through listening (see **aural skills**).
¡Échale ganas!	["Do your best!"; "Put your heart into it!"] This is an exclamation often heard by mariachi performers during a song as a form of spirit and encouragement.
eighth note	Eighth notes last half a beat or half of a quarter note. In Spanish this note value is called *corchea*.

El Charro Cantor	[The Singing Cowboy] Famous slogan associated with legendary ranchera singer Jorge Negrete (1911–1953). Negrete had a global career with over thirty-five movies, recordings, concerts, tours, and many songs. (see Chapter 8: Negrete Artist Interview).
elision	Elision refers to the slur marking that connects a word that ends in a vowel to another word that begins with a vowel, for example, "*ando̲ allá*." Elisions are common in Spanish, and the two vowels become a kind of diphthong without any separate phonation for the second vowel. Understanding this often gives singers a perfect accent in Spanish.
el pueblo	[the village] *El pueblo* refers to middle- and/or lower-class people representing typical villages in Mexico. The vocal style of José Alfredo Jiménez is directed to his market -*el pueblo*-the voice of the people of Mexico.
El Rey del Falsete	[The King of Falsete] This term is the slogan given to mariachi tenor Miguel Aceves Mejía for his effortless falsete extended high notes (see **falsete**).
empresario	[businessperson/entrepreneur]
ensemble	[at the same time] Group of musicians playing together at the same time.
Época de Oro del Cine Mexicano	[The Golden Age of Cinema] Charro or ranchera musicals were also called comedias musicales. They were popular in Mexico, Latin America, and Spain during the Golden Age of Cinema. This cinematic style was at its height between the 1930s and 1950s and was popular throughout Latin America. The mariachi solo-singing tradition and many ranchera songs became world famous through comedias musicales. One example is *Ay, Jalisco no te rajes*. Singers had to also develop characters and acting skills and were often the main feature for each movie. Singers Jorge Negrete, Pedro Vargas, and Lola Beltrán were among some of the many celebrity singers during this period.
escaramuza	A style of rodeo exhibition for women, achieved while riding side- saddle at *charreadas* (rodeos). Women's boots are called *escaramuzas*.
ethnomusicology	The study of music of different cultures. Practically speaking, the field of ethnomusicology addresses all non-Western cultures, including ranchera music. Ethnomusicological research includes historical, cultural, social, and sound aspects of music. The first US-based mariachi in academia began at UCLA in Los Angeles, California, in the early 1960s.

fach system	A German method of classifying primarily opera singers in voice types according to size, range, weight, and color of their voices. Some examples are lyric soprano coloratura, dramatic tenor, or soubrette soprano. The classification was associated with a specific repertoire for that type of voice. For example, a light lyric voice has a repertoire of opera roles that include small- to medium-sized orchestras rather than a huge one.
falsete	[false voice] Falsete in mariachi s a type of yodeling or vocal flip where the voice breaks between two registers and the break is accentuated with color contrast. In virtuosic *huapango* songs, falsete notes are sustained for four or more bars, showing off the singer's vocal dexterity. The longer singers can hold out falsete notes, the more the audience gets excited and involved. This term is related to the Italian male voice range called falsetto whereby certain male voices sing entire songs in their falsetto range about an octave above their regular range (see **countertenor**). Mariachi falsete makes use of this same range in a different way without singing entire songs or long runs in this range. Falsete is an important expressive gesture for every aspiring mariachi vocalist. When women flip into falsete, they accentuate timbre or color differences in registration when moving from chest to head voice range. Due to the smaller size of the vocal cords, it is already at a very high pitch, and there is no falsetto singing above the female range. (see Chapter 3).
falsetto	[false voice] Male singers have an upper range above their head voice (around a4 and roughly an octave above where men normally sing). This range has a unique color distinct from head voice. The same technique for the female voice in mariachi is called falsete. Women express falsete by accentuating the shift as a register break from their chest voice to head voice (roughly d4–b4). Contrary to men, women do not use falsetto range, although some women have a high coloratura whistle register between c6 and g 5 or 6.
fandango	In Mexico, a *fandango* is a party, *fiesta*, or celebration, and it usually includes singing. In Spain, the *fandango* is a musical rhythm and/or dance whose character varies widely depending on the region. In Spanish theatrical, *zarzuela*, and classical music, *fandango* is also referred to as a staged theatrical work.
Fantasia Ranchera	A film directed by Juan José Segura in 1947 with music and lyrics by Antonio Gomezanda taken from his script and opera ranchera entitled *MARIACHE: Primera opera ranchera mexicana,*. This mariachi opera was originally written by the same composer under a different name in 1929. The movie is a shortened form of Gomezanda's opera ranchera, and is, to date, the world's first documented mariachi opera (see Chapter 2: "Crossover Singing: Jorge Negrete and Operas Rancheras").

358 GLOSSARY

female mariachi fach	The female mariachi fach is a fixed range and timbre that authenticates the desired sound for women singers in this style. The range is approximately f3 to c4, between the contralto/tenor range (see **fach**; Chapter 3)
fermata	[stop/halt] When a fermata symbol appears over or under a note, the note can be held for at least two beats longer than normal or an indefinite amount, rather than its written value. It is called *calderón* in Spanish (see ***calderón***).
fiesta	Party, celebration, or *fandango* (see ***fandango***).
fingerpicking	A technique used to play guitar or string instruments with fingertips or fingernails instead of a pick.
flat	A musical symbol similar to the lowercase letter b, which lowers the pitch by half a step. In Spanish the term is *bemol* (see **half step**).
folk	Folk music is any oral tradition that passes songs down aurally from one generation to another. Folk songs describe cultures and social ideas, and can commemorate important moments in history. Ranchera songs are from an oral tradition.
forte	[loud] A musical symbol f to indicate a strong dynamic volume. *Fuerte* in Spanish.
gala	Refers to the design and shiny buttons that outline a *traje de charro*. The gala designs can be Aztec calendars, owl heads, stars, horse heads, logos, and initials. The buttons are also called *botonadura* or *plata* (silver).
gallo	[rooster] *Gallo* refers to early morning when the rooster crows and is a slang musical term for an early morning mariachi *serenata* (serenade).
genre	[style/category] Genres in music are categorized by style. Examples of music genres are classical, pop, rock, and mariachi. In Spanish, genre (used in English but originally a French word) is *género*.
gleno-humeral joint	One of the body's six natural points of balance and alignment. The gleno-humeral joint is a ball-socket articulation between the humerus and the glenoid cavity of the scapula. The joint falls under the shoulder and under the arm on the inside of the body. When this top joint is in alignment with five other joints, breath flows effortlessly through the air column. (see Chapter 3)
glottal	A glottal stop literally stops the air flowing in the vocal tract.
greca	A decorative pattern that repeats itself in a linear fashion. *Greca* patterns can be found on *trajes de charro*.
gritos	A yell or cry of exclamation. Mexicans are known for their unique *gritos* as a form of expression in appreciation during a live performance. *Gritos* are yelled by performers and audience alike.

GLOSSARY   359

guitarra	[guitar] A six-string wooden instrument originally from Spain. It is played by strumming its nylon strings with the right hand and placing the left-hand fingers down in different chordal combinations. The guitar, guitarrón, and *vihuela* make up the rhythmic section of the mariachi. There are typically one or two guitarists per mariachi ensemble and at least one *vihuela* player.
guitarrón	[large guitar] A large, six-string bass guitar with a humped back that is indigenous to the mariachi ensemble and to Mexico. Strings are often plucked in pairs with the right hand. The left hand does fingering on the strings with all fingers, sometimes including the thumb. By playing the bass line in octave pairs with the right hand, the guitarrón's sound cuts across the mariachi ensemble. The guitarrón's function is to serve as an anchor or foundation for the group's challenging rhythms, syncopation, and fast tempos. It is the hardest instrument to play while soloing as a singer.
género chico	A name for short one-act comedic or dramatic *zarzuelas* often performed in Mexico City during Spanish rule of Mexico between 1521 and 1821 (see **zarzuela**).
habanera	The *habanera* is one of the oldest song rhythms from Hispanic song literature, namely the 1879 title "La Paloma" (The Dove) by Sebastián Yradier (Iradier). Yradier was a Spanish Basque composer who wrote the song around 1860 after a visit to Cuba. He registered it in Madrid in 1879 as a "Canción americana con acompañamiento de piano" (song from the American continent with piano accompaniment).
hacienda	A large estate, ranch, or plantation.
half note	A half note is a round white-colored note that is sustained for two beats. In Spanish this note value is called a *blanca*.
half step	The half step or semitone is the smallest interval in Western music (Eastern music uses 1/4 tones). Each fret on many string instruments represents a half step. On the piano, from C to C# is a half step and E to F is also a half step; half steps can be any combination of white and black keys on the piano.
harmony	Two or more notes sounding simultaneously indicate some kind of harmony, although triads (three notes) and chords (triads with one note doubled) are more common indicators of harmonic chords. Harmony is vertical, and melodic movement is horizontal (see **melody**).
head voice	[*voz de cabeza*] The higher register above chest voice that is made with the crico-thyroid muscle (see Chapter 3).

huapango	A rhythmic and singing style from the Huasteca region of Eastern Mexico in 6/8 meter. It is easily distinguishable with falsete yodel-like flips in and out of chest to head register. Musical characteristics from the Huasteca region include virtuosic melodic runs on violin, alternating in call-and-response fashion with the voice. Vocal lyrics are often improvised within fairly repetitive vocal lines with non-sustained vocal flips. The huapango transformed into a contemporary urban virtuosic style in Mexico City between approximately 1920 and 1950. Classical and operatic vocal styles clearly influenced the singers and songwriters. Singers since this time are expected to sustain falsete flips in a high register, while focusing on a long, legato singing line in urban-style huapangos. Huapangos are generally the most difficult vocal parts of the mariachi repertoire.
huaraches	Mexican sandals that are usually made from rubber or straps of leather.
huastecos	Huasteco is a style of vocal and instrumental music from the Huasteco region of Mexico influenced by a mix of Spanish, African, and indigenous traits. The Huastecos are indigenous people residing in the Mexican states of San Luis Potosí, Veracruz, Hidalgo, and Puebla.
hymns	Religious songs or poems sung in praise of God.
improvisation	This term implies making up notes or rhythms spontaneously and in the moment. Most mariachi songs are not improvised, although older *huastecas* and related styles often improvise call-and-response patterns with improvisation led by the lead singer.
inflection	Inflection is the emphasis or stress upon the pitch, which can affect the intonation of a note or phrase.
intercostal muscles	Muscles around the outside of the rib cage. They expand as a singer inhales, along with the diaphragm lowering to create more space for air in the lungs. (see Chapter 3).
interludes	Break or space in the music, usually in the middle of a song, that serves as an instrumental transition from one lyric idea to the next.
interval	The distance between any two notes is an interval. As an example, from note C to E (or do to mi) is a third, or three steps counting step number one as C.
intonation	Accuracy of pitch.
IPA	[IPA; alfabeto fonético internacional] International Phonetic Alphabet. A language of international symbols and sounds that allow singers, speakers, and linguists to travel between languages with near perfect pronunciation. It is used in vocal training. In Spanish, the acronym for IPA is AFI (see AFI earlier in Glossary).

jarabe	[syrup] *Jarabe* is a Mexican *son* rhythmic style in 12/8 meter that usually links several sections of different *son* melodies and rhythms together into one piece (mixing flavors or syrups). It is often performed instrumentally with dancers, although some songs have the ensemble singing in parts. The most famous Mexican piece is the *Jarabe Tapatío*, danced by a woman in *china poblana* costume and man in *traje de charro*, similar to the mariachi ensemble (see https://gabrielamendozag arciafolklorico.com/2018/02/18/performing-nation-the-jarabe-tapa tio-of-1920s-mexico/). The *Jarabe Tapatío* is from Guadalajara, Jalisco. A tapatio is a person from this region of Mexico.
jarana	Small fretted string instrument shaped like a guitar used to play traditional music from Veracruz. It is also the name used for a couple's dance native to Yucatán, including a combination of waltz and zapateado steps. This instrument is not used in mariachi ensembles.
jaripeo	A form of bull riding within a rodeo or *charreada* and/or *fiesta*. It is a competitive sport with live music and other attractions. This term is used often in songs about rodeos such as "El jaripeo" and "La charreada" (The Rodeo).
key signature	[*armadura*] Key signatures let performers know what key the song is in with a set of symbols on the left-hand side of each line of music on the staff. The key signature lists all the flats or sharps together to the right of the clef but before the time signature. Key signatures can be major or minor (see **major keys**; **minor keys**).
largo	[slow speed] A tempo marking for slow. *Lento* in Spanish.
larynx	The larynx is also called the voice box. It is formed by cartilage, ligaments, and muscles. The larynx helps with breathing, swallowing, talking, and singing. Sound is produced by vibrations that happen when the air passes through the vocal cords within the larynx (see **voice box**).
legato	[*ligado*/smoothly connected] Italian term for a style of singing in a smooth, connected manner by linking the vowels.
lento	[slow] A tempo marking meaning slow in both Spanish and Italian.
lyric	Lyric voices tend toward a lighter sound quality and fast-moving agility. Miguel Aveces Mejía was a lyric tenor.
lyric diction	Articulation, pronunciation, enunciation of words to ensure natural singing that sounds authentic in the language being sung.
maestro	[teacher] Music or dance teachers are often referred to as maestro as a term of respect. While its use in this regard is common, technically, when a professor finishes their master's degree in México, they earn the term maestro as opposed to *profesor*. Upon earning the doctorate teachers are then addressed as *doctor/doctora*.
major	A chord, interval, or scale whereby the third note of the scale (mi) is the interval of a major third above the tonic, or root.

major key	Major keys are the most common keys chosen in music. They are based on scales that include a major third interval above the tonic, or root, with half steps between 3-4 and 7-8. These scales often portray a happy message, as in Cielito Lindo. (see **key signatures**; **minor key**).
maquillaje	[makeup] Traditional mariachi makeup is bold for stage makeup.
mariache	Historically interchangeable word with the word "mariachi," which is now more commonly used. *Mariache* is also the name of the world's earliest documented mariachi opera, by Antonio Gomezanda, first written in 1928 under the name *La Virgen de San Juan* (The Virgin of San Juan). The title and some lyrics were later changed and copyrighted in 1943 in both Mexico and the United States under the name *Mariache: Primera opera ranchera Mexicana* (Mariache: First Mexican Ranchera Opera). This historical landmark has never been performed live, although a shortened version was filmed and released as part of the 1947 movie *Fantasía ranchera* (Ranch Fantasy) (see Chapter 2).
mariachi	Mariachi refers to a Mexican folk music tradition within a larger genre called ranchera music (music from the ranch). Mariachi refers to many things: a certain body of repertoire, a musical style, a robust singing style, a solo singer or performer in a *charro* suit, and/or an ensemble. Mariachi originated on the Western coast of Mexico during the 1830s. It is documented as far north as San Francisco, California. The ensemble includes players that both sing and play the violin, guitar, *vihuela*, *guitarrón*, harp, and, since the 1940s, the trumpet. The term is historically interchangeable with the word mariache. The terms mariachi or mariache can also refer to a *fiesta*, a *fandango*, or a mariachi.
mariachi antiguo	Ranchera music is often defined as having two broad periods in its history; the first, a rural, older, regional Mexican mariachi style, also called *mariachi rural*, or *mariachi antiguo*. It is documented back to the 1830s up until the Mexican Revolution (1910–1921) (see ***mariachi rural***).
mariachi fach	A register and timbre named by author that is unique to the female voice in mariachi. The female mariachi fach lies below the mezzo-soprano range and sits in the contralto range but closer to the male tenor range with female color. The bulk of the range sits in the chest register. To stay healthy and provide projection, the upper end from e4 to c5 should be blended with training in soft-belt production.
mariachi moderno	Ranchera music after the Mexican Revolution is called contemporary, urban, or *mariachi moderno*. During this period, ranchera singers employed vocal techniques that included classical bel canto influences and folk bravío singing.
mariachi rural	The first period in mariachi music history featuring rural and regional Mexican mariachi trends before the Mexican Revolution. *Mariachi rural* is also called *mariachi antiguo*.

mariachi urbano	After the Mexican Revolution (1910–1921) ranchera music centralized in Mexico City and evolved into a style called contemporary, urban, or *mariachi moderno*. During this period, ranchera singers employed vocal techniques employing both classical bel canto influences and folk bravío singing.
master class	A performance class given by a voice professional to work with students to polish interpretation, repertoire, acting, and/or technique.
mayordomo	[foreman, chief laborer, team leader, mayor] *Mayordomo* and *caporal* are common words in mariachi song lyrics.
measure	A measure is a unit of time. A measure will contain four beats if the time signature is 4/4. In the time signature of 3/4 there are three beats in each measure. A measure of music is also called a bar of music. Each measure is divided by a bar line. In Spanish a measure is called *compás* (see **time signature**).
melismatic	Melodic movement is melismatic when many notes are sung quickly on a single syllable. From the word "melisma."
melody	A single musical line evolving note by note consecutively. Solo vocalists sing the main melody of a song. The melody is usually the main theme in a song. Melodic movement moves horizontally note by note while harmony sounds vertically, usually accompanying the melody (see **harmony**).
meter	Meter is the overall measurement of time throughout the song. The meter is intrinsically linked to the rhythmic genre and/or style. For example, the polka is always in 2/4 meter and is conducted by repeatedly counting 1, 2 throughout the song. The ranchera valseada is in 3/4, and singers should count 1, 2, 3 throughout the song. The huapango is in 6/8, which can be felt in either 1, 2, 3 or 1, 2 simultaneously.
metronome	A device that produces a clicking sound to help keep a strict tempo, or speed. The speed is adjustable for musicians to practice both slow and fast songs at different tempi (see **tempo**).
mezzo-soprano	A female vocal range lower than soprano and higher than alto. The female mariachi fach lies below the mezzo-soprano range but can intersect slightly with it.
minor	A key, chord, interval, or scale whereby the third note of the scale (mi) is a minor third above the tonic. Minor scales also include other note alterations depending on what kind of scale it is.
minor keys	These keys are based on the minor scales that include a flattened third step, among altered steps 6 and 7 depending on the scale type. These scales often express sadness and melancholy. The Mexican folk song "La Llorona" is in a minor key (see **key signatures**; **major keys**).

mixed voice	Mixed voice includes employing a blend of head (crico-thyroid) and chest (thyroid-arytenoid) muscles, instead of leaning exclusively on one or the other. Mixed voice with a higher percentage of chest can also be used in lieu of belt voice in the upper chest register for bravío songs, when properly supported with breath compression. Mixed voice is effective in the high notes of the bolero "Amor eterno," for example, as it provides a mellow timbre that fits the mood of the song. Bravío belt is best expressed in the high-energy *son* entitled "Pelea de Gallos."
Mixteco	[Mixtec] This term refers to a Mesoamerican indigenous group speaking the Mixtec language from La Mixteca region, located mainly in Oaxaca, Mexico.
moño	An untied bow that hangs around the collar used as part of the *traje de charro*.
música regional Mexicana	[regional Mexican music] A broad genre of Mexican folk music that includes rancheras. This term also includes Mexican songs from Northern Mexico and south Texas. Ranchera songs under this regional umbrella may be accompanied by tuba and brass instruments, while mariachi songs are accompanied by string and brass instruments. The vocal styles also vary in that norteño (from the north) and Tejano (Tex-Mex) regional Mexican songs in Spanish often make use of a nasal twang in the vocal delivery.
music fundamentals	Every musician begins their music degree by studying music fundamentals with general note reading, rhythms, musical structure, harmony, and melody.
music theory	Music theory teaches concepts and methods that allow musicians to comprehend, write down, listen acutely, and create music. These studies begin after music fundamentals and include dictation, sight-singing, and aural skills.
Náhuatl	[Nahuatl] Náhuatl is a Uto-Aztecan language spoken by about 1.5 million people, mostly in central Mexico. Náhuatl was the language of the Aztecs, existing prior to the arrival of the Spanish in 1521. Náhuatl is still spoken in Mexico City (D.F.), Hidalgo, Morelos, Puebla, and also in parts of Oaxaca, Guerrero, Veracruz, and even the country of El Salvador.
NATS	National Association of Teachers of Singing.
Neapolitan songs	Songs in the Neapolitan Romance language from Southern Italy. Singers training with Maestro Jose Pierson in Mexico City received training in this song style alongside Mexican rancheras and opera arias.
negra	[black] A Spanish term used for a quarter note. The note is black in the shape of a circle and is sustained for one beat.

GLOSSARY 365

noches mexicanas   [Mexican evenings] This term is a synonym of *revistas teatrales*. In the early 1900s, Mexican nationals organized staged performance troupes offering variety shows. The revues toured rural Mexico presenting shows under outdoor *carpas* (tents) with ranchera singers, orchestras, comics, and a wide assortment of entertainers (see ***revistas teatrales***).

nodes   Nodes are well-defined small individual structures within the connective tissue of the vocal folds. They interfere with speaking and singing and are a sign of an unhealthy voice.

nodule   Nodules are a swelling or a small aggregation of cells appearing on the vocal folds. They interfere with singing. Vocal rest is recommended to avoid further growths.

norteño   [northerner] *Norteños* refers to people that live in northern Mexico. *Norteño* is also the term used to describe music from Northern mexico. *Norteño* rhythms showcase the polca and vals rhythms.

octave   [*octava*] An octave is an interval of eight notes—for example, middle C (C4) up eight notes to C5 is one octave.

opera   [work] The term opera is derived from the word *opus* in Latin. Opera began in Italy around 1597–1600 as sung, staged dramas. Opera composers often based their music upon literary works. Opera includes sung speech, or recitative, which furthers the action. Recitative is alternated with virtuosic arias, duets, trios, and choruses with highlight singers to the accompaniment of the orchestra. The earliest ranchera opera is *Mariache: Primera opera ranchera mexicana* by Antonio Gomezanda, ca. 1929 (see Chapter 2) with two more contemporary ones since 2012, almost 100 years later.

operachi   A crossover mix between opera and mariachi. Dr. Juanita Ulloa's personal training and style earned her the title of first female operachi singer. Male ranchera singers from the 1930s were also trained by Maestro José Pierson in a crossover style that included elements of opera within the ranchera vocal style. Jorge Negrete's singing exemplifies this crossover training (see Chapter 2).

operas rancheras   The exploration of classical and folkloric music, namely mariachi, in Mexican song. There was natural crossover in classical and folk music, as well as vocal training in Mexico City during the 1930–1940s when mariachi took the global stage in the Golden Age of Cinema and Song. The earliest documented ranchera opera is *Mariache: Primera opera ranchera mexicana* by Antonio Gomezanda, ca. 1929 (see Chapter 2). The term is also known as mariachi opera.

operetta	A combination of theater and light opera. Operettas include dance, singing, and dialogue, similar to musical theater but with singers in a sound unique to operetta. In opera, all dialogues are generally sung as recitative, and the singers use a fuller sound. In Spain, zarzuelas are similar to operettas but with substantial folk flavor. Zarzuelas were commonly staged in Mexico City during Spanish reign and Mexican song and dance selections were featured during interludes.
ornaments	Ornaments are musical embellishments or decorations. They consist of musical notes added to the existing melody line to add variety, beauty, and virtuosity.
Orquesta Típica Mexicana	Touring orchestra formed in 1884 by Carlos Curti and followed by Miguel Lerdo de Tejada. They may have been the first to wear the traje de charro and include ranchera songs within their umbrella of diverse musical styles. Pedro Vargas also toured with this group.
palenque	A party, *fiesta*, or *fandango*, usually refers to an outdoor celebration.
passaggio	A term used in classical singing to describe the transition area between chest and head voice and other register changeovers.
pedagogy	Pedagogy is the study, development, and practice of teaching voice. Vocal pedagogy comes from a many-centuries-old Italian classical tradition whereby singers practiced exercises sometimes for years before tackling bigger songs, opera arias, or full roles.
pentagrama	[music staff] Five parallel lines used in standard music notation used to delineate the location of music notes. Pitches vary depending on whether notes are placed on spaces or lines and on which line in the staff.
phonation	From the word "phone" meaning sound. This term refers to the activation of sound through song or speech that emanates from the vocal cords or voice box.
phonator	The phonator is the source of sound within the human body. The vocal folds/voice box are the phonator responsible for producing human sound.
piano	[soft] A symbol p requesting soft volume. Both the Italian and Spanish word *suave* are used in English and Spanish music worlds.
pitch	Pitch describes how high or low a tone is. Pitch is also a sound quality governed by the rate of vibrations that produce it.
polca	[polca/polka] The polca is a lively dance in 2/4 meter especially popular in Northern Mexican *norteño* music. It comes from the polka in the European region of Germany-Austria. "Palomitos de ojos negros" is a polca ranchera.

GLOSSARY   367

polyp   A blister, lesion, extra piece of tissue, or growth located on the vocal cords that can cause constant vocal fatigue, graininess, excessive air release, and progressively less and less control over one's sound.

popote   [straw] *Popote* is a Mexican Spanish word. Straws, or *popotes*, are often used to practice many kinds of breath exercises. By inhaling a small amount of air quickly from a straw, one can observe the lower intercostal and abdominal muscles responding immediately to support the request activated by the *popote* for air and breath support.

popurri   [potpourri/medley] A medley of songs arranged together. Mariachi arrangers often enjoy creating elaborate arrangements for the ensemble that tie together contrasting ranchera songs that are favorites to the audience. This is related to multi-sectioned *jarabes* and multi-sectioned vocal solos such as "Mexico Lindo y Querido" (see *jarabe*).

posadas   A Christmas vocal-music tradition celebrated between December 16th to January 6th of each year in Mexico and Latin America. The journey of Mary and Joseph to Bethlehem is reenacted with songs asking for lodging. Christmas villancicos are often sung, and the celebration can involve festivities connected to the church.

ranchera/ranchero   [from the ranch] Ranchera music generally refers to folk music, dance, and a rural lifestyle that celebrates life on the ranch and beyond in Mexico. More specifically, ranchera songs are often played in waltz, huapango, *son*, or polca rhythms. Time signatures vary between 2/4, 3/4, 4/4, 6/8, and 12/8, usually in a major key. In the United States, the term "mariachi singer" has more common usage than the term "ranchera singer." In Mexico it is the reverse. Ranchera has rural Western Mexico folk origins dating back to the early 1800s. Ranchera songs are first documented in the 1830s along Mexico's western coast.

quarter note   Quarter notes last one beat. In Spanish this note value is called *negra* because the note is colored black with a stem.

quinceañera   [fifteen] A birthday celebration for fifteen-year-old girls in Mexico. This celebration is similar to the coming-of-age sweet sixteen birthday celebration for girls in the United States, but usually more elaborate. Mariachis typically perform at either the church service and/or ensuing party celebration.

rallentando   [gradually slower] *Atardando* or *deteniendo* in Spanish. This Italian term is similar to ritardando. Both Italian terms are widely used in Spanish and English music circles.

ranchera lenta [slow ranch song] A slow ranchera speed and style usually written in 2/4 meter. The bass *guitarrón* plays on downbeat counts 1 and 2, and the other string accompaniment, or *armonía*, *plays* on offbeats. Popular songs in this rhythm include "El Rey," "Por un amor," and "Volver, Volver."

368 GLOSSARY

ranchera valseada [ranch waltz] The ranchera waltz is in 3/4 meter and can be counted like a regular waltz. The bass *guitarrón* plays on count 1, and the guitars and vihuela or *armonía* play on counts 2 and 3. Singers usually vary the rhythms around the 3 count to provide interesting musical phrasing of the lyrics. Popular songs in this rhythm are "Cielito lindo" (which has the popular Ay, ay, ay chorus), "Tres días," and "La barca de oro."

rancho [Ranch] *Rancho* refers to a plot of land in rural areas for farming and for raising cattle and horses. Many folk ranchera songs reference rural Mexico's cultural and lifestyle traditions on ranchland with nostalgia. Owning land is also an important topic in Mexican history.

range Range is the musical distance from the lowest to highest pitch in a singer's voice. Vocal range varies greatly from person to person, depending on many factors, beginning with the size of the vocal cords, gender, musical style, and the amount of vocal training one has had, to name a few.

recital Recitals are performances where singers and musicians showcase musical repertoire. Recitals are more formal than concerts and can be classical. Ranchera singers more often appear in concerts than recitals.

redonda [round] Spanish music term for a whole note. A whole note resembles a round circle and lasts four beats.

register The voice actually changes registration every five or six notes. Most consider three main registers of head voice (includes falsetto voice for falsete for men), middle voice (upper register for men), and chest voice. Women naturally have a large head-voice range above a smaller chest voice range (Men are opposite) Women have no falsetto voice, but some high coloratura females have a whistle register above C6 above their head-voice range. There is an additional vocal-fry register or modal voice that all people have as well. (see **falsetto**; **falsete**).

repertoire List of songs or musical numbers, or a body of songs from any given style.

resonation The acoustic effect of sound. With respect to the voice, the resonating chamber is primarily located within the mouth, back part of the nose passageway into the throat, and part of the throat. Resonation can be secondarily felt in the chest and head areas as well. The less the sound or air is pushed, the more it can resonate if supported by the breath. Healthy vocal production with full breath support produces a full, reverberating, resonant sound.

revistas teatrales [theatrical revues In the early 1900s, Mexican national empresarios organized touring staged performance troupes with variety shows called *revistas teatrales*. Performers toured many regions in Mexico under outdoor *carpas* (tents). Shows included ranchera singers, orchestras, comics, and a wide assortment of entertainers.

ritmo	[rhythm] In music theory, rhythm consists of repeating patterns that indicate how long notes should last. Rhythmic styles are deeply important in Latin American music as a whole, and rancheras are no exception. Each repeating mariachi accompaniment rhythm constitutes a style or genre in a specific rhythmic groove. Some examples are: *sones* from many regions, huapango, ranchera lenta, ranchera valseada, polca, and bolero. (see Chapter 5)
ritardando	[gradually slower] *Ralentizar* in Spanish. To slow down gradually. This marking is common at the end of songs.
rodeo	[rodeo] The Spanish word "rodeo" is a regular part of the English language. *Charreada* is a synonym for rodeo. The United States rodeo tradition comes from Mexico. Mexico's charreada tradition comes from Spain. In Mexican charreadas the charros compete to demonstrate excellent style and skillsmanship, while in the United States they race against the clock. Mexico's strong equestrian tradition features show horses, bull riding, mariachi music, dance, and competitions.
rote	Rote learning describes songs through repetition and memorization. Ranchera music has historically been an oral tradition whereby the songs are memorized and passed down from generation to generation. The songs and style were traditionally taught and learned aurally by rote memorization.
rubato	[*rubare*] This Italian term means "to rob". The term is often used in both Spanish and English. A rubato marking signals to soloists, conductors, or directors that they may temporarily stretch or release the tempo or speed of the song to add personal musical expression. This is a temporary marking, and the singer should subsequently return to the regular speed of the piece in strict tempo.
rural huapango	The huapango comes from Mexico's eastern coastal state of Veracruz. During the nineteenth century, huasteca and huapango songs existed primarily in this region, with huastecas in the north and huapangos from the city of Veracuz to the south. In rural huapango style, falsete flips are a constant with one, two, or more flips per phrase. In many rural huapangos the falsete notes are traditionally quick, and the second note is a throwaway note without re-phonating the vowel. The top note is not sustained. This style can include improvised solos with call-and-response choral responses in harmony. Singers often accompany themselves instrumentally, alternate solos, and/or dance.. These huapangos are very different from urban mariachi virtuosic huapangos with sustained long falsete notes that emerged in Mexico City during the 1930s.
sabor	[flavor] A term in Spanish used to describe the "flavor" or expressive sound of the music. Similar to the term soul or soulful in English.

sainetes	*Zarzuelas* in Mexico were often called *sainetes, tonadillas, comedias musicales, or comedias rancheras.* (see **zarzuela**). These terms were interchangeable. The structure of comedias musicales was used when creating charro musicals, also called *comedias musicales or comedias rancheras.*
scale	A successive series of eight notes, one at a time, that start and end on the same note. An example is: C-D-E-F-G-A-B-C. In *solfege*, the equivalent notes are do-re-mi-fa-sol-la-si-do. (The letter "ti" in English is "si" in Spanish.)
semicorchea	Note name in Spanish for a sixteenth note. It lasts a quarter of a beat, and four sixteenth notes equal one quarter note.
sharp	[*agudo/aguda*] A sharp in music theory indicates a half step higher, usually indicated by a sharp symbol #. When a singer is singing sharp they are slightly higher than the desired pitch but not necessarily a full half step (see **half step**).
¡Si, eso es!	A vocal exclamation often used by singers at the end of a mariachi song, meaning "Yes, that's it!" Another exclamation with identical meaning is "*¡Así se hace!*"
Siglo de Oro del Cine Mexicano	Golden Age of Cinema, also known as *Época de oro del cine mexicano*, which could also be called *Época de oro del cine y canto mexicano* (Golden Age of Cinema and Song). During this period (between the 1930s and 1950s), Mexican charro musicals (comedias rancheras or comedias musicales) were quite popular throughout Latin America. Mariachi solo-singing technique was at a high level high, and at this time many ranchera songs became classics worldwide. One example is the movie and song "Ay, Jalisco no te rajes." Singers had to develop acting skills and were often the main feature for each movie. Singers Jorge Negrete, Pedro Vargas, and Lola Beltrán were among the long list of celebrity singers in movies during this period.
singer/songwriter	[*cantautor*]. Beginning in the 1950s, Mexican ranchera singer-songwriter José Alfredo Jiménez (1926–1973) pioneered a new earthy solo ranchera songwriting style. His songs delivered an intimate message combined with down to earth gutsy singing. Singers in the previous generation had accentuated more in-depth vocal training for vocal beauty and virtuosity with character development and high acting skills for roles in comedias rancheras. José Alfredo's new style opened up a path for new and different kinds of solo singers while adding voluminous songs to the mariachi canon. His work culminated in a third period of mariachi vocal history.
¡Sí, señor!	A vocal exclamation often used by singers at the end of a mariachi song, meaning "Yes, sir!" "*¡Sí, señores!*" is also used.

solfege	[*solfegio*] A term in French and Spanish used in English to describe the notes of a scale with syllables: do-re-mi-fa-sol-la-ti-do. It is also a musical system used to teach aural skills in music theory. An example of a song that teaches this skill is the song "do-re-mi" from the musical *The Sound of Music*. In ranchera music it is common to work with a fixed do system, meaning that do is always the letter C.
sombrero	A Spanish term for "hat" that comes from the word *sombra*, or "shadow." It is the largest and perhaps most noticeable part of the mariachi outfit and can be found in many different colors, materials, and décor.
sombrero de greca	This felt-covered cardboard sombrero is embroidered with various patterns.
sombrero de paja	This sombrero is made from straw and is sturdier than cardboard sombreros. It is covered in felt, embroidered in greca, and is custom fitted.
sombrero de trapo	This cloth-covered, cardboard sombrero is popular with school groups, ballet folklórico dancers, individuals, and groups on a budget.
sombrero sevillano	This sombrero is the finest type available as it is made with rabbit fur. It is usually custom fitted and can come in various colors, with or without greca design. It may have originated in Sevilla, Spain; hence the name *sombrero sevillano*.
son	The term *son* literally means "sound" but in Latin American music designates a type of song rhythm. A *son* is quite complex rhythmically. In Mexico *sones* have styles described by regions, as in the *son huasteca* (Tamaulipas, Veracruz, Hidalgo, Queretaro, Puebla, San Luis Potosi) or *son jarocho* (Veracruz with close ties to Cuba, African countries from slave trade, and Spain). In ranchera music, ensembles perform *sones* from different regions of Mexico as well, for example the *son jaliscience* (Jalisco) or the *son veracruzano* (Veracruz) but linked to mariachi instrumentation and interpretation. It is usually in in 6/8 or more often in 12/8 meter. Many mariachi *sones* are chorally sung in call and response with the instrumental sections.. Important standards in the *son* are "*La Negra*" and "*El Sinaloense*." Sones sung by solo singers include *Pelea de gallos, La Charreada, El Sinaloense*, and the third and final section of *Mexico lindo y querido*.
son Huasteco	A rhythmic genre of mariachi music in 6/8 time with hemiola rhythmic patterns. It is traditionally from the Huasteca region north of Veracruz and farther along the Gulf of Mexico. (see *son*).
son Jalisciense	Arguably the most traditional song form from the mariachi genre. This rhythmic genre originates from the state of Jalisco. It can have a 3/4 or 6/8 feel but is typically in a 12/8 with high levels of syncopation. It is said to be from the Nayarit and Jalisco areas in Mexico. Key songs from the mariachi canon include this rhythm. The rhythmic interplay of parts is complex for singers. The song "Guadalajara" is an example of *son Jalisciense*.

son Veracruzano	Folk music from Veracruz, Mexico. Also known as *son Jarocho*. It is a mix of Husatecan, Spanish, and African music. Song examples of the style are "La bamba" and "La Bruja,".
soprano	The highest female vocal register. It sits above the mariachi female fach, contralto, and mezzo-soprano register. Classical sopranos sing with a head-voice-dominant blend, while female mariachi singers sing with more chest-dominant blend. Some celebrated classical sopranos who recorded in Spanish include Victoria de Los Angeles and Monserrat Caballé. Most female mariachi singers do not cultivate the soprano range as it does not feature the warm chest-voice timbre desired in mariachi singing. This higher range is used by all female singers to sustain falsete notes, however. Opening up the full range helps keep the entire voice healthy and balanced.
sotto voce	[quiet voice] This Italian term is commonly used in the voice world for supported, intentional soft singing. It is one of the hardest techniques for a singer to learn.
staccato	Notation for musical articulation that indicates short detached notes. The musical symbol is a period/dot over or under any given note.
staff	Five parallel lines used in standard music notation used for expressing different pitches. Pitches vary depending on whether notes are placed on spaces or lines and higher up or lower down on the staff. The staff is called *pentagrama* in Spanish.
strum	Strumming is a technique used to play guitar, *vihuela*, and other string instruments by brushing fingertips against the strings, either upward or down. Each style of music has different sets of strumming patterns that help distinguish musical styles within mariachi song repertoire..
subdominant	Based off the fourth note of the scale. In the mariachi world it is known as *tercero* (IV-third) as it is the third-most-important chord, after the tonic and dominant chords. In written music it is represented by the Roman numeral (IV).
syncopated	Strong beat displacement from where one expects, or suddenly accenting off beats. In 4/4 meter, accents normally occur on beats one and three. Syncopation occurs if the accents are marked on beats two and four.
tapatío	Someone singing or dancing music from Jalisco. The famous song and dance *Jarabe Tapatío* is a song collection consisting of various rhythmic styles in different sections, all from Jalisco. (see manuscript of son publication from 1800s in Chapter 2: Manuel M. Ponce "The Father of Mexican Song")
telenovela	Soap opera aired on television. Beloved late mariachi singer "Chente" or Vicente Fernández also acted and sang on television with *telenovelas*.

GLOSSARY 373

tempi

[time] Plural in Italian for tempo (see **tempo**).

tempo

[time] The rate of speed at which a song should be played.

tenor

A high male vocal range above the bass and baritone ranges. The only higher range is that of a countertenor, and they sing complete songs performed in falsetto range. This style of singing was popular in opera during the Baroque period (1600–1750). A typical mariachi tenor is the voice of Mariachi Camperos soloist Raul Cuellar (see Chapter 8 Interview: Raul Cuellar), many soloists for Mariachi Vargas including Steevan Sandoval, or the somewhat higher Miguel Aceves Mejía. Vicente Fernández also had a tenor vocal color, but he sang more comfortably in baritenor range. Some classical tenors who recorded mariachi and other Mexican songs in Spanish include José Mojica from Mexico and from Spain, Alfredo Kraus, Placido Domingo, and José Carreras.

tertulias

[musical gatherings] A common Mexican term for musical, artistic, and cultural informal performances often held at cultural centers or as house concerts. In South America the term *peña* is similar.

tessitura

[texture] Italian musical term used in English and Spanish. The tessitura refers to the notes within a singer's range that are the easiest for them to sing and sound the best. Some call them "money notes".

timbre

Timbre is a French musical term commonly used to describe the color of a voice or instrument. Adjectives such as bright, dark, silvery, and rich are descriptions of timbre. Singers often strive for chiaroscuro, or light-dark, whereby the voice simultaneously expresses both colors simultaneously in perfect, equal balance.

time signature

[*marca de tiempo* or *compás*] A musical symbol with two numbers denoting a fraction listed at the beginning of a song in standard music notation. The top number expresses how many beats per measure will occur in a song. The bottom number expresses what kind of note, rhythmically speaking, will receive one beat. Note that the Spanish word *compás* can mean time signature, one measure or bar of music, or the general rhythmic feel of the song.

tonadillas

Zarzuelas in Mexico were often called *sainetes, tonadillas,* or *comedias musicales* (see **zarzuela**). In ranchera music *comedias musicales* were used as a structure for *comedias rancheras* in the Golden Age of Movies, Singers, and Songs (*Siglo de oro del cine, la cancion y el cantante mexicano*).

tonic

[root] The tonic is the name of the key, main chord and central note of whatever key one is singing in. It is based upon the first note of the scale. In ranchera music the tonic or root chord is known as *primero* (I—first) as it is the most important chord. In written music theory it is represented by the Roman numeral (I).

tono

[musical key] This term refers to the name of the musical key of a song, although the word has other musical meanings.

¡Tóquense una!	["Play a song!"] An exclamation often used by singers to alert the accompanists to be ready to play a song or have them play an instrumental solo.
torear	[to bullfight] verb.
torero	[bullfighter] noun.
toro	[bull] noun.
traje	[outfit] This linguistic term can mean an outfit for either gender, but in the mariachi world *traje* refers to a male *charro* suit. Every mariachi ensemble chooses their own matching *traje de charro*. Solo singers can choose any *vestuario* (costume) from colorful representations from any of Mexico's thirty-two states to customized, personally designed dresses that evoke Mexico's colors or the *charra* tradition.
traje de charro	[*charro* costume] Attire with gold or silver *botonadura* traditionally worn by mariachi solo singers and ensembles (see **charro**; **vestido de charro**). (see Chapter 4 section: "Costumes, Make-up, and Microphones").
traje de gala	[elegant *charro* outfit] A highly decorated *traje de charro* with a jacket, vest, pants, or skirt. It also includes a set of *gala* or *botonadura* (décor/side buttons) and a *broche* (jacket brooch). *De gala* indicates a high degree of décor. (see Chapter 4 section: "Costumes, Make-up, and Microphones").
traje con greca	[*charro* outfit] A less elegant *traje de charro* embroidered with simple sewn white lines down the sides to contrast the black outfit in lieu of gold or silver *botonadura* (see **botonadura**). (see Chapter 4 section: "Costumes, Make-up, and Microphones").
trajes típicos	[traditional costumes] This outfit describes costumes indigenous to a particular region or country that represents the traditions of the people from that location. Mexico has many *trajes típicos* for each region and state. One traje *típico* is the *chinaco*, a Mexican peasant attire (see *chinaco*).
transcribe	Transcription is the notation of sound written down as sheet music.
transpose	Transposition refers to changing the pitches into a new key. Finding the right key for each song and maintaining a list of keys alongside song titles is of utmost importance for every mariachi soloist.
treble clef	[G clef] The treble clef symbol curves around the second-to-bottom line of the staff indicating the pitch "G." It is also called a G clef, or in Spanish, *clave de sol*. This symbol notates music for all treble-pitched mariachi instruments such as the trumpet, violin, vihuela, and guitar.
trumpet	A brass, treble, three-valve wind instrument. In Mexico City's mariachi scene in the 1940s, the trumpet became popular on radio programs. The trumpet's sound was a color contrast to the voice and string instruments. Today, one or two trumpeters typically form part of a mariachi ensemble.

UNESCO	UNESCO stands for the United Nations Educational, Scientific and Cultural Organization. In 2011, UNESCO declared mariachi music a Mexican symbol of worldwide cultural heritage.
vals	[waltz] The waltz is a European dance in triple meter (3/4). The European waltz originated in Germany-Austria with Franz Schubert's *Lendler* folk dances in the early 1800s. The waltz was at first slower and considered a scandalous couple's folk dance because the dancers touched as partners. It was later accepted in ballroom court music and was brought to the Americas by Germans into Northern Mexico, along with the accordion. Northern Mexico at this time included Texas, Arizona, and Southern California, until the end of the Mexican-American War in 1848. The *ranchera vals* rhythmic style remains extremely popular in mariachi repertoire as well as *norteño* or Northern Mexican music (see **waltz**). "Amanecí en tus brazos" is a popular ranchera valseada by José Alfredo Jiménez.
vestido de charra	This female *charra* attire is similar to that of the *traje de charro*, usually with a skirt instead of pants, although women wear either.
vibrato	[to vibrate] Vibrato is the natural vibration of a note. It is part of musical expression. A normal vibrato occurs naturally when the larynx is relaxed and properly supported by breath support. The Spanish word *vibrar* means to vibrate, but the Italian term vibrato is commonly used in both English and Spanish. Vibratos can vary widely depending on the style being sung but also depending on the technical vocal production of the singer.
vihuela	This string instrument is a small, five-string guitar variant with a humped back. The vihuela and *guitarrón* (largest guitar) are the only mariachi instruments indigenous to Mexico. The vihuela is the smallest string instrument in the ensemble and forms part of the *armonía* or rhythm section of the mariachi ensemble. Each group typically has one *vihuela* player. It has a high-pitched, brilliant tone that strums actively and cuts through the mariachi.
violin	A four-stringed, curved wooden instrument with a horse-hair bow from Europe. The sound is produced by drawing a bow across the strings or by plucking them. A typical mariachi will have from three to nine violinists.
virtuosic	Performance or performer that shows exceptional skill, beauty, fast moving agility, and technique.
¡*Viva México*!	["Long Live Mexico!"] An exclamation often used by singers at the end of a mariachi song.
¡*Viva La República*!	["Long live the republic!"] An exclamation often used by singers at the end of a mariachi song.

vocal coaching	Vocal coaches in commercial music generally guide singers with repertoire, interpretation, and presentation skills. In classical music they work a singer's diction and their musical and interpretive skills, unlike a voice teacher, who trains singers technically and builds the voice slowly.
vocal fatigue	The voice can tire when misused or overused and fatigue sets in. If the voice is not properly produced and rested on a continual basis, nodes can appear on the vocal folds, producing an airy sound, a grainy sound, or coarseness.
vocal flip	[yodeling/falsete] When singers change from one vocal register to another they switch with a vocal flip similar to the change in color with yodeling. In the mariachi vocal tradition, the falsete flip is done with color contrast. Falsete flips can be quick or sustained. Falsete is most often used in the huapango style of singing (see **falsete**; **huapango**).
vocal folds	Vocal cords or vocal folds are ligaments located in the larynx or voice box on top of the windpipe. The vocal folds are small (usually no longer than a penny for a woman and up to the length of a quarter for a low-voiced man); nevertheless, they generate all sound needed for speech and singing. The length of the vocal folds can change; when activated they stretch longer for high notes, or shorter and thicker for lower notes.
vocal pedagogy	The field of vocal study and teaching: repertoire, voice function, and technique.
vocal register	The voice changes registers every five to six notes. The most common delineations for overall register changes are popularly called the chest voice, falsetto (men only), head voice, and whistle tone (women only).
voice box	The voice box is also called the larynx. It is located in the neck and is a cylindrical group of cartilages, muscles, and soft tissue that contain the vocal cords. The voice box helps with breathing, swallowing, talking, and singing. Sound is produced by vibrations that happen when the air passes through the vocal cords (see **larynx**).
voice break	Transition spot between different two vocal registers of the voice. In mariachi singing accentuating color contrasts with breaks revolves around discovering ones' register breaks as a singer.
voz de cabeza	[head voice] In reference to falsetto. The part of the voice activated by the crico-thyroid muscle from within the voice box. In ranchera singing, learning to use this muscle strengthens all high notes and falsete.(see Chapter 3).

GLOSSARY   377

waltz [dance, turn, revolve] *Waltzen* is the original German term for this style in 3/4 meter. In Germany, the waltz was originally considered risqué as it was a couple's dance initiated by the working class. The waltz was quickly adopted by all classes and morphed into an elegant ballroom dance. In Mexico, while the ballroom waltz was cultivated by aristocrats, at the same time the ranchera valseada was and is the popular staple, symbol, and musical accompaniment structure to many ranchera songs.

warm-ups Similar to athletes, singers also warm-up and warm-down their voices to activate the connection between the air in their bodies and the desired sound through vowels. Typical examples of warm-ups are lip buzzing, humming, and sirens, although warm-ups should also include breath coordination beyond this.

whistle range Some female singers have an upper range extension above their head voice with a change in timbre. The range falls between c6 and g6.

whole note Whole notes have no stems and are sustained for four beats. In Spanish this note value is called *redonda*.

whole step The distance from one note to the next (two half steps). Whole steps can begin and end on either white or black keys (see **half step**).

yodeling A form of singing or calling out with projection while accentuating a register break between two vocal registers. In Mexican mariachi falsete flips also accentuate color differences between the vocal registers.

zarape Colorful Mexican striped blanket often draped over the shoulder of performers.

zarzuela A staged musical genre from Spain originating in the early 1600s. While *zarzuela* is idiomatic to Spain, it also shares Italian operatic elements, such as bel canto singing style. *Zarzuela* is not unlike operetta but with folk-music elements and rhythms from Spain, spoken dialogue, and always in Spanish. *Zarzuelas* could be a short one act comedic or dramatic in nature, called *género chico*, or three-act musical dramas, called *género grande*. *Género chico* was often performed in Mexico City during Spanish rule of Mexico between 1521 and 1821. In Spain, *Zarzuela* got its start as musical interludes within larger presentations of plays during Spain's *Siglo de oro* (Spanish Golden Age). Later in Mexico, Spaniards allowed indigenous Mexican songs and dances as interludes within presentations of Spanish *zarzuelas*. *Zarzuelas* in Mexico were often called *sainetes, tonadillas,* or *comedias musicales*. *Comedias rancheras* during Mexico's Golden Age of Cinema and Song were originally structured around *comedias musicales,* or *zarzuelas*.

RESOURCES AND BIBLIOGRAPHY

Resources

Diction, International Phonetic Alphabet (IPA), and Linguistic Resources

Listening Tip: When isolating Spanish pronunciation in any source or on YouTube, seek Mexican or Latin American Spanish (not Castilian Spanish) with preference always for native speakers and singers.

Castel, Nico. *A Singer's Manual of Spanish Lyric Diction.* New York: Meyerlee Publications, 1994. (While the emphasis is Castilian and not Latin American or Mexican Spanish, it is the best existing general guide to date by a foremost linguist.)

Introduction to the International Phonetic Alphabet: Train Students with Identifying Symbols for Sounds. https://youtu.be/6sUmVMEwY0w.

Short Introduction to Spanish Alphabet: Sounds on YouTube with Rocket Languages. https://youtu.be/FUvG3XHuh-8.

Pronunciation Tracks and Arrangements for Rancheras for *The Mariachi Voice* coming in 20: https://www.juanitamusic.com/

Advanced Introduction to International Phonetic Alphabet (IPA) for Spanish alphabet. Each symbol appears below the alphabet letters in brackets. https://youtu.be/-YbcFf7MqpM.

linguistic: *Academia Mexicana de la Lengua*

http://www.academia.org.mx/

http://www.linguee.com/

Real Academia española

https://www.rae.es/

Mariachi and Mexican Voice Study*

1. https://themariachiconservatory.org/mariachieducation/
led by Ricardo Mata, Los Angeles, CA

2. https://sonesdemexico.com
Mexican Folk and Traditional Music School and Grammy
Nominated Performance Ensemble. Led by Juan Dies, Chicago, Ilinois.
New Applied Voice/Ethnomusicological Curriculum with Voice Consultant,
Dr. Juanita Ulloa.

* Competitions and select community-based locations with voice teaching. University programs at UTRGV and Texas State University in Texas also have vocal options.

3. https://www.musicedconsultants.net/mariachi-education.html
Del Sol Academy of Performing Arts, Led by Lupe and Fernando Gonzalez
Las Vegas, Nevada.

4. https://www.210mariachi.com Led by Juan Ortiz
Mariachi Campanas de América/ Alamo Community College,
San Antonio, Texas

5. https://www.loscenzontles.com
Mexican Traditional Music Los Cenzontles Center
Led by Eugene Rodriguez, San Pablo, Northern California

6. https://www.juanitamusic.com https://laney.edu/
Mariachi voice master classes/private voice training/performances
Led by Singer/Professor of Voice Dr. Juanita Ulloa
Laney Community College Music, Oakland, California
Voice with Mariachi Track (Online) and Private Voice Studio, Stockton, California (in person/online)

7. http://www.mariachiacademyny.org
Mariachi Academy of New York led by Ramón Ponce
Two Locations, New York City, New York

8. https://www.facebook.com/EscuelaMunicipalDelMariachi/
Escuela Municipal de Mariachi Led by Fernando Briseño
Guadalajara, Jalisco, Mexico

9. https://www.cultura.cdmx.gob.mx/recintos/emoyg
Escuela de mariachi Ollin Yolitztli Led by Vanessa Velazco
Mexico City, Mexico

Mariachi Voice Competitions
https://mariachimusic.com/events/mariachi-extravaganza/competitions/vocal/
Mariachi Extravaganza National Voice Competition led by Cynthia Muñoz,
San Antonio, Texas

https://mariachiusa.com/talent-search/
Mariachi USA Talent Search, Hollywood Bowl, Los Angeles, California

https://www.mariachiheritagesociety.com
led by José Hernandez Walnut, California

https://www.tamemariachi.com
Texas Association of Mariachi Educators (TAME): workshops,
showcases, competitions

NATS (National Association of Teachers of Singing)
https://nats.org (National)

Voices Competition (Commercial Voice Category. Many chapters can now include mariachi.
Check your local chapter)
https://calwestnats.org (West Coast Chapter)
https://sfbacnats.com (San Francisco Chapter)
https://www.facebook.com/CCCNATS/ (California Capital Chapter)

Vocal Pedagogy and Mexican Song Literature Resources

Avendano, Luvi. "Mexican Song and the Genesis of 20th century Mexican Modernism: The Case for a virtual repository of Mexican Song of the Early 20th century." PhD diss.,University of California, Santa Barbara, 2021.

Bunch Dayme, Meribeth. *Dynamics of the Singing Voice*. Fifth edition. New York: Springer Wien, 2009.

Bunch Dayme, Meribeth. *The Performer's Voice*. New York: W.W. Norton & Company, 2005.

Castel, Nico. *A Singer's Manual of Spanish Lyric Diction*. New York: Meyerlee Publications, 1994.

Gagné, Jeannie. *Belting: A Guide to Healthy, Powerful Singing*. Boston: Berklee Press, 2015.

Hoch, Matthew. *So You Want to Sing World Music*. Chapter 6 on "Mariachi Vocal Music Tradition" by Dr. Juanita Ulloa. Lanham, Maryland: Rowman & Littlefield, 2018. pp.126-143. https://www.nats.org/SYWTS_World_Music_-_Online_Resources.html

Hoch, Matthew. *So You Want to Sing Contemporary Commercial Music*. Lanham, Maryland: Rowman & Littlefield, 2018.

Lamperti. Arranged by William E. Brown. *Vocal Wisdom: Maxims of Giovanni Battista Lamperti*. Eastford, Connecticut: Martino Publishing, 2010.

Miller, Richard. *The Structure of Singing*. Boston: G. Schirmer, 1996.

Nix, John. "A Hole in the Sky." *The NATS Journal* (January–February 2018).

Popeil, Lisa. *The Total Singer*. California: Voiceworks, 1997, 2013. Warm-up CD for commercial singers.

Rosas Lira, Jessica Ariana. "Doce Canciones Mexicanas": A Singer's Guide to Manuel M. Ponce's (1882–1948) Romantic Mexican Art Song as Described in His Essay "La Canción Mexicana." PhD diss., University of North Texas, 2021. https://digital.library.unt.edu/ark:/67531/metadc1833452/m1/29/

Saunders-Barton, Mary. "Bel Canto Can Belto." *Classical Singer Magazine* (March 2014). https://www.csmusic.net/content/articles/bel-canto-can-belto/.

Spivey, Norman, and Mary Saunders-Barton. *Cross-Training in the Voice Studio*. San Diego: Plural Publishing, Inc., 2018.

Titze, Ingo. "The Mariachi Voice." *The NATS Journal* (March–April 1996): 29–30.

Ulloa, Juanita M. *The Songs of Mexican Nationalist, Antonio Gomezanda*. Published doctor of arts diss., University of Northern Colorado, 2016. https://core.ac.uk/download/pdf/217307335.pdf.

Ulloa, Juanita M. "The Mariachi Vocal Tradition" (chapter) *So You Want To Sing World Music*. Published by National Association of Teachers of Singing and Rowman & Littlefield, 2018.

https://rowman.com/ISBN/9781538112281/So-You-Want-to-Sing-World-Music-A-Guide-for-Performers

Vaccai, Nicola. *Practical Method of Italian Singing*. New York/London: G. Schirmer, 1975.

Ranchera/Bolero Sources for Song Sheets and Sheet Music (Not Arrangements)

www.musicnotes.com

www.sheetmusicplus.com

www.classicalvocalreprints.com

Gomezanda Mexican Song Collection. Three Volumes, *High and Low Keys*. Besides art songs and two arias from Mariache: Primera Opera Ranchera Mexicana by Gomezanda, this collection includes 3 Rancheras with full piano accompaniment.

https://www.halleonard.com/

Romance (Boleros from Mexico/Latin America) Hal Leonard Publishing Company

https://www.jwpepper.com/

http://www.elmariachi.com

http://mariachi.org

https://themariachiconservatory.org/

https://www.mujeresenelmariachi.com

Repertorio MacDowell (sheet music for Mexican songs)
Cuadrante de San Francisco 197-B, San Francisco, 04320
Mexico City, Mexico Tel: 011-52-55-5554-9653

Women in Mariachi History

Dr. Leonor Xóchitl Pérez
https://www.mariachiwomen.org/about-the-founder
https://www.sobrino.net/mer/
https://www.juanitamusic.com
https://www.mariachiwomen.org/

General Resources

https://www.tamemariachi.com
https://www.tmea.org/teaching-resources/
https://virtuosomariachi.com
Ponce Music Archive (resources for Mexican song)
Biblioteca Cuicamatini-Cuicamatini Library
Facultad de Música.UNAM Mexico City, Mexico

Resources for Music Theory and Costumes

Theory: http://etheory.com/
https://www.musictheory.net/
Trajes de charro and Mexican Regional Costumes:
El Charro—Rosario
Guadalajara, Mexico
charro_centro@hotmail.com
www.elcharroweb.com
El Charro
El Paso, Texas
http://www.elcharro1.com
(915) 534-7956
Charro Azteca, Los Angeles, California
https://charroazteca.com
(323) 676-0834
J. G. Ara (handcrafted earrings for mariachi)
San Antonio, Texas
(210)-680-9809
Jorge Nuñez (Tailer)
Guadalajara, Jalisco Mexico
(33) 3613-7754
Sastreria Garibaldi—Sara, Mariachi
Mexico City, Mexicohttps://www.facebook.com/eltrajecharro
+1 (323) 715-2985 Cell# USA

+5215548487901 Cell# México

Sastrería Jalisco—Eduardo Garcia E. (Tailor)

(656) 612-2109

Ciudad Juárez, México

Sombreros Castillos

(0133) 3618-65-88

Guadalajara, México

The Mariachi Connection, Inc.

San Antonio, Texas

http://www.mariachiconnection.com

Trajes de Charro García, Mexico City, Mexico

Mauro García

www.Facebook.com/Trajesdecharrogarcia

Trajes de Charro Reyes, Mexico City, Mexico

http://ww25.trajesdecharro.com/?subid1=20231212-1603-5818-a304-f0849df4151e

Bibliography (Spanish-English)

Archer, Christon I. "Fashioning a New Nation." In *The Oxford History of Mexico,* edited by Michael Meyer and William H., 301–338. Beezley. New York: Oxford University Press, 2000.

Avendano, Luvi. "Mexican Song and the Genesis of 20th Century Mexican Modernism: The Case for a Virtual Repository of Mexican Song of the Early 20th Century." University of California, Santa Barbara, California: its a dissertation. Doctor of Musical Arts, 2021.

Béhague, Gerard. *Music in Latin America: An Introduction.* New Jersey: Prentice-Hall, Inc., 1979.

Brill, Mark. Music of Latin America and the Carribean. New Jersey: Prentice-Hall, Inc., 2011.

Bunch Dayme, Meribeth. *Dynamics of the Singing Voice.* 5th edition. New York: Springer Wien, 2009.

Bunch Dayme, Meribeth. *The Performer's Voice.* New York: W.W. Norton & Company, 2005.Cardon, Hugh. "Twentieth-century Mexican Art Song." *NATS Journal* (January/February 1991): 15–20.

Cardon, Hugh. "Survey of Twentieth-Century Mexican Art Song." DMA diss., University of Oregon, 1970.

Castel, Nico. *A Singer's Manual of Spanish Lyric Diction.* New York: Meyerlee Publications, 1994.

Curl, John. "The Flower Songs of Nezahualcóyotl: Nahua [Aztec] Poetry." *Bilingual Review* May–December 26, no. 2/3 (2001–2002): 1–54.

Escorza, Juan José. "Opera, Cine y mariachi. La Virgen de San Juan del compositor Laguense Antonio Gomezanda." In *Memorias del Coloquio.el mariachi, patrimonio cultural de los mexicanos,* edited by Arturo Camacho Becerra, 21–38. Guadalajara: Secretaríade Cultura-Gobierno de Jalisco, 2012.

Gagné, Jeannie. *Belting: A Guide to Healthy, Powerful Singing.* Boston: Berklee Press, 2015.

Garmabella, José Ramón. *Pedro Vargas "Una vez nada más": Recuerdos y Confesiones del Tenor de las Américas.* México D.F.: Compañía Editorial Electrocomp, 1984.

Geijerstam, Claes. *Popular Music in Mexico.* Albuquerque: University of New Mexico Press, 1976.

Gibson Taylor, Christina. *The music of Manuel M. Ponce, Julian Carrillo, and Carlos Chávez* in New York, 1925—1932. College Park: University of Maryland, PhD Dissertation, 2008.

Gradante, William. "El Hijo del Pueblo: José Alfredo Jiménez and the Mexican Canción Ranchera." *Latin American Music Review* 3, no. 1 (Spring/Summer 1982): 36–59.

Henriques, Donald. "Performing Nationalism: Mariachi, Media, and Transformation of a Tradition (1920–1942)." PhD diss., University of Texas at Austin, 2006.

384 RESOURCES AND BIBLIOGRAPHY

Hoch, Matthew. *So You Want to Sing Contemporary Commercial Music*. Lanham, MD: Rowman & Littlefield, 2018.

Hoch, Matthew. *So You Want to Sing World Music*. Chapter on "Mariachi Vocal Music Tradition" by Dr. Juanita Ulloa. Lanham, MD: Rowman & Littlefield, 2018. Icaza, Claudia de. *Gloria y Jorge: Cartas de amor y conflicto*. México: Edamex, 1994.

Jáuregui, Jesús. *El Mariachi: Símbolo Musical de México*. México, D.F.: Santillana Ediciones Generales, 2007.

Jiménez, José Azanza. *Mis Vivencias con José Alfredo Jiménez*. México: Edamex, 1999.

Joseph, Gilbert M., and Timothy J. Henderson. *The Mexico Reader: History, Culture, Politics*. Durham, NC: Duke University Press, 2002.

Lamperti. Arranged by William E. Brown. *Vocal Wisdom: Maxims of Giovanni Battista Lamperti*. Eastford, Connecticut: Martino Publishing, 2010.

López, Rick A. "The India Bonita Contest of 1921 and the Ethnicization of Mexican National Culture." *Hispanic American Historical Review* 82, no. 2 (2002): 291–328.

Martinez, Miguel. *Mi vida, mis viajes, mis vivencias. Siete décadas en la música de mariachi*. México, D.F.: Consejo Nacional para la Cultural y las Artes, 2012. 2nd ed. 2013.

Mendoza, Vicente. *La Canción Mexicana: Ensayo de Clasificación y Antología*. Mexico City: Tezontle, 1961. Reprints 1982, 1988.

Meyer, Michael C., and William H. Beezley, *The Oxford History of Mexico*. New York: Oxford University Press, 2000.

Miller, Richard. *The Structure of Singing*. Boston: G. Schirmer, 1996.

Miranda, Ricardo, and Manuel M. Ponce. *Ensayo sobre su vida y obra*. México: Consejo nacional para la cultura y las artes, 1998.

Monsiváis, Carlos, et al. *Bolero Clave del Corazón*. México, D.F.: Fundación Alejo Peralta, 2004.

Montemayor, Cecilia. *El Lied Mexicano*. Monterrey, Mexico: Universidad de Nuevo León, 2009.

Mora, Erick. *La guitarra de Mariachi. Completa Aproximación Técnico-Estilística*. Guadalajara, Jalisoc, México: Secretaría de Cultura de Jalisco, 2016.

Negrete, Diana. *Jorge Negrete*. México: Editorial Diana, 1987 [1989]. Ocasio, Rafael. Literature in Latin America. Westport, Connecticut: Greenwood Press, 2004.

Nesme, Nayeli. *María Grever. Reflexiones sobre su obra*. Universidad de Guadalajara, México: Editorial Universitaria, 2009.

Nix, John. "A Hole in the Sky." *The NATS Journal* (January–February 2018). Start page 273.

Pareyón, Gabriel. *Diccionario Enciclopédico de Música en Mexico*. 2nd ed. [2 vols.]. Guadalajara: Universidad Panamericana, 2007.

Ponce, Manuel. *Doce Canciones Mexicanas: Obras para Canto y Piano*. Revised by Guadalupe Campos Sanz and Gonzalo Ruiz Esparza Torres. México, D.F.: Universidad Nacional Autónoma de México, 2008.

Ponce, Manuel. "El Folk-lore musical mexicano." *Revista Musical de Mexico* 1, no. 5 (September 15, 1919): 5–9.

Ponce, Manuel. "La música y la canción Mexicana." *Revista de Revistas* (December 21, 1913): 17–21.

Popeil, Lisa. *The Total Singer*. California: Voiceworks, 1997, 2013. Warm-up CD for commercial singers.

Rico Salazar, Jaime. *Cien Años de Boleros*. Bogotá, Colombia, 2000. 5th ed.

Rivas, Yolanda Moreno. *Historia Música Popular Mexicana*. Mexico City: Editorial Oceáno de México, 2008.

Rodriguez Lee, María Luisa. *María Grever: Poeta y compositora*. Washington, DC: Scripta Humanística, 1994.

Ronstadt, Linda. *Simple Dreams. A Musical Memoir*. New York: Simon & Schuster, 2013.

Rosas Lira, Jessica Ariana. "Doce Canciones Mexicanas": A Singer's Guide to Manuel M. Ponce's (1882–1948) Romantic Mexican Art Song as Described in His Essay "La Canción Mexicana." 2021 Phd Dissertation. Dallas: University of North Texas, 2021.

Saavedra, Leonor. "Of Selves and Others: Historiography, Ideology, and the Politics of Modern Mexican Music." PhD diss., University of Pittsburgh, 2001.

Saavedra, Leonor. "Race, Religion, and History in Mexican Opera of the 1940's." *Opera Quarterly* 23, no. 1 (Winter 2007): 1–27.

Saavedra, Leonor. "Spanish Moors and Turkish Captives in fin de siècle Mexico: Exoticism as Strategy." *Journal of Musicological Research* 31, no. 4 (October 2012): 231–261.

Saunders-Barton, Mary. "Bel Canto Can Belto." *Classical Singer Magazine* (March 2014). https://www.csmusic.net/content/articles/bel-canto-can-belto/.

Sheehy, Daniel. *Mariachi Music in America: Experiencing Music Expressing Culture*. New York: Oxford University Press, 2006.

Sosa, José Octavio. "El centenario de Ramón Vinay." *Revista Opera [Proopera]* 14, no. 2 (March–April 2011). www.proopera.org.mx.

Sosa, José Octavio. *La Ópera en México de la Independencia al inicio de la Revolución (1821–1910)*. México D.F.: Instituto Nacional de Bellas Artes y Literatura, 2010.

Spivey, Norman, and Mary Saunders-Barton. *Cross-Training in the Voice Studio*. San Diego, CA: Plural Publishing, Inc., 2018.

Stevenson, Robert. *Music in Aztec and Inca Territory*. Berkeley: University of California Press, 1968 [1977].

Stevenson, Robert Louis. *Music in Mexico: A Historical Survey*. New York: Thomas Y. Crowell Co., 1952.

Sturman, Janet. *The Course of Mexican Music*. New York: Routledge, 2016.Titze, Ingo. "The Mariachi Voice." *The NATS Journal* (March–April 1996): 29–30.

Ulloa, Juanita M. *The Songs of Mexican Nationalist, Antonio Gomezanda*. Published doctor of arts dissertation, University of Northern Colorado, 2016. https://core.ac.uk/download/pdf/217307335.pdf.

Ulloa, Juanita M. "The Mariachi Vocal Tradition". *So You Want TO Sing World Music*. ed. Matthew Hoch. Rowman & Littlefield, Lahnam, Ct. (2019) pp.126–143.

Vaccai, Nicola. *Practical Method of Italian Singing*. New York/London: G. Schirmer, 1975.

Velazco, Jorge. "Antonio Gomezanda y el Nacionalismo Romántico Mexicano." *Latin American Music Review* 12, no. 1 (Spring–Summer, 1991): 65–73.

Yubaile, Charbel. *The Multicultural and Eclectic Art Songs of Manuel M. Ponce*. Published doctoral dissertation, University of Houston, 2020.

INDEX

For the benefit of digital users, indexed terms that span two pages (e.g., 52–53) may, on occasion, appear on only one of those pages.

Tables and figures are indicated by an italic *t* and *f* following the page number.

"See glossary for further explanation of specialized music or linguistic terms"

Aceves Mejía, Miguel, 35–36
acting in mariachi, 101
Aguilar, Josefina "Cha Cha," 45
Aguilar, Pepe, 49
Alavéz, José López, 28
alignment, 85–86
Allá en el rancho grande (Over There on the Big Ranch) (1936), 30
Arceo, Sergio Mendez, 18–20
Azcárraga Vidaurreta, Emilio, 35

basic chords, 271–72, 273*f*, 274*f*
bass clef, 267–69, 268*f*, 269*f*
Beltrán, Graciela, 54
Beltrán, Lola, 29, 51, 119, 139*f*
belt voice, 95–96
bilingual music theory, 7, 264–69
bolero/boleros, 45–48, 51–52
bravío ranchera singing, 52–55
breathing exercises, 75–76
breathing lessons, 85–86
breath support, 71, 73, 86, 89, 91, 95–97, 98, 100, 103, 105, 106–7, 112

call-and-response singing, 49, 92
Callas, María, 134
Camarena, Enrique, 42
"Cancion mixteca," 167–69
"¡Canta mi son!," 170–73
canto singing, defined, 21
Carrillo, Debbie, 13*f*
Carrillo, Steve, 8, 118–19
charreadas (rodeos), 39, 53
charro outfits. *See trajes de charro*
Chávez, Lidia, 10*f*
Chiapanecas costume, 2*f*, 143*f*
china poblana costume, 3*f*, 120
chords, basic, 271–72, 273*f*, 274*f*
"Cielito lindo," 174–76
classical singing, 9–10, 23, 43, 55, 70, 71, 88–89, 92–93, 99–100, 101, 110–11, 263–64, 274
classical voice, 9–11, 21, 71, 88–89, 99–101, 317, 333–34
clave rhythm pattern, 133, 134, 266–69, 269*f*

coaching *vs.* teaching, 87–88
comedias musicales, 23, 29, 64
comedias rancheras, 29, 55, 64
commercial singing (CM), 9–10, 71, 110
"Como México no hay dos," 177–82
composers, female, 51–52
Contemporary Commercial Singing (CCM), 9–10
"Corazón de Chapulín," 183–90
corridos, 27, 28*f*, 133, 145, 147, 203
Cortazar, Ernesto, 47
costumes
    Chiapanecas costume, 2*f*, 143*f*
    china poblana costume, 3*f*
    description of, 1–2, 2*f*
    jarocho style, 22*f*, 31*f*
    mariachi song/singing preparation, 120–30
    regional differences, 121*f*
    song studies, 120–30
    trajes de charro, 1–2, 16–17, 26, 29, 46, 120–23
    vestido de charro, 120
    zarape (blanket), 19*f*, 35–36, 46, 120
"Cuando canto," 191–95
Cuellar, Raul, Jr.
    advice for young singers, 339–41
    early singing, 337
    evolving style of, 338
    feeling and interpretations, 338–39
    introduction to, 336*f*, 336–37
Curiel, Gonzalo, 47

danzón rhythm, 46
diction
    IPA (International Phonetic Alphabet), 144–47, 156–261
    lessons in, 150–52
    literal translations and, 156–261
    memorizing lyrics, 149–50
    Mexican Spanish, 146–49
    song studies, 153–54
    in vocal music, 4, 5, 99
dietary behaviors, 77
Dominguez, Alberto, 47
Downs, Lila, 26
dynamics in music fundamentals, 276

education programs, 5–8
"El Corrido de Higaditos," 196–203
"El Pastor," 204–7
ensemble soloists, 116, 117*f*
Esperón, Ignacio Fernández, 29
Esperón, Ignacio "Tata Nacho," 47
Esperón, Manuel, 47, 263

falsete/falsetto
　defined, 4, 90–95, 101
　development of, 91–92
　exercises for, 94–95
　flips, defined, 2, 4
　learning of, 92–93
　practice of, 93
　Ronstadt, Linda and, 320–21
　roots of, 92
　as vocal exercise, 81
female. *See* women
female key, 88–90, 98, 109–10, 110*f*, 112–13, 274
female mariachi fach, 8, 43, 45, 51, 71, 88–90, 101, 108–9,
　110*f*, 274, 275*f*
female ranchera singers, 51–55
female voices in mariachi singing, 88–90
Fernández, Vicente, 146–47
Flores, Juan Diego, 42–43
Fogelquist, Mark, 5
folk music/songs, 3–4, 5, 11, 20–21, 23, 24*f*, 26, 27, 31, 33*f*,
　33–34, 39, 48–49, 71, 164–66, 208–16, 242–50, 262,
　271, 317, 323
Fuentes, Ruben, 263

Gabriel, Juan, 50–51
gender differences
　key, 88–90, 98, 109–10, 110*f*, 112–13, 274
　mariachi vocal pedagogy, 79*f*, 79–85
Gomezanda, Antonio, 12, 39–41, 40*f*, 41*f*
Gormé, Edie, 51
graded song lists, 140–43
Grever, María, 47–48
group singing, 116
Guerra, Dahlia, 8

hair for stage, 123–25, 124*f*
"Hay unos ojos," 208–12
health habits/maintenance, 76–79, 84
Hermanas Nuñez (Nuñez Sisters), 51–52
Hermanas Padilla (Padilla Sisters), 51–52, 53–54
Hispanic song, 5–11
huaraches (sandals), 17, 120, 328
humming warm-ups, 102

Infante, Pedro, 46
inflection, 4, 84, 135
instrumentalists, 1–2, 3, 4–5, 13, 49
interpretation exercises, 135
interpretation in mariachi, 101
intonation, 49, 97, 100, 101–2, 135–36, 147, 154
IPA (International Phonetic Alphabet), 144–47,
　156–261
Italian opera/opera singers, 20–21, 22, 32–33, 37–38,
　55, 57, 64

jarocho style, 22*f*, 31*f*
jaw warm-ups, 102
Jiménez, José Alfredo, 46, 50–51, 55, 119–20

key/key choice
　exercises for, 111
　with falsete, 112–13
　for females, 88–90, 98, 112–13, 274
　finding of, 108–13
　finding singer's keys, 274–76
　literal translations of ranchera songs, 156–261
　for men, 111
　popular keys, 272–74
　quizzes for, 111

"La Adelita," 158–63
"La barca de oro," 164–66
"La Golondrina," 217–23
"La negra noche," 224–28
"Las Gaviotas," 213–16
"Las Mañanitas," 229–33
leadership by directors, 98–99
Leclerc, Juan Marco, 18–20
lifestyle behaviors, 77
lip warm-ups, 102

make-up for stage, 120–25, 124*f*
male key choice, 111
male vocal exercises, 80–81
mariache, defined, 11–13, 12*f*
mariachi antiguo, 20
Mariachi Aztlán, 8, 9*f*
Mariachi Cobre, 8, 116, 118–19, 320
Mariachi Divas, 8, 47–48, 52, 116
mariachi fach. *See* female mariachi fach
Mariachi Flor de Toloache
　advice for students, 334–35
　arranging music, 333
　introduction to, 329–35, 330*f*
　learning and balancing vocals, 332–33
　lesson plan for, 335
　musical backgrounds of singers, 329–32
　voice training, 333–34
mariachi moderno, 20
mariachi opera, 12*f*, 39, 41
mariachi rural, 20
mariachi song/singing
　defined, 1–5, 4*f*, 8, 11
　early twentieth century, 27–29
　for female voices, 88–90
　graded song lists, 140–43
　growth of, 5–11
　Hispanic song, 5–11
　introduction to, 16*f*, 16–17
　Ponce, Manuel M., 31–34, 32*f*, 33*f*, 34*f*
　rural folk origins, 17–29
　Siglo de oro del cine mexicano, 16–17, 29–30
　understanding terminology, 11–13
　vocal roots, 20–26
　See also ranchera singers/singing
mariachi song/singing preparation
　costumes, 120–30

ensemble soloists, 116, 117*f*
group singing, 116
hair for stage, 123–25, 124*f*
make-up for stage, 120–25, 124*f*
microphone singing, 120–30, 126*f*, 127*f*
solo singers, 117–20, 118*f*, 119*f*
tips for, 128–30
voice as shared, 115*f*, 115–16
Mariachi Uclatlán, 5
Mariachi Vargas de Tecatitlán, 5, 36, 41, 116, 118–19,
119*f*, 156, 263, 322, 323, 336*f*, 336–41
mariachi vocal pedagogy
addressing common problems, 81, 82*t*
alignment, breath, and vowels, 85–86
belt voice, 95–96
breathing exercises, 75–76
breath support, 71, 73, 86, 89, 91, 95–97, 98, 100, 103,
105, 106–7, 112
class exercises and discussion, 73
classical voice production *vs.*, 99–101
dietary and lifestyle behaviors, 77
exercises, 80–81
falsete and, 91–95
gender differences, 79*f*, 79–85
health habits/maintenance, 76–79, 84
introduction to, 70–72
leadership by directors, 98–99
medication management, 78
mindfulness development, 96–99
performance challenges, 97–98
production and care, 72*f*, 72–76
rehearsal pacing, 78–79
song excerpts and, 104*f*, 105, 106*f*
teacher *vs.* coach, 87–88
teaching by example, 83–84
traveling, 77–78
understanding vocal instrument, 73–76
vocal fatigue, 96–98
warming up, 101–3
Martinez, Miguel, 263
medication management, 78
Mejía, Miguel Aceves, 117
memorizing lyrics, 135, 149–50
Mendoza, Amalia, 18*f*, 36*f*, 55
Mexican opera/opera singers, 12, 21–22, 29–30, 42
Mexican *Posadas* Christmas sung celebration, 18, 20*f*
Mexican Revolution (1910–1921), 16, 17, 20–21, 26, 27,
31, 39–41, 47, 55, 57, 92, 146, 262–63
Mexican Spanish, 146–49
microphone singing, 120–30, 126*f*, 127*f*
mindfulness development, 96–99
Misa Panamericana (Panamerican mass), 18–20
Mojica, José, 26
Molina, Heriberto, 5, 6*f*, 7*f*
Monge, Jesus "Chucho," 47
Morel, Jorge del, 47
motor, 72*f*, 72–73, 86, 102–3
movement in mariachi vocal music, 4
Murúa, Veónica, 10–11
música regional, 11–13
music fundamentals
basic chords, 271–72, 273*f*, 274*f*

bass clef, 267–69, 268*f*, 269*f*
bilingual music theory, 7, 264–69
dynamics, 276
key/key choice, 272–76
lesson plans, 278–314
notes values, 269
in schools, 263–64
sheet music, 156–261, 262–63, 265
solfege/solfegio, 265
tempo, 276
transcriptions of melodies and rhythms, 270*f*, 271*f*, 271
treble clef, 266*f*, 266–67, 267*f*, 268*f*
musicianship, 116, 120, 134, 138, 143, 263, 264, 319,
321–22

Nahua indigenous cultures, 23
National Association of Teachers of Singing (NATS), 9–10
Neel, Marcia, 8
Negrete, Jorge
boleros, 46
celebrity status of, 26, 30, 35–36, 37–39, 43–44
introduction to, 37*f*, 325*f*, 326–29
issues with biographies about, 327
Metropolitan Opera audition, 327–28
movie myths, 328–29
popularity with female fans, 326–27
sheet music and, 263
solo singing, 117
Nix, John, 73, 92
notes values, 269

Oaxacan culture, 26, 124*f*, 129*f*, 131*f*
opera
Italian opera/opera singers, 20–21, 22, 32–33, 37–38,
55, 57, 64
mariachi opera, 12*f*, 39, 41
Ronstadt, Linda and, 323–24
Operachi style, 38
Opera Rancheras, 39–43
Ortíz, Juan, 7
Oteo, Alfonzo Esparza, 47

phonator, 72*f*, 72, 73, 85, 86
See also vocal folds
Pierson, José Eduardo, 26, 43–45, 44*f*, 117
"Plegaria de una indita morena a la virgencita Morena,"
234–36
poetic translations of ranchera songs, 156–261
Ponce, Manuel M., 31–34, 32*f*, 33*f*, 34*f*, 118–19,
262
Ponce, Ramón, 21*f*
popote warm-ups, 103
popular keys, 272–74
"Por un amor," 237–41
posture warm-ups, 102–3
practicing
advanced growth in, 108
day and time for, 107–8
locations for, 107
schedule ideas, 108
by singers, 106–8
song excerpts, 104*f*, 105, 106*f*

390 INDEX

Quintanilla, Selena, 54

ranchera singers/singing
    bolero/boleros, 45–48
    bravío ranchera singing, 52–55
    chronology of, 57–58
    defined, 1–5, 11
    early twentieth century, 27–29
    females, 51–55
    folk origins, 17–29
    graded song lists, 139–43
    history of singers/songs, 48–49, 59
    Jiménez, José Alfredo, 20, 42, 46, 50–51, 55, 58, 62, 67,
        119–20, 153
    literal translations of, 156–261
    Negrete, Jorge, 35–36, 37*f*, 37–39
    Opera Rancheras, 39–43
    Pierson, José Eduardo, 26, 43–45, 44*f*
    solo celebrity singers, 35–36
    style of, 48–49
    understanding terminology, 11–13
    vocal roots, 20–26, 58
ranchera valseada, 26–28, 48, 50, 132, 133, 140–42, 147,
    255–61, 269, 271
ranchera vocal pedagogy. *See* mariachi vocal pedagogy
"Rancho alegre," 242–50
range of singers, 274–76
rehearsal pacing, 78–79
resonator, 72*f*, 72, 73, 79
Reyes, Lucha, 26, 51, 52–55
rhythm styles
    choosing mariachi repertoire, 136–38, 137*f*, 138*f*
    clave pattern, 133, 134, 266–69, 269*f*
    exercises for learning, 134–36
    listening by singers, 133–34
    overview of, 132–33
    six basic rhythms, 136
Rodriguez, Jizelle, 4*f*
Ronstadt, Linda
    breath and harmony, 320
    breathing and vocal issues, 324–25
    crossover to opera, 323–24
    falsetto and falsete, 320–21
    favorite music, 319
    gender differences while touring, 323
    Grammy-winning Mariachi recordings, 322–23
    heritage, 316–17
    introduction to, 315*f*, 316
    musicianship, 321–22
    rhythmic style, 132
    as solo singer, 117–18, 118*f*
    spiritual aspect of singing, 325
    teachers, 317–19
    vocal background, 316–19
    vocal production, 320
Rossini, Giacomo, 21
Ruiz, Gabriel, 47

Sandoval, María Elena, 47
Santa Ana, Cosme, 18

sheet music, 156–261, 262–63, 265
Siglo de oro del cine mexicano (Mexico's Golden Age of
    Cinema), 16–17, 29–30
Siglo de oro (Golden Age), 16–17, 30, 117
Silvestre, Flor, 49
singer-songwriters, 50, 54, 55, 58, 93, 119–20, 153
slides in warm-ups, 103
solfege/solfegio, 265
Solis, Javier, 29, 46–47
solo singers, 117–20, 118*f*, 119*f*
song excerpt practicing, 104*f*, 105, 106*f*
song studies
    acting study in, 155
    advanced projects in, 155
    composer study in, 156
    costumes, 120–30
    diction, 153–54
    history of, 153–54
    lyrics and translations, 154–261
    performing artist study in, 155–56
"Soy Mexicana," 251–54
Spanish language, 23–26, 49, 145, 154
style in mariachi, 101, 135–36
syncopation, 3, 4, 23, 50, 67, 107, 134, 135–36, 155

teaching by example, 83–84
teaching *vs.* coaching, 87–88
Tehuana culture, 27*f*, 131*f*
tempo in music fundamentals, 276
tertulias, 39
tessitura, 54, 71, 88–89, 109, 110*f*, 111, 114, 264, 274–76, 275*f*
Texas Association of Mariachi Educators (TAME), 8
Tirado, Alfonso López, 26
Toloache, Flor de, 121–23, 122*f*
tongue warm-ups, 102
trajes de charro, 1–2, 16–17, 26, 29, 46, 120–23, 261*f*, 342*f*
transcriptions of melodies and rhythms, 270*f*, 271*f*, 271
traveling risks, 77–78
treble clef, 266*f*, 266–67, 267*f*, 268*f*

Ulloa, Juanita, xxiii–xxiv, 1*f*, 123*f*

Valdelamar, Ema Elena, 44–45, 48
Vargas, Pedro, 26, 40–41, 42*f*, 43–44, 70–71, 87–88, 117, 263
Vasconcelos, José, 29
Velásquez, Consuelo, 48
vestido de charro, 120
Vila, Irma, 53–54
Villa, Lucha, 51
"Vivo añorando," 255–61
vocal cords, 51, 73, 74–75, 76, 85, 95–96, 97, 103, 125, 320,
    324, 341
vocal expression, 4, 23, 49
vocal folds, 73, 74–75, 76–77, 78, 79, 80, 113, 320
    See also phonator
vocal pedagogy/training. *See* mariachi vocal pedagogy
vocal projection, 2
voice classes, 5, 100, 116, 145–46
vowel lessons, 85–86, 148–49
voz de cabeza (head voice), 90–91

warming up vocals, 101–3
women. *See also* female
    female ranchera singers, 51–55
    female voices in mariachi singing, 88–90
    mariachi and, 8
    vocal exercises, 80, 81
    voice pedagogy, 71

XEW Radio, 29, 35–36

yodeling exercises, 93–94
yoga breath warm-ups, 103

zarape (blanket), 19*f*, 35–36, 46, 120
zarzuelas, 20–21, 22–23, 43, 55

The manufacturer's authorised representative in the EU for product safety is Oxford University Press España S.A. of El Parque Empresarial San Fernando de Henares, Avenida de Castilla, 2 – 28830 Madrid (www.oup.es/en or product.safety@oup.com). OUP España S.A. also acts as importer into Spain of products made by the manufacturer.

Printed in the USA/Agawam, MA
April 11, 2025

885760.009